ePedagogy in Online Learning:

New Developments in Web Mediated Human Computer Interaction

Elspeth McKay
RMIT University, Australia

T0338691

Managing Director:	Lindsay Johnston
Editorial Director:	Joel Gamon
Book Production Manager:	Jennifer Yoder
Publishing Systems Analyst:	Adrienne Freeland
Development Editor:	Myla Merkel
Assistant Acquisitions Editor:	Kayla Wolfe
Typesetter:	Christina Henning
Cover Design:	Jason Mull

Published in the United States of America by
Information Science Reference (an imprint of IGI Global)
701 E. Chocolate Avenue
Hershey PA 17033
Tel: 717-533-8845
Fax: 717-533-8661
E-mail: cust@igi-global.com
Web site: http://www.igi-global.com

Library of Congress Cataloging-in-Publication Data

EPedagogy in online learning : new developments in web mediated human computer interaction / Elspeth McKay, editor.
    pages cm
 Includes bibliographical references and index.
 Summary: "This book provides approaches on adopting interactive web tools that promote effective human-computer interaction in educational practices"--Provided by publisher.
  ISBN 978-1-4666-3649-1 (hardcover) -- ISBN 978-1-4666-3650-7 (ebook) -- ISBN 978-1-4666-3651-4 (print & perpetual access) 1. Internet in education. 2. Web 2.0. 3. Human-computer interaction. I. McKay, Elspeth (Associate professor), editor of compilation. II. Title: E-pedagogy in online learning.
 LB1044.87.E75 2013
 371.33'44678
                            2012041387

British Cataloguing in Publication Data
A Cataloguing in Publication record for this book is available from the British Library.

All work contributed to this book is new, previously-unpublished material. The views expressed in this book are those of the authors, but not necessarily of the publisher.

Editorial Advisory Board

Table of Contents

Section 1
Technology and Change Management for the Web 2.0 Environment:
Strategies to Enhance eLearning in the Web 2.0 Environment

Section 2
Social Networking and Collaborative Learning through HCI:
Synchronous and Asynchronous Learning

Section 3
ePedagogy and Students' Use of HCI Interactive Learning Environments:
Performance Measurement Issues – How Can We Tell that People Have Learned Anything?

Detailed Table of Contents

Section 1
Technology and Change Management for the Web 2.0 Environment:
Strategies to Enhance eLearning in the Web 2.0 Environment

Chapter 1
Jo Coldwell-Neilson, Deakin University, Australia

Expectations of, and by, students and staff in the classroom have been well researched. Yet, still there is a gap between the expectations of students and what they experience in their studies. The classroom itself is changing with the introduction of Web 2.0 technologies into the mix. Further changes are being driven by the changing profile of a tertiary student in the twenty first century. Education will not fulfill its goal if the gap in expectations is not addressed. The discrepancy in expectations is explored from the perspective of students and staff and strategies for bridging the gap and enhancing eLearning in the Web 2.0 environment are offered. The chapter begins with a scenario that demonstrates the issues and concludes with suggestions to avoid them in the future. In doing so, the key drivers of change in the learning landscape in Australia are identified and the impact these may have on staff and student expectations is explored.

Chapter 2
Carole A. Bagley, The Technology Group, Inc., USA & University of St. Thomas, USA
William H. Creswell III, The Technology Group Inc., USA

The use of Web 2.0 social media such as Wikipedia, YouTube, Facebook, Twitter, and virtual worlds is rapidly increasing and transformational modes of communication are emerging (Greenhow, Robelia & Hughes, 2009; Godwin, 2008; O'Reilly, 2005). Public and private sector organizations are faced with the challenges of adapting their communication practices to the rapidly changing demands of the social media environment that present risks to both information security and privacy, changes to long-established policies and organizational culture, and the rewards of deeper involvement and collaboration with users. As social media transforms communication within all organizations, its potential to transform learning is also becoming apparent. This chapter promotes a better understanding of the effects social media has on learning and the importance to learners and the learning process, with special emphasis on its effect when combining face-to-face and distance learning. The subtopic for this chapter, HCI for the Web 2.0 environment seen through a corporate training lens, is emphasized with education and training examples from corporate, K-12, university and government sectors.

Chapter 3

This chapter shows how the online environment is used to promote quality teaching within a research project conducted by the Assessment Research Centre at the University of Melbourne. The project investigates how teacher teams use assessment data to inform teaching decisions and extensive efforts are made to check their learning through performance assessment procedures that monitor their discipline and pedagogy skills development. Teachers from the project are involved in a professional development course. The ways in which they adopt the knowledge, skills, and attitudes addressed by the course are tracked, along with assessment data from their students. The online environment is used to deliver the professional development course and to deliver online assessments for students and teachers. The authors are careful to ensure that the online experience for both teachers and students reinforces the ideas of the project. These include the notions of developmental approach rather than deficit, evidence rather than inferential decision making and collaboration rather than isolation.

This chapter describes an approach to assessment task design and delivery from the Assessment and Teaching of 21st Century Skills project (ATC21S). ATC21S is an example of an innovative, international, multi-stakeholder partnership involving industry, academics, governments, and educators that is aimed at shifting the direction of assessment and teaching towards a model more suited to the development of skills that students need in the 21st century. Within ATC21S, assessment design and delivery is just one component of a holistic framework in which assessment, teaching, resourcing, and policy work in unison to improve student outcomes. This chapter outlines this developmental framework and the impetus for ATC21S and partnerships which drive and support the project, sets the scene for dealing with performance measurement issues – how can we tell that people have learned anything? The focus of the chapter is on the technology-based design and delivery of assessments of one of the key skill areas of interest in the project - collaborative problem solving.

Siew Mee Barton, Deakin University, Australia

This chapter examines the impact of eLearning and Web 2.0 social media in a socially conservative environment in Indonesia that has nevertheless proven surprisingly adroit at change management. Web 2.0 social media has proven enormously popular in Indonesia but traditional Islamic schools (which are known in Java as pesantren but elsewhere in the Muslim world as madrasah) the focus of this study is often unable to access Web 2.0 or the Internet in general. Progressive non-national government organizations (NGOs) seek to remedy this situation by providing satellite broadband links to remote schools and this chapter examines one particular project. Despite the impoverished and conservative nature of their community, the leaders of this school have led their students in a surprisingly enthusiastic reception of eLearning technology, recognizing its great capacity to produce and enhance social networks and provide new opportunities for learning. Particular attention in this case study is given to factors relating to social capital, attitudes, and patterns of behavior in leadership and change management. A case study approach was chosen to enable a richer and more finely-grained analysis of the issues. The case study is based on semi-structured interviews and observations conducted over several years. This research shows that whilst the adoption and uptake of eLearning with emerging technologies is strongly shaped by cultural and social factors, it plays out in very different ways than might first have been expected.

Kathy Jordan, RMIT University, Australia
Jennifer Elsden-Clifton, RMIT University, Australia

Web 2.0 technologies are frequently represented as collaborative and interactive tools, and these capacities are particularly attractive to education. This chapter analyses how 26 beginning teachers in Victoria, Australia, used Elluminate Live!® (Elluminate) to support their professional learning. Drawing on Third Space theory and a case study approach, this chapter explores issues around change and emerging technologies. In particular, how beginning teachers appropriate features of this tool to engage in both receptive and collaborative learning spaces, ultimately transforming their professional learning space. It raises numerous issues and challenges for eLearning in the Web 2.0 environment.

Section 2
Social Networking and Collaborative Learning through HCI:
Synchronous and Asynchronous Learning

Saman Shahryari Monfared, Simon Fraser University, Canada
Peyman Ajabi-Naeini, Simon Fraser University, Canada
Drew Parker, Simon Fraser University, Canada

Social Networking, or the so-called Web 2.0 phenomenon, is changing the way we use the Internet. In turn, the way we use the Internet is changing the way we work, learn, communicate, and research. This chapter outlines a series of issues, tools, techniques, and pedagogy that may lie behind the process to bring social media into a learning environment. It then concludes with a four-year experience bringing these concepts into a senior undergraduate seminar, and offers observations and conclusions about the efficacy of our approach. Social networking has brought the Web into a conversation. Similarly, the chasm between synchronous and asynchronous learning is closing as the classroom becomes one part of a larger, continuous learning experience.

Chapter 8
Jennifer Martin, RMIT University, Australia

This chapter explores the use of information communications technology (ICT) to support international work integrated learning to provide more understanding of Web-mediated communities. The findings of a study of ICT use by students enrolled in a student mobility course on campuses in Australia and Vietnam reveal that students used a range of university provided commercial software as well as freely available ICT services and tools, particularly social networking sites, during their studies. A major challenge for universities is to provide access to the latest technologies at a cost that is affordable to the institution and its students, which provides the necessary level of reliability, availability, accessibility, functionality, and security. An online central management system or base camp can assist students to navigate the complex technical, social, cultural, and knowledge building opportunities that work integrated learning abroad offers.

Section 3
ePedagogy and Students' Use of HCI Interactive Learning Environments: Performance Measurement Issues – How Can We Tell that People Have Learned Anything?

Chapter 9
Long V. Nguyen, The University of Danang, Vietnam

The focus of this chapter is to explore if the collaborative potential offered by wikis translates into actual practice. The study examines the peer review process of 20 groups of English as a foreign language (EFL) students from two classes, i.e. a paper-based class and a wiki class, of a Bachelor of Arts (BA) in a Teaching English as a Foreign Language (TEFL) programme in a large university in Central Vietnam. Data analysis shows that the user-friendly wikis afford learning opportunities in two levels of analysis, namely participation and interaction, which lead to a high degree of information synthesis in the collaborative learning process. In terms of quantity, the multi-way nature of wiki-based exchanges confirms its characteristic of an architecture of participation. Likewise, the quality of the online peer review process is confidently affirmed in all three themes of collaborative interaction, i.e., socioaffective, organizational, and sociocognitive. It is concluded that the online platform of wikis turns the peer review process into a networking of both the academic and the social, and that wikis support a non-linear nature of collaborative learning.

Chapter 10
Sultana Lubna Alam, University of Canberra, Australia
Catherine McLoughlin, Australian Catholic University, Australia

With Web 2.0 technologies becoming increasingly integrated into all facets of higher education and society, it is vital to use the digital communicative tools and digital media so that students develop appropriate digital literacy and human-computer interaction (HCI) skills to enable them to become participatory citizens in our future society. In this case study, Web 2.0 tools and scenarios for learning are used in learning tasks to connect learners, share ideas, communicate, and-co create content within a university learning environment. The context for the study is social informatics – a composite class comprising 25-30 postgraduate and 3rd year undergraduate students within the Faculty of Information Sciences and Engineering.The study of social informatics examines the impact of technology upon social processes and learning. In order for students to gain a more comprehensive understanding of the topic, they engaged in range of tasks that enabled them to engage in collaborative dialogue and knowledge creation. In this case study, a Moodle mashup (the integration of information from different sources into one Website) is used to amalgamate information from the class and external sources such as blogs, wikis, and Twitter. The integration of HCI and Web 2.0 technologies into the learning process is examined, highlighting how social media tools can improve student engagement, collaboration, and digital literacy and e-citizenship skills.

Chapter 11

This study used a single-group pre-test/post-test design for a quasi-experimental study to implement a 12-week teaching activity. The research tools included a learning achievement test, a learning attitude scale, a portfolio assessment scale, a response and observation record form on Facebook, and a teaching reflection log. Each tool helped to identify the effect of problem-based learning on students' learning effectiveness and attitude. The following statistical methods were used to analyze quantitative data: descriptive statistics, one-way analysis of variance (ANOVA), nonparametric tests, single sample t-tests, dependent sample t-tests, Pearson product moment correlations, and Kendall harmony coefficients. The research results are as follows: (1) the teaching model of problem-based Facebook learning has a significant effect on the learning effectiveness of some students and has a positive effect on learning attitude; (2) there is a significant difference in the effectiveness of problem-based Facebook learning among students with different Website hosting experiences and among those who used Facebook's message function to varying degrees; (3) the problem-based Facebook learning has a significant impact on the effectiveness of the learning portfolios for students with different Website hosting experiences and message function utilization; (4) the problem-based Facebook learning method used for plant identification has a significant effect on the learning attitude of students; and (5) there is a significant positive correlation among the problem-based Facebook teaching of plant identification, students' learning effectiveness, and learning attitude.

This chapter reviews the concept of personalised eLearning resources in relation to integrating interactivity into asynchronous learning. Personalised eLearning resources are learning resources which are selected to suit a specific student or trainee's individual learning requirements. The affordance of personalised eLearning would provide educators with the opportunity to shift away from eLearning content that is retrieved and move towards the provision of personalised interactive content to provide a form of asynchronous learning to suit students at different degree levels. A basic introduction to the concept of ePedagogy in online learning environments is explored and the impacts these systems have on students learning experiences are considered. Issues, controversies, and problems associated with the creation of personalised interactive eLearning resources are examined, and suggested solutions and recommendations to the identified issues, controversies, and problems are reviewed. Personalised interactive asynchronous learning resources could potentially improve students' learning experiences but more research on the human computer interface of these authoring tools is required before personalised eLearning resources are available for use by non-technical authors.

Section 4
Rich Internet Applications and HCI in Educational Practice- Educational and Training Design: Support Systems, Models, Case Studies, etc.

Chapter 13

Fáber D. Giraldo, University of Quindío, Colombia
María Lilí Villegas, University of Quindío, Colombia
César A. Collazos, University of Cauca, Colombia

This chapter is written as one method to supply the necessary support systems for educational and training design. As such, the authors propose their global development software (GDS) methodology emerges as a revolutionary discipline. It is based on the externalization of software development between geographically distant places in order to reduce development costs. Traditional educational and training process in software engineering must be advocated to consider (or enhance) this new trend, with its respective challenges and necessary skills (multicultural interaction, effective communication, distributed software project management), into curriculums. GDS therefore demands the presence of supporting systems to provide permanent user interaction and enhanced communication tasks. The presence of such interactions is a key aspect to promote the performance and knowledge acquisition processes among globally distributed software development teams. The main goal of such interactions into platforms that support distributed contexts is to reduce the impact generated by the tyranny of distance. This work exposes some human-computer interaction (HCI) principles applied by the authors' research team in order to structure a supporting user interface environment that reflects the distributed computer supported collaborative learning (CSCL) practice in software engineering. The chapter describes several services that are provided for managing the interaction between participants, such as synchronous interactions through Microsoft © LiveMeeting and Adobe © Connect, and asynchronous interactions such as Moodle forums. In this way, the authors implement effective HCI into educational professional practice scenarios for a distributed CSCL within the specialized domain of software engineering.

Chapter 14

C. Candace Chou, University of St. Thomas, USA
Rama Kaye Hart, University of St. Thomas, USA

This chapter aims at examining, through a case study, student perceptions of interactive learning activities based on the experiential learning model in Second Life (SL). Undergraduate students in an Honors Program reflected on their learning experiences in a blended learning course that took place both in person and in SL for four weeks. Student reflections on two main learning tasks: discussion about assigned readings and SL field trips which include simulating and gaming, were recorded in weekly journals. Sixty journal entries were the data source for coding. Student experiences of the learning tasks are predominately positive with some challenges. Positive views include: excitement, enhanced confidence, motivation for learning, and increased knowledge. Challenges were mostly due to technical issues. Instructor interventions, including ground rules for online conversation and tech support, were important in minimizing barriers to student learning in virtual worlds.

Foreword

New technologies are now delivering for us the groundswell of interest in online learning that for many years has been predicted but never fully realised. Few institutions now, can avoid the need to provide students with the flexibility and opportunities of online learning. There still remains, however, large differences in the quality of online learning programs brought about in many cases by the way our understanding of how best to apply technologies to learning lags behind the opportunities the new technologies are bringing.

This book seeks to bridge this gap by providing access to contemporary and innovative research-based approaches to the application of technologies in online learning. The book represents a collection of ideas and examples of effective learning and teaching where the learner and learning takes precedence over the technology. The book provides an excellent blend of theory and practice drawing from the minds of eminent teachers and researchers from all corners of the world. What is particularly useful about this book is that it contains the broadest possible set of examples and ideas. The book is organised around themes which recognise the ways in which contemporary technologies can support and enhance online learning through a focus on important issues of pedagogy.

I am confident that through this book, readers will become well informed about the capabilities of contemporary learning technologies, enlightened by the ideas and examples it contains and inspired by the many opportunities which are represented. The book continues the excellent work of the many researchers and teachers exploring and applying online learning. It provides a strong supports for extending our capabilities and outcomes for effective and efficient online learning.

Ron Oliver
Deputy Vice-Chancellor (Teaching, Learning and International)

Ron Oliver *is Deputy Vice-Chancellor (Teaching, Learning and International) and Professor of eLearning at Edith Cowan University in Western Australia. Throughout his teaching career he has used emerging technologies to engage and motivate his students and has a particular interest in learning and the need for relevance and engagement in curricula. He has been an active researcher and publisher in the area of instructional technologies and eLearning for the past thirty years, and has experience in the design, development, implementation and evaluation of a diverse range of technology-facilitated learning settings. Ron has been recognised for his innovative teaching and research with learning technologies through a number of awards including: Australian Award for University Teaching (1997); Australian Learning and Teaching Council Fellowship (2006); Fellowship of the Association for the Advancement for Computer in Education (2007); and Fellowship of the Australasian Society for the Use of Computers in Learning in Tertiary Education, (2009).*

Preface

OVERVIEW

In many places around the world, Web 2.0 continues to be promoted as the new incarnation of the Internet because of the social networking aspects afforded by the supporting technologies. This general acceptance may be due to the evolutionary nature of the ripple effect of the human-dimensions of the whole Internet environment. As a result, there are many ways to view the term *Web 2.0*. Firstly, in the sense that it represents both a range of information and communications technology (ICT) tools that enable businesses to profit. Secondly, it is by its meme-like characteristics that are emerging as cultural dogma in new ideas and values, or patterns of behavior, which are passed from one person to another as if by symbiotic imitation. It is the latter definition that sets a broader context for this book, expanding the discussion beyond the popular generation of Web-based tools and educational sites. This book sets out to predict what the future holds in store for both the corporate sector and educational institutions alike, through Web-mediated education and training environments that enable openness, interaction, and teach communities to flourish.

OBJECTIVES OF THE BOOK

The overall objective of this book is to follow on from the previous Premier Reference Source book published in 2007 *Enhancing Learning Through Human Computer Interaction* to provide a useful handbook on adopting interactive Web 2.0 tools that promote effective human-computer interaction (HCI) in ePedagogical practice for education and training. Its main purpose is to provide a design manual for the novice educational-HCI designer. Web 2.0 tools are often described in an endless list of discussion or blogging type tools, ignoring the need for finding new ways to improve our ePedagogical strategies.

The chapters in this book are devised to focus interest on eLearning best practice in corporate performance that is applicable to the education sector. In so doing, it brings forward traditional instructional design frameworks, which involve interactivity on the Internet that have succeeded in the business arena, in a language that is familiar for teaching and learning institutions in schools and higher education.

TARGET AUDIENCE

Industry training developers, corporate trainers, courseware designers, government sector specialists, infrastructure policy makers, educational technology practitioners and researchers (school teachers, higher education), and post graduate students.

INTEGRATING ePEDAGOGY INTO ONLINE CLASSROOMS

For many of us, knowing how to learn is something that improves as we grow older. For the most part, as we travel along our lifelong learning path, it becomes easier to differentiate which instructional strategies are likely to suit us best. The ICT tools of digital age are redefining pedagogy such that many of us simply cannot keep abreast of the emerging instructional space we are calling ePedagogy in this book. The difficulties we are likely to face with online instruction may depend upon whether there are suitable instructional strategies to cognitively fast-track the learning tasks. It is well known that novice learners require the full range of rules and information related to learning something new, whereas an experienced learner might only require a quick revision (McKay, 2008). Research has clearly demonstrated that beginners or novice learners will respond best to measured amounts of guidance through progressively more complex instructional/learning content with strategic opportunities for interactive practice examples along the way (Merrill, 2002). Alternatively, a person possessing a more complete grasp of the task online will likely want to experiment first, preferring to refer to the rules and basic information only when they need assistance. Unfortunately there are many online programmes that do not cater for both modes of learning. When instructional systems cannot adapt to this important requirement, they run the risk of demotivating both groups of learners (Tennyson & Bagley, 1991). The result may be confusion for novices when the primary rules and examples are not sufficiently explicit, and boredom and frustration for the experienced learner who is forced into following the complete instructional strategy.

In seeking answers to the dilemma of how to provide such flexible ePedagogies, our attention should turn to the valuable body of work that is relevant to our discussion by Repovs and Baddeley (2006). They say that working memory has proven to be an important part of the human's cognitive system, providing the ability to maintain and manipulate information in the process of guiding and executing complex cognitive tasks. With ePedagogy, such cognitive tasks may need to involve past experiences that are encoded and held in our memory as retrievable information (or prior domain knowledge). An important principle for unlocking this prior domain knowledge is to integrate the screen-based information into our working memories while our prior experiences/knowledge is held in our long-term memories, according to Kalyuga (2005).

Therefore, this book proposes that the design of instructional materials or the ePedagogy must include consideration of the level of expertise (prior domain knowledge) of the learners. Research shows that most adults have relevant experiences that either drive them or demotivate them to learn, and that when the content and design of instructional materials do not challenge or interest them, they may become demotivated.

THE HUMAN-DIMENSIONS OF HCI

While many organisations have eLearning Websites that include courseware and other online learning artefacts, they often lack a coherent and effective broad-based eLearning strategy (Rosenberg 2001). We are suggesting that the human-dimensions of HCI offer the strategic glue for successful online training which Rosenberg notes is lacking. The human-dimensions of HCI are but one piece of the complicated computer-usability or techno puzzle that involves two distinct contexts. One relates to the human-dimension or social context of computing, while the other relates to the machine side, with people's perspectives shaped by the performance of the technical computing components (McKay 2008). The literature deals more often with the latter. It is only in recent times that a voice has been given to computer-usability issues that involve the human-dimensions.

Considering the human-dimensions of HCI provides a useful framework for understanding how adult learners prefer to participate in online training. Attention to their prior knowledge increases learners' willingness to participate. Yet, there is little evidence that instructional design in the government sector includes recognition of the factors that encourage a positive attitude towards participation. We discuss some of these issues below.

WEB-MEDIATED EDUCATION/TRAINING

Web-mediated learning programmes require flexible interaction depending upon whether the learning event involves instruction – then implement a training programme that facilitates improved performance outcomes; if it is purely an information giving exercise, the Web-mediated ePedagogy will require a *knowledge management strategy* instead.

TERMINOLOGY

A short word is given here to afford a more comfortable reading stance; this is necessary as the ICT paradigm extends across so many philosophical fields. Authors may at times refer to the following terms without providing satisfactory clarification. For instance:

- **Synchronous/Asynchronous:** The former usually refers to a ePedagogy that requires interaction (facilitator/trainee) occurring in the same timeframe; while the latter refers to situations where the facilitation and learner/trainee interact at different times.
- **Face-to-Face:** Refers to the more traditional classroom pedagogy where there is a one-to-one interaction between the instructional facilitator and the learner/trainee.
- **HCI:** There are some authors who refer to this term to mean human computer *interface* (instead of interaction). This simply identifies that they describe the screen-based characteristics, rather than the interaction.
- **LMS:** Refers to the proprietary *learning management systems* that are accepted as off the shelf software management applications.
- **Wiki:** This term usually refers to a Website that is developed collaboratively by a community of users, allowing any user to add and edit content.
- **Blog:** Or *Weblog* describes a personal online journal - intended for public viewing that is frequently updated by the blogger/author.

SCHOLARLY VALUE AND CONTRIBUTION

The chapters in this book directly compare traditional pedagogy with emerging ePedagogies in a variety of higher educational, corporate and elementary/secondary school settings. These instructional forums provide a diverse range of positive outcomes linking information management techniques that enhance the leverage of ICT tools in a specialist educational context. Through the global nature of the authorship contribution, this book reveals the impact of increased awareness for promoting more effective HCI in the classroom/training sessions that benchmark ePedagogy.

CONTRIBUTIONS

This book is organized into 14 chapters, which fall into four main themes, including: *Technology and Change Management for the Web 2.0 Environment*; *Social Networking and Collaborative Learning Through HCI*; *ePedagogy and Students' use of HCI Interactive Learning Environments*; and *Rich Internet Applications and HCI in Educational Practice*.

SECTION 1: TECHNOLOGY AND CHANGE MANAGEMENT FOR THE WEB 2.0 ENVIRONMENT

The corporate environment is shifting instructional design away from taking a more traditional approach to their online training, which previously relied upon adopting ICT tools in face-to-face sessions, to concentrate on developing ePedagogies that encourage customized Web 2.0 enriched courseware. In recent years the adoption of Web 2.0 enhanced tools (otherwise referred to as multi-media) has been researched by a diverse mix of professional disciplines. Accordingly adoption of these enhanced ICT tools is defined here as the decision to implement an online solution to solve an educational need as well as business workforce training/reskilling. Many of the authors of this book are describing operational ePedagogy design, which means they are concentrating on a set of *user-centred activities* that people and their computers need to perform upon their educational/corporate information resources. ICT adoption can therefore be studied at three operational design levels. The first level relates to the need for developers of online education/training programmes to understand how corporate-level investment decisions in online training are made. The second level applies to the user-centred perspective of the trainee/learners to explain what people do with their online experiences. The third level is closely connected to the previous, which examines the information systems (IS) design and development process to evaluate why online training adoption rates are not keeping pace with Web 2.0 advances.

Chapter 1: *Managing Expectations: A Changing Landscape* – This opening chapter writes about adopting practical strategies to enhance eLearning in the Web 2.0 environment. As such, it serves as an excellent example of how to deal with the changing nature of asynchronous ePedagogies. It highlights the need to plan for the changing profile of our 21st century tertiary students; describing both sides of the specialist online educational equation, to highlight discrepancies in both student and staff expectations. Set in an Australian University, the author describe an educational scenario that will be of interest to online facilitators in both the corporate and educational settings alike.

Chapter 2: *The Role of Social Media as a Tool for Learning* – Set in the USA, this chapter describes the theoretical basis for social media effects upon learners' adoption of Web 2.0 tools as seen through the corporate training practice lens of the authorship. It speaks of a social presence and the perils of transactional distance; while taking a constructivist approach towards dealing with community and the socio-cultural context of knowledge.

Chapter 3: *Assessment and Learning Partnerships in an Online Environment* - Set within an Australia university's research study, this chapter shows how the online environment is used to promote quality teaching in a professional development course and online assessments for students and teachers. This data is used to inform teaching decisions by drawing on performance assessment procedures that monitor the teacher's discipline and pedagogy skill development.

Chapter 4: *Development of the Assessment Design and Delivery of Collaborative Problem Solving in the Assessment and Teaching of 21st Century Skills Project* - This chapter describes effective HCI strategies for the Web 2.0 environment seen through a corporate training practice lens, as it involves academe with industry and government stakeholders. It outlines a developmental framework that indicates whether people have learned anything; shifting the direction of assessment towards a unified model of skills that people require for the 21st century. The context for this Australian research involves a technology-based design and the delivery of assessments that relate to collaborative problem solving skills.

Chapter 5: *Facilitating Learning by Going Online: Modernising Islamic Teaching and Learning in Indonesia* - This chapter describes a study conducted in Indonesia. It is the first of the two chapters in this book, which describe emerging technology and change management issues for ePedagogies in a Web 2.0 environment. This chapter concentrates on the impact of eLearning social media tool adoption in a socially conservative environment. There is an interesting discussion on progressive non-governmental organisations as they seek to increase ICT access to the learning institutions that normally miss out on such Internet access.

Chapter 6: *Rethinking Web 2.0 Learning via Third Space* - Set again within an Australian university. Like the previous chapter, this is the second chapter which deals with the emerging technology and change management issues for eLearning in the Web 2.0 environment. These authors analyse novice teachers' use of collaborate software through interactive social learning experiences that include: virtual classrooms, online conferencing and instant messaging. This research raises issues that challenge the approach to adoption of such ICT tools in an educational/training setting.

SECTION 2: SOCIAL NETWORKING AND COLLABORATIVE LEARNING THROUGH HCI

Creating collaborative work space is certainly not a mere theoretical dream anymore; it is now a reality brought about with the advent of eCommunities. More and more we are seeing how the corporate workplace is engaging directly with information through social networking to such an extent that it is giving rise to the term information or knowledge worker. In a sense, collaboration is a bread and butter skill for most people in the workforce – where the triple bottom line matters the most. For those readers who may not be aware – triple bottom line is derived from the accounting profession; it means expanding the traditional reporting framework to reflect the ecological and social performance in addition to financial performance. Some of us believe that collaborative work space is therefore a commercial necessity, if we are to survive in a global business environment. However, there are major hidden costs in such global networking. According to Felman, Marcobella, Duhl, and Crawford (2005), the hidden costs to a corporation for their information work with 1,000 information workers - with an average salary of US$60,000 each per year, plus benefits - is US$30 million for wasted time. There can be no doubt this is telling us there is enormous potential for software developers to come up with more efficient and effective collaborative ICT-tools that are easy to understand and use. In keeping with this approach to collaborative learning through effective HCI, this section contains two chapters that concentrate on the synchronous/asynchronous ePedagogies in building Web-mediated communities.

Chapter 7: *Bringing Web 2.0 into the Learning Environment* - Canada provides the backdrop for this interesting chapter. It has been written through the personal experience of the undergraduate student/ authors and their facilitator. They provide commentary on their four-year online learning programme. They propose that the gap between synchronous and asynchronous environments is closing due to the classroom becoming "one part of a larger, continuous learning experience."

Chapter 8: *Networked Learning and Teaching for International Work Integrated Learning* - The setting for this chapter involved two universities in Australia and Vietnam. It describes the role of ICT services and tools that support international work integrated learning in building Web-mediated communities, pointing out where improvements to their ePedagogy will enhance their instructional outcomes. The researcher utilized a qualitative methodology to provide detailed student feedback.

SECTION 3: ePEDAGOGY AND STUDENTS' USE OF HCI INTERACTIVE LEARNING ENVIRONMENTS

Content and quality of ePedagogies need to be designed with the utmost consideration for effective learning/training. To achieve this, it is useful to think that the 'e' in eLearning refers to how an online course is digitised, while the 'learning' refers to what the course content involves and the instructional strategies (ePedagogies) required to achieve the expected learning outcomes. Following on from thinking about the what, in terms of instructional content - is to consider that the why is about helping individuals achieve their educational goals or assisting organisations to improve employee skills and workforce performance (Clark & Mayer 2008). For employees/corporate trainees to engage more intuitively with eLearning, it is therefore important for designers to consider the impact of HCI on adult learners; that is, to measure their learning outcomes effectively. Jasinski (2007) asserts that eLearning may facilitate highly valuable training and skills development. Yet if the learning achievement is not measured, employers and employees will be less inclined to participate or believe in the potential of eLearning. Moreover, it is difficult to measure the effectiveness of eLearning; however, this goal is a design challenge shared by other types of training and workplace strategies (Jasinski 2007). If effectiveness is not measured appropriately, there will be no legitimate evidence that eLearning occurred. The next five chapters reflect this approach as they tell us how they have gone about integrating HCI into their ePedagogies that include: solutions through their classroom use of multi-media and integrating interactivity into their asynchronous strategies.

Chapter 9: *Wiki-Mediated Peer Review Process: Participation and Interaction* – Set in Vietnam the author of this chapter writes about how the research dealt directly with performance measurement to explore whether the collaborative potential offered by Wikis translates into actual practice. The research adopts a mixed method that includes qualitative and quantitative data analysis.

Chapter 10: *E-Citizenship Skills Online: A Case Study of Faculty Use of Web 2.0 Tools to Increase Active Participation and Learning* – An Australian university's higher-education course-unit on social informatics sets the context for this chapter which explores the impact of informatics in our society.

Chapter 11: *A Study on a Problem-Based Learning Method Using Facebook at a Vocational School* – Set in an agricultural college in Taiwan, this chapter explores the effectiveness of a problem-based ePedagogy using Facebook to enhance the attitudes towards learning for sophomore students. Research findings are given, followed by suggestions for future studies.

Chapter 12: *Web-Mediated Education and Training Environments: A Review of Personalised Interactive eLearning* – This chapter reviews the literature to provide us with a comprehensive and interesting description of such strategies which amount to an emerging ePedagogy. It points out there are many issues, concerns, and obstacles that prevent personalised eLearning realizing its true potential.

SECTION 4: RICH INTERNET APPLICATIONS AND HCI IN EDUCATIONAL PRACTICE

To introduce the final two chapters, a small word or two is necessary to explain this rather sophisticated or high-end IS computing environment in simple language for the uninitiated reader of this educational technology book. The current range of ICT tools provide a range of powerful features that include: easier access, updating capability, scheduling of tasks, and flexible environments for both learning facilitators (teachers and corporate trainers) and their students. There are three ICT elements that represent a rich Internet application (RIA) that are necessary to drive a successful ePedagogy. These RIA elements include: rich client technology, server technology, and development tools. The so called rich client technology (the Flash player is a good example) provides all the hidden operating benefits of the Web by keeping costs to a minimum (automatic compression and loading of components on demand). In addition there is: client-side scripting, high performance connectivity, real-time server communication. Server technology provides the markup languages to connect to the rich client technologies; for example Web database language tools. Development tools offer an environment that provides the ability to create the various pieces of an application - from user interfaces to server-side logic. Staffing this type of ICT production event requires a mixture of IT professionals: an application architect to integrate the ICT tools into an existing environment, a multi-media expert to develop the interactive graphical user interface and communications service with the application server, and a Web-designer in the initial stages of a system's development project to consult on the user interface specifications, and act as the conduit between the architect and multimedia practitioner. A successful RIA can offer a range of benefits that include: distributed, server-based internet applications that extend the interactive capabilities of desktop applications. As such, they should enhance the user's interactivity and manipulation of data, rather than behave as fancy graphical page-turners. They should provide the user with a real-time status check mechanism whenever background processing is underway. This way, informed users can understand and stay oriented during a lengthy activity. Finally, because a RIA can store client-side data, this allows customization of their interaction during a system processing cycle.

Chapter 13: *The Use of HCI Approaches into Distributed CSCL Activities Applied to Software Engineering Courses* – This chapter deals with educational/training design as it relates to RIA support systems described above. The authors describe this educational technology environment in easy to read language that belies the complex nature of the RIA it represents for managing their synchronous/asynchronous interactions necessary for their software engineering course.

Chapter 14: *A Case Study of Designing Experiential Learning Activities in Virtual Worlds* – The last chapter ends the book as it provides the reader with a generous and interesting insight into a virtual classroom experience. This chapter is certainly a fitting one to complete the contributions. It treats us to an undergraduate online experiential model that took place in Second Life, where the ePedagogy challenges were mostly due to technical issues.

Elspeth McKay
RMIT University, Australia

REFERENCES

Clark, R., & Mayer, R. (2008). *E-learning and the science of instruction: Proven guidelines for consumers and designers of multimedia learning* (Taff, R., Ed.). 2nd ed.). Pfeiffer.

Felman, S., Marcobella, J. R., Duhl, J., & Crawford, A. (2005). *The hidden costs of information work.* Retrieved from http://scribd.com/doc/6138369/Whitepaper-IDC-Hidden-Costs-0405

Jasinski, M. (2007). *Innovate and Integrate: Embedding innovative practices.* Retrieved from http://www.flexible-learning.net.au

Kalyuga, S. (2005). Prior domain knowledge principle in multimedia learning . In Mayer, R. (Ed.), *The Cambridge handbook of multimedia learning* (pp. 325–337). Cambridge, UK: Cambridge University Press. doi:10.1017/CBO9780511816819.022

McKay, E. (2008). *The human-dimensions of human computer interaction. The Future of Learning Series* (*Vol. 3*). Amsterdam, The Netherlands: IOS Press.

Merrill, D. (2002). First principles of instruction. *Educational Technology Research and Development, 50*(3), 43–59. doi:10.1007/BF02505024

Repovs, G., & Baddeley, A. (2006). The multi-component model of working memory: explorations in experimental cognitive psychology. *Neuroscience, 139*, 5–21. doi:10.1016/j.neuroscience.2005.12.061

Rosenberg, M. J. (2001). *E-learning: Strategies for delivering knowledge in the digital age.* New York, NY: McGraw-Hill.

Tennyson, R. D., & Bagley, C. A. (1991). *Structured versus constructed instructional strategies for improving concept acquisition by domain-experienced and domain-novice learners.* Annual Meeting of the American Educational Research Association, Illinois.

Acknowledgment

A special note of thanks is given to the following researchers, who through their expertise in special education joined the Editorial Advisory Board, assisting the Editor in the manuscript peer reviewing process. In particular, their care and attention to details was appreciated when there were conflicting chapter submission reviews.

Mandi Axmann, *Open Universities Australia*
Professor Sandra Jones, *College of Business, RMIT University, Australia*
Professor Toshiaki Honda, *Faculty of Education, Ibaraki University, Japan*
Professor Kuldip Kaur, *Open University Malayasia*

Each chapter underwent a strict double-blind review process between authors to evaluate the submissions for this book. There is a special thank you that is due to the generosity of some of these authors who agreed to review extra submissions – due to the promised anonymity they cannot be singled out – all the same, they will know who they are.

Section 1
Technology and Change Management for the Web 2.0 Environment:
Strategies to Enhance eLearning in the Web 2.0 Environment

Chapter 1
Managing Expectations:
A Changing Landscape

Jo Coldwell-Neilson
Deakin University, Australia

ABSTRACT

Expectations of, and by, students and staff in the classroom have been well researched. Yet, still there is a gap between the expectations of students and what they experience in their studies. The classroom itself is changing with the introduction of Web 2.0 technologies into the mix. Further changes are being driven by the changing profile of a tertiary student in the twenty first century. Education will not fulfill its goal if the gap in expectations is not addressed. The discrepancy in expectations is explored from the perspective of students and staff and strategies for bridging the gap and enhancing eLearning in the Web 2.0 environment are offered. The chapter begins with a scenario that demonstrates the issues and concludes with suggestions to avoid them in the future. In doing so, the key drivers of change in the learning landscape in Australia are identified and the impact these may have on staff and student expectations is explored.

SETTING THE SCENE

It is Friday afternoon. Jane is heading home after a busy week at work. She has an assignment due on Monday morning so is keen to get started once she has cooked dinner for the family. While on the train she downloads the assignment onto her smart phone and starts reading it. She decides that it is relatively straightforward but there is one section she is not sure how to tackle. So she sends her lecturer a short email from her phone confident that she will have plenty of time to

DOI: 10.4018/978-1-4666-3649-1.ch001

complete the assignment by 9am on Monday. On Monday morning Dr Johns arrives at his office before his first lecture with enough time to check his messages. He had intended to have a relaxing weekend bushwalking but had a PhD thesis to examine (the report was due in today) and four conference papers to review (also due today). He is surprised to find a number of emails from one of his students. The first had arrived on Friday at about 5:15pm, a short message obviously sent from a smart phone. The second email had been sent later that evening with a rather longer explanation of the information and guidance the student required in order to complete the assignment which was due before 9am today. The third email had been sent on Saturday morning. The student was showing signs of concern as Dr Johns had not yet responded to her enquiry. There were yet more emails from Jane sent on Saturday and Sunday, each using language more irate than the last, the final one indicated that she was extremely upset at the lack of communication from Dr Johns. This one also indicated that she had not expected a university, which claimed to be student-centred and flexible, would treat their students in such a disrespectful manner and that she would be lodging a formal complaint about the matter.

INTRODUCTION

Managing student expectations in a classroom setting is a well researched area with many pedagogical and administrative processes having been developed by teachers since teaching began! In the late twentieth century information and communications technology (ICT) tools were introduced into the classroom with dramatic effect. Suddenly students and teachers were expected to be computer literate and be willing and able to use these new, innovative tools to support teaching and learning. Hiltz (1994, p. 259) suggested that "what we are going to see in the future are more virtual universities", that the "meaning of the 'university' will change, and the idea of a

'campus' as we know it may disappear. It is now possible to run a university from a closet". This expectation that the bricks and mortar classroom would disappear in favour of technology supported virtual learning centres for example, has proved to be unfounded and, as Burdett (2003, p. 84) suggests, "despite anticipated benefits ... ICT is not embraced enthusiastically nor completely by all academics".

With hindsight we know that these changes in the classroom are an ongoing process. Face-to-face teaching is still the core business of educational institutions at all levels. But the classroom has been enhanced and, in many cases, transformed with the introduction of ICT tools. Interactive white boards, laptop computers and social media for example are used extensively to enhance the learning experience of students throughout the education system (see for example Preston & Mowbray, 2008; Hemmi, Bayne & Land, 2009). Learning management systems (LMS) have also been widely adopted providing opportunities for students to gain access to learning resources and activities without temporal or geographic boundaries. There are opportunities for students and staff to communicate with each other and for students to be supported in ways that are just not possible in a traditional face-to-face setting alone.

At the same time as these changes have been occurring in the classroom, the profile of a tertiary student has also changed. The ideal traditional student who is supported financially and culturally to study full-time, who is eager to learn, is dedicated to their studies, is interested in academic debate, is engaged fully with the university community, is self-motivated and takes responsibility for their learning and whose goal is to achieve at the highest level possible is mostly a student of the past. The modern student has to work to support themselves and to support the lifestyle they have chosen. Full-time students are often working part-time; many students are working full-time while studying part-time. Some attempt full-time study while continuing to work full-time. The goal of their studies is to achieve employment in their chosen area rather than the acquisition of knowledge per se. The distinction between campus-based learners and distance learners is becoming blurred with many students enrolling on-campus but accessing the learning resources through online technologies rather than attending face-to-face classes. Many students are juggling work, family and social commitments while attempting to meet their study commitments. Unfortunately many students are not successful jugglers and can fall by the wayside if institutions do not have strategies in place to identify such students in a timely manner. Institutions also need to have interventions at the ready to assist these students to address their difficulties and to give their studies an appropriate priority in their busy lives. Students also expect a much greater level of support from the university that bears little or no resemblance to what was available 20 or 30 years ago (ACER, 2011a).

These technology and student driven changes in higher education are causing friction within institutions. Staff expect students to be motivated to learn and to understand what is expected of them. Students expect to be informed fully as to what they need to learn to complete their studies successfully and they expect a level of flexibility in recognition of the many commitments, other than education, in their lives. Unfortunately the discrepancies between staff and student expectations have unwanted outcomes which can lead to staff becoming disillusioned with teaching and the perceived poor attitude of students, and students becoming disillusioned with the realities of life at university and the apparent inflexibility of the education system. Students may even reject the opportunity of completing their studies. All these factors contribute to creating a stressful environment which is not conducive to a positive learning experience.

Education will not fulfill its goal if the mismatch between staff and student expectations is not addressed and managed. The increasing emphasis universities, as well as their funding bodies, are placing on student engagement, retention and pro-

gression means that we can no longer sweep these pockets of disillusionment and discord under the carpet. Continuing changes in the higher education sector suggest that addressing any discrepancies in expectations requires urgent attention. The expectations of students by staff, and of staff by students, are an ongoing issue. As the range of ICT tools change and increase, the demands of, and by, both sides change. Managing expectations requires constant attention and, with increasing diversity in the classroom, innovative solutions.

The overall objective of this chapter is to explore the expectations of staff and students with respect to: each other; the technology that supports teaching and learning; and the support provided by the institution. The key drivers of change in the tertiary sector in Australia are identified, which sets the scene in which the expectations of staff and students are investigated. Strategies to manage staff and student expectations are explored in the context of the author's personal experience, providing practical insights into how good practice can be successfully implemented in a technology-supported learning environment. Although good teaching and learning practice will be discussed in the context of a wholly online learning environment, it should be noted that the principles and strategies to engage students are relevant to any teaching situation whether or not they include elements of online delivery. This chapter concludes with a response to the opening scenario.

DRIVERS OF CHANGE

A review of higher education commissioned by the Australian Government in 2008 is having a major impact on the tertiary education sector within Australia. The Bradley Review, as the report is known, made a number of recommendations, some of which will have a significant impact on the profile of students entering into tertiary education in the years to come. The two most significant recommendations in this context are (1) that the percentage of 25- to 34- year olds completing an undergraduate degree is expected to rise from 29% to 40% by 2020; and (2) that 20% of students enrolled in higher education are expected to be from low socio-economic backgrounds (Bradley, Noonan, Nugent & Scales, 2008). These targets reflect the view that "the reach, quality and performance of a nation's higher education system will be the key determinants of its economic and social progress" (Bradley et al., 2008, p. xi). The Australian Government is supporting the outcomes of the Bradley Review indicating that the proposed changes will:

provide the foundation for a new student centred higher education system, which will enable students to develop richer learning and employment pathways. The focus on students and how to provide them with the best possible experience and educational outcomes involves a renewed emphasis on quality in teaching and research, underpinned by robust standards and accreditation (Commonwealth of Australia, 2009, p. 8).

In Australia, and many other countries, increasing emphasis is being placed by higher education institutions on improving student engagement and their learning experience as evidenced by the variety of student surveys that are currently being undertaken in the Australian tertiary sector. These include (but are not limited to):

- **The Australian Survey of Student Engagement (AUSSE):** Focuses not only on student engagement and experience but also on improving student retention (ACER, 2011b);
- **The Course Experience Questionnaire (CEQ):** Seeks information from recent university graduates about their perceptions of the quality of the course they have just completed as well as the skill set they have acquired as an outcome of their programme of study (McInnis, Griffen, James & Coates, 2000); and

- Various instruments implemented by tertiary institutions to provide students an opportunity to evaluate their learning experiences such as the Student Evaluation of Teaching Units (SETU) which is completed by students at the conclusion of each teaching period at the author's own institution.

This focus is not entirely of the institutions' own making. A further recommendation of the Bradley Review indicates that tertiary institutions are expected to administer the Graduate Destination Survey, CEQ and the AUSSE and report annually on the findings, emphasizing the importance being placed on student engagement, retention and progression. This focus is reflected within institutions with increasing emphasis being placed on responding to the students' voice.

The annual Horizon reports (produced by The New Media Consortium) provide an interesting insight into the rapidity of technological change and acceptance of change over the last five to 10 years within the higher education sector. The 2005 Horizon Report suggested that over a period of one to five years a number of technologies would have a significant impact on teaching and learning (NMC, 2005). These included:

- Over one to two years, extended learning and ubiquitous wireless;
- Over three to four years, intelligent searching and educational gaming; and
- Over five or more years, social networks and knowledge webs as well as context-aware computing.

By 2010, the 2005 predications were in place with most if not all higher education institutions utilizing at least some aspects of the technologies mentioned. According to Johnson, Levine, Smith and Stone, (2010) in 2010 the predications were:

- Over one to two years, mobile computing and open content;
- Over three to four years, electronic books and simple augmented reality; and
- Over five or more years, gesture-based computing and visual data analysis.

Already the short and mid-term predictions for technology change are evident in higher education while gesture-based computing is evident in the current crop of games consoles. The rapidity of change does not provide many opportunities for a new technology to be introduced, accepted and then bedded-down to become common-place in the portfolio of technologies that are available to support teaching and learning. The acceptance of technology in a social or entertainment setting seems to be more rapid than in an educational institution setting.

It is evident that the general climate of technology acceptance in our everyday lives is having an impact on student expectations. The availability of the Internet in the home, and the increasing use of mobile devices such as smart phones, wireless enabled devices such as iPads, various eReaders, as well as very affordable netbooks has led to the expectation that delivery of education will, in some part at least, utilize such devices (Johnson et al, 2010). Most, if not all, tertiary institutions have recognized the benefits of facilitating learning through the increasing use of ICT tools. LMS for example are now commonplace as a standard part of universities' portfolio of educational technologies (e-technologies) to support teaching and learning, with many institutions up to their second or third generation of LMS. Students expect to be able to use the technologies that they do in their everyday lives and may well be disappointed that this is not always the case.

Academics are being exposed to the same drivers for everyday use of technology but not all are as ready to accept ICT tools more broadly into their teaching practice. Differences in the levels of use between academics further exacerbates perceptions amongst students that teachers are not delivering quality programs and are not meeting their (the students') expectations; "students have high expectations for faculty members' technology knowledge and skill" (Roberts, 2005, pp. 3.3-3.4).

Managing student expectations in a classroom setting is a well researched area. In 1987 Chickering and Gamson published their Seven Principles of Good Practice in undergraduate education which very rapidly became the benchmark for higher education teachers at that time. Sorcinelli (as cited in Prebble et al., 2005) suggested that these principles were well supported by 50 years of research. Prebble et al. (2005) further suggest that there are few sources cited as frequently as these principles.

The seven principles are:

1. Encourage contact between students and faculty;
2. Develop reciprocity and cooperation among students;
3. Encourage active learning;
4. Give prompt feedback;
5. Emphasize time on task;
6. Communicate high expectations; and
7. Respect diverse talents and ways of learning (Chickering & Gamson, 1987).

Chickering and Gamson's teaching environment was not necessarily technology enhanced but rather the traditional face-to-face classroom. But in a subsequent paper Chickering and Ehrmann (1996) document a number of cost effective, appropriate ways of using ICT tools to advance the seven principles. The range of technologies available at that time was described as 'staggering' with most falling into one of three categories:

- **Asynchronous Communication:** Participants in the communication do not need to use the communication tool at the same time as messages are permanently available to be read. Email and discussion boards are commonly used asynchronous communication tools.

- **Synchronous Communication:** Communication occurs in real time and is not normally available to be read thereafter. Online chat is one such example. This is the closest technology-supported communication mode to face-to-face communication.
- **Simulations:** ICT tools or application that allow a real world situation or environment to be modeled or represented with the aim of providing opportunities for learners to experience the situation or practice processes that may not otherwise be available to them.

Since 1996 the acceptance and range of technologies being used in educational settings has grown dramatically placing increasing demands on teachers and students to not only be ICT literate but also be effective online teachers and learners as well. Coldwell, Craig and Goold (2011) have developed a categorization of educational technology tools consisting of 14 categories, rather more than Chickering and Ehrmann's staggering number, which extend the broader categories of virtual learning environments, online learning environments and LMS to include a range of tools that are often included or can be used in conjunction with these broader categories.

Although the incorporation of technology into the teaching portfolio has changed the way that we teach in many ways, face-to-face teaching is still the primary mode of knowledge transfer. However, this has been extended and enhanced to include use of e-technologies although the level of adoption varies considerably depending on a range of factors including: the discipline; the teacher's preferences; the teacher's perception of the value of adding technology into the mix; the availability of the technology itself; and the expectations of the students as perceived by the teacher. There may also be institutional expectations on minimum standards for use of technology to deliver learning resources (see for example Coldwell & Newlands, 2004). A student however may not recognize these drivers. Their expectations of technology use and availability of learning resources outside the classroom are set by their

'best' experience leading to dissatisfaction with learning experiences that they perceive as having a lower level or quality of service.

Managing staff and student expectations of each other within the context of institutional expectations are thus key to a positive learning and teaching experience for the stakeholders, these being the students, teachers and ultimately the institution (Newlands & Coldwell, 2004). But how can these be managed in the context of the ongoing changes to higher education that are now occurring? The following sections will explore the barriers to and facilitators of positive learning and teaching experiences and review Chickering and Gamson's seven principles in the context of the twenty first (technology enhanced) century.

MANAGING EXPECTATIONS

In order to better understand, and hence be in a position to adequately manage, the expectations of a modern student we need to consider who they are and what they expect. We also need to consider what an academic's commitments are and what they expect of a modern student.

A Student of the Twenty First Century

There are, of course, many students who do not fit the somewhat extreme profile being presented here but have more traditional educational priorities with traditional support both culturally and financially from their family and friends. The students of most concern are those who seem to have the loudest voice and often are the ones most in need of support by the university as they don't get it from elsewhere. Often, these are the students who are the first in family to attempt tertiary education, students from low socio-economic backgrounds, who are struggling financially to support their education, the students who perceive tertiary education as the key to a successful career yet don't know what career choice to make. These are the students who are most at risk of failing in their studies, not because they are not academically capable but rather through the pressures placed on them outside of the education system. It is therefore incumbent on the university system to recognize these pressures and accommodate them to enable these students to successfully achieve their goals.

So what do students of today look like?

- Their first priority is to their family and friends.
- Their second priority is to work.
- Their third (final) priority is to education.
- They consider higher education as a right, not an opportunity.
- They are comfortable using ICT tools such as smart phones, Facebook, email and seeking information on the Internet, regarding themselves as digital natives. (Oblinger & Oblinger, 2005).

How does this translate to their immediate expectations of tertiary education?

- They don't expect to have to turn up for every class.
- When they do turn up for class they expect to be entertained.
- They expect to have everything they need to pass provided online, in a number of different formats.
- They expect to be informed of exactly what they need to do.
- They don't expect to have to read a lot – they don't have time.
- They expect to find the answers on the Internet.
- They expect the university (and hence teaching staff) to be sufficiently flexible so that their education can fit into their busy schedules rather than their busy schedules being adapted to fit educational requirements.
- They consider a 'pass' to be OK.

Students no longer immerse themselves in their studies. They have other demands and priorities on their time. They are easily distracted. Even if they turn up to class, their phone takes priority rather than participating, or even listening, to what is going on in the classroom. They are provided with comprehensive resources, so they don't take notes. In other words they don't engage with their education. More significantly, students arrive at university unprepared for independent learning yet they perceive a degree to be the ticket to getting a job, i.e. the process of completing a degree is vocational. This view is supported by the increasing emphasis being placed on, and in, institutions on the attainment of graduate attributes through the completion of a degree.

Students expect their classroom to be technology-enhanced, increasing pressure on teachers to adopt an ever increasing range of technology-based educational tools. Although some students come to campus keen to engage with their learning in new ways, they often find faculty who are "reluctant to alter their traditional and entrenched teaching approaches" (Dey, Burn & Gerdes, 2009, p. 377). Students expect to find their learning resources online; they expect to be able to undertake research activities online; they expect to be able to find the answer to their questions online; and they expect to have their questions answered promptly, online. They want to be told what they need to know in order to pass the course, a passing grade being more than adequate for some.

An Academic of the Twenty First Century

As has always been the case an academic is expected to have a role in teaching, research and service. However, there does appear to be greater demands in all portfolios. All academics are expected to contribute at some level to the running of their department or school. As far as research is concerned obtaining funding is a very competitive process with less money to go further. With less university-based funding available, there is a growing expectation that research has to be self funded. There are greater demands in the teaching portfolio too, with students demanding greater accountability from staff with service availability that matches their timelines. Staff expect to have a life outside of their work commitments, although if they are high profile researchers, their life outside work is probably their research.

Increasingly academics are accepting the just-in-time approach to teaching preparation as the norm rather than the exception. During teaching periods there seems to be less time to allot to research or service activities as students are more demanding of an academic's time. In fact just-in-time is becoming the norm across all aspects of an academic's life.

Staff also expect students to be eager to learn, to be dedicated to their studies, be self-motivated with a desire to achieve at the highest level possible, taking advantage of every learning opportunity that is presented to them, to be willing to communicate and take responsibility for their own learning. They also expect students to not only 'read the instructions' but also follow them. They expect students to access the learning resources in a timely manner, and deal with them in a traditional manner – reading them from cover to cover, following up on the extra readings and learning activities that are suggested to them.

Bridging the Gap

Although the typical student and academic presented here are somewhat extreme, these profiles capture the essence of the issues that have to be addressed in a modern, technology supported learning environment. The key is for all parties to develop an understanding of the facilitators and barriers to engagement, and to take these into account in all types of interactions.

With the increased emphasis on retention and progression of students, most institutions have implemented various orientation and transition programmes to assist students to assimilate into tertiary education. Articulation of expectations is a key component for students to understand their role as a student, as well as to develop realistic expectations of their teachers (Craig, Goold, Coldwell & Mustard, 2008). Typically, teachers would like students to engage with their learning, "to share our enthusiasm for our academic discipline and find our courses so compelling that they willingly, in fact enthusiastically, devote their hearts and minds to the learning process" (Barkley, 2010, p. 5). This can be challenging, particularly when face-to-face contact with the student is removed (as in online courses) or minimized (when students do not turn up for classes). Barkley (2010, p. 11) further suggests that students "must have confidence that, with appropriate effort, they can succeed". She concludes that "motivation is the portal to engagement" (Barkley, 2010, p. 15). Expectations are often articulated formally in the form of a Student Charter (see Deakin University, 2008 for example), yet it is unclear how many students are aware of the Charter and if they are, whether they fully comprehend or even take notice of the expectations that are articulated within the document (Newlands & Coldwell, 2004).

As early as 2005 it was evident that the increasing use of technology in the learning environment would impact significantly on how students and staff communicated with a perception that "it is a virtual certainty that new forms of communication, collaboration, and learning will follow [the technology trends]" (NMC, 2005, p. 3). Communication between students and teachers is paramount. Unfortunately this is often where the cracks appear first. In an online course the primary mode of communication to individual students is via email. However, they need to be accessing their emails in order for the communication to at least be noted. Although it is a requirement that they access their official university email regularly at the author's institution, many students don't. Others choose to redirect university emails to their preferred, non-institutional email address. This has some unfortunate consequences. They have to negotiate the redirection process successfully to ensure emails arrive. Further, the free email services that they seem to prefer to use often have limited capacity so there is no guarantee that they will even receive redirected messages, never mind act upon them.

With the increased dependence on mobile technologies, students are not limited to normal business hours when engaging with learning activities. When they get stuck on an assignment at midnight, they would appreciate assistance at midnight. Since they are up and about at that time it is not unreasonable to expect that their tutor or lecturer is also available to answer their questions – no? As the scenario posed at the start of this chapter articulates, students do expect support when they need it rather than when the academic can provide it. It is incumbent on the academic, therefore, to make it very clear from the start of the teaching period when they are available to students. In a face-to-face situation the academic's office hours would be published prominently, perhaps on their office door. Similar information should also be published about online communications. For example the following message is quite clear and if it had been posited in the context of face-to-face office hours would seem very generous:

Queries posted between Monday and Thursday will be responded to within 24 hours. Queries posted between Friday and Sunday will normally not be attended to until the following Monday.

Although the message is quite unambiguous, we can unintentionally reinforce an expectation amongst students of far faster service. For example if the teacher regularly responds to messages within a few hours then students have their expectations raised to believe that this is 'normal service'. Similarly, responses to messages posted at the weekend quickly become an expectation, particularly if an assignment is due on Monday morning. Therefore any information about what students can expect in

the way of online communication must not only be reasonable from the students' point of view, but is also sustainable from the academic's perspective.

There is an expectation that students will have sufficient computer literacy skills to be able to negotiate learning technologies. This expectation continues to be articulated despite the increasing evidence of computer use in our day-to-day lives. The issue today is what is meant by computer literacy? There is ongoing debate on this topic and also, where computer literacy skills should be acquired.

The Australian Computer Society (ACS) has stated that:

ICT literacy has moved from being a fringe issue to the centre stage of the school education platform. While ICT has become embedded into all aspects of our home and work lives, this has not yet been achieved in the nation's classrooms (ACS, 2005, p. 2).

The ACS further suggests that:

The aim should be for all students to be not only fluent in the use of ICT but able to use it to their advantage in learning. It is a skill they will need regardless of their career paths, whether it is University, TAFE, or a trade (ACS, 2005, p. 2).

The policy document further suggests that ICT literacy consists of a number of components including:

- **Using ICT:** Being critical, reflective and strategic in the use of ICT.
- **Accessing Information:** Knowing how to access, research and collect information.
- **Managing Information:** Applying/reconfiguring existing organisational or classification schemes.
- **Integrating Information:** Interpreting, integrating and representing information.

- **Evaluating Information:** Making judgements about the quality, relevance, usefulness, or efficiency of information.
- **Creating New Information:** Generating information by adapting, applying, designing, inventing or authoring information.
- **Communicating:** Transmitting, exchanging or transforming information using ICT. (ACS, 2000, p. 5).

Most students are confident about using email, searching the Internet, using a mobile phone for far more than making phone calls, using Instant Messenger and sending text messages known as short message service (SMS). Very few students would be confident that their ICT literacy skills stand up to the ACS suggested standard. Students' computer literacy skills also do not necessarily equate to what an academic understands as computer literacy. This may involve the ability to post a message in a discussion forum in English (or whatever the teaching language is), to be able to follow any email protocols that may have been established, be able to download or upload a file in a specific format and be able to determine whether the process has completed successfully to name just a few elements of computer literacy. They also expect students to be able to use sources other than Wikipedia to find accurate information. So who is responsible for ensuring students acquire adequate computer literacy skills? As with so many generic skills, including essay writing, study management skills, exam preparation skills and so on, support services within the university are taking on the responsibility for ensuring students have opportunities of gaining or improving such important, but often lacking, study skills. Students need to be informed that such services exist, (they often are, during orientation when they first start their tertiary studies but out of context, it has no meaning or relevance), and need to be directed to take advantage of the services, as and when appropriate. Most importantly, students should be informed as to what skill set is required within their course and, as with discipline specific learning, when and how they will be required to acquire the skills. This is becoming more evident in the formulation of learning outcomes for units of study. Not only are the discipline-based learning outcomes being specified, but so too are the generic attributes with links to assessment, providing a well articulated skill-set mapping for students.

Academics have an expectation that students will engage with the learning resources and activities. With increasing use of technology to support and enhance the learning experience, students are being required to participate in a range of learning activities that could not be implemented easily in a face-to-face setting. Multiple choice quizzes with immediate feedback on demand, are relatively straight forward to set up in an LMS for example, although the process is very time consuming. Once built, quizzes can easily be deployed to students. There is an increasing expectation too that students will collaborate with each other on learning activities in the online environment. The collaboration per se is not innovative, after all students are expected to work in teams on major projects for example, in a face-to face environment. The innovation rather lies in the ability to more easily assess the collaboration process, as well as the final artifact. Using online discussion forums for example captures students' conversations in textual form, allowing assessment of participation as well as contribution. Even audio conversations can be recorded for later assessment, if tools such as Elluminate Live© or Skype© are used to facilitate the conversation.

More interestingly is the ability to facilitate collaboration between students who would normally have little or no contact with each other, such as between students on different campuses or with distance education students. However this type of collaboration has significant impacts on the students themselves. Those who study at a distance have historically been 'the lone learner' with no expectation of contact with other students and only minimal contact with academics. They usually received paper-based learning resources at the beginning of the study period and would work through these in a time frame that allowed them to submit assessment according to the university's requirements. In a technology enhanced environment they can talk with academics regularly as well as with other students in the class. No longer are they left to their own devices with almost full control of their study time. Now they are expected to participate in online discussion, communicate regularly with staff and students and to collaborate with other students to produce pieces of assessable work, just like on-campus students. These activities impose significant constraints on a distance education student's study time management, as no longer are they the lone learner but rather are expected to be an active member of their class – which could number 100's of students.

Ensuring students are fully aware of the scheduling requirements of their studies, is something that needs to be addressed at least by the start of each teaching period. This is not a new requirement yet the level of detail that is required in an online environment is much greater. In practice it is more effective to publish a schedule of learning activities before the learning activities themselves are published, allowing students to focus on the big picture time management issues, before becoming embroiled in the detail of completing assessment tasks.

The 2010 Horizon Report (Johnson et al, 2010, p. 4) suggests that "people expect to be able to work, learn and study whenever and wherever they want", with this being one of the key drivers of educational technology adoption in the next one to five years. However this is proving challenging at an institutional level as the role of the academy is changing. From a teaching perspective, the demands that the increasingly diverse population of students is placing on academics is stretching the limits of what an individual teacher can do. In an online environment it is just as important to ensure effective student learning is taking place, as in any other learning environment, but now

how this can be achieved is changing (Craig, Coldwell & Goold, 2009). Academics need to develop effective strategies to provide support to students within the time frames that the students require. Although the suggestions here are in the context of a wholly online unit, these can easily be utilized in other learning environments.

Key times when students are likely to need extra learning support are at the commencement of their studies and when assessment is due. The norm seems to be for students to start work on assessment items just a few days before they are due, and many have an unrealistic view of how long the task is likely to take. In an online unit, this results in a rush of queries in the evening or late at night, rather than during the day. Often the most urgent sounding queries are the ones that are posted just a day or two before the deadline. The nature of an online unit means that there is no face-to-face contact and students have full control of the scheduling of their study time, fitting this schedule around higher priority activities. Naturally they would like a response to their questions within a 'reasonable' time frame. Unfortunately the urgency of the enquiry determines the students' perception of what a reasonable time frame is.

Where tutor support is available, a good use of their time is to provide support for students online in these extra busy periods. Since the support is provided online with the tutors having a virtual presence, it is often possible to schedule their presence online to align more closely with the times students are online. Further it is often not necessary to schedule large blocks of time but more frequent short blocks. Being online for 15-30 minutes around 9 pm can often be more effective from the students' perspective than being available for two to three hours from midday! Another useful strategy is to use synchronous communication tools to provide scheduled, small group support. However, any scheduling has to have some flexibility built in. For example a weekly one hour drop-in session could occur at different times from week to week, making the sessions accessible to a greater number of students.

In exploring the impacts on expectations, the author has offered some strategies for managing them. This is by no means an exhaustive presentation; it only scratches the surface. Every teacher will develop strategies that work for them and the suggestions included here can be used as a sound basis to develop more.

FUTURE RESEARCH DIRECTIONS

As the student profile changes and the range of technologies to support teaching and learning increases, ongoing research will be required to assist academics to make informed decisions regarding adoption of educational technologies and to develop strategies for a continued positive learning experience. Good change management practices, as in any dynamic situation, are often the key to successful implementation of innovation. What these practices are in a teaching and learning environment requires further investigation to ensure that expectations of all stakeholders continue to be recognized and addressed.

The ongoing changes in the student population will further increase pressure on academics to deliver education in new and innovative ways, using an ever increasing portfolio of educational technologies. This field is providing, and will continue to provide, a seemingly bottomless pit of research opportunities.

CONCLUSION

So, what about Dr Johns and student Jane? What could have been done to avoid the inevitable confrontation on Monday?

An immediate response would be to suggest that Jane should not have left commencing the assignment until the last minute and should have at least reviewed the requirements days ago. Probably from Jane's perspective she has not left it until the last minute with a full weekend being more than sufficient time to complete the tasks and, based on her previous experience of responses from Dr Johns, expected him to be available to respond to her initial email on Friday night. If Dr Johns had made a habit of responding to students' enquiries promptly, even after hours, then this was not the weekend to plan to be away or have so much work to do that he was unable to check his emails during the weekend.

Obviously there are areas that could have been handled better on both sides of the academic fence. As Jane has family commitments, it would not have been unreasonable for her to anticipate that Dr Johns may also have commitments that would take him away from his computer during a weekend. On the other hand, unless Dr Johns is a very new academic and this was his first experience of how a typical student would approach an assessment task, it would not have been unreasonable for him to anticipate that at least some students would require assistance with the assignment, in the days leading up to the deadline.

A simple confrontation avoidance tactic would have been for Dr Johns to inform students earlier in the week that he would be unavailable during the weekend and any queries should be sent to him before Friday. Another tactic (funds allowing) is to schedule a tutor to be online at certain times immediately prior to a submission deadline to deal with such emergencies as described in the scenario. However, this does require some planning (and money) to ensure that queries can be accessed by the tutor.

What this scenario demonstrates is how the gap in expectations can become a chasm very rapidly. Here the expectations were probably perceived as being quite reasonable, given the prior history. Staff need to realise that the university of old is no longer viable and today's students have different priorities. Academic rigour is still of paramount importance, yet academics have to articulate what they expect of students more clearly and precisely, as well as be more flexible. Students of today are seeking flexibility of their institutions, yet they need to recognize that they too have to compromise – they need a realistic approach to a balance of study, work and play, they have to manage their time to ensure reasonable lead times to complete tasks and they cannot expect 24/7, or even after hours service, from academics (unless the academic happens to be a night owl too).

In terms of Chickering and Gamson's seven principles, one may ask, are these still relevant in the twenty first century? From the perspective of managing and meeting expectations they are essential. How the principles are implemented is now very different from Chickering and Gamson's learning and teaching environment. Web 2.0-enabled communication channels are now the norm. Being able to collaborate with others without being in the same physical space is expected. Having a real time conversation using asynchronous tools seems to be a skill that students have mastered, yet academics generally have not. Being fully engaged in their learning is not a high priority for many students. Providing prompt feedback is becoming a more automated task and is therefore an expectation by most students. The opportunities to deliver learning in a variety of ways, including face-to-face, is opening up learning opportunities to many who may have felt that higher education was not possible for a variety of reasons, which will further widen the gap in expectations.

In an ideal world, the gap between student and staff expectations should be minimized, given our increasing understanding of what created the gap initially. However, as the 2011 Horizon Report points out "keeping pace with the rapid proliferation of information, software tools, and devices is challenging for students and teachers alike". (Johnson, Smith, Willis, Levine & Haywood, 2011, p. 4) This, together with the ongoing challenges higher education institutions need to address as a result of the adoption of the recommendations from the Bradley Review, will put pressure on maintaining, never mind improving, a positive learning experience for all stakeholders.

REFERENCES

ACER. (2011a). *Dropout DNA, and the genetics of effective support.* Australian Council for Educational Research: Research Briefing 11. Retrieved from http://www.acer.edu.au/documents/AUSSE_Research_Briefing_Vol11.pdf

ACER. (2011b). *Australasian survey of student engagement (AUSSE).* Australian Council for Educational Research. Retrieved from http://www.acer.edu.au/research/ausse

ACS. (2005). *Policy statement on computer literacy.* Australian Computer Society. Retrieved from http://www.acs.org.au/acs_policies/docs/2005/ComputerLiteracy.pdf

Barkley, E. F. (2010). *Student engagement techniques: A handbook for faculty.* San Francisco, CA: Jossey-Bass.

Bradley, D., Noonan, P., Nugent, H., & Scales, B. (2008). *Review of Australian higher education: Final report.* Australian Government: Department of Education, employment and workplace Relations. Retrieved from http://www.deewr.gov.au/HigherEducation/Review/Pages/default.aspx

Burdett, J. (2003). A switch to online takes time: academics' experiences of ICT innovation. In G. Crisp, D. Thiele, I. Scholten, S. Barker, & J. Baron (Eds.), *Interact, Integrate, Impact: Proceedings of the 20th Annual Conference of the Australasian Society for Computers in Learning in Tertiary Education* (pp. 84-93). Adelaide, 7-10 December.

Chickering, A., & Ehrmann, S. C. (1996). Implementing the seven principles: technology as a lever. *American Association for Higher Education Bulletin*, October, 3-6.

Chickering, A. W., & Gamson, Z. F. (1987). Seven principles for good practice in undergraduate education. *American Association for Higher Education Bulletin*, March.

Coldwell, J., Craig, A., & Goold, A. (2011). Using e technologies for active learning. *Interdisciplinary Journal of Information. Knowledge and Management, 6*, 1–12.

Coldwell, J., & Newlands, D. A. (2004). Deakin online: An evolving case study. *Journal of Issues in Informing Science and Information Technology, 1*, 1–10.

Commonwealth of Australia. (2009). *Transforming Australia's higher education system.* Canberra, Australia.

Craig, A., Coldwell, J., & Goold, A. (2009). The role of the online teacher in supporting student learning: A case study. In T. Bastiaens, J. Dron, & C. Xin (Eds.), *World Conference on E-Learning in Corporate, Government, Healthcare, and Higher Education* (pp. 1181–1187). Vancouver, Canada: AACE.

Craig, A., Goold, A., Coldwell, J., & Mustard, J. (2008). Perceptions of roles and responsibilities in online learning: A case study. *Interdisciplinary Journal of E-Learning and Learning Objects, 4*, 205–223.

Deakin University. (2008). *Student charter.* Retrieved from http://theguide.deakin.edu.au/ TheDeakinGuide.nsf/7264c32fe71924374a2566f 3000a65de/60045aea1a0c4d47ca2574d3008361 c1?OpenDocument&Highlight=0,student,charter

Dey, E. L., Burn, H. E., & Gerdes, D. (2009). Bringing the classroom to the web: Effects of using new technologies to capture and deliver lectures. *Research in Higher Education, 50*(4), 377–393. doi:10.1007/s11162-009-9124-0

Hemmi, A., Bayne, S., & Land, R. (2009). The appropriation and repurposing of social technologies in higher education. *Journal of Computer Assisted Learning, 25*, 19–30. doi:10.1111/j.1365-2729.2008.00306.x

Hiltz, S. R. (1994). *The virtual classroom: Learning without limits via computer networks.* Norwood, NJ: Ablex Publishing Corporation.

Johnson, L., Levine, A., Smith, R., & Stone, S. (2010). *The 2010 horizon report.* Austin, TX: The New Media Consortium.

Johnson, L., Smith, R., Willis, H., Levine, A., & Haywood, K. (2011). *The 2011 horizon report.* Austin, TX: The New Media Consortium.

McInnis, C., Griffen, P., James, R., & Coates, H. (2000). *Development of the course experience questionnaire (CEQ).* Department of Education, Training and Youth Affairs. Retrieved from http://www.dest.gov.au/archive/highered/eippubs/ eip01_1/01_1.pdf

Newlands, D. A., & Coldwell, J. (2004). Managing student expectations online. *Lecture Notes in Computer Science, 3583*, 355–363. doi:10.1007/11528043_37

NMC. (2005). *The 2005 horizon report.* Austin, TX: The New Media Consortium.

Oblinger, D. G., & Oblinger, J. L. (2005). Is it age or IT: First steps toward understanding the NET Generation. In Oblinger, D. G., & Oblinger, J. L. (Eds.), *Educating the net generation* (pp. 3.1–3.7). EDUCAUSE.

Prebble, T., Hargraves, H., Leach, L., Naidoo, K., Suddaby, G., & Zepke, N. (2005). *Impact of student support services and academic development programmes on student outcomes in undergraduate tertiary study: A synthesis of the research.* Report to the Minister.

Preston, C., & Mowbray, L. (2008). Use of SMART boards for teaching, learning and assessment in kindergarten science. *Teaching Science, 54*(2), 50–53.

Roberts, G. (2005). Technology and learning expectations of the net generation. In Oblinger, D. G., & Oblinger, J. L. (Eds.), *Educating the net generation* (pp. 3.1–3.7). EDUCAUSE.

Sorcinelli, M. D. (1991). Research findings on the seven principles. *New Directions for Teaching and Learning, 47*, 13–25. doi:10.1002/tl.37219914704

ADDITIONAL READING

Aarsvold, J. A. (2009). *Attitudes, expectations and adoption of education technology in higher education. Unpublished Masters*. Duluth, Minnesota: University of Minnesota.

Butcher, M. F. (2010). *Online social networks and their impact on student expectations of university-provided learning technology*. Unpublished Doctoral Thesis, Northern University of Arizona.

Cinar, M., & Torenli, N. (2010). Redesign online courses with student expectations: A case study with a new infrastructure. *Procedia Social and Behavioral Sciences, 9*, 2013–2016. doi:10.1016/j.sbspro.2010.12.438

Coldwell, J. (2003). Mapping pedagogy to technology - A simple model. In W. Zhou (Ed.), *International Conference on Web-based Learning,* Melbourne, Australia, (pp. 180 – 192). Springer.

Coldwell, J., Craig, A., & Goold, A. (2006). *Student perspectives of online learning. ALT-C 2006.* Edinburgh, Scotland: Association for Learning Technology.

Coldwell, J., & Newlands, D. (2003). A model of online teaching and learning. In Constantinou, C., & Zacharia, Z. (Eds.), *Computer based learning in science* (pp. 77–85). Nicosia, Cyprus: University of Cyprus.

Collins, A., & Halverson, R. (2010). The second educational revolution: Rethinking education in the age of technology. *Journal of Computer Assisted Learning, 26*, 18–27. doi:10.1111/j.1365-2729.2009.00339.x

Crisp, G., Palmer, E., Turnbull, D., Nettelbeck, T., & Ward, L. (2009). First year student expectations: Results from a university-wide student survey. *Journal of University Teaching and Learning Practice, 6*(1), 11–26.

Doiron, R., & Asselin, M. (2011). Exploring a new learning landscape in tertiary education. *New Library World, 112*(5/6), 222–235. doi:10.1108/03074801111136266

Ellis, A., & Newton, D. (2009). First year university students' access, usage and expectations of technology: An Australian pilot study. In T. Bastiaens, J. Dron, & C. Xin (Eds.), *World Conference on E-Learning in Corporate, Government, Healthcare, and Higher Education 2009* (pp. 2539–2546). Vancouver, Canada: AACE.

Ertmer, P. A., & Ottenbreit-Leftwich, A. T. (2010). Teacher technology change: How knowledge, confidence, beliefs, and culture intersect. *Journal of Research on Technology in Education, 42*(3), 255–284.

Goold, A., Coldwell, J., & Craig, A. (2010). An examination of the role of the e-tutor. *Australasian Journal of Educational Technology, 26*(5), 704–716.

Goold, A., Craig, A., & Coldwell, J. (2007). Accommodating culture and cultural diversity in online teaching. *Australasian Journal of Educational Technology, 23*(4), 490–507.

Holmes, C. (2005). Changing expectations for higher education. In Apple, D. K., & Beyerlein, W. (Eds.), *Faculty guidebook: A comprehensive tool for improving faculty performance* (2nd ed., pp. 3–6). Lisle, IL: Pacific Crest.

Lau, M. C. F., & Tan, R. B. N. (2002). *Minimum computer literacy at tertiary institutions – Whose responsibility is it?* International Conference on Computers in Education. Auckland, New Zealand: IEEE Computer Society.

Lavy, I., & Or-Bach, R. (2011). ICT literacy education—College students' retrospective perceptions. *Inroads, 2*(2), 67–76.

Littlejohn, A., Margaryan, A., & Vojt, G. (2010). Exploring students' use of ICT and expectations of learning methods. *Electronic Journal of e-Learning, 8*(1), 13-20.

Ramanau, R., Hosein, A., & Jones, C. (2010). Learning and living technologies: A longitudinal study of first-year students' expectations and experiences in the use of ICT. In L. Dirckinck-Holmfeld, V. Hodgson, C. Jones, D. McConnell, & T. Ryberg (Eds.), *7th International Conference on Networked Learning*, Aalborg, Denmark, (pp. 1–8).

Scott, A., & Ryan, J. (2009). Digital literacy and using online discussions: Reflections from teaching large cohorts in teacher education. In Gibbs, D., & Zajda, J. (Eds.), *Comparative information technology: languages, societies and the internet* (pp. 103–120). Springer. doi:10.1007/978-1-4020-9426-2_8

Smith, P., Coldwell, J., Smith, S. N., & Murphy, K. L. (2005). Learning through computer-mediated communication: A comparison of Australian and Chinese heritage students. *Innovations in Education and Teaching International, 42*(2), 123–134. doi:10.1080/14703290500062441

Spivey, R., Collins, L., & Bishop, H. (2003). Opening Doors with a New Set of Keys. *Electronic Journal for the Integration of Technology in Education, 2*(2), 81–92.

Tricker, T. (2003). *Student expectations – How do we measure up?* 2nd Global Conference on The Idea of Education, United Kingdom.

van der Klooster, M., & Coldwell, J. (2005). Real time, perceived time and time online: A review of student experiences of time over thirty years of distance and online education. In A. Burge (Ed.), *3rd Annual Hawaii International Conference on Education*, (pp. 1–14). Honolulu, Hawaii.

Watson, G., Proctor, R. M. J., Finger, G., & Lang, W. (2004). *Education students' views on the integration of ICT into their undergraduate learning experiences.* Effective Teaching and Learning Conference 2004. Brisbane, Australia: Griffith University.

Waycott, J., Bennett, S., Kennedy, G., Dalgarno, B., & Gray, K. (2010). Digital divides? Student and staff perceptions of information and communication technologies. *Computers & Education, 54*, 1201–1211. doi:10.1016/j.compedu.2009.11.006

Willis, L., & Wilkie, L. (2011). Student expectations and perceptions of instructor email response rates by college students enrolled in online courses. In M. Koehler & P. Mishra (Eds.), *Society for Information Technology and Teacher Education International Conference 2011*, (pp. 848–852). Nashville, TN: AACE.

Zhang, Z. (2008). ICT in teacher education: Examining needs, expectations and attitudes. *Canadian Journal of Learning and Technology, 34*. Retrieved from http://www.cjlt.ca/index.php/cjlt/article/viewArticle/498/229

KEY TERMS AND DEFINITIONS

Computer Literacy: The level of competency required to use ICT efficiently and effectively to meet an individual's needs.

Good Practice: A teaching environment in which students encounter a positive learning experience ultimately resulting in the intended learning outcomes being achieved.

Online/Wholly Online: Using e-technologies to support learning and teaching, minimizing or eliminating the need for face-to-face contact to complete learning activities.

Staff Expectation: An individual staff member's interpretation of what they expect of a student based on their previous experiences and understanding of the responsibilities of a typical student.

Student Engagement: The student's involvement with learning resources and activities which are likely to result in quality learning.

Student Expectation: An individual student's interpretation of their rights and responsibilities (as a student) based on their previous experiences and personal situation.

Chapter 2
The Role of Social Media as a Tool for Learning

Carole A. Bagley
The Technology Group, Inc., USA & University of St. Thomas, USA

William H. Creswell III
The Technology Group Inc., USA

ABSTRACT

The use of Web 2.0 social media such as Wikipedia, YouTube, Facebook, Twitter, and virtual worlds is rapidly increasing and transformational modes of communication are emerging (Greenhow, Robelia & Hughes, 2009; Godwin, 2008; O'Reilly, 2005). Public and private sector organizations are faced with the challenges of adapting their communication practices to the rapidly changing demands of the social media environment that present risks to both information security and privacy, changes to long-established policies and organizational culture, and the rewards of deeper involvement and collaboration with users. As social media transforms communication within all organizations, its potential to transform learning is also becoming apparent. This chapter promotes a better understanding of the effects social media has on learning and the importance to learners and the learning process, with special emphasis on its effect when combining face-to-face and distance learning. The subtopic for this chapter, HCI for the Web 2.0 environment seen through a corporate training lens, is emphasized with education and training examples from corporate, K-12, university and government sectors.

INTRODUCTION

While logos of Facebook, Twitter, Flickr, and YouTube are increasing on corporate, government and educational institution websites, the strategy guiding these initial implementations limits social media's full impact. Social media are utilized as just another channel to disseminate news briefs and provide links to draw the reader to the main website for more information, rather than providing a conduit of interactivity between the reader and the content (Gordon-Murnane, 2010). By fully

DOI: 10.4018/978-1-4666-3649-1.ch002

enabling the interactive aspects of social media that will enhance learning, this invites a radical degree of open information-sharing with the public, and legal and regulatory risks that accompany such changes to long established communication practices. Even when the benefits of openness and transparency are weighed and risks accounted for, implementation of social media is difficult because it calls for not only new practices and policies, but new corporate and institutional culture. Kundra (2009) states that the full implications of social media use by government will change the nature of government information-sharing to and with the public and will require a massive transformation of practices to ensure that authorities can deal with this new reality.

The arrival of social media on the front pages of private and public sector education and corporate training websites indicates the earliest stage of this new reality of public information sharing, and the effects are beginning to be recognized. Social media are opening new dimensions of public communications and accelerating change. The role social media played and continues to play in the political upheavals in Tunisia, Egypt, and other countries in the 'Arab Spring' of 2011 demonstrates that it is becoming the political pamphlet of the 21st century, capable of accelerating and spreading protest and even revolution (Gustin, 2011). The effect social media has on other forms of communication is less dramatic but no less potent. Educators and trainers are facing the new reality that social media poses to disrupt the traditional learning paradigm, by experimenting with different social media to supplement traditional face-to-face learning to test the suitability of social media as a formal tool for workplace learning (Losey, 2010; Lipowicz, 2010). As with information-sharing practices and policies, implementing social media for educating and training requires a transformation of institutional pedagogy and culture. For learning, social media represents a radically new paradigm of literacy and collaboration, changing the normative

relationship between learners and instructors to the open collaboration found in Web 2.0 environments (Greenhow et al., 2009).

What is required to make this reality is a new educational philosophy and pedagogy that will tame social media by "bringing its public, fragmented and slippery form ... within the constrained and relatively rigid framework of formal assessment practice" (Hemmi, Bayne & Land, 2009, p. 25).

Emerging research on the potential of social media for distance learning is being applied in theoretical models and new normative contexts of use. In different settings, experimental stand-alone social-media-integrated courses and models blending social media with live instructor support are being tried, measured, and evaluated against traditional face-to-face (F2F) instruction (Väljataga & Fiedler, 2009; So & Brush, 2009; Bagley & Chou, 2007). Advocates of social media in learning are applying this new knowledge in producing learning and training courses integrated with social media.

This chapter will further describe and provide the theoretical basis for social media effects on the learner, particularly emphasizing: social presence; transactional distance; and community/socio-cultural context of knowledge. The effect of social media on the learning process will also be described and supported: feedback and interactivity; cognitive load; human-computer interaction (HCI); and instructional design. Examples of social media use and solutions for dealing with issues and controversies will be provided from multiple learning sectors including K-12 education, university, corporate and government.

THEORETICAL FRAMEWORK

The potential of social media for learning is increasing as a greater understanding of the technologies and emerging patterns of use is explored and justified. Social media integration into K-12 and university education as well as corporate and government training is still in its infancy, however, the patterns of use for social media in learning in each of these institutions are beginning to identify and define a theoretical framework for cognitive learning and the effects on the learner and learning environment. The emerging digital literacies of social media differ and include a wide variety of applications from text-based wikis to three-dimensional avatars in virtual worlds, making the effects more complex and challenging to classify and measure. Educators often view the learning environment differently than corporate and government trainers. However, the impact of social media is on 'learning' and therefore, crosses the boundaries of both education and training. Kaplan and Haenlein (2010) suggest one method of classifying each social media by plotting its learning effects on two dimensions: the level each requires of the user's self-presentation/disclosure to the community of collaborating learners (low, medium, or high) and social presence (low, medium, or high) established in its use. The degrees of the two dimensions mark differences between social media, how a specific tool usage engages learners, and how each form of social media can fill specific roles in a framework of a collaborative learning environment (CLE) (See Table 1) (Palvia & Pancaro, 2010).

Distance-learning research shows that CLE's can work effectively in supporting learning and that learners in CLE's aren't necessarily disadvantaged compared with learners in traditional F2F environments, supporting Schramm's observation that learners are more affected by the content of learning, rather than the delivery me-

dium (Schramm, 1954; Benson & Samarawick-rema, 2009). The common outcome of social media use is the broadening of the concept of knowledge to a collective agreement that may include facts, opinions, values and spiritual beliefs, validated and co-constructed through collaborative interaction in the CLE (Greenhow et al., 2009, p. 247).

Research into the effects of social media use is needed to define factors ranging from the effects on learners, the transformation of the learning process, and even how social media potentially changes academic scholarship itself. Instructors' own lack of knowledge and experience with social media hamper scholars from participating and collaborating with their students to guide them to appropriate and educative uses of social media in a blended learning environment (Benson & Samarawickrema, 2009)

An understanding of social media begins with how learner interactions with social media and social-media-enabled learning processes compare to established metaphors of traditional learning. Research is needed to define systematic methods of application to bring together the best practices of social-media-integrated learning and measure the results. The ultimate goal is a process and methodology (an instructional design and pedagogy) that will deliver the benefits of the social workplace (or productivity), and the benefits of the social-media marketplace (or collaboration), in a way that meets curricular and regulatory requirements and objectives (Hibbets, 2010).

The effects of social media that research has identified as important to factors affecting the learner are: social presence; transactional distance;

Table 1. Social media classification

Social Presence/Rich Media		Self Presentation/Disclosure		
		High	**Medium**	**Low**
	High	Virtual worlds (e.g. Second Life)		Virtual game worlds (e.g. World of Warcraft)
	Medium	Social networking (e.g. Facebook)		Entertainment (e.g. YouTube)
	Low	Blogs		Collaborative (e.g. Wikipedia)

and community/socio-cultural context of knowledge. The effects of social media important to factors effecting the learning process are feedback and interactivity, the cognitive load, the human-computer interaction (HCI), and the instructional design/pedagogy (Fanning, 2009).

SOCIAL MEDIA: EFFECT ON FACTORS IMPORTANT TO LEARNERS

Social Presence

In any learning environment, learners must establish their identity (or social presence), as a starting point to begin interaction and collaboration. This is done physically and psychologically in F2F classroom interactions, but distance learners lack these clues, and in a text-only environment must rely on language to establish identity and discern meaning (So & Brush, 2009). Compared with F2F interaction, language-only interaction achieves a relatively low level of self-disclosure and involvement, yet even this low level of social presence supports the emotional and psychological states of the learner, and it contributes to forming the group social structure necessary for productive interactions among distance learners (Delfino & Manca, 2007).

In both F2F and distance collaborative learning environments (CLE), social presence begins to form as a learner processes sensory and social cues forming unique maps or schema, defining roles, interplay, and behavioral modes of the individual and the group (Slagter van Tyron & Bishop, 2009, pp. 291-292; Kirschner, 2002). Schema assists the learner to navigate a path within the group by providing a social context or web of interactions, perceptions, expectations, and behaviors that connect them (Slagter van Tyron & Bishop, 2009, pp. 336-337). Schema makes the learning space more immediate and familiar

to the user and enables individuals to trust each other and the group. Group trust builds structure, and learners in a structured environment are more likely to actively participate in social interactions and cognitive, task-oriented activity, which leads to higher individual performance and feelings of satisfaction (So & Brush, 2009; Gunawardena & Zittle, 1997). The authors have significant practical experience that supports increased participation and trust over time, given a facilitator/instructor who focuses on a specific topic or set of questions when using discussion boards and blogs.

Kreijns, Kirschner, and Jochems (2003) contend a CLE depends on social interactions based on trust, cohesion, and a feeling of belonging and that the lack of these inhibits social presence and structure-building, resulting in fewer interactions per learner and lower overall group activity.

The frequency and number of successful interactions are important as social activity in groups tends to be complex, based on both task-oriented communications and social interactions. The latter interactions may seem unrelated and less important, but both task and social interactions contribute to building shared knowledge and consensus that guides groups toward collaboration in problem-solving (Yamada, 2009; Chen & Wang, 2009; Bagley & Chou, 2007).

The Asia-Pacific Economic Cooperation (APEC) Cyber Academy (http://linc.hinet.net/apec/) is a CLE used by K-12 students world-wide. In addition to students' engagement in multimedia learning and projects, social media is incorporated through the use of synchronous dialog between the instructor and students and among students. The platform provides online prompts periodically for students to plan and activate their prior knowledge while learning a specific topic, provides prompts and feedback if ineffective learning strategies have been used by learners.

This includes a monitoring system to indicate what goals have been met or not met with a clear time frame. This synchronous dialog between the instructor and students and between students has a significant effect on the learner's social presence and their learning (Lin, Chou & Bagley, 2007).

Research shows that social presence improves when multimedia (animations or 'rich media' with audiovisual capabilities) is added to the environment (Homer, Plass & Blake, 2008). Social media with multimedia capabilities, or affordances, like Facebook and YouTube, and avatar-driven virtual-worlds applications like Second Life, provide different examples of multimedia that improve social presence (So & Brush, 2009; Chen & Wang, 2009; Iqbal, Kankaanranta & Neittaanmaki, 2010). The affordances of social media that support social presence of learners and groups are vital because inadequacies at the social level of interactivity are even more likely than technical problems to lead to failure of a CLE (Gunawardena & Zittle, 1997; Kreijns, Kirschner & Jochems, 2003).

Technology is dramatically changing the learning landscape with the Web 2.0 social media technologies. Over six million users from more than 100 countries have become residents in the virtual-worlds communities of Second Life (Pence, 2007). Second Life (SL) and other virtual-world platforms provide a near-real-life, immersive environment and allow users to experience objects or phenomena impossible to observe or examine in real life. Wang and Hsu (2009) list examples of instruction incorporated into virtual worlds of the International Spaceflight Museum, where users can play with scientific objects such as a lunar landing module, and the National Oceanic and Atmospheric Administration's (NOAA) Earth System Research Laboratory, where users can experience a tsunami and observe the process of glacier retreat. Virtual worlds are not always fantastic in scope: Sony-Ericson built a virtual exhibit in SL for virtual field trips for teachers and students similar to the company's real exhibit at the 2008 Barcelona Mobile World Congress (Wang & Hsu, 2009, p. 77).

Another use of virtual world simulation is in emergency response training. The Disaster Emergency Medical Personnel System (DEMPS) has created emergency management training in an immersive virtual world environment that simulates real-world situations that responders to an emergency face, such as a hurricane, where changing environmental conditions impact responders' decision-making (Greci et al., 2009; Greci et al., 2010; Smith, Bagley & Greci, 2010). Virtual world collaboration adds a high sense of presence for group interaction and collaboration and team work is a strong component of the DEMPS virtual world.

In a virtual world, users interact with each other through the virtual agency of an avatar. Avatar refers to an identity that is customized by the user. The user can create an avatar that is similar to his or her appearance, or totally different, such as an alien or a rabbit. Jung's (2008) study of avatar usage revealed that social presence has a direct relationship with users' intention to participate in the SL online community. Students in SL feel a strong attachment to their avatars (Pence, 2007) and users' social presence is established through the interaction between near-real avatars in SL, which yields SL great potentials to strengthen online learners' sense of community (Wang & Hsu, 2009). For a class conducted in a pure asynchronous online environment, the instructor should consider meeting synchronously with all students several times in the SL to help them sense the social presence of all participants in the class. Asynchronous environments are those where the learner is communicating with the environment and other individuals at a time that is convenient and all learners may not be in the environment at the same time. Synchronous environments are those where the learner is communicating with others in real-time and everyone is actively engaged at the same time. In this context, other social media tools are used synchronously in a virtual world, including chatting, video, blogging, and Twitter, to collaborate with others in the environment (Wang & Hsu, 2009).

Among the newer virtual-worlds technologies are three-dimensional massively multiplayer online games (MMOG). The MMOG evolved from 1980s digital 3-D text-based, multiuser dungeons, or domains, (MUD) that connected multiple players in a computer role-playing game to an immersive virtual world. In a MMOG such as EverQuest II and World of Warcraft, groups of four or more users are pitted against sophisticated artificial intelligence in simulated battles. Complex collaboration results as users form teams and pursue strategy based on accumulation of points in skill-based games or balance strengths and weaknesses among teams in class-based games. Collaboration of teams in task-oriented problem-solving is facilitated by fantasy or reality-based avatars that, along with text, create the users' social presence and facilitate social interactions (Yee, 2006).

Adapting an MMOG and network into a 3-D virtual world with social networking features, yields a multiuser virtual environment (MUVE), also called virtual spaces or virtual worlds, for short. Since the early 2000s, a number of virtual-worlds' applications have been launched, including: Active Worlds; OLIVE; OpenSim; Teleplace; Torque; Unity3D; SL, and others.

An early corporate adopter of virtual worlds was IBM, which continues to maintain an island in SL. Started in 2003, SL, from Linden Labs, was conceived as a customizable environment with built-in social networking features for user-designed avatars to interact, play, and create and market unique goods and services to each other, earning 'Linden Dollars' along the way. Users in SL live in an overall larger world ('the grid') within which they own regions of 256 by 256

meters, which can be divided and have a different owner. The owner sets permissions to control access to parcels, and can choose to enable media features such as text and video for communicating (Cherbakov, Brunner, Smart & Lui. 2009).

SL users automatically gain social presence with social networking attributes, including text chat, voice functions, and avatar customization (Cherbakov et al., 2009). These strengths attract corporations, government agencies, and even embassies to create 3-D spaces in SL, and though activity has leveled off since the peak in 2007, SL continues to grow and has evolved beyond its beginnings as a space for virtual conferences and demonstrations (Hansen, 2009).

A MUVE's value as a learning environment lies in learning subjects and behaviors in an authentic environment that enables interaction and collaboration between users whose social presence is enabled. Allowing users to create a personalized online social presence with social networking capabilities reduces transactional distance and promotes connectedness and intimacy (Edirisingha, Nie, Pluciennik & Young, 2009). In a study of a corporate MUVE, users reported that the experience was deeply engaging and helpful for creative collaboration (Larach & Cabra, 2010). Given these factors, a virtual world's potential for enterprise distance learning is great for collaborative learning distributed across time zones (Larach & Cabra, 2010) (Table 2).

While measurable results of using a MUVE in education and training is only beginning to be defined, experimental MUVE developments

Table 2. Virtual worlds opportunities for education and training (Larach & Cabra, 2010)

	Features introduced	**Enterprise opportunities suggested by the features**
MMOG	Avatar (presence)	Individualization, exploration of multicultural environments. Demonstrations, rehearsals, team-building exercises, test-oriented learning.
Social Spaces	Social interactions and connections	Connecting time and geographically distributed teams. Expertise location, remote mentoring, social networking, collaboration.
Virtual Worlds (MUVE)	Persistent 3-D spaces Co-creation voice over Internet protocol VoIP	Immersion, 2-D/3-D, and real-life integration. Data visualization, collaborative learning. Multipurpose events.

continue to serve to inspire others. A MUVE developed by Idaho State University for training first responders in emergencies came to the attention of the Deptartment of Veteran's Affairs (VA) physicians in the Northern California Health Care Network who faced a similar need, and have continued work on emergency management training (Greci et al., 2009). In addition to the MUVE, the emergency management training also includes Twitter, using tweets to communicate informally with the volunteers and later, during the training scenario, make changes, or 'injects' in real time. One exercise included a series of 28 different 'injects' to a hurricane simulation. Each inject was a 'tweak' of the original simulation, done as the exercise progressed. The purpose was to train the volunteers to manage a hurricane simulation with realistic changes happening.

What was unique was the use of social media to communicate to and connect volunteers. Of the 325 signed up volunteers, 176 were Twitter subscribers and received Twitter 'tweets' alerting them about the simulation and to each 'inject' during the simulation. The other 149 volunteers were contacted by other media channels. The Twitter-connected volunteers first received a tweet that 'something was brewing in the Caribbean' followed by a 'tweet' for each 'inject' as it happened.

Studies of the MUVE in middle schools compare virtual worlds favorably with traditional classroom learning by higher gains of learning and achievement on tests and retention, although the overall highest results came from the blended MUVE, with instructors providing guidelines and feedback (Ketelhut, Nelson, Clarke & Dede, 2009). Other improvements were noted, as virtual worlds improved learner motivation and behavior during school hours, with more learners volunteering for extra learning activities even without extra credit.

Transactional Distance

Transactional distance refers to the lack of connection learners experience in a distance-learning environment. The lack of immediate feedback in an asynchronous CLE is only one form. Transactional distance is felt by the learner in inverse proportion to the amount of support or structure present in the CLE. Too little structure increases transactional distance and eventually lowers learners' rates of cognitive performance and knowledge retention (Powers, Janz & Ande, 2006; Means, Toyama, Murphy, Bakia & Jones, 2009).

Structure is created formally from instructor-supplied directions, the course syllabus, assignments, and course materials. Informal structure building takes place through interactions between the learner and these course materials, and between one learner and another. Kearsley and Lynch (1996) contend informal structure, or dialogue, is as important as formal structure because it is learner-focused, personalized, and interactive, and represents the synthesis of understanding between a learner, instructor, and other learners. Dialogue-formed structure lessens transactional distance for the learner, while too little dialogue increases transactional distance and corresponding lower levels of learner performance and satisfaction (Kearsley and Lynch, 1996; Lee & Rha, 2009; Powers et al., 2006). Therefore, there is support for both structured and unstructured dialogue among learners and instructors.

The APEC Cyber Academy incorporates both structured and unstructured online prompts for students to plan and activate their prior knowledge while learning a specific topic. This provides an environment where learners connect with one another and with the instructor thus decreasing their transactional distance and impacting the learning and confidence of the student (Lin et al., 2007).

Community and the Socio-Cultural Context of Knowledge

In constructivist learning philosophy, a community refers to a specific group united through established social presence and common interests. Each learner constructs social presence and a narrative relating their 'story' to the group, forming a shared context or metacognition around issues of concern and interest, or learning (Pachler & Daly 2009; Gunawardena et al., 2009). Thus forms the collaborative community of practice (CoP). Whether the shared learning is cooperative or collaborative depends on one's perspective on the process. Cooperative learning advocates state the importance of learners establishing and following individual roles within the group is a critical step to achieving assigned tasks together (Ochoa & Robinson, 2005; Dillenbourg, 1999). Others believe role formation may not be required and that collaborative learning itself is the most important factor, whether achieved by cooperation, instructor-led mediation, or from other conditions (McIsaac & Gunawardena, 1996). To simplify, the term 'collaborative learning' will be used here.

Wegner and Vallacher (1977) describe the collaborative learning of a CoP as social cognition, the process of people making sense of the social environment. Learners interact freely, self-disclose, negotiate, and collaborate, leading to development of a common or shared knowledge (Jaworski, 1996; Yamada, 2009; Chen & Wang, 2009). Kreijns and others state the nature and quality of group collaboration is more important than the quality of the composition of the group, (Kreijns et al., 2003, p. C38) and ideal collaborative environments don't require specific skills or expertise if the CoP enables broad social cognitive interaction (Gunawardena et al., 2009; Jaworski, 1996).

The theory of socio-cultural learning attempts to define the computer-mediated communication effect with social cognition theory. Based on the work of Vygotsky, it states that collaborative learning and other higher order critical functions develop not solely from the individual's own experience but out of external social interactions with others that require cognitive and communicative functions (DeValenzuela, 2007). The point of individual and group interaction is the 'zone of proximal development', the difference between what an individual can achieve acting alone and what is accomplished when acting collaboratively

with others (Lantholf & Thorne, 2000: 17). Jaworski (1996) believes both socio-cultural learning and constructivist learning coexist in a CoP and lists five relationships as evidence (Table 3).

The APEC Cyber Academy provides the opportunity for students to engage and collaborate with other students located around the world. The students participate in social interactions within the CLE environment by sharing their knowledge with others. This small group collaboration increases social presence and decreases transactional presence as the students spend time in discussion of topics and building projects (Lin et al., 2007).

SOPHIA (http://www.sophia.org) is a new startup social teaching/learning company. The site, boasting 77,000 users from 147 countries and 1,400 education institutions, describes itself on its home page as 'a mashup of Facebook, Wikipedia, and YouTube focused solely on teaching and learning'. The site provides teachers and learners with access to learning content and methods by which they may exchange and share knowledge, skills

Table 3. Constructivist and socio-cultural learning relationships in a CoP (Jaworski, 1996)

Constructivist & Socio-Cultural Learning Relationships In a CoP
1. Learning is a process of comparing new experience with knowledge constructed from one's previous experience, resulting in the reinforcing or adaptation of that knowledge.
2. Social interactions within the learning environment are an essential part of this experience and contribute fundamentally to individual knowledge construction.
3. Shared meanings develop through negotiation in the learning environment, leading to the development of *common* or 'taken-as-shared' knowledge (metacognition).
4. Knowing is a participatory action of the learner, not received from an external source.
5. Learning is a process of comparing new experience with knowledge constructed from previous experience, resulting in the reinforcing or adaptation of that knowledge. (Vygotsky's 'zone of proximal development')
6. Social interactions within the learning environment are an essential part of this experience and contribute fundamentally to individual knowledge construction.

and know-how. Homework help and connections with students, teachers and tutors are provided as well as the opportunity for students and teachers to socially interact and compare their knowledge with others.

Socio-cultural learning takes place through daily interactions that create and reinforce a shared reality of what is true. Social media like Facebook and Twitter demonstrate socio-cultural learning at a high frequency as users check in and make contributions minutes and even seconds apart, incrementally adding to their shared worldview and supporting their CoP (Warshauer, 1997; Gunawardena, et al., 2009).

SOCIAL MEDIA: EFFECT ON FACTORS IMPORTANT TO LEARNING

The factors important to learners are only some of the capabilities or affordances of social media. Other factors are important to the learning process. These are feedback and interactivity, the cognitive load, the HCI, and the factor of how social media effects instructional design and pedagogy (Fanning, 2009).

Feedback and Interactivity

The learner relies on feedback and interactivity to support collaborative learning in both F2F learning and a distance-learning environment. Kreijns, Kirschner, and Jochems (2002) state that social media promotes social interactions in two ways: a reciprocal relationship forms when the learner perceives a social affordance of the technology and the CLE supports the following action (e.g. initiating a communication), and next, when a fellow learner perceives the affordance to respond (a 'perception-action coupling') that results in a collaborative interaction.

The social media (discussion boards, blogs, Facebook, Twitter, Flickr) enables the CLE to make a learner's perception of 'e-mmediacy' real by providing a seemingly continuous or ubiquitous connection and a shared context of understanding. To the learner, the CLE is capable and can be relied upon for further use. But to the educator or trainer, the CLE's reliability still rests on meeting requirements of cognitive load and the HCI.

Cognitive Load

Studies beginning in the 1970s of why learners struggled with the process of problem-solving exercises in algebra and geometry led to the cognitive load theory (CLT) of learning.

The most complex of these problem-solving exercises put a heavy demand on a learner's working memory. The learner must proceed step by step while keeping different goals and states in mind at the same time, such as the problem state, goal state, any sub-goal states, and any operators affecting these states (Sweller, 1988). CLT considers that the inherent limitations of human cognition are reached when too many factors must be kept in mind at once and a cognitive 'bottleneck' slows down the transfer of information in short-term memory to long-term memory. Different types of cognitive load occupy working memory different ways, as when complex visual and verbal information is processed. Schnotz and Kürschner (2007, p. 470) argue that cognitive load is exaggerated by traditional teaching methods and that improved instructional design can manage cognitive load more effectively. If instead of solving actual problems requiring the overload on working memory, learners can first practice 'worked-out' equations and concentrate on learning the 'goal-free' process of problem-solving. After practice on existing problems and application to the problem-solving process, the next appropriate step in learning would be to move on to solving new problems.

Cognitive load occurs in contexts other than problem-solving for the learner. Research shows that the effects of multimedia can reduce cognitive load through improving visualization, but too much visualization can increase cognitive load. The affordances of social media may distract and add to cognitive load, or reduce load and support knowledge retention. Multimedia in distance learning increases a learner's social presence, another load-decreasing factor (Homer et al., 2008) and in the proper context, social media with multimedia affordances could be useful in lessening cognitive load on knowledge creation.

The Human-Computer Interaction

HCI is one of the most dynamic factors effecting online distance education, and is critical in successfully implementing social media in a CLE. The primary goals of HCI are designs that minimize the barrier between the human's cognitive model of what they want to accomplish and the computer's understanding of the user's task. HCI principles include: consistency in layout and function, screen readability, navigation, user control, aesthetic value, and directions (Nielsen, 2006; Shneiderman, 1998).

The intuitive interface capabilities of Facebook to connect the user to their CoP and enable interactions are social affordance properties the learner perceives useful for actions they afford (Gaver, 1995). Well-designed virtual worlds will also provide an environment that allows a learner's participation and interaction with the learning to be natural and intuitive. The degree of popularity social media enjoys is in large part due to intuitive and adaptable interfaces, and a leading argument for adapting social media to learning is this superiority of effective HCI that differs markedly from learning management system (LMS) designs that are 'pedagogically and interaction negligent' (Bonk & Dennen, 2003). According to Dix, Roselli, and Sutinen (2006), social media engages novice users more easily, through more flexible and intuitive HCI, anywhere and at any time. Social media provides the models for the types of LMS needed for an effective distributed learning environment: eLearning applications smart enough to adapt themselves to the students' learning styles which assure high standards of accessibility and usability, to make learners' interaction with the systems as natural and intuitive as possible (Dix, Roselli & Sutinen, 2006, p. 1).

Social media HCI afford many types of actions, ranging from simple text tweets to immersive, 3-D virtual-worlds multiplayer experiences. The most successful interface designs deliver the goal of learner-centered interactions. The APEC Cyber Academy platform provides a learner-centered approach that is constructivist, rooted in social-cognition theories and self-directed learning (Lin et al., 2007), as well as group learning, or distributed cognition, enabled through distance-learning technology and the interface (Hollan, Hutchins & Kirsh, 2000).

Self-directed learning typically comes with a high degree of learner control over the interface, which benefits cognition by involving the learner, but has its disadvantages by increasing load. Studies have shown that a high degree of learner control over various aspects of instruction can reduce the level of learning achievement (Hannafin & Sullivan, 1995). Social-media interfaces are intuitive by design in their original context, yet they can impose an additional cognitive load in an instructional context of use, though experienced users are less affected. The author's experiences indicate that experienced learners appreciate and excel when allowed to control their learning; however, those with less prior knowledge will experience cognitive load issues and will take considerably longer to learn (Tennyson & Bagley, 1992; Bagley & Chou, 2007).

In adapting the social media HCI to an instructional context, the intuitive nature of the social media affordances must be balanced with the cognitive load imposed by the instructional content and the overall context of use (So & Brush, 2009).

Effect on Instructional Design and Pedagogy

Social media is recognized as enabling learning activity that fits two established definitions or metaphors of learning: learning by acquisition of knowledge, called 'know that' and learning by participation or application of the knowledge, called 'know how' (Hong & Sullivan, 2009: 618; Sfard, 1998). The metaphors define distinctly different cultures of knowledge-building that are sequential. An example of 'know that' is a primary school student memorizing multiplication tables, while a middle school student uses multiplication to solve a 'know how' problem (Hong & Sullivan, 2009, p. 615).

In practice, both acquisition and participation/application metaphors dominate instructional design, which is primarily oriented toward building knowledge and problem-solving. For accomplishing a task, knowledge acquisition is fast and efficient and participation routines guide problem-based learners from hypothesis to solution. Hong and Sullivan (2009) argue that these metaphors limit higher level learning by being concerned with efficient, not innovative, learning. A third metaphor of the instructional-design model that will support higher levels of learning is needed, to move beyond acquisition and participation learning to building and disseminating knowledge within a CoP (Hong & Sullivan, 2009, pp. 613-614). From simple fact-gathering and application of the facts to a procedure, this higher level moves the learner to complex knowledge-creation learning, a higher form of learning that relies on meaningful constructivist activities (Hong & Sullivan, 2009, p. 614).

Hong and Sullivan (2009) note that while collective effort is important to all acquisition and participation learning metaphors, collaboration is essential in a knowledge-creating community in which "the knowledge goal is not merely to achieve individual knowledge growth or to promote distributed knowing, but to collectively advance community knowledge" (Hong & Sullivan, 2009, p. 614). This describes 'distributed cognition' theory, like socio-cultural learning, an offshoot of constructivist learning philosophy. Where constructivists believe that individuals build knowledge through many influences, including prior knowledge, distributed cognition theory looks at the collective influence of CoPs, or discourse:

Intelligence is not solely an attribute within individuals, but is generated collaboratively within discourse communities. Tools in the physical environment serve as mediating structures that shape and direct human activity; and human activity emerges from human need (Cifuentes, Sharp, Bulu, Benz & Stough, 2010, p. 381).

Any instructional design model for integrating social media must consider individual learning styles if the focus is to match the technology to the learner's cognitive preference. In addition, the multimedia creation and manipulation afforded by social media photo and video-sharing applications such as Flickr and YouTube bring into play privacy issues, and raise ethical questions over whether images should be shared by learners, and the concerns of those learners from conservative societies and cultures that do not share images of the opposite sex (Greenhow et al., 2009) which would lead these learners to be underrepresented.

Nonetheless, researching social media and learning styles shows promise. In an experimental web-building course, teachers combined types of social media that included blogs, audio, and video, which were matched to learners' surveyed preferences in learning style and technology (Saeed, Yang & Sinnappan, 2009). Students were categorized as those who learn best visually, orally, or by written words, and matched to social media affordances (See Table 4).

Table 4. Technology preferences for various learner types (Saeed et al., 2009)

Learning style	Technology preference	Learning style	Technology preference
Active	Social bookmarks	Reflective	Podcast
Sensing	Email	Intuitive	Blog
Visual	Vodcast	Verbal	Podcast
Sequential	Podcast	Global	Blog

Academic performance of learners was measured, and findings showed that matching learning styles and technology preferences did improve performance, and that learners were flexible and balanced, combining styles of reflective and verbal, or intuitive and global (Saeed, 2009). Learners preferred both traditional synchronous (instructor-presented) media and asynchronous, user-controlled media and had well-balanced academic preferences across all learner types. Learners were "ready to experience new technologies in their study routines and willing to collaborate using multiple communication channels" (Saeed, 2009, p. 105).

Solutions and Recommendations

On the front lines, learning advocates are continuing their experiments with social media. Much of this activity reflects frustrations with conservative, cumbersome Learning Management Systems (LMS) that slow down the delivery of online learning. Instructors migrate to social media such as blogs, wikis, and virtual worlds seeking a more participatory and transparent environment for learners and do-it-yourself affordances for instructors to control the pace of learning (Hemmi et al., 2009; Yang & Liu, 2004, pp. 340-341). Whether conducted in a traditional F2F classroom setting by instructors interacting synchronously with learners or an asynchronous CLE with media delivered through the use of social media tools, learning cannot be taken for granted if adequate instructor-provided guidance or structure is lacking.

Instructional design must also acknowledge the importance of the social-psychological dimension of social interaction in learning (Yang & Liu, 2004, pp. 341-344). Instructional designs that are focused on CoP are about more than task execution. Collaborative learning depends on learners shifting smoothly between formal, task-related interactions and informal, social, non-task interactions that build the social structure and connect the learners to the community (Chen & Wang, 2009). These points argue that a blended form of social media instruction that combines social media and asynchronous networks both to scale effectively and to reach more learners, but with a live instructor providing mediation and formal and informal support, may be the most applicable instructional design for most social media-enabled learning environments (Wang, 2007; Charskey et al., 2009).

Social media and its integration into learning is increasing. The description of a CLE as a flexible, collaborative group of learners interacting in both task-related and non-task social communications, illustrates how social media-enabled learning ideally works. Wikis, blogs, and webcasts are the 'low hanging fruit' of social media that seem most adaptable to existing constructivist learning principles and instructional designs. Yet the more complex virtual-worlds applications like SL cannot be downplayed as they both extend the traditional (and proven) classroom model while adding unique affordances beyond the classroom experience, which are beneficial to both learner and the learning process.

Once a particular form of social media is selected for use as a tool for instruction, the instructional design and pedagogy, grounded in effective eLearning instructional strategies, is required. These strategies should align with what is known to be effective from research in 'visible learning' (Hattie, 2009), to put educational aims in the foreground, yet keep open and adaptable to possibilities beyond what we currently know (Greenhow et al., 2009). Clark lists these nine strategies to produce high levels of learning in a CLE (Table 5).

Little progress has been made on identifying a general framework design for learning spaces and experiences integrating social-media affordances, and much more work should be done in this area (Bower, Hedberg & Kuswara, 2009). The types and effects of cognitive load created by different social media need further study, as social-media applications range from the immediate and responsive microblogging applications to 3-D virtual-worlds immersions. Turning to applied research, the most exciting developments appear to be in hybrid blended models that combine different social media, such as Twitter and SL, with live instructor support.

Table 5. Nine strategies to produce high levels of learning (Clark, 2004)

Nine Strategies to Produce High Levels of Learning
1. Providing learner control of instructional navigation.
2. Strategies based on providing worked examples and practice.
3. Strategies based on effective feedback during learning.
4. Strategies based on increasing student motivation by encouraging active engagement and persistence.
5. Strategies based on increasing student motivation: Helping learners invest maximum mental effort.
6. Strategies based on teaching concepts.
7. Strategies based on teaching process knowledge.
8. Strategies based on teaching causal principles.
9. Strategies based on teaching procedural (how-to) knowledge.

CONCLUSION

Social media changes information-gathering from a commodity developed by experts and delivered through established one-way channels, to a commodity created by all and shared in unexpected and unplanned ways (Gilroy, 2009). Social media changes the 'one-to-many' paradigm in many ways: Newspaper content transmitted one-way to readers on newsprint or a web page, is blogged and tweeted, updated and altered. Readers interact with different forms of content and extend it into a collaborative, organic body of knowledge.

In learning, social-media-enabled instruction changes the paradigm by allowing learners to personalize and customize course content and comment with observations and questions. Students interact and collaborate with their instructor in building knowledge, blurring the roles between instructor and learner (Thompson, 2007; Magnolda & Platt, 2009). Educators, trainers and instructional designers are challenged with implementing social media. Although examples of social-media integrated with blended learning are appearing, the systematic transformation of practices and culture has not been codified and the new pedagogy is not formed (Carr, 2009; Meister & Willyerd, 2010).

Current technical barriers of security and privacy as well as more experimentation and refinement of collaborative learning, interactivity, and task focused and unfocused dialog will positively increase the impact of social media on learning (Kreijns, Kirschner & Jochems, 2003). We have learned that social-media blended courses based on socio-constructivist and dialogic learning pedagogy seems to improve rates of learning and retention (Ketelhut et al., 2009; Bower et al., 2009) and both collaborative and self-directed learning are possible in CoPs (Väljataga & Fiedler, 2009). Some form of summative evaluations are needed to better measure social media's effects and ambiguities in learning in CoPs (Fanning,

2009), however social media doesn't need any further justification as a viable set of tools for facilitating legitimate learning.

REFERENCES

Bagley, C., & Chou, C. (2007). Collaboration and the importance for novices in learning Java computer programming. *ACM SIGCSE Bulletin, 39*(3), 211–215. doi:10.1145/1269900.1268846

Benson, R., & Samarawickrema, G. (2009). Addressing the context of e-learning: Using transactional distance theory to inform design. *Distance Education, 30*(1), 5–21. doi:10.1080/01587910902845972

Bonk, C., & Dennen, V. (2003). Frameworks for research, design, benchmarks, training, and pedagogy in web-based distance education. In Moore, M. G., & Anderson, W. G. (Eds.), *Handbook of distance education* (pp. 329–348). Mahwah, NJ: L. Erlbaum Associates.

Bower, M., Hedberg, J., & Kuswara, A. (2009). Conceptualizing Web 2.0 enabled learning designs. In *Same Places, Different Spaces: Proceedings Ascilite* Auckland 2009. Retrieved from http://www.ascilite.org.au/conferences/auckland09/procs/bower.pdf

Carr, N. (2009). New media mayhem. *The American School Board Journal, 196*(10), 45–47.

Charskey, D., Kish, M., Briskin, J., Hathaway, S., Walsh, K., & Barajas, N. (2009). Millennials need training too: Using communication technology to facilitate teamwork. *TechTrends, 53*(6).

Chen, F., & Wang, T. (2009). Social conversation and effective discussion in online group learning. *Education Tech Research, 57*(5), 587–612. doi:10.1007/s11423-009-9121-1

Cherbakov, L., Brunner, R., Smart, R., & Liu, C. (2009). Enable far-reaching enterprise collaboration with virtual spaces, Part 1: Introduction to the opportunities and tchnologies. *Convergence*, 1–22.

Cifuentes, L., Sharp, A., Bulu, S., Benz, M., & Stough, L. (2010). Developing a Web 2.0-based system with user-authored content for community use and teacher education. *Educational Technology Research and Development, 58*(4), 377–398. doi:10.1007/s11423-009-9141-x

Clark, R. (2004). What works in distance learning: Instructional strategies. In O'Neil, H. (Ed.), *What works in distance learning: Guidelines.* Greenwich, CT: Information Age Publishers.

Delfino, M., & Manca, S. (2007). The expression of social presence through the use of figurative language in a web-based learning environment. *Computers in Human Behavior, 23*, 2190–2211. doi:10.1016/j.chb.2006.03.001

DeValenzuela, J. (2007, August 22). *Sociocultural theory.* Retrieved from http://www.unm.edu/~devalenz/handouts/sociocult.html

Dillenbourg, P. (1999). What do you mean by 'collaborative learning. In Dillenbourg, P. (Ed.), *Collaborative-learning: Cognitive and computational approaches* (pp. 1–19). New York, NY: Elsevier Science, Inc.

Dix, A., Roselli, T., & Sutinen, E. (Eds.). (2006). eLearning and human-computer interaction: Exploring design synergies for more effective learning experience. *Journal of Educational Technology & Society, 9*(4), 1–2.

Edirisingha, P., Nie, M., Pluciennik, M., & Young, R. (2009). Socialisation for learning at a distance in a 3-D multi-user virtual environment. *British Journal of Educational Technology, 40*(3), 458–479. doi:10.1111/j.1467-8535.2009.00962.x

Fanning, E. (2009). Instructional design factors as they relate to the creation of a virtual learning environment. *Journal of Interactive Instruction Development, 21*(2), 24–42.

Gaver, W. W., Smets, G., & Overbeeke, K. (1995). A virtual window on media space. In I. R. Katz, R. L. Mack, L. Marks, M. B. Rosson, & J. Nielsen (Eds.), *Proceedings of the ACM CHI 95 Human Factors in Computing Systems Conference,* May 7-11, 1995.

Gilroy, M. (2009, September 21). Higher education migrates to YouTube and social networks. *The Hispanic Outlook in Higher Education, 19*, 12–14.

Godwin, B. (2008). *Matrix of Web 2.0 technology tools and government.* U.S. GSA Office of Citizen Services and Innovative Technologies. Retreived from http://www.usa.gov/webcontent/documents/Web_Technology_Matrix.pdf

Gordon-Murnane, L. (2010). We need your input. *Searcher, 18*(3), 26–88.

Greci, L., Ramloll, R., Hurst, S., Garman, K., Beedasy, J., & Pieper, E. Agha, Z. (2009). *Disaster planning.* Best practice poster session presented at the California Hospital Association's Fifth Annual Disaster Planning for California Hospitals Workshop, Sacramento.

Greci, L., Ramloll, R., Hurst, S., Garman, K., Beedasy, J., Pieper, E., et al. (2010). *Pandemic flu patient surge planning and practice in a virtual environment.* 2010 Integrated Training Summit, Las Vegas, Nevada.

Greenhow, C., Robelia, B., & Hughes, J. (2009). Learning, teaching and scholarship in a digital age. [ProQuest Hospital Collection.]. *Educational Researcher, 38*(4), 246–259. doi:10.3102/0013189X09336671

Gunawardena, C., Hermans, M., Sanchez, D., Richmonds, C., Bohley, M., & Tuttle, R. (2009). A theoretical framework for building online communities of practice with social networking tools. *Educational Media International, 46*(1), 3–16. doi:10.1080/09523980802588626

Gunawardena, C., & Zittle, F. (1997). Social presence as a predictor of satisfaction within a computer-mediated conferencing environment. *American Journal of Distance Education, 11*(3), 8–26. doi:10.1080/08923649709526970

Gustin, S. (2011, February 11). *Social media sparked, accelerated Egypt's revolutionary fire.* Retrieved from http://www.wired.com/epicenter/2011/02/egypts-revolutionary-fire/

Hannafin, R., & Sullivan, H. (1995). Learner control in full and lean CAI programs. *Educational Technology Research and Development, 43*, 19–30. doi:10.1007/BF02300479

Hansen, L. (2009). *What ever happened to Second Life?* Retrieved from http://news.bbc.co.uk/2/hi/8367957.stm

Hattie, J. (2009). *Visible learning: A synthesis of over 800 meta-analyses relating to achievement.* London, UK: Routledge.

Hemmi, A., Bayne, S., & Land, R. (2009). The appropriation and repurposing of social technologies in higher education. *Journal of Computer Assisted Learning, 20*(1), 19–30. doi:10.1111/j.1365-2729.2008.00306.x

Hibbets, J. (2010, April 11). *A chat with Cheryl McKinnon.* Retrieved from http://opensource.com/life/10/4/leadership-culture-innovation-with-cheryl-mckinnon

Hollan, J., Hutchins, E., & Kirsh, D. (2000). Distributed cognition: Toward a new foundation for human-computer interaction research. *ACM Transactions on Computer-Human Interaction, 7*(2), 174–194. doi:10.1145/353485.353487

Homer, B., Plass, J., & Blake, L. (2008). The effects of video on cognitive load and social presence in multimedia-learning. *Computers in Human Behavior, 24*(3), 786–797. doi:10.1016/j.chb.2007.02.009

Hong, H., & Sullivan, F. (2009). Towards an idea-centered, principle-based design approach to support learning as knowledge creation. *Educational Technology Research and Development, 57*(5), 613–627. doi:10.1007/s11423-009-9122-0

Iqbal, A., Kankaanranta, M., & Neittaanmäki, P. (2010). Engaging learners through virtual worlds. *Procedia - Social and Behavioral Sciences, 2*(2), 3198-3205. Retrieved from http://www.sciencedirect.com/science/journal/18770428

Jaworski, B. (1996). *Constructivism and teaching: The socio-cultural context.* Retrieved from http://www.grout.demon.co.uk/Barbara/chreods.htm

Jung, Y. (2008). Influence of sense of presence on intention to participate in a virtual community. *Proceedings of the 41st Hawaii International Conference on System Science*, Vol. 325. Retrieved from http://www.computer.org/comp/proceedings/hicss/2008/3075/00/30750325.pdf

Kaplan, A., & Haenlein, M. (2010). Users of the world, unite! The challenges and opportunities of social media. *Business Horizons, 53*(1), 59–68. doi:10.1016/j.bushor.2009.09.003

Kearsley, G., & Lynch, W. (1996). Structural issues in distance education. *Journal of Education for Business, 71*(2), 167–191.

Ketelhut, D., Nelson, B., Clarke, J., & Dede, C. (2009). A multiuser virtual environment for building and assessing higher order inquiry skills in science. *British Journal of Educational Technology, 41*(1), 56–68. doi:10.1111/j.1467-8535.2009.01036.x

Kirschner, P. (2002). Cognitive load theory: Implications of cognitive load theory on the design of learning. *Learning and Instruction, 12*(1), 1–10. doi:10.1016/S0959-4752(01)00014-7

Kreijns, K., Kirschner, P., & Jochems, W. (2002). The sociability of computer-supported collaborative learning environments. *Journal of Educational Technology & Society, 5*(1), 8–22.

Kreijns, K., Kirschner, P., & Jochems, W. (2003). Identifying the pitfalls for social interaction in computer-supported collaborative learning environments: A review of the research. *Computers in Human Behavior, 19*, 335–353. doi:10.1016/S0747-5632(02)00057-2

Kundra, V. (2009). The nation's new chief information officer speaks. *New York Times Business and Technology Blog, Bits.*

Lantholf, J., & Thorne, S. (2000). *Sociocultural theory and second language learning.* New York, NY: Oxford University Press.

Larach, U., & Cabra, J. (2010). Creative problem-solving in Second Life: An action research study. *Creativity and Innovation Management, 19*(2), 167–179. doi:10.1111/j.1467-8691.2010.00550.x

Lee, H., & Rha, I. (2009). Influence of structure and interaction on student achievement and satisfaction in web-based distance learning. *Journal of Educational Technology & Society, 12*(4), 372–382.

Lin, C., Chou, C., & Bagley, C. (2007). APEC cyber academy: Integration of pedagogical and HCI principles in an international networked learning environment. In McKay, E. (Ed.), *Enhancing learning through human-computer interaction* (pp. 154–177). Hershey, PA: Idea Group Publishing, Inc. doi:10.4018/978-1-59904-328-9.ch009

Lipowicz, A. (2010). vGov for feds aims to be a more engaging online environment. *Federal Computer Week.* Retrieved from http://fcw.com/Articles/2010/07/12/FEAT-QandA-Paulette-Robinson-NDU-vGov.aspx

Losey, S. (2010). Government to launch 'Fedspace,' a social media site for feds. *FederalTimes.com*. Retrieved from http://www.federaltimes.com/ article/20100427/DEPART-MENTS07/4270302/-1/RSS?sms_ss=email

Magnolda, P., & Platt, G. (2009). Untangling Web 2.0's influences on student learning. [Academic Search Premier.]. *About Campus, 14*(3), 10–16. doi:10.1002/abc.290

McIsaac, M., & Gunawardena, C. (1996). Research in distance education. In Jonassen, D. (Ed.), *Handbook of research for educational communications and technology* (pp. 403–437). New York, NY: Scholastic Press.

Means, B., Toyama, Y., Murphy, R., Bakia, M., & Jones, K. (2009). *Evaluation of evidence-based practices in online learning: A meta-analysis and review of online-learning studies*. Washington, DC: U.S. Department of Education. Retrieved from http://ctl.sri.com/publications/displayPublication.jsp?ID=770

Meister, J., & Willyerd, K. (2010). Looking ahead at social learning: Ten predictions. *T+D, 64*(7), 34-41.

Nielsen, J. (2006). *Ten usability heuristics*. Retrieved from http://www.useit.com/papers/heuristic/heuristic_list.html

O'Reilly, T. (2005). *What is Web 2.0? Design patterns and business models for the next generation of software*. Retrieved from http://oreilly.com/pub/a/web2/archive/what-is-web-20.html?page=1

Ochoa, T., & Robinson, J. (2005). Revisiting group consensus: Collaborative learning dynamics during a problem-based learning activity in education. *Teacher Education and Special Education, 28*(1), 10–20. doi:10.1177/088840640502800102

Pachler, N., & Daly, C. (2009). Narrative and learning with Web 2.0 technologies: Towards a research agenda. *Journal of Computer Assisted Learning, 25*(1), 6–18. doi:10.1111/j.1365-2729.2008.00303.x

Palvia, S., & Pancaro, R. (2010). Promises and perils of Internet-based networking. *Journal of Global Information Technology Management, 13*(3).

Pence, H. E. (2007). The homeless professor in Second Life. *Journal of Educational Technology Systems, 36*(2), 171–177. doi:10.2190/ET.36.2.e

Powers, S., Janz, K., & Ande, T. (2006). Using theories of social presence and transactional distance to understand technology enhanced instruction. In C. Crawford, et al., (Eds.), *Proceedings of Society for Information Technology & Teacher Education International Conference 2006* (pp. 502-505). Chesapeake, VA: AACE. Retrieved from http://www.editlib.org/p/22087

Saeed, N., Yang, Y., & Sinnappan, S. (2009). Emerging web technologies in higher education: A case of incorporating blogs, podcasts, and social bookmarks in a web programming course based on students' learning styles and technology preferences. *Journal of Educational Technology & Society, 12*(4), 98–109.

Schnotz, W., & Kürschner, C. (2007). A reconsideration of cognitive load theory. *Educational Psychology Review, 19*, 469–508. doi:10.1007/s10648-007-9053-4

Schramm, W. (Ed.). (1954). *The process and effects of communication*. Urbana, IL: University of Illinois Press.

Sfard, A. (1998). On two metaphors for learning and the dangers of choosing just one. [Academic Search Premier.]. *Educational Researcher, 27*(2), 4–13.

Shneiderman, B. (1998). *Designing the user interface: Strategies for effective human-computer interaction* (3rd ed.). Reading, MA: Addison-Wesley.

Slagter van Tryon, P., & Bishop, M. (2009). Theoretical foundations for enhancing social connectedness in online learning environments. *Distance Education, 30*(3), 291–337. doi:10.1080/01587910903236312

Smith, R., Bagley, C., & Greci, L. (2010). *Disaster emergency medical personnel system (DEMPS) selection of a virtual world platform to address human performance requirements.* Retrieved from http://ntsa.metapress.com/app/home/contribution.asp?referrer=parent&backto=issue,52,170;journal,1,18;linkingpublicationresults,1:113340,1

So, H., & Brush, T. (2009). Student perceptions of collaborative learning, social presence, and satisfaction in a blended learning environment: Relationships and critical factors. [Academic Search Premier.]. *Computers & Education, 51*(1), 318–336. doi:10.1016/j.compedu.2007.05.009

Sweller, J. (1988). Cognitive load during problem-solving: Effects on learning. [Academic Search Premier.]. *Cognitive Science, 12*(2), 257–285. doi:10.1207/s15516709cog1202_4

Tennyson, R., & Bagley, C. (1992). Structured versus constructed instructional strategies for improving concept acquisition by domain-competent and domain-novice learners. *Journal of Structural Learning, 11*(3), 255–263.

Thompson, J. (2007). Is education 1.0 ready for Web 2.0 students? *Innovate: Journal of Online Education, 3*(4). Retrieved from http://www.innovateonline.info/vol3_issue4/Is_Education_1.0_Ready_for_Web_2.0_Students

Väljataga, T., & Fiedler, S. (2009). Supporting students to self-direct intentional learning projects with social media. *Journal of Educational Technology & Society, 12*(3), 58–69.

Vygotsky, L. S. (1978). *Mind in society: The development of higher psychological processes.* Cambridge, MA: Harvard University Press.

Wang, Q. (2007). Designing a web-based constructivist learning environment. *Interactive Learning Environments, 17*(1), 1–13. doi:10.1080/10494820701424577

Wang, S., & Hsu, H. (2009). Using the ADDIE model to design Second Life activities for online learners. *TechTrends, 53*(6), 76–81. Retrieved from http://edtc6325teamone2ndlife.pbworks.com/f/6325+Using+the+ADDIE+Model.pdf doi:10.1007/s11528-009-0347-x

Warshauer, M. (1997). Computer-mediated collaborative learning: Theory and practice. *Modern Language Journal, 81*(3), 470–481. doi:10.1111/j.1540-4781.1997.tb05514.x

Wegner, D., & Vallacher, R. (1977). *Implicit psychology: An introduction to social cognition.* New York, NY: Oxford University Press.

Yamada, M. (2009). The role of social presence in learner-centered communicative language learning using synchronous computer-mediated communication: Experimental study. [Academic Search Premier.]. *Computers & Education, 52*(4), 820–833. doi:10.1016/j.compedu.2008.12.007

Yang, Z., & Liu, Q. (2004). Research and development of web-based virtual online classroom. [Academic Search Premier.]. *Computers & Education, 48*(2), 171–184. doi:10.1016/j.compedu.2004.12.007

Yee, N. (2006). Motivations for play in online games. *Cyberpsychology & Behavior, 9*(6), 772–775. Retrieved from http://www.liebertonline.com/toc/cpb/9/6 doi:10.1089/cpb.2006.9.772

ADDITIONAL READING

Barnett, M., Yamagata-Lynch, L., Keating, T., Barab, S., & Hay, K. (2005). Using virtual reality computer models to support student understanding of astronomical concepts. *Journal of Computers in Mathematics and Science Teaching, 24*(4), 333–356.

Boulos, M., Hetherington, L., & Wheeler, S. (2007). Second Life: An overview of the potential of 3-D virtual worlds in medical and health education. *Health Information and Libraries Journal*, *24*(4), 233–245. doi:10.1111/j.1471-1842.2007.00733.x

Brooks, L. (2009). Social learning by design: The role of social media. *Knowledge Quest*, *37*(5), 58–60.

Carr, D. (2009). Constructing disability in online worlds. *London Review of Education*, *8*(1), 51–61. doi:10.1080/14748460903557738

Churchill, D. (2007). Web 2.0 and possibilities for educational applications. *Educational Technology*, *47*(2), 24–29.

Clarke, J., Ketelhut, D., Nelson, B., Erlandson, B., Dieterle, E., & Dede, C. (2007). *Investigating students' behaviors, patterns, and learning in a multiuser virtual environment designed around inquiry*. Paper presented at the 2007 American Educational Research Association Conference, Chicago, IL.

Fiedler, S., & Pata, K. (2009). Distributed learning environments and social software: In search for a framework of design. In Hatzipanagos, S., & Warburton, S. (Eds.), *Handbook of research on social software and developing community ontologies* (pp. 45–158). Hershey, PA: IGI Global. doi:10.4018/978-1-60566-208-4.ch011

Galagan, P. (2009). Twitter as a learning tool. Really. *T+D, 63*(3), 28-31.

Hill, J. R., & Raven, A. (2000). *Online learning communities: If you build them, will they stay?* Instructional Technology Forum. Retrieved from http://it.coe.uga.edu/itforum/paper46/paper46.htm

Hsu, J. (2007). Innovative technologies for education and learning: Education and knowledge-oriented applications of blogs, wikis, podcasts, and more. *International Journal of Information and Communication Technology Education*, *3*(3), 70–89. doi:10.4018/jicte.2007070107

Huang, H. (2002). Toward constructivism for adult learners in online learning environments. *British Journal of Educational Technology*, *33*(1), 27–37. doi:10.1111/1467-8535.00236

Jonassen, D., Davidson, M., Collins, M., Campbell, J., & Haag, B. B. (1995). Constructivism and computer-mediated communication in distance education. *American Journal of Distance Education*, *9*(2), 7–26. doi:10.1080/08923649509526885

Kelliher, A., Birchfield, D., Campana, E., Hatton, S., Johnson-Glenberg, M., & Martinez, C. Uysal, S. (2009). SMALLab: A mixed-reality environment for embodied and mediated learning. *American Journal of Physics*, 1029-1031. Retrieved from http://portal.acm.org/citation.cfm?id=1631272.1631504

Kemp, J., & Livingstone, D. (2006). *Putting a Second Life 'metaverse' skin on learning management systems*. Paper presented at the Second Life Education Workshop at the SL Community Convention, San Francisco, CA. Retrieved from http://cmapspublic3.ihmc.us/rid=11668488586 87_1820623091_2414/whitepaper.pdf

Ketelhut, D. J., Dede, C., Clarke, J., Nelson, B., & Bowman, C. (2007). Studying situated learning in a multiuser virtual environment. In Baker, E., Dickieson, J., Wulfeck, W., & O'Neil, H. (Eds.), *Assessment of problem-solving using simulations*. Mahwah, NJ: Lawrence Erlbaum Associates.

Lesser, E., & Storck, J. (2001). Communities of practice and organizational performance. *IBM Systems Journal*, 40(4), 831–841. Retrieved from http://ieeexplore.ieee.org/stamp/stamp.jsp?tp=&arnumber=5386944 doi:10.1147/sj.404.0831

Martinez-Jimenez, P., Pontes-Pedrajas, A., Polo, J., & Climent-Bellido, M. (2003). Learning in chemistry with virtual laboratories. *Journal of Chemical Education*, 80(3), 346–352. doi:10.1021/ed080p346

Oliver, M., & Carr, D. (2009). Learning in virtual worlds: Using communities of practice to explain how people learn from play. *British Journal of Educational Technology*, 40(3), 444–457. doi:10.1111/j.1467-8535.2009.00948.x

Pata, K. (2009). Modeling spaces for self-directed learning at university courses. *Journal of Educational Technology & Society*, 12(3), 23–43.

Scarpelli, N. (2009, July 30). Social media's effect on learning. *Digits*. Retrieved from http://blogs.wsj.com/digits/2009/07/30/social-medias-effect-on-learning/

Singh, H. (2003). Building effective blended learning programs. *Educational Technology*, 43(6), 51–54.

Smith, M. (2003, 2009). Communities of practice. Infed.org. *The Encyclopaedia of Informal Education*. Retrieved from http://www.infed.org/biblio/communities_of_practice.htm

Thorpe, M. (2002). Rethinking learner support: The challenge of collaborative online learning. *Open Learning*, 17(2), 105–119. doi:10.1080/02680510220146887a

Tu, C., Blocher, M., & Roberts, G. (2008). Constructs for Web 2.0 learning environments: A theatrical metaphor. *Educational Media International*, 45(4), 253–269. doi:10.1080/09523980802588576

Warburton, S. (2009). Second Life in higher education: Assessing the potential for and the barriers to deploying virtual worlds in learning and teaching. *British Journal of Educational Technology*, 40(3), 414–426. doi:10.1111/j.1467-8535.2009.00952.x

Wenger, E. (1998). *Communities of practice: Learning, meaning, and identity*. London, UK: Cambridge University Press.

Windschitl, M. (1998). The WWW and classroom research: What path should we take? *Educational Researcher*, 27(1), 28–33.

Zhao, C., & Kuh, G. (2004). Added value: Learning communities and student engagement. *Research in Higher Education*, 45, 115–138. doi:10.1023/B:RIHE.0000015692.88534.de

KEY TERMS AND DEFINITIONS

Asynchronous Learning: A student-centered teaching method that uses online learning resources to facilitate peer-to-peer information sharing outside the constraints of time and place among a network of people.

Cognitive Load: A measurement of the amount of information the human mind can effectively process. Because human working memory is limited with respect to the information it can hold, and thus the number of operations it can perform on that information, the amount of information presented during instruction must be managed to maintain a reasonable cognitive load.

Community/Socio-Cultural Context of Knowledge: Social interaction and community have profound implications for increasing learning and higher-order function.

Feedback: Output from or information provided by teacher or learner about a learning event will influence new events or learning.

Human-Computer Interaction: The study, planning, and design of the interaction between people (users) and computers.

Instructional Design: The practice of prescribing optimal methods of instruction to bring about desired changes in learner knowledge and skills.

Interactivity: Using social media to communicate or collaborate so as to engage in learning in an active rather than passive way.

Social Media: A group of Web 2.0, Internet-based media applications used for social interaction.

Social Presence: A measure of the feeling of community a learner experiences in an online environment.

Transactional Distance: A psychological and communication space to be crossed; a space of potential misunderstanding between the inputs of instructor and those of the learner.

Chapter 3
Assessment and Learning Partnerships in an Online Environment

Patrick Griffin
The University of Melbourne, Australia

Judith Crigan
The University of Melbourne, Australia

Esther Care
The University of Melbourne, Australia

Nafisa Awwal
The University of Melbourne, Australia

Pam Robertson
The University of Melbourne, Australia

Masa Pavlovic
The University of Melbourne, Australia

ABSTRACT

This chapter shows how the online environment is used to promote quality teaching within a research project conducted by the Assessment Research Centre at the University of Melbourne. The project investigates how teacher teams use assessment data to inform teaching decisions and extensive efforts are made to check their learning through performance assessment procedures that monitor their discipline and pedagogy skills development. Teachers from the project are involved in a professional development course. The ways in which they adopt the knowledge, skills, and attitudes addressed by the course are tracked, along with assessment data from their students. The online environment is used to deliver the professional development course and to deliver online assessments for students and teachers. The authors are careful to ensure that the online experience for both teachers and students reinforces the ideas of the project. These include the notions of developmental approach rather than deficit, evidence rather than inferential decision making and collaboration rather than isolation.

INTRODUCTION

Teacher teams use assessment data as evidence to inform teaching intervention decisions. They undertake an online professional development programme which encourages the idea of collaboration, challenge, evidence-based decision making, peer accountability, targeted and differentiated teaching directed at a developmental construct and an emphasis on skills rather than scores. The ways in which they adopt the knowledge, skills and attitudes addressed by the course are tracked,

DOI: 10.4018/978-1-4666-3649-1.ch003

along with assessment data from their students. The online environment is used to deliver the professional development course and to deliver online assessments for students and teachers.

During the professional development programme, teachers engage in an online environment to develop their skills in the use of data to teach literacy, numeracy and problem solving. In doing so the programme attempts to help teachers shift from a deficit model to a developmental approach. The project objective is to enable teachers, through a 10 session online professional development programme, to use data within a developmental framework to improve performance of all students. The professional development programme shows teachers how to work in a culture where evidence is challenged and discussed, rather than one where there is merely mutual endorsement of shared teaching strategies.

Participants become increasingly skilled in the theory and application of assessment and the developmental construct they are teaching and better able to link evidence of student learning readiness to targeted intervention. This professional development provision constitutes part of a larger research project which seeks to identify how teacher factors influence student learning outcomes. This chapter outlines how diverse skills such as leadership, information dissemination and influencing attitudinal change are taught in an online environment.

BACKGROUND

The Assessment and Learning Partnerships (ALP) project has its origins in a project conducted by the University of Melbourne, the Assessment Research Centre and the Catholic Education Office, Melbourne. In 2004, trials of a range of reading tests were conducted in 20 schools to examine how the test data could be used to improve student reading comprehension. The pilot study was known as the Learning Assessment Project

(LAP) (Murray & Rintoul, 2008). Professional Learning Teams (PLT) were led by the schools' literacy coordinators, with classroom teachers as team members.

Team members engaged in collaborative discussions based on challenging peer evidence of learning and links between intervention and learning gains. Gains in student reading comprehension were compelling (Griffin, Murray, Care, Thomas, & Perri, 2010). Several hypotheses were formulated and a large research study supported by the Australian Research Council and linkage partners was established to examine and systematically test those hypotheses, in order to generalise and scale up the procedures across systems, year levels and subjects.

The programme conducted for the Catholic Education Office involved face-to-face teaching. Due to high demand, an online professional development programme was developed to provide the course to larger numbers of school-based participants. This online programme was called the Assessment and Learning Partnerships Online System. To date, more than 280 schools and 400 teachers have completed the course. To provide teachers undertaking the professional development programme with a valid source of criterion-referenced data, an online testing programme for students was also developed. Approximately 100,000 tests have been administered to more than 30,000 individual students during the 2011 school year. This source of student achievement data also serves as a dependent variable in the research project, which aims to examine the approach's effect on student learning achievement.

The premise of the project is that teachers who use a specific style of evidence-based teaching and operate within a developmental learning paradigm have an increased effect on student learning outcomes. The online programme facilitates the role of collaborative teaching teams in the use of data to enhance decision-making about teaching and learning strategies. Team-based models have been shown to be an effective form of professional development compared to traditional workshop models (Care & Griffin, 2009). The programme encourages critical and collaborative discussions where teachers test their ideas, challenge inferences of student ability, and ensure assumptions about student ability and progress are based on observable evidence.

Pilot work in the project suggested that with a data-driven, evidence-based approach to teaching and learning, teachers could manipulate the learning environment and scaffold learning for every student, regardless of the student's development or intellectual capacity (Griffin, 2007; Timperley, Parr, & Bertanees, 2009). In the programme, teachers are led to differentiate between deficit and developmental teaching and learning approaches. When working with a deficit approach, skills that the student lacks are taught and problems are 'fixed'. This approach represents a 'rescue' package for low achievers. However, when using a developmental teaching approach, skills that the student is on the verge of acquiring are taught. This gives it a more forward looking and goal-driven focus.

Teachers administer standardised tests of reading comprehension, problem solving and mathematics to their students at two time points (six months apart) as part of their learning in the course. This is an important aspect of the approach because student ability is determined in part by these assessments and teachers use the results to identify student ability and plan teaching. A secondary use of this data is to assess the effectiveness of the online professional developmental programme: does the course promote change in practice leading to improved student outcomes?

CONTEXT

There are two characterising aspects of the model – team-based action, and interpretation and use of evidence for instructional intervention. These are the focus of the professional development provi-

sion. A normal practice in teacher professional development programmes and in pre-service training is to focus first on teaching strategy. However, the approach makes explicit it is student performance and readiness to learn that will define the focus of the course. The literacy study made it explicit that there was a prior student condition that had to be measured and generalised prior to deciding upon intervention and designing intervention strategies.

In the literacy study, teacher capacity to use data to improve student learning was linked to the way in which teacher teams developed data-driven instructional systems to improve classroom practice and monitor student learning. Griffin (2007) and Alton-Lee (2008) have shown how team leaders and teachers develop formative feedback systems. Timperley (2008) and Alton Lee (2008) have also shown that teachers in teams need to develop as members of their teams. The LAP project incorporated learning opportunities for teachers consistent with principles that underpinned the CLaSS project (Hill & Crévola, 1997) as a school improvement strategy (Hill, Crévola, & Hopkins, 2000). It was also consistent with the recommendations of Fullan, Hill and Crévola (2006) who highlighted the importance of professional learning. They identified three core elements that enhanced sustained change in schools: personalisation, precision, and professional learning. They argued that assessment for learning, although frequently spoken about, was not broadly or effectively practiced in schools. In the project reported here, the emphasis is placed on assessment for teaching.

ALP is not the only professional development initiative to focus on the use of assessment data. DataWise (Boudett, City, & Murnane, 2005) and Instructional Rounds (Fowler-Finn, 2009), for example, are programmes that direct primary attention to the use of data in education. There are some considerable similarities in approach and language used to describe data use across these initiatives. DataWise and Instructional Rounds are, however, directed primarily toward leadership teams, at system and school levels respectively. The ALP model is directed primarily toward the PLT leader, who is often synonymous with the teacher in the classroom. The focus of the project is specifically on the pedagogical use of student data by the teacher, rather than on the policy use of data.

Evidence-based approaches to teaching have at their disposal myriad sets of data. In the online course, the focus is initially on the interpretation of scored and scaled data. This does not imply, however, that such data are valued more highly than other sources of information about student learning and progress in that learning. The use of scaled data allows identification of student progress across time, but does require in-depth understanding by data users about the nature and origin of such data. In particular, it does not require teacher understanding of the nature of the developmental continua which such data are designed to indicate or represent. Consequently, information designed to ensure such understanding constitutes a major theme in the online course.

Merely having and using tests is insufficient to inform teaching and improve learning (Halverson, Grigg, Prichett, & Thomas, 2005). The way test data is interpreted is central. Using standardised assessments formatively requires that tests provide sufficient information to profile students' learning and to identify the zone of intervention for individual students. It also requires teachers to link their interpretation of data at both group and individual levels to teaching interventions to examine and explain any improvement in student learning. This has been enhanced by a process of critical and collaborative analysis and discussion of data (Griffin et al., 2010). The common theme across previous studies has been that it is essential to have a process by which teachers can be engaged in interpreting data, linking the information to their own teaching, and testing the links using the discourse of evidence and accountability among their peers.

THE PROFESSIONAL DEVELOPMENT PROGRAMME

The course delivers a series of online sessions enabling teachers in teams to structure evidence-based intervention for their own and their students' learning needs. Following procedures outlined by Griffin et al. (2010), teachers proceed through the course, accountable to their peers for the way they use evidence of student development, for decisions about interventions and resource use, and how these link to student development in key learning outcomes. The team leader maintains logs of these discussions to account for team strategies and their link to evidence of learning of both teachers and students. These logs represent records of the accountability process. They are collected online and analysed qualitatively to construct derived variables. Records of the teaching strategies that are used in the classroom are linked to student learning, which is assessed using an online student assessment system. In this way, the effectiveness of a range of teaching strategies can be analysed by the researchers. Participants are guided to apply the same process of developmental learning with themselves and other team members as they do with students in their care.

The course presents information to team leaders to explore theory, research, and information about practices in their own and in other schools, and to take this learning to their teams. Classrooms within schools are linked through the team members so they can learn from and guide one another, discussing, challenging and evaluating information and theory conveyed to them by their team leader from the leader's own experience in the course. The team leader returns material from this process online via the course facilitators to the researchers.

Participants in the course are working teachers, coaches and principals in schools. Their progress through the course and implementation of the approach in their practice is dependent on a range of factors. They need the support of their school's leadership to provide resources, such as time to meet, and access to further professional development. They also need other teachers willing to form a team and work with the approach. Essential prerequisites for engaging successfully with the approach have been identified. Schools wishing to participate need to be aware of these prerequisites and of the demands on their staff.

Developmental Framework

Teacher knowledge of the use and interpretation of test data is central for the success of any evidence-based approach to teaching and learning. It requires teachers to know how to link the interpretation of assessment data to teaching interventions and to be able to examine measured progress in student achievement critically. Within the project, student outcomes are interpreted in a developmental assessment framework as described by Griffin (2007).

Griffin combined the theories of Glaser (1963), Rasch (1960), and Vygotsky (1978) to show how probabilistic interpretation of competences can provide a basis for the link between assessment and teaching and learning. In this context, competences are defined in terms of achievement of a series of tasks of growing difficulty. This developmental framework provides teachers with the opportunity to interpret assessment data using a criterion-referenced framework and link student progress to points along the associated developmental continuum. This is the basis of the course; teachers are led to generalise information about what a student can and cannot do and place this within a reference frame in which to monitor progress.

Criterion-Referenced Framework

It can be misleading to interpret performance on a test by examining the raw score (the score obtained by adding together all the items answered correctly). This is because interpretation of the scores cannot be separated from the test. Consequently, interpretation is tied to the test's content. A high score on a test simply indicates that the student can respond correctly to those items. It explains little about the test-takers' skills. In a norm-referenced framework, performance of the test taker is compared to other test takers or to some other normative group. Interpretation in this manner simply shows a test taker's standing relative to others. Another model, the criterion-referenced framework, was brought about by the need to reference test scores to test taker performance or, more precisely, to what the person can or cannot do with respect to some instructional objective or particular skill set (Nitko, 1980).

Criterion-referenced interpretation of assessment data was first introduced by Glaser (1963). In his work he described performances and development in terms of the nature and order of tasks performed. The test item is described by skill or a single criterion that has to be demonstrated by the test taker. Performance is interpreted directly to a single fixed level of achievement and success is interpreted as either mastery or non-mastery, by reference to a single cut score. This definition led to an interpretation as simply being a list of individual tasks that the test taker can or cannot do, thus reducing the assessments to a checklist of skills with little use for educational instruction (Griffin, 2009). Responding to this, Glaser (2007) expanded and redefined the mastery/non-mastery approach, adjusting it to mean stages along a progression of increasing competency.

MAKING SENSE OF DATA

The type of evidence needs to be considered separately from the evidence itself. It can include things such as tests, direct observation, rubrics, work samples, and portfolios.

Before instructional decisions can be linked to evidence, it is necessary to find a way of interpreting the evidence and developing a system of coding our observations and generating records. It is surprising that much of this is done intuitively and often unsystematically. Records are typically codes devised to record observations. However, whenever a code is used, decoding is also required in order to attach meaning to it.

Consider an example of a multiple choice test item in Figure 1.

If a student chooses the correct answer to this question (B), what does this indicate about the student's skills, assuming that the student did not guess? The response is coded with a '1' to indicate that a correct answer was selected, but what does the '1' mean? It could mean only that the student chose the correct option. But it can provide more than just the scale. In order to score 1, the student must be able to calculate the number of times the central processing units (CPU) used (6), the number of monitors used (3), then calculate the difference (3). It is multi-step problem involving multiplication, division and subtraction, in the appropriate sequence. It is a complex skill and to code it as '1' without recording the full meaning (the skills required) detracts from the value of the assessment task, and provides little feedback information. The idea that a score is a code and needs to be decoded in terms of the skill underpinning the success is important for the teacher to understand how to scaffold learning, as explained by Griffin (2007).

Few if any instructional development programmes offer help to teachers regarding how to construct or interpret assessment codes for instructional purposes. When the '1's are summed and a

Figure 1. Multiple choice test item

A computer CPU needs replacing after 2.5 years. A computer monitor needs replacing after 5 years. Kamal worked with computers from the beginning of 1998 until the end of 2010. How many more CPUs than monitors did Kamal use over that time?

A. 2
B. 3
C. 6
D. 13

total score is obtained (and sometimes converted to a percentage) the loss of meaning is compounded. The total score is also a code for something, and it too needs to be decoded. Procedures do exist for decoding and interpreting. Teachers need help to achieve this level of interpretation. This is a major goal of the course. In many instances it is a simple process and can be done either using a human/computer interface or a simulation of it (Griffin, et al., 2010). If the scores are decoded within a developmental frame of reference the power of the information is magnified many times. The developmental framework is a critical and central aspect of the approach, despite that it is constructed empirically from a test analysis and skills audit of the test items. The test items are replaceable but the developmental framework is not. Emphasising test items can be avoided and as Griffin and Nix (1991) pointed out, once the progression is defined assessment data can be collected in a range of ways and used to locate a student on the continuum.

LATENT TRAIT OR ITEM RESPONSE THEORY

The codes for each item become the basic data for an item response analysis based on what is known as latent trait theory. The introduction of latent trait theory enabled the connection of student performance on an item with item difficulty. This is determined via the response function that defines how the probability of a person's correct answer to an item varies with a person's ability. The central assumption of latent trait theory is that the probability of answering the test item correctly depends only on the item and the person taking the test. More precisely, that person's ability to answer the item correctly is determined by the amount of the trait possessed by the person and by the item's parametric connection to the latent trait (Traub & Wolfe, 1981). Depending on the response function used, information on the person consists of just one parameter (ability) while information on the item may consist of one (difficulty), two (difficulty, discrimination) or three parameters (difficulty, discrimination, guessing).

A commonly used model for dichotomously scored items is one introduced by Rasch. It is a one parameter model where item difficulty is described by δ and each person's ability by θ, while the item characteristic function is defined as

$$p = P(X = 1) = \frac{\exp(\delta - \theta)}{1 + \exp(\delta - \theta)}$$

where X=1 indicates success on the item.

This relationship allows for the placement of both item and person on the same scale. The position of the items on the scale is defined by the ability value for which the probability of the correct answer is 0.5.

The item position on a latent trait map is where the probability of the correct answer for each person is 0.5. This can be directly linked to the Vygotsky's Zone of Proximal Development (ZPD) (Griffin, 2007). This is the difference between what a person can do on their own and what they can do with the help of a more knowledgeable other. It is the point where the individual cannot consistently achieve, but is on the verge of mastery. Translated to statistical terms, it is the point at which the student is achieving approximately 50% correct.

Developmental Progression

Combining criterion-referenced test interpretation and latent trait theory links a person's ability level to a scale of increasing competence. The scale clearly shows a progression of skills, and a person's position on this scale is pinpointed. This gives meaning to the score and helps establish the meaning of the underlying construct by interpreting skills required to answer the item correctly (Griffin, 2009). Figure 2 shows the position of the person and item on a common scale. This representation is also called a variable map and

is produced using item response software such as ConQuest (Wu, Adams, & Wilson, 1998).

The map shows the distribution of students on the left side, and the test items on the right. The items are distributed beside the students who had a 50% probability of successfully responding to that item. Items are represented by their question numbers on the right side of the map. It can be seen from the map that items cluster together, representing similar difficulty levels. Once clusters are identified the items are examined to determine if there is a skill common to the items in a cluster. These skills are then used to interpret the underlying variable and define a common developmental progression of learning. This interpretation allows the linking of student performance to Glaser's (2007) stages of increasing competence.

Students' positions on the map are represented by X on the left side of the figure. Because items and students are on the same scale, students can be viewed as groups with similar ability levels. Levels are separated by red horizontal lines. Students within a particular level have an approximately 50:50 chance of answering items within a level correctly. They have less than 50% chance of answering items above their level correctly and more than 50% chance of answering items in the level below correctly.

This representation enables teachers to link assessment data to the interpretation of what the student can or cannot do. The combination of a criterion-referenced framework, the Rasch model and Vygotsky's ZPD enables the teacher to define the point at which intervention should be targeted. The point where the student has 50:50 chance of answering an item correctly is the point where teaching intervention has the best chance of success (Griffin, 2007).

The assessment instruments used in the ALP project and the online course measure progress in the areas of literacy, numeracy and problem solving. For each of the subject domains, tests are mapped onto a single developmental continuum using item response theory.

Figure 2. Variable map

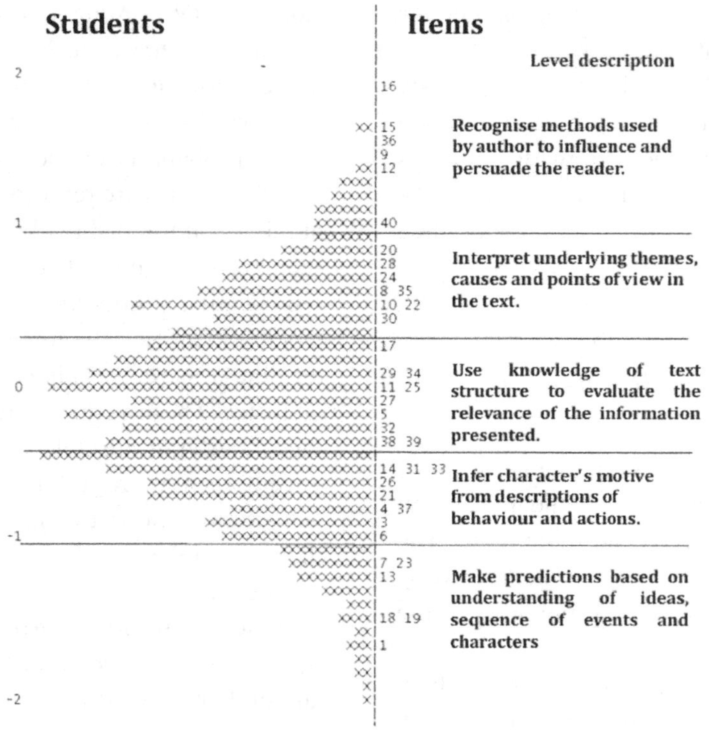

This provides teachers with a developmental learning framework that enables them to locate students' zone of proximal development and monitor student growth in terms of increasing levels of competence through the duration of the course and afterwards. For teachers participating in the project it is essential to develop their knowledge of data interpretation within the framework and to view instruction, assessment and learning as integrated components of their teaching.

STUDENT ASSESSMENT SYSTEM

An integral component of the ALP project, and the online course which supports it, is the online student testing system. It was developed in-house for the project as a comprehensive assessment system which maps student competency to an underlying developmental progression and reports ability level. It delivers a series of assessments through the year and consists of items selected from an item bank which are targeted to a range of ability levels approximately up to Year 10 in the Victorian education system. It also includes a reporting package which provides real time reports to teachers (Griffin, 2000).

The system is web-based and allows teachers to administer tests and other forms of assessment instruments online. The tests can be used to assess literacy, numeracy and problem solving for students at different levels of ability using a multiple-choice item format. For students with learning difficulties, teacher observation instruments are available through the system. The instruments for assessing students with additional needs (SWANS) address communication and literacy, interpersonal skills and intrapersonal skills. They provide observation schedules which are rubric, or judgement, based (Woods & Griffin, 2010).

The current suite of online assessments encompass the domains of reading comprehension (eight tests), mathematics (eight tests) and problem solving (three tests), with content from the Victorian curriculum for students in Year 3 through to Year 10. Each test consists of 40 items selected from the item bank and linked to a developmental progression for the appropriate learning domain. The tests are interactive and responses are recorded and scored automatically. Results are reported at individual and class levels in real time upon test completion. The use of such a system allows teachers to obtain detailed feedback about their students' performance that enables them to make informed instructional decisions within collaborative teacher teams. This feedback to teachers is not in the form of raw scores achieved by the student but in the form of individual or class level reports profiling the students' competency and their point of readiness to learn. The aim of the system is to provide teachers with assessment tools and results that allow them to monitor student progress over time and link that progress to successful teaching strategies.

The current testing system is quasi-adaptive, to help teachers target assessments and match the tests to the student ability level. The correct targeting of assessment is essential to determine precisely what a student can and cannot do. When a student responds accurately to too few items, the assessment does not adequately examine what they can do. Similarly, when a student responds to most of the items in a test accurately, their actual ability is also not known, as their ability level is higher than the test is assessing. Teachers learn how to determine the most appropriate test for their students. The tests overlap, so in reality a single student could be validly assessed by two or three different level tests. When a student responds accurately to too many items for their ability to be accurately determined, further items at a higher difficulty level are automatically delivered. This increases the validity of the reporting information for use in teaching intervention.

Access to the online system is available to schools that are part of the research programme and enrolled in the online course. The authentication process controls access to different parts of the system and its various functions for both the teachers and students (Figure 3). Teachers are in control of tests in order to make them accessible to students. This ensures that tests are supervised and cannot be administered without teacher authority. Teachers also have real-time access to the reporting and feedback module, various instruments, and longitudinal data from tests completed over a period of time by students in their school.

Students are permitted to view a number of tests in the three domains only after teachers have enabled the tests to be accessible to them. The system deals with unexpected interruption due to internet connection failures or other technical issues by allowing students to continue their tests at a later time, incorporating their earlier responses. In addition, students can view the progress of their completed work and edit their test responses. The system notifies teachers with suggestions on the appropriateness of the test targeted for the student in question and alerts the teachers to the time taken to complete the test and

Figure 3. The online assessment system (ARCOTS) design

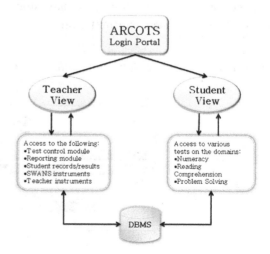

the number of items attempted by the student. Students' responses are automatically scored and fed back into the reporting module instantaneously to provide teachers with a rich source of evidence of their students' learning.

The online system makes test administration easy and accessible (Figure 4). It speeds up the process for delivering assessments and reporting online to schools with minimal technical requirements, and increases the effective use of assessment data to make targeted and differentiated instructional decisions. The system has far reaching implications for student learning. At the student level, it allows teachers to tailor their teaching to the point where the student will learn the most, and teaching will be most efficient. At the grade and school level, aggregate data provide system level information to monitor student growth and teaching effectiveness. At the regional or state level, information about curriculum implementation and teaching success can be monitored and evaluated.

How the Course Instills Change in Teaching Practice

To effect the changes in teaching practice, the online course addresses three main areas. First, the course provides teachers with knowledge of developmental assessment theory. This includes the selection and administration of assessments and competency-based interpretation. They are also introduced to procedures for the use of developmental assessment practices to locate the most appropriate point for teaching intervention. Second, the course encourages teachers to develop their skills in using this knowledge within their work. By building the knowledge and skills of teachers, we expect to influence their attitudes towards developmental assessment. This is the third area which the course addresses. Once teachers incorporate the developmental approach to assessment into their personal schema, they have a role in influencing the work of colleagues. The course also equips participants with the skills and knowledge necessary to support their colleagues in the use of developmental learning approaches.

The online delivery poses no problem for improving knowledge, but use of this medium in creating affective change is problematic. Affective change can come about in several ways. Chief among these is through a dynamic group process. The group processes most familiar to adults remain face-to-face rather than virtual. The online course uses information dissemination as the major tool to affect attitude change, rather than relying on the interpersonal group dynamic. In order for teachers to adopt the approach of relying on objective data analysis, changes in knowledge and skills need to occur. A primary requirement in adopting a developmental approach to teaching is the belief that all students can learn. Notwithstanding, the model does not presume specific amounts of change, nor that specific levels of competency will be achieved

Figure 4. Teacher view (left) and student view (right) of ARCOTS

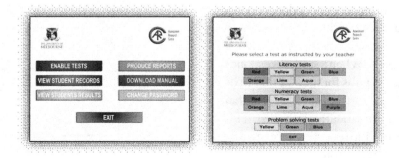

within specific time frames by cohorts of students. The model presumes that every student can move along the developmental progression. Consistent with individual differences, movement along these continua will vary in rate. Quality assurance in the course lies in student progress along developmental continua. Such progress of all students implies that the approach is being implemented at a high quality level. However, such outcomes do not occur concomitantly with knowledge, skills or attitudinal change in participating teachers. Change in teacher practices takes time, and the delay before student outcome change occurs can be considerable.

To help address the three domains of attitude, knowledge and skill, developmental frameworks are used to provide a basis for course structure and assessment. Although content material is delivered at a fixed level, with readings and exercises posted on the portal, assessment tasks provide the opportunity for participants to demonstrate different levels of understanding through commenting on evidence-based actions in their schools. The online course itself includes video presentations, readings, webinars and forums for 'virtual teams'.

There are two units in the online course – Leading a Professional Learning Team and Assessment for Teaching and Learning. Sessions pertaining to the two units are interspersed and team-based participants work through these as they simultaneously implement the data-driven approach in their teaching by having their students complete tests through online assessments and discussing the results in their team meetings. The students complete the tests twice – early and later in the school year. This provides teachers with practice at test targeting, administration and interpretation of the output reports.

In Leading a Professional Learning Team, participants are introduced to leadership skills specific to collaborative teams of teachers. As part of the course approach, each participant takes on a leadership role, leading a group of six to eight other teachers in their school. Their role is twofold – to

disseminate the knowledge learnt in the course, and to build a team which uses the approach to change teaching. The teaching of leadership skills is difficult in an online environment, and several processes have been incorporated into the course to facilitate it. A discussion forum is provided for interaction between participants. Leadership is also practiced in the school-based teams, with participants reporting back into the online environment by completing set activities. For example, participants identify their own positions and those of their team on a number of developmental progressions relevant to the adoption of beliefs about developmental learning and modes of operating within teams as a strategy for self-awareness and planning for self-development.

In Assessment for Teaching and Learning, participants are introduced to assessment and data interpretation skills. One of the basic tenets of the approach is that learning is most efficient when teaching is targeted to the point where a student is on the verge of learning, their zone of proximal development. If a student's skills are determined, and the normal learning progression is known, then teaching can be targeted – allowing each student in the class to learn at the point that is matched to their ability, and thus maximising learning for all.

To achieve this, teachers learn how to determine each student's skill level. They also examine subjects from the perspective of their underlying developmental progressions, in order to identify and understand the normal order in which skills are acquired, so they know what the student is ready to learn next. The course covers assessment administration, competency-based interpretation of assessment data, and the linking of this data to developmental progressions. The course provides an environment in which teachers work in a collaborative environment to examine the skills that are evidenced and to determine targeted teaching strategies.

A logical corollary of a developmental approach to teaching is the use of differentiated intervention strategies in the classroom. For some participants, moving from a whole class teaching approach to catering for sub-groups of or individual students requires major accommodations. To help in this process, each school allocates time for their teams to meet and examine the data and their connection to their intervention practices. The team leaders share teaching experiences with colleagues during team meetings and with leaders from other schools during project meetings with the facilitators.

Feedback to Course Participants

A rubric system is used to help participants monitor their own learning along the progressions relevant to the adoption of beliefs about developmental learning and modes of operating within teams. These rubrics are drawn from successive cohorts of participants' reporting of their practices and experiences in their PLTs. The rubrics typically contain four levels ranging from low to high skill. Course facilitators provide written feedback in response to participant self-reporting in order to draw out salient aspects of individuals' progress along the continua. The rubrics and feedback enable participants to see where they are in relation to the progressive acquisition of the skill. For example, rubric descriptions allow the participant to see what a response at a higher level would look like, and hence effectively explain how the participant can move forward in their learning.

For the early cohorts to complete the course the rubrics were created by the researchers. That is, a developmental level was assumed based on a theoretical understanding of the topic. Then, using the early cohort data, their responses were analysed using item response modelling to empirically determine the developmental progression participants exhibit in their responses. This is continually fine-tuned as additional cohorts provide their perceptions of their experiences and learning, leading to an accurate understanding of the progression of ability.

This process matches the developmental view we ask participants to take in their classrooms with their own students: determining the level, then targeting instruction at the appropriate level to move learning to the next level. The goal is that the programme is delivered in such a way that it mirrors the evidence-based practices the course is attempting to instil.

Developmental Frameworks to Guide Feedback

Attitude

A framework for the development of affective states or attitudes was developed by Krathwohl, Bloom and Masia (1964). Five levels – receiving, responding, valuing, organising and characterising – are described (Bloom, 1956). This progression of the acquisition of attitude forms the basis of structured feedback to participants. Griffin (2009) has added the lower level of rejecting to the bottom of this scale, to account for people who are not willing to engage. The six levels of the framework have been adapted to describe attitudes towards teachers' use of developmental assessment data within teacher teams.

The 'responding' level is where compliance occurs and participants are willing to carry out the set tasks in the workplace. An important motivation for teachers is the progress of their students. When course participants complete a task and discover that it benefits students, the bridge to the higher levels of the attitude progression is made.

Once participants reach the 'organising' level they incorporate the skills and knowledge from the course into their personal schemas and change has occurred. At the characterising level, participants will advocate for the new practices within their workplaces and encourage others to participate, maximising the chances of the new processes becoming sustainable within the school.

Knowledge

The framework which underpins the acquisition of knowledge has been adapted from Bloom (1956). It focuses on conceptual knowledge relating to developmental assessment and procedural knowledge of how to use developmental assessment within the Professional Learning Team to plan evidence-based teaching interventions collaboratively. Bloom describes six levels: 'remembering'; 'understanding'; 'applying'; 'analysing'; 'evaluating' and 'creating'. By the end of the course, the goal is that many participants will reach the upper levels where they are able to analyse and evaluate their use of the concepts and procedures.

Skill

Dreyfus and Dreyfus (1980) identified a framework for the development of skills consisting of five levels: 'novice'; 'advanced beginner'; 'competent'; 'proficient' and 'expert'. Within the course the framework has been applied to the skill with which participants use the knowledge gained through the course to lead their PLT. This is the most difficult to identify accurately online, as it can only be demonstrated through participants reporting and reflecting on what has happened as they have led their teams.

USE OF THE FRAMEWORKS

The use of developmental frameworks within the course parallels the processes participants use with their PLTs as they review their students' progress. Course facilitators review evidence of participant learning collected via the session tasks and discussion forums. They use this evidence to identify the current ZPD of the participants on the knowledge, skills and attitudes frameworks. The facilitators then provide feedback to the participants regarding actions that could be taken to progress.

The online professional development programme models the use of monitoring participants' progress along learning progressions, allowing them to experience it from the point of view of the learner. For each session, participants describe some elements of what is called 'Apply to Practice'. These exercises typically reflect actual practice as well as the theoretical content of the programme. This helps online participants to move from a theoretical understanding to practice. It also allows feedback targeted at improving practice to be provided.

A benefit of this practice for the course facilitators is that it allows course outcomes to be evaluated throughout the course. Facilitators meet weekly and analyse the experiences provided by participants to gain an understanding of the skills exhibited. Facilitators bring a range of samples to analyse and discuss to determine how the responses differ. They focus on what the underlying differences are that might account for the different forms and levels of practice and how these levels are being captured with the current rubrics for that content area.

Sometimes it is apparent from this process that key aspects of the course are not being transferred into the teachers' practice. When this happens the course content is analysed to determine what can be done to improve the transfer of knowledge.

Participant Engagement

Participants are encouraged to comment and discuss issues in an online forum. For this aspect, uptake has been minimal. The most common reason given for the lack of participation is that participants do not feel comfortable in an online environment. Participants are concerned that their comments or questions have more 'permanency' than conversing face-to-face. This has caused some issues because participants with concerns may not have them addressed quickly, potentially leading to negative feedback. Similarly, many participants do not contact their online facilitator directly, either through the Learning Management System portal or by email. They mention that they place the researchers and University staff in high regard and are worried about bothering them. This lack of communication between participants and facilitators is a systemic issue in provision of the course.

DISCUSSION

Information is easily disseminated through the web. Many adults who would not, some years ago, have thought of turning to a computer to seek information, now do it on a daily basis. Many adults, however, do not seek to learn through a structured course in an online environment. For those over 40, the internet remains a quick retrieval facility or an entertainment provider. In particular, for online learning which deals with matters of approach and attitude, it remains foreign territory. Increasingly, institutions and bureaucracies see web-based delivery of initiatives as an immediate solution, particularly when they are to be scaled-up. In the initiative described in this chapter, both sides of this perspective are seen. In terms of offering an environment in which information about theories can be delivered, it has functioned well. In terms of offering an environment in which affective change can be stimulated, monitored, and evaluated, it functions less well. Given that attitudes and beliefs are more ephemeral than information, this differential response to web-based delivery makes sense. There is permanence to the written word, even when electronic. Accordingly, those aspects of self which we see as less permanent, we are less likely to consign to permanent storage.

The online course was designed to provide a teaching and learning environment in which practices and approaches to the evidence-based teaching of students could be modelled. The course includes a major student test administration, scoring and reporting facility and component which

serves to provide a data-based platform for the professional development of participants. It is not clear, however, that the online environment is one amenable to the achievement of attitudinal change.

Where team-based action is valued, immediate questions concerning how the team is to be guided are raised. Where a culture is being promoted that requires collaborative practices, where those practices are evaluated by a group, and where they are the responsibility of a group, the logical question concerns how these practices can be modelled. When counsellors run a training programme in counselling, is it incumbent on them to treat their trainees as they would have their trainees treat their clients? Where a university runs professional development programmes that are designed to encourage dynamic, challenging and respectful team functioning designed to test their own practices, is it incumbent on the university to model these same practices? Where the goal of a course is to have its participants function as a team, should it also be a goal that the team members be mutually responsible for their engagement in the course and its requirements, rather than individually monitored and assessed?

The researchers in this project are promoting a culture of challenge, of team responsibility, and of examining evidence in order to make informed decisions concerning interventions. To the extent that it is appropriate to practice what one preaches, how would the actions inherent in this approach determine the researchers' own teaching practices, and what effects would this have on the course outcomes for its participants? By extrapolating the relevance and applicability of developmental learning progressions originally focussed on student outcomes to teachers, the researchers applied a logical paradigm. This requires the paradigm to be directed inward to the researchers themselves. The prime responsibility of each of these examples is to effect change, not just to deliver a programme or a set routine. This university professional development tries to change the behaviour of teachers and monitors the change rather than the delivery of content. The researchers are examining what best leads to change and are dependent on the programme to produce change in varying degrees.

REFERENCES

Alton-Lee, A. (2008). *Designing and supporting teacher professional development to improve valued student outcome.* Paper presented at the Education of Teachers Symposium, International Academy of Education Meeting.

Bloom, B. (1956). *Taxonomy of educational objectives: The classification of educational goals.* London, UK: Longman.

Boudett, K., City, E., & Murnane, R. (Eds.). (2005). *Data Wise: A step-by-step guide to using assessment results to improve teaching and learning.* Cambridge, MA: Harvard University Press.

Care, E., & Griffin, P. (2009). Assessment is for teaching. *Independence, 34*(2), 56-59.

Dreyfus, S., & Dreyfus, H. (1980). *A five-stage model of the mental activities involved in directed skill acquisition.* Washington, DC: Storming Media.

Fowler-Finn, T. (2009). *Instructional Rounds Australia.* Paper presented at the Instructional Rounds Conference, Harvard University, May.

Fullan, M., Hill, P., & Crévola, C. (2006). *Breakthrough.* Thousand Oaks, CA: Corwin Press.

Glaser, R. (1963). Instructional technology and the measurement of learning outcomes: Some questions. *The American Psychologist, 18,* 519–521. doi:10.1037/h0049294

Glaser, R. (2007). *Personal communication,* 28 June.

Griffin, P. (2000). *ARC learning profiles: User's manual.* Unpublished manuscript, Melbourne.

Griffin, P. (2007). The comfort of competence and the uncertainty of assessment. *Studies in Educational Evaluation, 33,* 87–99. doi:10.1016/j.stueduc.2007.01.007

Griffin, P. (2009). Teacher's use of assessment data. In Wyatt-Smith, C., & Cumming, J. (Eds.), *Educational assessment in the 21st cenutry.* Dordrecht, The Netherlands: Springer. doi:10.1007/978-1-4020-9964-9_10

Griffin, P., Murray, L., Care, E., Thomas, A., & Perri, P. (2010). Developmental assessment: Lifting literacy through professional learning teams. *Assessment in Education: Principles. Policy & Practice, 17*(4), 383–397.

Griffin, P., & Nix, P. (1991). *Educational assessment and reporting: A new approach.* Victoria, Australia: Harcourt Brace.

Halverson, R., Grigg, J., Prichett, R., & Thomas, C. (2005). *The new instructional leadership: Creating data-driven instructional systems in schools.* Madison, WI: University of Wisconsin-Madison, Wisconsin Center for Education Research.

Hill, P., & Crévola, C. (1997). The literacy challenge in Australian primary schools. *IARTV Seminar Series, 69.*

Hill, P., Crévola, C., & Hopkins, D. (2000). Teaching and learning as the heartland of school improvement. *IARTV Seminar Series, 100.*

Krathwohl, A., Bloom, B., & Masia, B. (1964). *Taxonomy of educational objectives: The classification of educational goals. Handbook II: The affective domain.* New York, NY: Longman Green.

Murray, L., & Rintoul, K. (2008). *The literacy assessment project: An initiative of the Catholic Education Office for continuous school improvement in literacy.* Paper presented at the Australian Councol for Educational Leaders.

Nitko, A. (1980). Distinguishing the many varieties of criterion-referenced tests. *Review of Educational Research, 50*(3), 14.

Rasch, G. (1960). *Probablistic models for some intelligence and attanment tests*. Copenhagen, Denmark: Danish Institute for Education Research.

Timperley, H. (2008). *Teacher professional learning and development. Education Practices Series-18*. Paris, France: International Bureau of Education.

Timperley, H., Parr, J., & Bertanees, C. (2009). Promoting professional inquiry for improved outcomes for students in New Zealand. *Professional Development in Education, 35*(2), 227–245. doi:10.1080/13674580802550094

Traub, R., & Wolfe, R. (1981). Latent trait theories and the assessment of educational achievement. *Review of Research in Education, 9*, 377–435.

Vygotsky, L. (1978). *Mind and society: The development of higher psychological processes.* Cambridge, MA: Harvard University Press.

Woods, K., & Griffin, P. (2010). *Teachers' use of developmental assessment to support communication proficiency for students with additional needs.* Paper presented at the AARE International Education Research Conference - 2010, Melbourne, Australia.

Wu, M., Adams, R. J., & Wilson, M. (1998). *ConQuest: Generalised item response modelling software.* Melbourne, Australia: ACER Press.

Chapter 4
Development of the Assessment Design and Delivery of Collaborative Problem Solving in the Assessment and Teaching of 21st Century Skills Project

Patrick Griffin
The University of Melbourne, Australia

Myvan Bui
The University of Melbourne, Australia

Esther Care
The University of Melbourne, Australia

Nathan Zoanetti
The University of Melbourne, Australia

ABSTRACT

This chapter describes an approach to assessment task design and delivery from the Assessment and Teaching of 21st Century Skills project (ATC21S). ATC21S is an example of an innovative, international, multi-stakeholder partnership involving industry, academics, governments, and educators that is aimed at shifting the direction of assessment and teaching towards a model more suited to the development of skills that students need in the 21st century. Within ATC21S, assessment design and delivery is just one component of a holistic framework in which assessment, teaching, resourcing, and policy work in unison to improve student outcomes. This chapter outlines this developmental framework and the impetus for ATC21S and partnerships which drive and support the project, and sets the scene for dealing with performance measurement issues – how can we tell that people have learned anything? The focus of the chapter is on the technology-based design and delivery of assessments of one of the key skill areas of interest in the project - collaborative problem solving.

DOI: 10.4018/978-1-4666-3649-1.ch004

THE CHANGING CONTEXT OF WORK

With ubiquity of telecommunications and the emergence of the information age, the role of information in society has changed, and with it the structure of the workforce. Many occupations that depended on the direct use of manual or routine labour that dominated the 20th century have disappeared or have been altered completely because of technology. Robots have replaced many specialised routine assembly skills. Unskilled labour occupations remain but in reduced quantity. A new set of occupations has emerged based on the production, distribution and consumption of information using technology. These occupations involve reasoning, collaboration, critical and creative thinking, and the capacity to learn while solving problems through the medium of technology.

In such occupations, individuals need the skills to create or analyse the credibility and utility of information, evaluate its appropriateness, and intelligently apply that information. A study by Autor, Levy and Murnane (2003) illustrates the substantial shifts in the structure of the workforce and how they might be conceptualised. From 1960 to 2000 there was an increase in abstract tasks with a corresponding decrease in both routine and manual tasks. Those without the skills to act as information producers, distributors and/or consumers will be disadvantaged, even if their related commodity skills are still in demand. Access to management and advisory roles has become dependent on information skills. Increasingly, people are relying on information and communications technology (ICT) as a medium of day-to-day exchange and interaction. At the individual level, the ability to learn, collaborate and solve problems in a digital information environment has become mandatory. There are also implications at the societal level. Economic growth depends on the synergies between new knowledge and human capital. New technological advances are of little value in countries that have few skilled workers to use them.

As a result, education faces the challenge of providing the populace with the information skills needed in a society that depends on the production, distribution and consumption of information. Education has to emphasise information and technology skills rather than those emphasising the manufacture, distribution and consumption of products, as is the current approach. There is also a corresponding need to rethink the way education is measured and monitored.

PROJECT BACKGROUND: A MULTI-NATIONAL, MULTI-STAKEHOLDER PARTNERSHIP TO DRIVE INNOVATION

In response to these changing workforce and education demands, three major companies - Cisco, Intel and Microsoft – commissioned a 'Call to Action' paper to prompt political, education, and business leaders to join a multi-national multi-stakeholder project to transform educational assessment and instructional practice. The paper highlighted the urgent need for education systems to respond to changes in technology and its increasing impact on employment, living and social interaction. This led to the creation of the ATC21S project, launched at the London Learning and Technology World Forum in January 2009. The goal of the ATC21S project is to develop ways of assessing 21st century skills, encourage curriculum change, and enable teachers to assess and teach these skills in the classroom.

Cisco, Intel and Microsoft negotiated with six national governments to join the project as founder countries. These were Australia, Finland, Portugal, Singapore, England, and the USA. Costa Rica and the Netherlands joined during a later period. An academic partnership was created with the University of Melbourne, with the directorate of the programme of research and development situated within its Assessment Research Centre. International teams of researchers were formed to produce a series of research papers and to complete field work in each country and data collection in schools. An advisory panel was also formed. This consisted of members of organisations with global concerns: the Organisation for Economic Cooperation and Development (OECD), the International Association for the Evaluation of Educational Achievement (IEA), the United Nations Economic, Social and Cultural Organisation (UNESCO), the World Bank, the Inter-American Development Bank, the National Academy of Sciences and the International Testing Commission. Close associations were formed with the OECD Programme for International Student Assessment (PISA) project and the IEA ICT literacy project. Guidelines were drawn up to allow other countries, organisations and other companies to join the project. Project work is organized around a series of international working conferences and meetings, online interactions, a knowledge sharing web portal, and social networking sites. In keeping with the spirit of open innovation, a crowdsourcing competition was hosted through http://www.innocentive.com/in early 2011. The aim of the competition was to gather ideas to assist in building an innovative platform that could handle the challenges associated with online delivery of interactive student assessments of collaborative work. ATC21S is intended to be a highly inclusive, collaborative venture using the diverse expertise of many individuals and groups sharing in the project's goals.

In the first year of this three-year project, the main products were five 'White Papers' that reviewed previous work, recognised research and development issues, and identified 21st century skills. The project's intended final products are new assessment strategies and the developmental learning progressions underpinning these strategies, tested and validated in the participating countries. The output materials will also include several prototype versions of assessments that will act as guides for operationalising the assessment strategies. The assessment strategies and prototype tasks are to be open access, open source, non-proprietary, prototype versions. They will be available to anyone seeking to develop assessments of 21st century skills, as defined in the project, and wanting to deliver them using ICT tools. The project is about new ideas, new approaches to assessment, and new and established relevant skills being assessed in different ways. The ATC21S project team predicts these skills will be in such demand that schools, governments, employers and large scale assessment programs will need to address them in the near future. There is an expectation that the new approaches developed by ATC21S will be of particular benefit for:

- OECD's PISA, Program for the International Assessment of Adult Competencies (PIAAC), and its Assessment of Higher Education Learning Outcomes (AHELO) project.
- IEA's Trends in International Mathematics and Science Study (TIMSS), Progress in International Reading Literacy Survey (PIRLS), and any possible extension of its Information Technology in Education studies to assess ICT competence.
- National surveys of student and adult achievement, either sample-based studies or full cohort assessments.
- Commercial test development by not-for-profit or for-profit organizations.

As well as responding to change, the ATC21S project aims to drive change. It is hoped that the project's focus on assessment will encourage a change in curriculum and pedagogy. Research has established the significant role assessment can play in setting new expectations and signalling priorities for curriculum and instruction, serving to focus the content of instruction (Raizen et al., 2012). The ATC21S project's focus on 21st century skills and their method of assessment is aimed at shifting the direction of assessment and teaching towards methods more suitable to the measurement and development of skills that people will need in the 21st century. This has been considered too difficult to do previously, due to technical constraints and gaps in methodological knowledge and innovation (Csapó, Ainley, Bennett, Latour & Law, 2011; Wilson et al., 2012). In order for meaningful, lasting changes to occur, several things must occur together. A holistic framework linking assessments, skills and teaching is required. This framework is outlined in the following section.

A HOLISTIC APPROACH TO TRANSFORMING EDUCATION TO DELIVER 21ST CENTURY SKILLS

One of the more radical changes associated with teaching 21st century skills is the emergence of a developmental model of learning. There is a need to be very clear about the difference between deficit and developmental learning approaches. Deficit approaches sometimes focus on those things that people cannot do and hence develop a 'fix-it' approach. Developmental models build on and scaffold existing knowledge bases of every student. They also need to be evidence based, focus on readiness to learn, and follow a generic thesis of student development. Acquiring 21st century skills will require people to work towards higher order thinking and problem solving. There will be a need for teams of people to work together in solving problems operating at high levels of thinking, reasoning, and collaboration. This has implications for the teaching and assessment of these skills. In order to become specialists in developmental learning, teachers need to have skills in using data to make teaching intervention decisions. They will need expertise in developmental assessment, in collaborative approaches to teaching, and a clear understanding of developmental learning models.

In a developmental framework there is a need to break the link between whole class teaching and instructional intervention. Teachers must focus on individual developmental and personalised learning for every student. Teachers need to work collaboratively and base their decisions on evidence rather than inference. When teachers pursue a developmental model, their theory of action and psychology of instruction is based on developmental learning theory. Being able to identify the Vygotskyian (1978) zone of proximal development (ZPD) is fundamental to the identification of where a teacher would intervene for improving individual student development. Teachers recognise and use evidence to implement and monitor student progress within a Vygotskyian approach. Specifically which developmental theory underpins the work is negotiable, but having a developmental theoretical basis is an important aspect of all forms of teacher education, both preservice and in-service, if teaching for individual developmental learning is to be realised.

When a developmental model of learning is used, the teacher has to reorganise the classroom and manipulate the learning environment to meet the needs of students. Manipulation of the learning environment is an important skill and the way in which a teacher links classroom management, intervention strategies, and the resources used to facilitate learning is a challenge. The divergence between students' classrooms and their technology-embedded external lives is one of the greatest challenges to the acquisition of skills they will need to manage their lives intelligently and consciously. However, as classrooms increasingly accommodate online resources, the use of web-enabled assessment will become a routine practice. The current incongruence of technology-assisted teaching with paper-based assessment is out of step with practices in the world of work and is not sustainable. However, it is important that what is taught in the classroom and how it is taught is consistent with what is assessed and how it is assessed. Curriculum content and assessment methods must reflect the needs and realities of the world outside the classroom. Where this content and method are consistent, we will not find the current tension between assessment for change, which informs learning and teaching, and assessment of a student's current status, which informs policy.

There is a parallel between this perspective and the aspirations of the ATC21S project. The project aims to provide both foreground information for use by teachers and background information for summative system-level analysis. Can we have the best of both worlds? The approach outlined in this chapter provides an indication of how this might be achieved. When complex tasks can be used as learning and assessment tools and administered on a large scale, there is the potential to avoid the sometimes negative effect of assessment on teaching. We have seen both in Australia's National Assessment Program – Literacy and Numeracy (NAPLAN) and the No Child Left Behind legislation in the USA how high-stakes large-scale testing programs can distort teaching practices such that 'teaching to the test' replaces 'teaching to a construct'.

Teachers have implicitly been encouraged to improve scores but not to improve skills. This is a direct outcome of the mismatch between the style of tests and the style of teaching and learning. What is outlined in this chapter is a model for congruence between these two elements.

In applying a formative assessment approach, teachers also develop skills in using assessment data to adapt their practices to meet students' learning needs. Numerous studies have shown this is effective at improving teaching and learning (see, for example, Griffin, Murray, Care, Thomas & Perri, 2010; Taylor, Pearson, Peterson & Rodriguez, 2005). Assessment data must be based on skills, not scores, and must have the capacity to reflect readiness to learn rather than achievements or deficits. These are the goals of the ATC21S project: linking assessment, teaching and skills of the 21st century.

ASSESSMENT OF COLLABORATIVE PROBLEM SOLVING SKILLS

The ATC21S project has identified skills of interest due to the role they are thought to play in negotiating the 21st century. One of these is collaborative problem solving. It is a skill brought to bear in face-to-face situations, is well entrenched in many workplaces, and is increasingly required as groups of people solve problems in virtual space. Collaborative problem solving has been seen primarily as an adult skill, rather than as an enabling skill similar to literacy and numeracy. It rests on the existence and development of sets of sub-skills, both cognitively and socially-based. It has been seen in the workplace as a set of skills that is desirable, yet has lacked clear definition. It tends to be associated with human resource training courses in team building and role playing, i.e. akin to social capabilities, rather than with higher order skill development. As the need for collaborative problem solving increases in virtual communities, the inadequacies of these workplace-based organisational psychology approaches have become apparent.

The ATC21S project sees collaborative problem solving as a 21st century skill made up of parts: collaboration, problem solving and the new technologies characterising the 21st century. The skill itself, although associated strongly with the workforce, is relevant to everyday life.

A primary element of collaborative problem solving is the problem itself. A focus in collaborative problem solving is on identifying and understanding the context of the problem, often referred to as the problem space. One element of problem solving to be considered is the degree to which knowledge or information needs to be brought to bear to solve the problem. Some problems are almost content or information free, whereas others may be 'knowledge rich'. Another important element of problem solving is whether a problem has a finite solution. Both of these elements, amount of knowledge/information required, and presence/absence of a finite solution, have implications for whether the problem can be solved by a single person or requires a number of people, each potentially able to provide unique contributions to the problem solving space.

Strategies used to solve problems vary with the kind of problems. A commonly-cited strategy is referred to as means-end-analysis (Newell & Simon, 1961), which can be used to solve simple and formalised problems. For more complex problems the organisation of multiple inputs and the ways in which these may be combined (the rules), require different analytic approaches. Where problem solving is dependent on human input and expert knowledge is needed to solve the problem, cooperation becomes pivotal. Problems may vary in effort demanded by virtue of the amount and type of knowledge required, the complexity of the problem space, and the number and skills of the participating persons.

We define 'collaboration' as the activity of working together toward a common goal. There are logical elements included in the activity. One is communication, the exchange of knowledge or opinions in a way that is designed to optimise mutual understanding. This element is a necessary, but not sufficient, condition for collaboration. Collaborative problem solving requires the process of communication to achieve a goal beyond mere exchange. A second element, cooperation, refers primarily to division of labour based on agreement. Collaborative problem solving goes beyond cooperation in problem solving, to nuanced and responsive contributions by the persons involved in the problem space. Responsiveness is an essential component of collaboration. It implies a more active and insightful participation than does cooperation.

Consequent upon this definition of collaboration, collaborative problem solving itself refers to working together responsively on a task or problem. This may involve exchanging ideas

to facilitate progress, completing activities, or sharing knowledge needed to solve a problem. Collaboration makes sense especially when different expertise is both available and needed for solving a problem. Collaboration rests on a number of factors such as readiness to participate, understanding the perspectives of others, and readiness to negotiate conflicts.

Collaborative problem solving (CPS) does not appear in school curricula; the world of education has yet to explore the possibilities of this skill. In the ATC21S project, CPS is conceptualised as being composed of social and cognitive skills, consisting of five broad strands (Griffin, Care & McGaw, 2012):

- Participation as a member of the group by contributing knowledge, experience and expertise in a constructive way.
- Recognition of the perspective of other persons in a group.
- Recognition of the need to manage contributions within the group.
- Identification and regulation of the problem space.
- Building of knowledge and understanding.

Each strand can be further subdivided into capabilities, some of which may contribute to more than one strand. For example, 'social regulation' may include capabilities such as 'negotiation', 'knowledge of self', 'knowledge of others' and 'responsibility'. Equally, some of these capabilities may contribute to 'participation' or 'perspective taking'. The capabilities must be defined in terms of indicators described by sets of observable, ordered quality criteria corresponding to novice through to expert performance on that indicator. Together, components, strands, capabilities, indicators and quality criteria can form a scoring rubric for making inferences about overall CPS skills and for informing further skill development.

The ATC21S project is developing both a task delivery system and the tasks for the assessment of CPS in students aged 11 to 15 years old. In order for empirical validation of the tasks to take place, CPS scenarios and tasks first need to be designed and constructed, not a trivial endeavour (Meier, Spada & Rummel, 2007). In the process of developing and field testing collaborative problem scenarios, three types of scenarios and tasks are being developed and trialled in the ATC21S project. Firstly, serious games have been identified as suitable for collaborative problem solving assessment. Existing leadership games were modified and reprogrammed to enable data capture pertinent to student performance in CPS. Serious games are game-like interactive systems developed with computer game technology and design principles for some purpose other than pure entertainment, usually for training and simulation (Kankaanranta & Neittaanmaki, 2009). Within the ATC21S project they represent a type of ill-defined, ambiguous problem that does not require knowledge of a school curriculum. They should elicit a range of collaborative and problem solving behaviours. The hope is that by demonstrating the feasibility of serious games for student assessment, the serious games industry will be motivated to create engaging virtual environments for enhancing and monitoring 21st century student learning outcomes.

A second approach involves a series of problem solving tasks that can be solved collaboratively and are linked to science and mathematics curriculum in schools. The hope for these tasks is that they will stimulate the development of assessable curriculum-linked problems that can be solved collaboratively and will connect with everyday teaching and learning in the mathematics and science curricula around the world.

As a third approach, the ATC21S project is developing collaborative problem solving tasks based on curriculum-free content, using clear and well-defined problems. It is expected that when requiring collaboration, the overall emphasis on reasoning will diminish and collaboration and general problem solving skills will dominate. It is hoped that understanding of the processes inherent in problem solving may lead to beneficial changes in instructional practice.

The tasks discussed in this chapter are from the third category described. These were designed to be undertaken by pairs of students engaged in real-time collaboration through instant messaging and shared object manipulation. Also described in this chapter are several implications for assessment design in terms of client and server technologies when moving from single-user to multi-user computer-based tasks. Tasks were constructed based on an established set of computer-based problem solving assessment tasks developed by Zoanetti (2010) for single-user administration. The conversion of these tasks from single-user to two-user tasks with differentiated screen views and real-time collaboration tools provides an environment within which to test the tasks' capacity to elicit collaborative problem solving skills.

ASSESSMENT DESIGN PRINCIPLES AND THEIR RELATIONSHIP TO TECHNOLOGY

Precursory steps in assessment design should include definitions of the assessment purpose and the psycho-educational construct of interest (Mislevy, Steinberg, Breyer, Almond & Johnson, 1999). Further, the construct of interest should be analysed in terms of what development might look like from novice to expert (Glaser, 1991). With these two components defined, it is then necessary to consider the types of evidence required for making inferences about the level a person is operating at on the construct (Williamson et al., 2004). Once the types of evidence are documented, consideration can be given to the nature of assessment tasks which would be suitable for eliciting the required evidence. The range of feasible task types then needs to be rationalised in terms of pragmatic factors such as time to develop, time to administer, cost to develop, stakeholder acceptance, and the practicality of administering.

Beyond specifying the types of tasks which might be suitable, it is also necessary to evaluate them throughout the task development cycle (Parshall & Harmes, 2009). One approach involves gathering survey information from assessment stakeholders. Another approach is panelling the tasks with subject-matter experts. Perhaps the most informative approach is to conduct cognitive laboratories with students from the intended target population. These labs involve making observations of students' behaviours as they undertake the tasks. One popular method is to record a student's utterances about what they are thinking and doing as they work through a task (Leighton & Gierl, 2007). Video recording can also be used. Data recording techniques such as logging student process data, using screen capture software, or using eye-tracking technology are among other options. The technology employed during cognitive laboratories is likely to be more expansive than that used in the operational assessment. Nonetheless, it is important to examine both situations. In the former, the focus is on gathering evidence concerning the validity and usability of the tasks. In the latter, it is about ensuring the scope of data collected during a single assessment instance is sufficient for supporting inferences about the student proficiencies of interest. For a final version of the assessment system to be practical for use in classroom settings, only unobtrusive data capture (of keystrokes and mouse events) via the task interface would be retained.

In the following section, we look at specific examples of assessment tasks that highlight the technology requirements needed to support them. The first example looks at a single-user, computer-based assessment task, originally designed to measure procedural aspects of problem solving. The second example examines the recently adapted version of this task into a multi-user online assessment task for measuring CPS.

FROM PRODUCT SCORING TO PROCESS SCORING

Computer-based assessments which go beyond being reproductions of existing paper-and-pencil assessments have recently emerged. These assessments record detailed interactions between the problem solver and the task environment, and thereby capture data describing salient solution processes in an unobtrusive way (Bennett, Jenkins, Persky & Weiss, 2003). The theoretical, or construct-related, benefits of this approach include the capacity to build tasks that assess aspects of problem solving that would be difficult to measure by other means (Mills, Potenza, Fremer & Ward, 2002). The recorded actions culminate in information that can be linked to theories of cognition and developing competence (Pelligrino, Chudowsky & Glaser, 2001; Williamson, Mislevy & Bejar, 2006). Importantly, this process data can be used to evaluate how systematic and efficient a problem solver is at solving a task (Wirth & Klieme, 2003). The central theme here is that tasks must be interactive so that data describing purposeful actions can be recorded. From the evidence arising from these interactions, interpretations can be made regarding which strategies and cognitive processes are carried out at which time to solve the problem fully, partially or not at all.

Next we examine a specific example of how interactive, technology-enabled assessment tasks have been used to describe student proficiencies which would be difficult to infer from traditional static tasks. The example in Figure 1 shows an interactive problem solving task that was used to assess procedural aspects of problem solving.

Figure 1. Single-user hot chocolate task

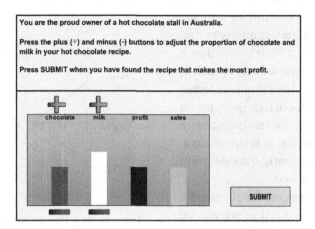

Specifically, this task examined how systematically an individual student applied trial and error. Students were expected to experiment with the recipe mixture by adjusting the relative quantities of milk and chocolate until the profit bar hit its maximum height. The sales bar was included as a distraction in this permutation of the problem.

Scoring the task as either correct or incorrect would not provide any information about how the student solved the problem. Instead, to support inferences about how the student solved the problem, it was also necessary to collect process data describing performance characteristics such as how many steps the student carried out, whether they carried out ineffectual steps, how long they spent between steps, how long they spent working on the task, and the sequencing of steps taken. Given that the intended measure concerned procedural aspects of problem solving, such as the capacity to sustain and carry out trial and error systematically, these process data provide evidence for generating profiles of procedural problem solving strengths, weaknesses and tendencies of an individual student. The task has since been adapted to measure collaborative problem solving. By examining it in its earlier form, a set of useful contrasts can be made in terms of changes to the task design and the technology platform necessary for measuring collaboration.

DEVELOPING THE TECHNOLOGY PLATFORM FOR SINGLE STUDENT PROBLEM SOLVING TASKS

Platforms for authoring and delivering computer-based assessments are now commonplace. The majority of these systems support traditional item types such as multiple-choice questions, matching tasks, 'fill in the blank', and so on. These systems provide all the usual benefits of a computerised medium including remote accessibility (if online), automated scoring, immediate feedback and convenient data storage. They do not, however, provide any psychometric advantages over traditional paper-and-pencil assessment forms. The development of computer-based assessments for the capture of information-rich student performance is in its infancy. In order to advance, it needs to provide a means for recording, storing and scoring richer data than that derived from conventional tasks and test item types. Such 'richer' data in the first instance consists of process data which might describe the type, order and quantity of interactions with a task, as well as a corresponding timestamp for each. Collection and recording of process data like these is relatively straightforward. A range of client interfaces can capture data describing discrete mouse and keyboard events. Likewise, relatively simple server-side scripts can be used to export these data to files or databases for subsequent access. In the present example, students were provided with identification numbers and were able to access the task at their convenience via any internet browser with a relatively up to date Flash Player plug-in. This architecture is depicted in Figure 2. Since the assessment requirements on the technology are essentially for capture, storage and processing of time-stamped click-stream data, many other client and server configurations could be used to achieve the same end.

For this particular exercise, on the client side, the single-user task was designed using Adobe Flash MX2004 and ActionScript 2. The Flash task was embedded in web pages using a minimum of HTML code. The server side scripting was written in PHP and served the primary function of directing students to the task and recording their process data into a MySQL database. These data were then available to other modular components of the system used for scoring and reporting. Student authentication was also handled by querying the MySQL database. All of these components were hosted on a Linux server. To summarise, the system utilised the free open source components of what is often referred to as the LAMP stack: Linux, Apache HTTP Server, MySQL and Perl/PHP/Python.

CONDUCTING COGNITIVE LABORATORIES FOR TASKS ASSESSING PROCEDURAL SKILLS

Cognitive laboratories provide information about the construct validity of assessment tasks in at least two ways: first, they are also carried out to ensure that the tasks elicit the intended subset of behaviours (Mislevy et al., 1999); and second, they are conducted to identify aspects of tasks with which students struggle that are not related to the construct. For the single-user 'Hot Chocolate' task, a verbal protocol method was used, as

Figure 2. Schematic diagram of the single-user system

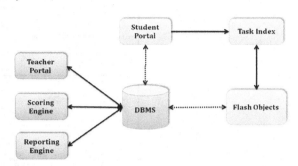

described by Ericsson and Simon (1993). This involved recording the utterances of students as they 'thought aloud' while working through the task. A single researcher would sit with an individual student throughout the process. A digital voice recorder was used to record the utterances and a notepad was used to record obvious behavioural cues. The additional technology requirements were modest, an attraction of the method (Parshall & Harmes, 2009). Ultimately the verbal data were transcribed into a spreadsheet called a *Temporal Evidence,* as described by Zoanetti (2010), alongside the corresponding click-stream data to reconstruct the solution attempt. This concurrent evidence approach allows the presence of *a priori* expected behaviours to be confirmed. The approach can also provide information about how sequences of click-stream data might relate to particular cognitive processes and behaviours. This information could be used to produce and refine automated scoring rules. Sequences of action data are likely to be interpretable independently, but with the addition of concurrent utterance data, the interpretation is more certain. When utterances are matched up to their concurrent click-stream data, an understanding of the structure of data corresponding to differentially sophisticated behaviours and levels of the construct emerges. This use of concurrent sources of evidence provides one approach to demonstrating the construct validity of the assessment tasks.

The 'Hot Chocolate' task records time-stamped mouse-event data which can be interpreted substantively based on problem solving theory and empirical information from cognitive laboratories. In order to extend its capabilities to the measurement of a more complex construct and to a multi-user environment, a more sophisticated architecture becomes necessary for task authoring, task delivery and data capture.

DESIRED FEATURES OF TASKS FOR ASSESSING COLLABORATIVE SKILLS

A collaborative construct has implications both for the types of features tasks should contain and also for the technology platforms used to deliver them. The types of evidence required to support inferences about CPS need to describe the interaction between individuals and their individual actions as recorded in the mouse-click stream. This requirement identifies several components the tasks must embed, and it also determines the sophistication of the web technologies needed to build the task delivery platform.

For a collaborative task, both users (students) must be engaged in the process via a number of dependencies. Providing students with a common goal, but with different information or resources, is the first task design requirement. Ensuring that the information or resources provided to one student are of some utility to the other student is a second task design requirement. Thirdly, students need to be able to communicate with each other to regulate the solution process. While other task design variables could be specified, these three conditions were seen as a sufficient set for simulating the nature of a task which requires collaboration. While it would be possible to make each task a 'What You See Is What I See' (WYSIWIS) scenario, this might nullify the need for collaboration, thereby weakening the capacity of the task to tap

into the construct. By ensuring that one student cannot solve the problem on their own efficiently, the need to collaborate is established.

Due to the complex nature of collaborative problem solving, with its multiple components, strands and capabilities, it is unlikely that one task which is limited to less than 15 minutes duration will have the capacity to indicate the full construct. Accordingly, in the first instance, the adaptation of the 'Hot Chocolate' task was designed to indicate capabilities such as 'contribution', 'task completion', 'responding', 'planning', and 'process', among others. These fall within the strands of 'participation', 'perspective taking' and 'task regulation'. To a lesser extent, the task also samples indications of other collaborative problem solving (CPS) capabilities including 'responsibility', 'negotiation' and 'learning' from the 'social regulation' and 'knowledge building' strands. The reconstructed task provided an instant messaging facility, and changes to all shared objects were updated in real-time for both clients to see. The two student perspectives for the two-user adaptation of the 'Hot Chocolate' task are shown in Figures 3 and 4 respectively. In this task, one student is presented with the 'left view' of the problem and the other student sees the 'right view'. The left view student is presented with a recipe grid, where different combinations of chocolate, sugar and milk can be selected by clicking on the graphics. After each selection, the sales and profit charts alter and both students see this change simultaneously. The right view student is presented with a four-page market research report with information about regional recipe preferences on each page. This student also has control of the region that the chart data apply to. This task enables good collaborators, who effectively share information and organise their respective roles, to expedite their solution. For instance, two good collaborative problem solvers will tend to explore and learn about their respective resources, use the chat box to share salient information, and frequently report back to each other. They will also tend to solve the problem correctly and in fewer moves. Poorer collaboration might consist of more activity and less interaction, leading to more moves and a reduced chance of successfully solving the problem. Data describing these performance differences, such as activity timing and counts, chat message timing and counts, region correctness and recipe correctness can be automatically scored. These scores can then be analysed using an appropriate statistical measurement model to determine the level at which students are operating on the construct.

DEVELOPING THE TECHNOLOGY PLATFORM FOR MULTI-USER PROBLEM SOLVING TASKS

The key client technologies used to develop the CPS tasks are described in this section. The tasks were programmed using Adobe CS5 with Action-Script 3. SmartFoxServer 2X was chosen as the socket server technology through which clients share communication and object manipulation data. This was chosen based on the existence of a number of easy-to-implement examples and the availability of a free and fully featured community version which could support up to 100 concurrent clients. Therefore, SmartFoxServer 2X Action-Script 3 libraries were imported into the Flash CS5 development environment for use throughout the programming effort. To support some of the animations within tasks, motion tweening utilities were also imported. These were the Tweenlite ActionScript 3 libraries by Greensock (available at http://www.greensock.com/). The tasks were to be delivered in four different languages in the first instance: English, Spanish, Finnish, and Dutch. The XML Strings Panel provided in the Flash IDE was used to embed the appropriate language in each task as determined by the client operating system. Appropriate fonts for each of the target languages were manually embedded in the chat messaging interface as well.

Figure 3. Student A view of the hot chocolate task

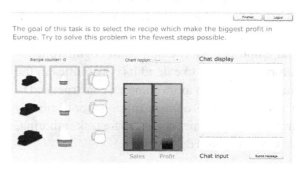

Figure 4. Student B view of the hot chocolate task

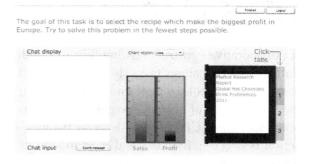

The server components once again included the LAMP stack described as part of the single-user architecture. This was implemented on a remotely hosted server and locally using the XAMPP package from Apache and Friends (available at http://www.apachefriends.org/en/xampp.html). Also on the server side, as mentioned, SmartFoxServer 2X was installed as a service. This product provided the open connection between the clients via the server. While the single-user architecture might be able to support turn-based games, it would have constrained design of real-time tasks which relied on real-time (or minimal lag) updating of each client following activity from one client. A number of custom Java classes were programmed and incorporated into the SmartFoxServer 2X platform to supply some of the assessment task logic and also to handle the flow of data between clients and from clients to the MySQL database. The MySQL database tables and fields were set to be UTF-8 encoded to support the four target languages.

The system was eventually expanded to incorporate Flash assessment tasks designed by third parties who used the Flash Media Interactive Server (FMIS) as the socket server technology. Therefore an instance of FMIS was also installed on the Linux operating system as a service. The system was also built to integrate with the established single-user system such that the authentication, scoring and reporting modules were common across all assessment environments. The established system is known as the Assessment Research Centre Online Testing System (ARCOTS). Whilst not yet IMS QTI standards compliant, and therefore not optimally interoperable, some modularity was built into the platform to help ensure that other assessment tasks could be accommodated.

The task was programmed similarly to a game within an online multi-user gaming architecture (Figure 5). The multi-user architecture for the task was as follows:

- Students log in against credentials (unique identifier and a team code or pairing key to assign collaborators) stored in the MySQL database.
- Successful login results in a student entering a virtual room called 'Lobby'.
- Students select a task to attempt.
- Students click on a user icon and a virtual room is created dynamically based on the combination of the unique task ID and the shared pairing key or team ID. The student is informed that the room is waiting for their pre-assigned partner to join them.
- If the student is the second in an assigned pair to click on a user icon, they will enter the virtual room created by the first student, and the task contents will automatically be presented to both students.
- Students then complete the task and are redirected either back to a task list or onto a self- and peer-assessment survey.

Given the intended proliferation of tasks in this project, programming re-usable client-side and server-side classes (packages) with ActionScript 3 and Java became an important goal to allow for efficient up-scaling. These classes managed the majority of processes common across tasks, including student login, real-time chat, data logging to the database, real-time sharing of information about task objects between students, and other aspects of game logic.

CONDUCTING COGNITIVE LABORATORIES FOR TASKS ASSESSING COLLABORATIVE SKILLS

Cognitive laboratories were undertaken for the 'Hot Chocolate' task in the collaborative mode in order to check construct validity of the measures of collaborative problem solving. The verbal protocol methodology used was similar to that for single-user tasks but differed in some key respects due to the collaborative nature of the task. Cognitive laboratories were run in classrooms using schools' computers. One researcher was present while two students completed the task simultaneously and collaboratively at opposite ends of the same room, facing away from each other, to prevent them from overhearing each other's 'think aloud' comments. While tasks are intended to simulate and capture behaviours of those collaborating at

Figure 5. Schematic diagram of the multi-user assessment platform

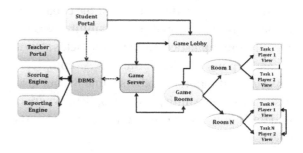

long distances (including separate countries), it was neither practical nor necessary to replicate this during the cognitive laboratory.

Screen and audio capture software was used to record the students' 'think aloud' comments as well as their on screen activities. This not only created useful records for later review, but was also necessary as a single researcher is not able to take notes on two students simultaneously. Comprehensive notes on students' behaviours were assembled after the event, using the audio and screen capture files. A data logger was built into the tasks to capture students' conversation logs, intermediate solutions, final solutions, as well as all other mouse clicks and key strokes; all with time stamps. Screen and audio files were useful additional tools for task refinement, particularly when students encountered aspects of the tasks that did not function as expected or intended. Such files are able to shed light on otherwise perplexing sequences of data and chat text comments. These data sources were all used to examine behaviour on the tasks in detail, as way of determining the degree to which the tasks were able to elicit the hypothesised skills contributing to collaborative problem solving.

Figure 6 is an extract from a chat log between two 13 year old students solving a task that required them each to contribute resources to which each has unique access. Each line of chat text can be evaluated based on rubrics that operationalise CPS into strands, capabilities, and indicators with their quality criteria for performance. Chat text can be classified under multiple capabilities, as illustrated by line 6, which is an example of a level of 'responsibility' and a level of 'planning course of action'. In this rubric, for the capability 'responsibility', 'assumes responsibility' is considered more sophisticated than 'completes activities and reports to others'. Student A 'completes activities and reports to others' (line 8), but also 'assumes responsibility' (lines 6, 10), whereas Student B only 'completes activities and reports

to others' (lines 7, 11). Thus, there is evidence that Student A has more advanced specific collaborative problem solving skills than Student B in terms of taking responsibility. This is evidence of the students' level of CPS development, but is also evidence that the task can stimulate different levels of performance in this skill area. When combined with students' problem solving actions captured by mouse event data, we are able to build evidence for differentiating between students in terms of the construct and evaluating the capacity of the tasks to elicit and record the information required for doing so.

This evidence provides a useful example for teachers to view the processes undertaken by students to solve problems collaboratively and thereby introduces them to the concept of collaborative problem solving. In an additional phase of the ATC21S project, teachers will participate in professional development workshops. These workshops will focus on understanding of the concept, familiarity with its strands and elements, and looking at evidence of student skills along the developmental learning progression. Using this progression, teachers will identify current functioning levels of students and the additional sophistication in skills required to move students forward. The workshops will provide an opportunity for teachers to identify strategies and lesson approaches that can be used across a range of discipline areas to facilitate student progress.

FUTURE GOALS

Automated Scoring

Current methods of scoring complex collaborative work with free flowing dialogue involve hand scoring by trained or expert evaluators. This is done either through coding individual lines of text using a rubric (Wilczenski, Bontrager, Ventrone & Correia, 2001) or assigning an overall rating of

Figure 6. Coding of collaborative problem solving behaviours using a rubric

Line	Student	Conversation Log	Strand	Capability	Quality Criteria
1	A	do you know what the anwser is ?	Participation	Interaction	Initiates interaction
2	B	no i am confused	Social Regulation	Knowledge of self	Notes own performance
3	A	same :)	Participation	Interaction	Responds to cues in communication
4	A	do you think that we have to write a number in the drop	Knowledge Building	Tolerance for ambiguity	Notes ambiguity and suggest options
5	B	maybe	Participation	Task completion	Maintains presence only
6	A	lets write a number	Task Regulation	Planning course of action	Identifies short sequences of actions for a task
			Social Regulation	Responsibility	Assumes responsibility
7	B	okay i wrote 10	Social Regulation	Responsibility	Completes activities and reports to others
8	A	i will write 5	Social Regulation	Responsibility	Completes activities and reports to others
9	B	k	Participation	Interaction	Acknowledges communication
10	A	did you write it in; did yours work?	Social Regulation	Responsibility	Assumes responsibility
11	B	yea	Social Regulation	Responsibility	Completes activities and reports to others

performance on several dimensions of CPS based on a rating handbook (Meier et al., 2007). Both methods are extremely time and labour intensive. While such methods are suitable for research purposes, they are unlikely to be viable options for scaling up measures of CPS for use in schools and large scale assessments.

The automation of scoring complex process data remains a motivating goal in educational assessment. The main attractions include immediate provision of feedback to students and educators and the potential to incorporate adaptivity into the selection of tasks. As demonstrated in the discussion of the single-user 'Hot Chocolate' task, methods which call upon theoretical frameworks in combination with empirical data can provide a productive starting point. The granularity of the observable variables to be scored will likely determine how difficult the development and programming of automated scoring rules will be. For example, it is relatively easy to automate the scoring of a well-defined problem or the scoring of whether a student carries out a particular single-step action or not. It is less straightforward when the observable variable is procedural and may include multiple steps and sequences.

Several of the behaviours that tasks should elicit to support inferences about CPS proficiencies are related to the content, timing and order of typed chat messages. These data are free-text transactions, the contents of which can vary a great deal across and within tasks. Establishing scoring logic for these data is seen as a hugely important step for advancing assessment. Building reliable scoring rules is dependent upon a theoretical framework combined with a bank of empirical data from task trials. One option for subsequent deployment of the tasks is to embed the most commonly transmitted text messages as pre-defined messages which might be selectable by students, via drop-down menus for example. This would simplify the task of automated scoring, but it might provide an undesirable level of scaffolding in guiding students to collaborate in predictable, pre-defined ways.

A potential supplement to automated scoring for large scale CPS assessment is the use of peer ratings, since the very direct target of CPS behaviours and their impact are on the collaborators' peers. Peer ratings are not uncommon in workplaces, and peer judgements are prevalent in society. However, given the relative lack of knowledge in the community about the collaborative problem solving construct, it is not clear whether students would be able to provide useful assessment data. Ratings of others are heavily dependent on the understanding and knowledge of the rater about the domain which is the subject of interest, as well as on the individual skill level of that rater on that domain. Thus, while the use of peer ratings to score CPS may be logistically easier than automated scoring of actual activity, research would be required to ascertain students' ability to rate their peers on dimensions of CPS.

Technology Integration

Technologies such as cloud computing, mobile devices, and natural language processing software are all likely to influence the way assessments are designed, delivered and utilised in the coming years. Cloud platforms provide a means for delocalising educational resources and making them available whenever a user is online. Resources hosted on cloud configurations enable high concurrency and high availability since part of their appeal is their capacity to scale on demand. The virtual storage of assessment data is another attractive feature which will allow monitoring of learning progress to continue even for students who relocate from their school or area. Over a billion mobile devices are produced each year. As these devices gain acceptance as part of educational technology integration in schools, they might also become part of the continuous assessment landscape. There are certain advantages with these devices: they are relatively cheap, many of them enable internet access, and they are extremely portable. There are disadvantages too: the size of the screen on mobile devices constrains the kinds of tasks that are sufficiently user-friendly and there are compatibility issues with certain device/software combinations. Nonetheless it is possible that certain elements of learning and assessment may become more convenient using mobile devices.

Real-time translation is another facility which is emerging in online environments. This feature, if integrated into assessment tasks, could provide the sense of a global classroom. Students from different countries could work together to solve problems without knowing each other's language. Microsoft's Lync platform is one example of a real-time translation technology, and several others are beginning to appear in beta form.

Technology in Schools

The technological difficulties in large scale assessment cannot be ignored. The issue of whether major resources are to be allocated to development and design for implementation now or in the future is of primary importance. Development of assessment tasks which have an eye on the future poses logistical and pedagogical challenges, not only for the developers but also for potential users of the technology. Schools do not always have the technology or the flexibility to test out technically-advanced tasks that require robust and up to date software and hardware, large bandwidth and fast download speeds, and broad-ranging internet access. This gap between state of the art technology-based assessment development and environmental conditions in the target locations has implications beyond the mere development of tasks. In addition, where students are not functioning in a technology-rich environment, the implications of technology-rich assessments will be different from those for students who are functioning in such integrated settings. From the pedagogical perspective, teachers are not familiar with the concepts underlying the 21st century skill tasks and the implications these will have for teaching and curriculum. The perspective that assessment will drive teaching and curriculum may be well-founded, but the time lags in the supporting structures for implementation pose interim challenges that can have serious consequences for take-up of the desired changes. The development of assessment procedures needs to be ahead of the technology and infrastructure that is available in schools. The immediate challenges this poses in developing the tasks and platforms for their delivery and for teaching and curriculum are considerable. We are not living in a pure research climate – we are dealing with real students, real teachers and real schools.

CONCLUSION

This chapter outlined the theoretical, technological and practical requirements and challenges associated with the design and delivery of CPS assessment tasks, using an example from the ATC21S project. This chapter also highlighted the implications that some emerging technologies could have on the scope of assessment design, delivery and participation. While these are exciting means for integrating assessment seamlessly in a learner's world, they are only one part of making substantive progress in technology-enabled assessment design. The most significant advances will relate to the automation of scoring and feedback for providing timely, valid and instructionally relevant information about student development on new and important learning areas. This chapter described the specification of technology requirements needed to support the evidentiary arguments of two different assessment systems designed to make inferences about two different aspects of problem solving behaviour. It is anticipated that assessment designers will continue to make progress on leveraging technology to support inferences about a broader range of 21st century skills. Ideally these inferences will provide valuable information for informing student instruction. This is a valuable goal if it helps students acquire the skills they will need to succeed in increasingly information-rich and globalised educational and vocational settings. There is scope for those interested in this area to make contributions to the field, both in development of technology and in investigation into skills such as collaborative problem solving.

A major challenge is presented here, not only in the identification and definition of 21st century skills, but in designing and developing assessment tasks that capture the skills believed to play a major role in how individuals engage with the new century. Within the traditional classroom, but with an eye to the use of skills beyond its borders, we have outlined an initiative being developed in Melbourne, and trialled across Asia, the Pacific, Europe and the Americas. The responses of both students and teachers to the assessment tasks will provide focus for continuing work in the use of the approach within mainstream education.

REFERENCES

Autor, D., Levy, F., & Murnane, R. (2003). The skill content of recent technological change: An empirical exploration. *The Quarterly Journal of Economics*, *118*(4), 1279–1333. doi:10.1162/003355303322552801

Bennett, R. E., Jenkins, F., Persky, H., & Weiss, A. (2003). Assessing complex problem solving performances. *Assessment in Education*, *10*(3), 347–359. doi:10.1080/0969594032000148181

Csapó, B., Ainley, J., Bennett, R., Latour, T., & Law, N. (2011). Technological issues for computer-based assessment. In Griffin, P., Care, E., & McGaw, B. (Eds.), *Assessment and teaching of 21st century skills*. New York, NY: Springer.

Ericsson, K. A., & Simon, H. A. (1993). *Protocol analysis: Verbal reports as data* (*rev. ed.*). Cambridge, MA: The MIT Press.

Glaser, R. (1991). Expertise and assessment. In Wittrock, M. C., & Baker, E. L. (Eds.), *Testing and cognition* (pp. 17–30). Englewood Cliffs, NJ: Prentice Hall.

Griffin, P., Care, E., & McGaw, B. (2012). The changing role of education and schools. In Griffin, P., Care, E., & McGaw, B. (Eds.), *Assessment and teaching of 21st century skills*. New York, NY: Springer. doi:10.1007/978-94-007-2324-5_1

Griffin, P., Murray, L., Care, E., Thomas, A., & Perri, P. (2010). Developmental assessment: Lifting literacy through professional learning teams. *Assessment in Education: Principles. Policy & Practice*, *17*(4), 383–397.

Kankaanranta, M., & Neittaanmaki, P. (Eds.). (2009). *Design and use of serious games*. New York, NY: Springer. doi:10.1007/978-1-4020-9496-5

Leighton, J., & Gierl, M. J. (2007). Verbal reports as data for cognitive diagnostic assessment. In Leighton, J., & Gierl, M. J. (Eds.), *Cognitive diagnostic assessment for education* (pp. 146–172). Cambridge, UK: Cambridge University Press. doi:10.1017/CBO9780511611186.006

Meier, A., Spada, H., & Rummel, N. (2007). A rating scheme for assessing the quality of computer-supported collaboration process. *Computer-Supported Collaborative Learning, 2,* 63–86. doi:10.1007/s11412-006-9005-x

Mills, C. N., Potenza, M. T., Fremer, J. J., & Ward, W. C. (2002). *Computer-based testing: Building the foundation for future assessments*. New Jersey: Laurence Erlbaum Associates, Inc.

Mislevy, R. J., Steinberg, L. S., Breyer, F. J., Almond, R. G., & Johnson, L. (1999). A cognitive task analysis with implications for designing simulation-based performance assessment. *Computers in Human Behavior, 15*(3-4), 335–374. doi:10.1016/S0747-5632(99)00027-8

Newell, A., & Simon, H. A. (1961). *GPS, a program that simulates human thought*. Los Angeles, CA: Rand Corporation.

Parshall, C. G., & Harmes, J. C. (2009). Improving the quality of innovative item types: Four tasks for design and development. *Journal of Applied Testing Technology, 10*(1), 1–20.

Pelligrino, J., Chudowsky, N., & Glaser, R. (Eds.). (2001). *Knowing what students know: The science and design of educational assessment*. Washington, DC: National Academy Press.

Raizen, S., Binkley, M., Erstad, O., Herman, J., Ripley, M., Miller-Ricci, M., & Rumble, M. (2012). Defining 21st century skills. In Griffin, P., Care, E., & McGaw, B. (Eds.), *Assessment and teaching of 21st century skills*. New York, NY: Springer.

Taylor, B. M., Pearson, P. D., Peterson, D. S., & Rodriguez, M. C. (2005). The CIERA school change framework: An evidenced-based approach to professional development and school reading improvement. *Reading Research Quarterly, 40*(1), 40–69. doi:10.1598/RRQ.40.1.3

Vygotsky, L. (1978). *Mind and society: The development of higher psychological processes*. Cambridge, MA: Harvard University Press.

Wilczenski, F. L., Bontrager, T., Ventrone, P., & Correia, M. (2001). Observing collaborative problem-solving processes and outcomes. *Psychology in the Schools, 38*(3), 269–278. doi:10.1002/pits.1017

Williamson, D. M., Bauer, M., Steinberg, L. S., Mislevy, R. J., Behrens, J. T., & DeMark, S. F. (2004). Design rationale for a complex performance assessment. *International Journal of Testing, 4*(4), 303–332. doi:10.1207/s15327574ijt0404_2

Williamson, D. M., Mislevy, R. J., & Bejar, I. I. (2006). *Automated scoring of complex tasks in computer-based testing*. New Jersey: Lauwrence Erlbaum Associates, Inc.

Wilson, M., Bejar, I., Scalise, K., Templin, J., Wiliam, D., & Irribarra, D. T. (2012). Perspectives on methodological issues. In Griffin, P., Care, E., & McGaw, B. (Eds.), *Assessment and teaching of 21st century skills*. New York, NY: Springer.

Wirth, J., & Klieme, E. (2003). Computer-based assessment of problem solving competence. *Assessment in Education*, *10*(3), 329–345. doi:10.1080/0969594032000148172

Zoanetti, N. P. (2010). Interactive computer based assessment tasks: How problem-solving process data can inform instruction. *Australasian Journal of Educational Technology*, *26*(5), 585–606.

KEY TERMS AND DEFINITIONS

21st Century Skills: Four skills: ways of thinking (Creativity, critical thinking, problem-solving, decision-making and learning), ways of working (communication and collaboration), tools for working (information and communications technology and information literacy), and skills for living in the world (citizenship, life and career, and personal and social responsibility).

Assessment Design: Assessment purpose and construct of interest defined, construct should be analysed to determine what development from novice to expert would look like. Appropriate evidence for making inferences considered. Feasible task types determined, based on pragmatic factors. Tasks evaluated via development cycle.

ATC21S Project: An international research effort aimed at empowering students with the skills to succeed in the 21st century workplace. ATC21S is developing methods to assess skills that will form the basis for 21st century curricula, with an emphasis on communication and collaboration, problem-solving, citizenship, and digital fluency. The project will offer curricula recommendations for education systems to support an improved workforce.

Automated Scoring: Benefits of automated scoring of complex process data include immediate provision of feedback to students and educators and the potential to incorporate adaptivity into task selection.

Cognitive Laboratories: Cognitive laboratories provide information about the construct validity of assessment tasks in at least two ways. They are carried out to ensure tasks elicit the intended subset of behaviours. They are also conducted to identify aspects of tasks that students struggle with that are unrelated to the construct. In a cognitive laboratory, a researcher sits with a student throughout the process with a voice recorder to record utterances and a notepad to record obvious behavioural cues. Concurrent sources of evidence can show assessment task construct validity.

Collaborative Problem Solving: Working together to solve a common challenge, involving the contribution and exchange of ideas, knowledge or resources to achieve a goal. Such skills are considered necessary for success in modern education and work environments.

Information and Communications Technology (ICT): Any communication device or application, encompassing radio, television, cellular phones, computer and network hardware and software, satellite systems and so on, as well as the various services and applications associated with them, such as videoconferencing and distance learning. Its importance centres on its ability to create greater access to information and communication.

Process Scoring: Recording detailed interactions between the problem solver and the task environment, thus capturing data describing solution processes in an unobtrusive way. The benefits of this approach include the ability to build tasks assessing aspects of problem solving difficult to measure in other ways.

Chapter 5
Facilitating Learning by Going Online:
Modernising Islamic Teaching and Learning in Indonesia

Siew Mee Barton
Deakin University, Australia

ABSTRACT

This chapter examines the impact of eLearning and Web 2.0 social media in a socially conservative environment in Indonesia that has nevertheless proven surprisingly adroit at change management. Web 2.0 social media has proven enormously popular in Indonesia but traditional Islamic schools (which are known in Java as pesantren but elsewhere in the Muslim world as madrasah) the focus of this study is often unable to access Web 2.0 or the Internet in general. Progressive non-national government organizations (NGOs) seek to remedy this situation by providing satellite broadband links to remote schools and this chapter examines one particular project. Despite the impoverished and conservative nature of their community, the leaders of this school have led their students in a surprisingly enthusiastic reception of eLearning technology, recognizing its great capacity to produce and enhance social networks and provide new opportunities for learning. Particular attention in this case study is given to factors relating to social capital, attitudes, and patterns of behavior in leadership and change management. A case study approach was chosen to enable a richer and more finely-grained analysis of the issues. The case study is based on semi-structured interviews and observations conducted over several years. This research shows that whilst the adoption and uptake of eLearning with emerging technologies is strongly shaped by cultural and social factors, it plays out in very different ways than might first have been expected.

DOI: 10.4018/978-1-4666-3649-1.ch005

INTRODUCTION: *E-PESANTREN*

Muslims have creatively applied Internet technologies in the interests of furthering understanding of their religion. It is only natural for a net-literate generation to seek out specific truths and affiliations online, especially when the information cannot be accessed in a local mosque or community context. Cooke and Lawrence (2005, p. 13) reflect Dawson's point in a discussion on religion and the Internet: 'the Internet is used most often to expand people's social horizons and involvement. Thus far, however, *pesantren* have mainly been using the Internet for the purposes of religious teaching. A recent initiative by the International Centre for Islam and Pluralism (ICIP) and the Ford Foundation, is aimed more at bringing general education to *pesantren* via the Internet. Started in 2007, a program called the Open, Distance and eLearning (ODeL) Program for *pesantren*, plans on giving *pesantren* students the equivalent of a high school education, which in Indonesia is split into two levels of lower middle school (Years 7–9), and higher middle school (Years 10–12).

LITERATURE REVIEW

Emerging Technologies

Veletsianos (2010) defines emerging technologies as follows: emerging technologies (ET) are not necessarily new technologies. According to Veletsianos, emerging technologies can be described as evolving organisms that exist in a state of 'coming into being'; experience hype cycles; satisfy the 'not yet' criteria of not yet being fully understood, and not yet being fully researched or researched in a mature way; and are potentially disruptive, but their potential is mostly unfulfilled. For the purpose of the discussion here, we will focus on the first criterion: emerging technologies are not necessarily new technologies. Veletsianos further

explains that a technology is still emerging if it is not yet a 'must-have'. Veletsianos (2010) further explains this criterion:

Newness, by itself, is a problematic indicator of what emerging technologies are, as older technologies can also be emerging (Veletsianos, 2010, p. 13).

We see this characteristic as compelling in the sense that it gives a broader view of the term 'emerging technologies' and can be taken to suit one's experiences and cultural nuances with technologies. Educators are constantly experimenting with various technologies to foster and explore learning processes, and we see this concept as an emerging way of using various technologies in an integrated manner. Internet technology is becoming more readily available and is allowing the integration of other technologies such as Internet-based video-conferencing, learning objects and podcasts. Internet video-conferencing has re-emerged as a result of technological advancements, cost savings, and climate change concerns (Veletsianos, 2010).

Emerging technologies are also seen as synonymous with Web 2.0. The term Web 2.0 refers to the changing trends in the use of the World Wide Web technology that enhance communication, information sharing, collaboration and creative use of the web. Web 2.0 concepts have led to the development and evolution of web culture communities and hosted services such as social-networking sites, video sharing sites, wikis, blogs, and folksonomies (Veletsianos, 2010).

Emerging technologies such as wikis, blogs, podcasts, social networking tools, virtual worlds and avatars are being widely used in higher education. Wiki pages can be used by anyone to publish new content direct to the Web, including text, images and hyperlinks; to edit existing content; and also, because the wiki is fluid and open to all, to 'roll back' if necessary to previous versions through a 'page history' utility. Students can develop their own knowledge content promptly using a wiki and seldom need to study alone because of participation in a technologically mediated social space conducive to the formation of communities of practice (Boulos, Maramba & Wheeler, 2006). Podcasts are also being increasingly adopted by distance learning institutions such as, for example, Indira Gandhi National Open University (IGNOU), which has created an IGNOU channel on YouTube.

Emerging technologies provide opportunities to increase learner engagement, promote authentic learning as well as presenting opportunities to allow learner control over content and interaction. However, educators who adopt these tools to support, or rather produce, learning among their students, must realize that technology, no matter how good it is, by itself does not guarantee better learning (Wagner, 2005). Web 2.0 offers great potential in enabling collaborative learning communities (Veletsianos, 2008, p. 65), and is a powerful learning situation for adult distance learners.

This chapter examines the experience of a traditional Islamic school known in Indonesia as a *pesantren* (but elsewhere in the Muslim world as a madrasah) in using the Internet to enhance learning. The contrast between the largely rural, largely poor, and overwhelmingly conservative nature of these traditional religious institutions and the technology of eLearning with its great capacity to produce and enhance new social networks and new opportunities for learning is very striking and makes this a particularly revealing case study.

Education

Indonesia's education system is run by public and private partnerships in all sectors (AusAid, 2007). Indonesia's Ministry of National Education (MNE) runs the public educational services and has decentralised offices at provinces, district

and sub-district levels. Indonesia's Ministry of Religious Affairs oversees the private and non-governmental sector, which is dominated by the Islamic institutions, mainly madrasah and *pesantren* (AusAid, 2007).

The CIA World Fact Book (2010) reported on statistics for Indonesia:

Aged 25 or over and having attained:

- No formal schooling 30.3%
- Incomplete primary 32.3%
- Primary 22.8%
- Incomplete secondary 6.4%
- Secondary 7.1%
- Higher 1.2%

Aged 15 or over and having attained literacy:

- Literate population 77.6% (Central Intelligence Agency, 2010)

Indonesia, as in other countries, established higher education policies and strategies to harness the use of ICTs for improving the country's national competitiveness. In 2000, the government took the initial step by establishing the Indonesian Telematics Coordinating Team (TKTI), which consisted of all cabinet ministers and was chaired by former President Megawati Soekarnoputri. In 2001, ICT national plan was formulated by Presidential Decree No. 6/2001 which is a Five-Year Action Plan for the Development and Implementation of ICT in Indonesia (TKTI, 2001) that stated the government's policy towards ICT, and commissioned TKTI to drive ICT implementation in Indonesia. Presidential Decree No. 6/2001, with its five-year action plan, set out an ICT plan for education that included the areas outlined in Table 1 (TKTI, 2001).

Waluyo (2006), in his report to the Ministry of Culture and Tourism (MOCT), presented the five-year plan for Indonesia's ICT projects (Table 2).

Table 1. Indonesian telematics coordinating team (TKTI, 2001, p. 5)

Action Plan	Time Schedule	Priority
Develop ICT networks for public and private universities as well as research and education networks in Indonesia.	2001–2005	B
Develop and implement ICT curricula.	2002–2004	A
Use ICTs as an essential part of the curricula and learning tools in schools/ universities and training centres.	2001–2005	B
Establish distance education programs including participation in Global Development Learning and other networks.	2001–2005	A
Facilitate the use of Internet for more efficient teaching and learning (e.g., School, 2000).	2002–2005	A

Table 2. ICT projects

ICT Projects	
2005: ICT Familiarisation	To familiarise the uses of computers, networks, and other peripherals as daily supporting tools; Train selected people in the use of related applications in their lines of duty; Reinforce the use of e-mails as main communication tools both internally and externally; Manage the e-mail traffic and follow-ups.
2006: ICT Automation	To identify processes that could be auto-mated or calculated by the use of ICT; To design a new business process improved by these ICT automations; Actively campaign internally to find any potential benefits by using ICT.
2007: ICT Empowerment	Form new organisational charts for the new ICT-automated business processes; Delegate clear and direct responsibilities for each and every person involved; Train these very people to acquire the needed competency; Empower human resources, therefore, ICT human resources will be distributed to each unit, instead of centralised on Data and Information Centre (DIC) (a 3-year plan).
2008: ICT Simplification	Focus on paperless transactions and docu-mentation, that is, simplify processes and de-bureaucracy.
2009: ICT Organisation	Empower ICT human resources, therefore ICT human resources will be distributed, instead of centralised on DIC (final year in a 3-year plan); Reinvent the Ministry as an ICT organisa-tion, one that uses ICT as an organisational advantage, not merely as technology.

Indonesia's ICT five-year projects plan (Waluyo, 2006)

DISTANCE EDUCATION IN INDONESIA

In 1955, distance education was being introduced in Indonesia (Belawati, 2007). Distance education was first established as a correspondence program with the aim of upgrading teaching qualifications. Not until 1981 was there widespread distance education, when two projects on in-service train-ing for secondary and tertiary-level teachers were introduced (Belawati, 2007). These projects later became a major part of the Universitas Terbuka (UT) (Indonesian Open Learning University) (Belawati, 2007). UT is a state-owned university. It was established in 1984 with three main mis-sions: 1) to increase access to higher education; 2) to train increasing numbers of students in areas demanded by the economic and cultural development of the country; and 3) to upgrade the qualifications of primary and secondary school teachers who had graduated from the short-term programs to enable them to obtain a full teacher training degree (Belawati, 2007). UT was set up to be a flexible and inexpensive university for people who were unable to attend on-campus face-to-face classes. UT is the only university that is a wholly distance education institution in Indonesia (Belawati, 2007).

Pesantren, Madrasah, and eLearning

It is commonly assumed that *pesantren* and madrasah, being traditional Islamic educational institutions, must be overwhelmingly socially conservative and committed to propagating a narrow worldview. Whilst there is some truth in this, the reality is much more complex. Scholars of modern religious movements have observed that those movements that can be best described as fundamentalist tend to be led by those with only limited religious education in their tradition. In other words, fundamentalist movements tend to be lay movements. Conversely, those who have obtained a deep level of scholarship in the religious tradition, whilst conservative, tend not to see the world in black and white terms. They have been trained to understand the complexity and ambiguity when interpreting texts and, are accustomed to the fact that respected scholars can take opposing views on many issues.

The *pesantren* are Islamic boarding schools. In the past, the *pesantren* taught a non-formal religious curriculum, for which the students are not given state-recognised certificates. They differ from schools that simply concentrate on Qur'an recitation and memorisation, and are similar to the religious that can be found in the Middle East (Pohl, 2007, p. 92). Before examining the relationship between the Internet and Islamic education within Indonesia, it is important to understand what a *pesantren* is.

The *pesantren* has a strong foundation in traditional Indonesian society. M. Dawam Rahardjo (Jabali & Jamhari, 2003, p. 81) stated that the *pesantren* is a cultural symbol of Indonesia's indigenous education system. Historically, the approach to education developed at the *pesantren*, and it has its roots in the traditional religious instruction that predominated when Hinduism and Buddhism were prevalent in Indonesia.

Contrary to the popular image of traditional Islamic education being medieval and backward, these educational institutions have undergone extensive reforms since the early twentieth century. Further, not all these institutions are called *pesantren*, but vary in name according to location. In Java and South Kalimantan, they are called *pesantren*, but in Aceh they are called *dayah*. In other parts of Kalimantan, South Sulawesi, Malay and parts of Sumatra, they are called *pondok*, while in West Sumatra, they are called *surau*. The

unifying feature of these institutions was is that they are traditional in nature, in that their curriculum consists almost entirely of instruction in classical Islamic traditions of knowledge. Another defining feature is the fact that they were run by the *ulama* or *kyai* as they were known in Java. These *pesantren* are dedicated to the study of the Qur'an and Hadith, jurisprudence, mysticism and Arabic sciences, amongst other things. However, since the early twentieth century, subjects such as mathematics, history and English have also been offered, a practice that was the norm by the 1950s. By the 1970s, the Indonesian government had mandated that *pesantren* students also complete a general elementary education at the very least (Azra et al., 2007, pp. 174–176).

Many of these reforms were initiated because of the introduction of another type of Islamic school, the madrasah. First established in West Sumatra and south-central Java, madrasahs are actually self-consciously more modern than *pesantren*. In the Middle East, a madrasah refers to an institute of higher Islamic learning, but the word is used differently depending on its location. In Indonesia, a madrasah is different from a *pesantren* because most are primarily concerned with general educational courses. Further, the teaching methods of a madrasah in Indonesia are different from that of a *pesantren*. The latter conduct classes by utilising study groups that circle the teacher, while the classes and courses themselves often do not have a formal structure. In a madrasah, this has all been replaced with classrooms, whiteboards, textbooks and exams. Moreover, unlike the *pesantren*, madrasah have more closely followed government regulations in terms of education standards (Azra et al., 2007, pp. 176–177).

Even more recently, modern institutions of Islamic learning have been introduced, and have simply been called Islamic schools, offering an even greater proportion of general educational courses than both *pesantren* and madrasah. Ever since the 1990s, Islamic schools have become the preferred choice for many middle-class Muslims in Indonesia, despite their higher fees. Islamic schools offer specialised programs in science, history, social sciences and foreign language studies (Azra et al., 2007, p. 177).

Being the oldest institution of education, *pesantren* are now faced with numerous challenges, such as declining enrolments in recent years. On top of this, many of the 25,000 *pesantren* are located in some of the poorest regions of Indonesia, filling in the gaps that the Indonesian public school system cannot cover. It is important to note here that traditionalist does not always equal conservative, and this is evident in the willingness of a large number of *pesantren* to embrace the Internet.

The word madrasah has gained a bad reputation, especially since the al-Qaeda attacks of 11 September 2001, because a minority of Pakistan's madrasahs is associated with violent Islamist movements, including the Taliban and al-Qaeda. Moreover, a larger number of madrasah in Pakistan and elsewhere in South and West Asia teach a limited range of subjects confined to matters of religious learning and practice. Thus, they have acquired a reputation for being supportive of violently reactionary movements, at worst, and at best, as belonging to a bygone age at odds with the modern world. Across the Muslim world, there are many madrasah that belie this widely-held stereotype. However, it is particularly in Indonesia that this image of madrasah, or *pesantren*, begins to break down. The vast majority of Indonesia's *pesantren* today teach the standard state curriculum from the secular schooling system. Their classes in religious matters are often conducted in the late afternoon or evening and, effectively, run in addition to the day school classes. This was not always the case but the last three decades have seen the transformation of the *pesantren* system. Thus, graduates of *pesantren* can matriculate to regular tertiary institutions and go on to professional careers that are not limited to the exercise of specialist religious knowledge and skills. This is of great benefit to both *pesantren* students and

to Indonesian society as a whole, as approximately 20 per cent of all school-age students receive their education in the *pesantren* system. Therefore, like many religious schools around the world including Christian denominational schools in both the developed and developing world, these Islamic schools are making a vital contribution to the education of many.

Nevertheless, the stereotypical prejudice about *pesantren* being remote from modern society and marked by social conservatisms does have some foundation. For a start, many of the *pesantren* students come from the poorest elements of Indonesian society. Many either do not pay for their *pesantren* education in cash, or pay very modest amounts and attend *pesantren* because their families cannot afford to send them to regular schools, in a system where even the state schools require significant cash payments each term to cover costs. In addition, many of these *pesantren* are located in very remote rural areas or, at the very least, are situated largely outside the larger urban communities, and are linked to rural communities dependent upon agriculture. A very small number of *pesantren* are associated with violent Islamist movements. Around 250 of Indonesia's approximately 25,000 *pesantren*, or about one per cent, have a clear association with extremist ideas. Perhaps one tenth of this group, that is to say, around two dozen *pesantren* have well-established links with terrorist groups like *Jemaah Islamiyah (JI)*. Therefore, in terms of *pesantren* representing a security problem, the threat is greatly exaggerated. Certainly, the one per cent of *pesantren* with extremist tendencies do need to be kept under surveillance, but authorities are increasingly becoming aware that traditionalist Islamic institutions in Indonesia and beyond, such as *pesantren*, are much more part of a solution to combating extremism than they are part of the problem.

Some of Indonesia's most significant progressive Islamic intellectuals, who are also some of the worlds' leading Islamic thinkers, have been schooled in Indonesia's *pesantren* system. The researcher will briefly examine the biographies of several of Indonesia's leading progressive, or as they are sometimes called, liberal, Islamic intellectuals and reflect upon the social factors that were formative in the development of their thinking.

A large proportion of Indonesia's *pesantren* can, essentially, be described as moderate. They are committed to teaching a tolerant and sophisticated understanding of Islam that is respectful of Indonesia's social, cultural and religious diversity, and encourage constructive engagement with broader society. There is also a significant section of the *pesantren* community that, while engaged neither with extremist religious teaching nor with supporting violent movements, is nevertheless somewhat isolated from society and given to reinforcing the sort of social conservatism that sets them in opposition to many aspects of modern Indonesian society. Evidence of this conservatism is readily available from recent social surveys. During the Suharto era, there was very little reliable social surveying done in Indonesia apart from market research in industries such as the tobacco industry. Over the last decade following Suharto's resignation in May 1998, however, there have been a number of very credible regular social surveys initiated.

One of the best, which pertains to attitudes regarding religion and society, is conducted annually by the Center for the Study of Islam in Society (Pusat Pengkajian Islam dan Masyarakat) (PPIM) located in the State Islamic University (UIN) of Jakarta, in conjunction with the Indonesian Survey Institute. Each year, a series of surveys is conducted intended to ascertain social attitudes across the whole of Indonesian society. In 2007, three surveys were conducted as part of a set intended to understand attitudes to political Islam, Islamism, democracy and secularism. Significantly, these surveys showed the extent to which there was a stark contrast between teachers and senior students in *pesantren* madrasah and Islamic schools and members of the general society. The surveys revealed a somewhat surprisingly high level of support (around 30 per cent of respondents) at least nominally, for Islamism. Therefore, for example, a relatively high number of general respondents indicated support for the application of Sharia, or Islamic law, including the more debatable aspects associated with corporal punishment. Significantly, when the same questions were asked of scholars and senior students in the Islamic institutions, the response rate in the affirmative in support of Islamic law and the creation of an Islamic state was double (around 60 per cent of respondents) that in the general population.

Most commentators suggest care needs to be taken in interpreting these affirmative responses too literally. Nevertheless, it would appear that the *pesantren*, madrasah and other Islamic institutions are markedly more conservative than general Indonesian society. For this reason, many of Indonesia's leading civil society activists who contribute to progressive Islamic thought and discourse, and who are concerned about extremism affecting religious freedoms, define the *pesantren* as being key institutions in shaping Islamic thought, practice and attitudes in Indonesia. Many of Indonesia's progressive Islamic non-governmental organisation (NGO)—and Indonesia has more progressive Islamic NGO than any other Muslim majority country—are closely connected with the *pesantren* community. A significant majority of the *pesantren* and their leaders play a key role in the development and socialisation of progressive Islamic thought. Moreover, some of Indonesia's key Islamic leaders and scholars have arisen out of this nexus, as can be seen in the next section. There is significant online engagement from these progressive *pesantren* and NGO. In fact, they form the backbone of online activity propagating a tolerant and inclusive understanding of Islam that is productively engaging with modernity.

ISLAMIC EDUCATION AND THE INTERNET IN INDONESIA

From the earliest days, Internet development across the globe revolved around tertiary education institutions and Indonesia has been no exception to this. Consequently, there is a history of synergetic relations between the Internet and education in Indonesia. University campuses are typically surrounded by *warnets*, or Internet cafés. Within 500 meters of the main Universitas Indonesia campus, for example, there were as many as 20 *warnets* at the beginning of this decade (Hidayatullah & Dharmawan, 2003, p. 22) and numbers have grown steadily since in response to unabated demand. Moreover, the link between places of learning and Internet usage is not limited to élite institutions such as UI, but occurs across the entire sector and includes even the most traditional institutions of education such as the Islamic boarding schools known as *pesantren*.

A recent survey conducted by the Indonesian Centre for Agricultural Library and Technology Dissemination; found that at least 39 *pesantren* s had official websites (with another seven *pesantren* -related websites not being linked to any specific *pesantren*). These 39 *pesantren* were located across seven different provinces within Indonesia, as follows:

- East Java (16 *pesantren*, 41.03%)
- West Java (9 *pesantren*, 23.08%)
- Central Java (5 *pesantren*, 12.82%)
- DKI Jakarta (4 *pesantren*, 10.25%)
- DI Yogjakarta (3 *pesantren*, 7.69%)
- Riau (2 *pesantren*, 5.13%)
- Aceh (1 *pesantren*, 2.56%)

This represents a significant increase from the tally of 15 *pesantren*s with websites observed in the year 2000 and, yet, almost certainly underestimates by a large measure the total number of *pesantren* -related websites.

At the same time, there has also been significant growth in the range of technologies used. In the year 2000, there were only seven main applications being widely used: websites, e-mail, Usenet, newsgroup, listserve, chat rooms and Internet searches. This has increased to at least 16 core application types today, with *pesantren* now taking advantage of the following technologies: membership, streaming, downloads, polling, rating, links, guest book, calendar functions, counter and statistics.

Out of the 46- *pesantren* websites observed, the report found that at least 27 of them used the Internet to conduct teaching activities related to Islamic topics. This phenomenon is not, of course, limited to Indonesia, as countries such as Malaysia and Singapore have also seen *pesantren*, or madrasah (the Arabic name for schools used widely for traditional Islamic institutions across the world), establishing their own websites. Of course, students are not the only ones to benefit from the Internet, as teachers and Islamic scholars also have much to gain. Whereas it would have taken many days to travel to another institute of learning, or many days to send letters, the communication between scholars and teachers is now near instantaneous. Teachers, Islamic scholars and students can now connect and link to each other, forming bonds and bridges with one another. This shows how social capital and education have become inherently linked.

Cooke and Lawrence (2005) argue that a broad spectrum of Islamic hyper-textual approaches and understandings can be, and are, located in cyberspace, created by Muslims seeking to present dimensions of their religious, spiritual, and/or political lives online.

Muslims have creatively applied the Internet in the interest of furthering the understanding of their religion for other believers, especially those affiliated to a specific worldview and, in some cases, a wider non-Muslim readership. It may be a natural phenomenon for a net-literate generation to seek out specific truths and affiliations online, especially when they cannot be accessed in a local mosque or community context.

WHAT MAKES THE INTERNET ISLAMIC?

According to contemporary Muslim scholars, especially those who are proactively engaged with Internet technologies, there is no incompatibility between Islam as a religion and its representation on the Internet (Castells, 1997, p. 25). That vision is dependent on the purpose and intent for which the medium is applied.

The Prophet Muhammad is said to have urged his followers to 'seek knowledge even as far as China' (Haddad, 2005, p. 1). Many Muslim scholars argue that the Internet can be used as an extension of that quest (Haddad, 2005). Nevertheless, it has to be noted that access to the Internet, while improving for many Muslims, is still relatively low. There has been resistance to aspects of the Internet from some Muslim quarters. This has been tempered by pragmatism, given that there is an educated generation that has grown up fully conversant with the application of computer interfaces as part of leisure, education, business, and now religious expression and understanding (Castells, 1997, p. 26).

INDONESIAN CASE STUDY BACKGROUND

In Indonesia most traditional Islamic schools, or *pesantren*, teach the secular national curriculum alongside classes on religion. But some of the poorest and most conservative of these schools lack the means and resources to to teach the state curriculum. The International Centre started an initiative, known as the Open, Distance and eLearning (ODeL) program in 2007 for Islam and Pluralism (ICIP) and the Ford Foundation with the aim of bringing general education to *pesantren*

students via the Internet. The project was intended to facilitate the transformation of *pesantren* into becoming more modern, open, communities.

The project started with a needs assessment study in the community regarding alternative education and their online readiness. After undertaking a couple of workshops, the installation of the technology for the program began. ICIP provided support of the smooth running of the ODeL program by providing 15 desktop computers, 1 server, 5 CPUs, I LCD, 1 printer, 1 scanner, 1 DVD RW, a set of CD programs and a set of study DVDs. The primary activity of OdeL is to promote the use of Information and Communications Technology (ICT) as a primary medium of instructions for teachers and students in *pesantren*. Besides this, another activity in this program is the provision of equivalent ICT education for *santri* who have not taken part in conventional education and people surrounding the *pesantren* through the equivalent education Packets B and C programs. For *santri* and others who have already had formal education, ICT in the form of the Internet is used to obtain as broad access as possible for their needs and empowerment, so that they can be agents for change for the advancement of their respective regions.

For this study, a total of ten one-on-one interviews at ICIP in Indonesia were conducted over a 12-month period. The qualitative approach was applied through a selected case study of particular Indonesian institutions. Data were collected using focus group interviews and observation of selected teachers from Indonesia.

Stories from Teachers at ICIP

Experiences from Sanwar

One of Indonesia's leading progressive Islamic NGO is ICIP, led by 'Sanwar'. Sanwar has a long history of activism and leadership in Islamic society and in civil society. In his career he has been senior editor of some of Indonesia's leading Islamic magazines and publications such as the magazine Ummat. His PhD thesis from the University of Melbourne examined the nature of politics and Islamic activism surrounding Suharto's final decade in office, and his attempt to manufacture a support base from the conservative Islamic leaders that he had previously opposed and alienated. After completing his doctoral studies in Melbourne, Sanwar established ICIP driven by a concern that extremist teaching and energetic activism threatened to tip the balance in Indonesian society and establish greater acceptance of extremist Islamist ideas. Like many in his position, Sanwar remains optimistic that tolerant and inclusive Islamic thought and practice will continue to prevail in Indonesia, but argues that this will only be the case if moderate and progressive elements become active in promoting a counter-narrative to the extremist one that increasingly prevails, particularly on university campuses and amongst the young people. Sanwar explained that: "Many years ago I thought that new opinions could be learnt or accessed through travelling long distances to be with scholars and experts. Now I can access many of them from my mobile phones, desktop computers. I can also share and exchange ideas from colleagues and expert globally." Sanwar recognized that "surfers increasingly access the "Islamic libraries and information resources of the world and make up their minds on issues" (Bunt, 2000, p134).

In 2008, ICIP launched a new project targeting conservative *pesantren*. Sanwar has a background in Islamic activism and publishing and enjoys has a strong reputation with Muslim leaders across the spectrum. Because of this, he was able to gain the trust of some of the more conservative elements of the *pesantren* community to engage in his new e- *pesantren* project.

This new program marks a more concentrated effort in tackling the issue of education in Indonesia. Through the website, www. *pesantren* global.org, students can register themselves, and then access educational materials such as text-book exercises and online tests free of charge. This provides the students with the government's standardised Packet A (7–12 years old), Packet B (13-15 years old) and Packet C (16–18 years old) curricula, as well as skill and citizenship-based learning programs. This site would then be administered by eight different *pesantren* participating in the program.

The previous *pesantren*s were chosen precisely because they were linked to communities with low levels of education, high levels of poverty, and a low rank on the Human Development Index. This program is intended to increase the number of high school graduates who not only possess the skills needed by their communities, but who can also go on to university. This new eLearning program can be seen as the result of government efforts since 1997 to promote distance learning programs.

Students use computers to access equivalent education Packet C materials from the Internet and materials provided by their teachers (Figure 1). Upon completion of the eLearning program, the *pesantren*s provide the students with a certificate.

One student commented:

This gives us the freedom of expression as individuals and enables us to engage with other internet communities. This also helps me be aware of what's out there and learn to share and get more knowledge. Books and printed materials are very limited and some are very old and cannot be read. But with access to the internet, I can get a lot of materials to learn and teach my friends, families and communities.

Following the 9/11 attacks in the USA and the Bali Bombings of October 2002 in Indonesia, much has been said and written about *pesantren* and madrasah. They were given a variety of labels, from 'schools of terror' to 'jihad factories' (Noor, 2007, p. 2). In the wake of these attacks, an attempt was made to modernise the *pesantren* and madrasah,

Figure 1. Students accessing computers at the library

especially in Pakistan, through US monetary aid. Many have talked about the importance of education in creating a more tolerant, plural, moderate, and forward-looking community, and while that is essential, it is only half of the equation. The other, equally important half, in such an endeavour, is the involvement of social networks and life experiences. Sanwar acknowledges, "that technology alone is insufficient, and there is a real need and issue of educating the students at the *pesantren*s on the medium and use of the Internet, to ensure that they have broad knowledge and experience." The presence of the Internet at the *pesantren* has improved and enhanced literacy developments. He has observed that there has been an improvement in students' learning and increase interest in learning and finding out more things from their online learning the students at the *pesantren*s about Muslim cyberspace and communities globally. The *pesantren* students grouped together and share a computer.

The e-*pesantren* project developed by ICIP is very much the visionary work of one individual: ICIP founder and director, Sanwar. Sanwar has a long association with Islamic thought and education in Indonesia. He worked for several decades as a journalist and as an editor of publications written for pious urban readerships. For example, throughout the 1990s, he was editor of Ummat magazine. Ummat magazine was aimed at a readership of urban professionals who had come from a non-practicing, or non-*santri*, background but had become observant, or *santri* Muslims in recent years.

Before that, he had worked for Republika newspaper, which was aimed particularly at modernist urban Muslims. Republika was closely associated with the Indonesian Association of Muslim Intellectuals, or ICMI, which had been led by Suharto's protégé, BJ Habibie, since its formation in 1990 until Suharto's resignation in May 1998 following the economic crisis of the previous year and serious social unrest. The formation of ICMI and the associated politics were the subject of Sanwar's PhD thesis at an Australian university.

Throughout his career, he had become increasingly concerned about sectarianism in Indonesian society and politics. Sanwar's PhD thesis is sharply critical of Suharto's manipulation of radical Islamist sentiment in an attempt to buy political support. Sanwar is a determined and hard-working individual, and sold his family home to move his wife and family to Melbourne whilst he was completing his doctoral dissertation. After he completed his PhD in Melbourne, he returned to Indonesia. It is a mark of his idealism that when he returned to Jakarta, he channeled his energy into establishing ICIP in order for him to put into practice the theoretical observations of his doctorate.

Owing to his long association with Islamic publishing, Sanwar has excellent connections across Indonesia's diverse Muslim communities. Although his own background lies with Islamic modernism and the mass-based organisation Muhammadiyah, Sanwar was also close to the many progressive Islamic thinkers associated with the traditionalist organisation Nahdlatul Ulama (NU) and, in particular, with the charismatic NU leader and former Indonesian President, Abdurrahman Wahid (Barton 1996, 1997). This background is significant because when Sanwar decided to engage with grassroots Muslim communities via the traditional schools known in Java as *pesantren*, but elsewhere referred to as madrasah, he needed to draw the support of the largely rural traditionalist communities that are most closely associated with *pesantren*.

Sanwar chose to work with the *pesantren* because he recognised that these institutions formed a natural cultural bridge between rural village life and, via modern education, the prospects of white-collar work in the cities. Moreover, whilst most of his colleagues were associated with activism in support of progressive Islamic thought aimed at countering Islamist extremism, Sanwar worked primarily in the large cities of Indonesia such as the national capital, Jakarta. Sanwar recognised that for his work to be effective, he needed to tap into grassroots networks, and the most effective way of doing this was to engage the *pesantren*. He was also convinced that working with the *pesantren* was strategic because he recognised that ideas and the formation of thought through education was key to social transformation within the highest Muslim communities in Indonesia.

Sanwar decided that there was an opportunity to give value to traditional *pesantren* (Figure 2) by introducing them to distance and eLearning to help them access curriculum material and social networks that would otherwise be outside their reach. At the same time, he also recognized that the social connectivity that came from helping these *pesantren* go online would be transformative for students and teachers alike.

At the beginning of the project, ICIP lacked financial resources and had poor infrastructure. Komisi (similar to ABA licensing station—regulatory) became involved in the setting up of a new body to regulate the learning management content materials. This was a 'top-down approach' by management, which was necessary as staff at ICIP were very used to the traditional ways of teaching. That is, face-to-face teaching and a one-to-many approach was an 'old habit'. The students were also very traditional, showing respect to staff.

Curricula, RoteLearning, and eLearning

Pesantren in Indonesia are generally thought of as being the equivalent of madrasah elsewhere in the Muslim world. They are primarily concerned with imparting religious learning and specific skills, such as the ability to read the Koran in its original Arabic. In fact, *pesantren* in Indonesia are generally more advanced than is generally the case for madrasah in Muslim majority societies.

Under the leadership of progressive thinkers such as Abdurrahman Wahid and more senior scholars in earlier decades, Wahid's father and both of his grandfathers, were co-founders of NU and, thus, were serious *pesantren* pioneers in their own right. They introduced education to female students and also the teaching of European languages (Figure 3). The *pesantren* had been steadily modernising, in both the way they went about teaching and learning and the nature of the curriculum material they taught.

Beginning in the 1970s, traditionalist *pesantren* began to incorporate teaching of the national secular curriculum and established secular day schools within their communal boarding school walls, which were known as *madrasah aliah*. The madrasah aliah curriculum ran parallel to the *pesantren* religious studies programs that were known as the *madrasah diniyah*. The idea was that the students would study in the secular school in the morning and early afternoon and, in the late afternoon and evening, would study religious subjects in the traditional religious school program of the madrasah diniyah. The students were rewarded for doing this by being able to receive Indonesian government funding for attending the *madrasah aliah*. There continue, however, to be some *pesantren* that refuse all government funding and focus entirely upon delivering a religious education, but the vast majority of *pesantren* contain a *madrasah aliah* program. This has been a very important development for Indonesia because the *pesantren* constitute a significant pro-

Figure 2. Traditional pesantren classroom

Figure 3. Female students learning of European languages

portion of all the schools in this poor archipelago nation.

As mentioned before, it is estimated there are around 20,000 *pesantren* in Indonesia today that educate around 20 per cent of Indonesia's primary school students. The state curriculum in Indonesia is divided into three stages associated with three different levels of schooling: primary schools, junior high schools, and senior high schools. The curricula associated with these three stages are known in Indonesia as Packet A, Packet B, and Packet C.

Associations between social capital and education have been investigated in the contexts of vocational and educational training (VET) (Kilpatrick, 2003), early childhood education (Farrell, Tayler & Tennent, 2004), and non-formal education (Shrestha, Wilson & Singh, 2008).

Sanwar and his staff were confronted with overcoming the traditional rote learning method of teaching and learning in order to implement eLearning. Sanwar had noted that older students tended to be more resistant to changes in learning styles. The younger the group the more open they were, "maybe this is a generation thing".

Sanwar confided that one way of improving the attitude to eLearning is to recruit younger staff as they were easier to motivate and could adapt to eLearning. He continually found that older and non-IT background staff felt embarrassed when asked to attend basic computer courses and became confused when too much information was provided to them.

In the eight- *pesantren* chosen by ICIP for the ODEL *pesantren* program, a common characteristic was the low socio-economic status of the communities they served and the limited capacity of the *pesantren* as a result. The eight *pesantren* had previously taught Packet A, or primary school material, and attempted to teach Packet B or junior high school. However, they struggled with Packet B of the material, and most of them were not able to teach at Packet C junior high school level. One of the practical contributions made by the ODEL *pesantren* project was that, via the Internet and other digital means including DVD material, *pesantren* were provided with comprehensive teaching and learning material at Packet B and Packet C levels.

Organic Rice Farming

Teachers and students alike within the *pesantren* communities have positively received the very practical and helpful contribution made by the ODEL *pesantren* program to formal education. Nevertheless, the impact of the *pesantren* program is not limited to four more curricula matters. Over the several years that the *pesantren* program has been running, a number of very interesting phenomena have been observed that have arisen spontaneously as a result of the social connectivity and access to knowledge that has been produced by bringing the *pesantren* online.

For example, in one of the *pesantren* communities in Java, Sanwar reports that the *pesantren* has been able to increase its revenue significantly by switching from the cultivation of regular rice crops to organic rice farming. Generally, students at *pesantren* pay little or no fees and instead rely upon contributions in kind by families and communities associated with the *pesantren*. The *pesantren* also produces basic products for their own consumption and for sale within what is, effectively, a co-operative farming community immediately associated with the *pesantren*. Typically, *pesantren* grow their own rice crops and run a small number of animal flocks as well as raising ducks and chickens. In the case of this *pesantren*, Sanwar was pleased to discover the leader of the *pesantren* talking enthusiastically about their new project in organic rice farming. When he asked where the idea came from and how they managed to start it, the teacher explained that they had learnt about organic rice farming from material they found on the Internet and had discovered, by their own initiative, that there was more than sufficient material to guide them through the process of converting their own rice fields to organic rice farming.

Online teaching and learning took off with distance learning in Indonesia and then moved onto online learning. Sanwar said that staff and students are keen to use the Internet for online teaching, and are particularly keen to implement the use of the material they learnt from the Internet such as, for example, organic rice farming. Initially, he set up web pages used for teaching and the delivery of course materials and found them to be an effective and efficient method of course delivery. He began to teach his other colleagues in

Indonesia from what he had learnt from his time in Australia when he studied his PhD.

Social Connectivity

Sanwar documented another incident that illustrated the social connectivity of this kind of spontaneous autonomous learning that had occurred as a product of bringing the Internet to the *pesantren* in Cianjur. It was a particularly socially conservative *pesantren*, more so than many of the others associated with the project, and like most economically poor *pesantren*, tended towards social conservatism. In this *pesantren*, the teacher instructed his female students that they should not only veil their heads but they should also cover their faces with a second veil known as the *nikab*. Thus, Sanwar was rather surprised when he met with female students from this *pesantren* at a workshop in Jakarta in which he had invited them to participate, and found them to be veiled in the traditional fashion without their faces covered. When he politely inquired of them why they had changed the usual practice, they explained that in their own research online, they had come across the instructions and teaching of the *grand mufti* of Cairo, a relatively progressive figure but still very much respected within conservative traditionalist societies around the world, on the topic of veils.

In the material that they discovered online, the *mufti* explained from classical Islamic texts that it was not necessary for women to veil their faces and that merely covering their hair was sufficient to comply with the Koran's commandment for modesty in dress (Figure 4). The girls were so impressed by the logic and scholarship of this argument that they decided amongst themselves that it was correct. Nevertheless, they explained with a laugh to Sanwar, that when they returned to their *pesantren* they would continue to wear their veils across the lower face as was expected of them by their teachers, but that they knew privately now that their teachers' position on this matter was incorrect.

Figure 4. Santri girls browse the Internet for their study

Sanwar gave many other similar examples of unexpected insights obtained through autonomous eLearning made possible by having an Internet connection and computer access in poor schools. Realising the important role *santri* have to play in the economy, the *pesantren* provides *santri* with life skills through online learning by searching and browsing for learning resources, which are focused on agribusiness such as farming, fishery and animal husbandry. These new learning initiatives are managed by *santri* as a part of their skills learning. Sanwar hopes that when the *santri* return to society, they will not only practice the religious knowledge they have obtained, but also be creative with the skills and expertise they have acquire through open, distance and eLearning through the *pesantren*.

Both students and teachers are being transformed by the social online social media connections they formed with other *pesantren* communities and with communities across the Muslim world, and by the learning material they find readily provided online. At one *pesantren*, Sanwar experienced a semi-serious rebuke from the wife of the senior teacher who explained to him that she had now lost her husband's attention in the evening between sunset and late-night prayers because he was constantly online. When

asked about this, and why it was that he spent so much time online, the teacher excitedly explained that he was encountering enormous amounts of useful teaching material that could be correctly applied at his *pesantren*, and that he had never before had access to such richness and was excited to continue exploring and to collect material of value to his community.

Through ODeL program, the *pesantren*s have been able to start Packets B and C programs complete with Internet (Figure 5), blended learning and computer skills. There are 253 students participated in the equivalent education Packet B program, 407 people in the Packet C program and there are 1650 computer users. The Packet C program, 80% of which are still of school age (17-20 years old).

The Packet C program has become an alternative source of formal education for the large number of students who dropped out from school due to financial difficulties. Many of these students ended up studying in *pesantren*s and could access Packet C program through the Open Distance eLearning program. There are new online activities of the equivalent education program, which include films, podcasts and online forums with the local communities. The films displayed are part of their educational and encourage students

Figure 5. Packet C students showing great enthusiasm in their studies

to strive for change towards a better world. The students then self reflect on what they have watched and applied to their educational programs.

DISCUSSION AND ANALYSIS

This chapter builds upon the different themes derived from the research and discusses the narratives from each of the themes. As mentioned earlier in this chapter, data from the case study are presented first in the form of vignettes and, then later, in the form of aggregated assessments of key variables relating to attitudes and approaches to social capital, leadership, entrepreneurialism, attitude and behaviour, and teaching.

There is reason to believe these findings are not just generally applicable to the stories in the case study in question, but also reflects on broader national tendencies. In Indonesia, the value of innovation and striking out in new directions is highly regarded because the need is great and the rewards can also be great when pioneering innovation pays off.

The sort of extreme isolation and poverty observed in the *pesantren*, in this case, would be relatively unknown in many parts of South East Asia. Consequently, the necessity to reach out and engage these communities is much stronger in Indonesia. For these reasons, in general terms, eLearning can deliver even greater rewards in Indonesia.

There is lesser emphasis on specific cultural communities when it comes to leadership in the division case study where cultural brokering (Geertz, 1960) is regarded as very important. Perhaps this is because, in the Indonesian context, serious cultural brokering is required when going from urban to rural communities even in their commonalities of language and religion.

Top-down leadership in the division case study was regarded as desirable, but not as being very important. However, directive leadership, the sort of leadership found in the teacher context that is

sometimes associated with herding cats, and reciprocal trust-based leadership, are both regarded as very important. Leadership by example, in Indonesian stories, is regarded as essential.

However, entrepreneurialism and a particularly can-do mindset were essential in these Indonesian stories. In the same manner, visionary or strategic thinking entrepreneurialism was regarded as very important in Indonesia, as was having a creative mindset. Even more strikingly, an active approach to globalisation was regarded as essential in the context of this Indonesian case study. The use of Web 2.0 technologies (Figure 6) has contributed to the student learning experience and teachers are enhancing their teaching practices as a result of the use of different Web 2.0 tools. One teacher explained that she finds that the use of the technologies has empower her in her engagement with her students, "Using of YouTube, chat, facebook is very interactive and gives a whole new way and meaning to community learning."

Attitudes and practice relating to teaching in Indonesia are regarded as very important. Thus, teaching by example, teaching as learning, and teaching from life experience are all regarded as essential in this Indonesian case study.

Broadly speaking, the uptake of the Internet in the education sector especially in the *pesantren*

Figure 6. The use of Web 2.0 technologies: A computer class at the pesantren

community is driven by the demand to access information and participate in social networks and collaborative learning (Figure 7).

This is seen, in particular, in the ICIP program, where the power of the technology to facilitate change is most important, and not technology for technology's sake. To understand what is happening with the use of the Internet in traditional Islamic learning, one needs to understand the social context and cultural factors to appreciate why Internet usage is so attractive. The appeal of the uptake of e- *pesantren* lies in the connectivity provided by the technology and the access to knowledge that otherwise may not be readily accessible. This chapter discusses the social and cultural influences on the uptake of e- *pesantren* in Indonesia.

The primary finding of this case study is that progressive individuals, working within a system that remains largely conservative but is nevertheless more adaptable than often thought, chose to engage various kinds of eLearning technologies primarily because of the capacity of those technologies to facilitate learning in all of its forms. In other words, these key pioneers were motivated not so much by a deep interest in

Figure 7. Collaborative online learning at the pesantren

the technology, or even a deep understanding of its elements, but primarily by a desire to do all they could to encourage transformative learning experiences and environments. They used eLearning technologies because they could be introduced more quickly, efficiently, and economically than other alternatives.

The diagram (Figure 8) seeks to summarise the key elements that emerged in the case study discussions.

Figure 8. Key elements arising from the interview discussions

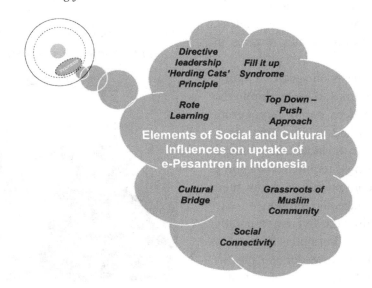

REFERENCES

Australian Government AusAid (2007). *Australian agency for international development: Indonesia education program strategy 2007ystem.*

Azra, A., Afrianty, D., & Hefner, R. (2007). *Pesantren* and madrasa: Muslim schools and national ideals in Indonesia. In Hefner, R., & Zaman, M. Q. (Eds.), *Schooling Islam: The culture and politics of modern Muslim education* (pp. 172–199). Princeton, NJ: Princeton University Press.

Barton, G. (1996). The liberal, progressive roots of Abdurrahman Wahid's thought. In Barton, G., & Fealy, G. (Eds.), *Nadhlatul Ulama, traditional Islam and modernity in Indonesia* (pp. 190–226). Clayton, Australia: Monash Asia Institute.

Barton, G. (1997). Indonesia's Nurcholish Madjid and Abdurrahman Wahid as intellectual Ulama: The meeting of Islamic traditionalism and modernism in neo-modernist thought. *Islam and Christian-Muslim Relations, 83,* 323

Belawati, T. (2007). Open and distance education in the Asia Pacific region: Indonesia. In Shive, G., Jegebe, O., Haynes, P., & Smith, J. L. (Eds.), *Online learning and teaching in higher education: Indonesia* (pp. 171–188). Hong Kong: Open University of Hong Kong.

Boulos, M., Maramba, I., & Wheeler, S. (2006). Wikis, blogs and podcasts: A new generation of web-based tools for virtual collaborative clinical practice and education. *BMC Medical Education, 6*(41). Retrieved from http://www.biomedcentral.com/1472-6920/6/41

Bunt, G. (2000). *Virtually Islamic: Computer mediated communication and cyber Islamic environments.* Cardiff, UK: University of Wales Press.

Bunt, G. (2003). *Islam in the digital age: E-jihad, online fatwas and cyber Islamic environments.* London, UK: Pluto Press.

Bunt, G. (2009). *iMuslims: Rewiring the house of Islam.* Chapel Hall, NC: University of North Carolina Press.

Castells, M. (1996). *The rise of the network society.* Cambridge, MA: Blackwell Publishers.

Central Intelligence Agency. (2010). World fact book: Australia. Retrieved from https://www.cia.gov/library/publications/the-world-factbook/geos/as.html

Cooke, M., & Lawrence, B. B. (Eds.). (2005). *Muslim networks from Hajj to hip hop.* Chapel Hill, NC: University of North Carolina Press.

Farrell, G. (Ed.). (2001). *The changing face of virtual education.* Vancouver, Canada: Commonwealth of Learning.

Geertz, C. (1960). The Javanese Kijaji: The changing role of a cultural broker. *Comparative Studies in Society and History, 2*(2), 228–249. doi:10.1017/S0010417500000670

Geertz, C. (1988). *Works and lives: The anthropologist as author.* Cambridge, UK: Polity Press.

Haddad, S. G. F. (2005). Seek knowledge as far as china. *Living Islam: Islamic Tradition.* Retrieved August 8, 2012, from http://www.livingislam.org/n/skx_e.html

Hidayatullah, S., & Dharmawan, Z. (2003). *Islam virtual: Keberadaan Dunia Islam di Internet.* Ciputat, Indonesia: Penerbit Mifta.

Indonesian Telematics Coordinating Team. (2001). *Five-year action plan for the development and implementation of information and communication technologies (ICT) in Indonesia.*

Jabali, F., & Jamhari. (Eds.). (2003). *The modernization of Islam in Indonesia: an Impact Study on the Cooperation between the IAIN and McGill University.* Jakarta, Indonesia: Indonesia-Canada Islamic Higher Education Project.

Noor, F. A. (2007). *Ngruki revisited: Modernity and its discontents at the pondok pesantren al-Mukmin of Ngruki. Surakarta, S.* Singapore: Rajaratnam School of International Studies.

Pohl, F. (2007). Islamic education and civil society: Reflections on the *pesantren* tradition in contemporary Indonesia. In Kadi, W., & Billeh, V. (Eds.), *Islam and education: Myths and truths.* Chicago, IL: University of Chicago Press.

Shrestha, M., Wilson, S., & Singh, M. (2008). Knowledge networking: A dilemma in building social capital through non formal education, *Adult Education Quarterly, 58*(2), 129 58.

Veletsianos, G. (Ed.). (2010). *A definition for emerging technologies in education, emerging technologies in distance education.* Athabasca University Press.

Wagner, E. (2005). Enabling mobile learning. *EDUCAUSE Review, 40*(3), 40–53.

Waluyo, H. (2006). *General ICT overview: Data and information centre.* Ministry of Culture and Tourism, Republic of Indonesia.

Chapter 6
Rethinking Web 2.0 Learning via Third Space

Kathy Jordan
RMIT University, Australia

Jennifer Elsden-Clifton
RMIT University, Australia

ABSTRACT

Web 2.0 technologies are frequently represented as collaborative and interactive tools, and these capacities are particularly attractive to education. This chapter analyses how 26 beginning teachers in Victoria, Australia, used Elluminate Live!® (Elluminate) to support their professional learning. Drawing on Third Space theory and a case study approach, this chapter explores issues around change and emerging technologies. In particular, how beginning teachers appropriate features of this tool to engage in both receptive and collaborative learning spaces, ultimately transforming their professional learning space. It raises numerous issues and challenges for eLearning in the Web 2.0 environment.

INTRODUCTION

If ICT is to be successfully and effectively used for educational purposes ... it is essential that the myth of omnipotent teaching and learning technologies is challenged by those within the educational community and ICT's are (re) constructed and (re) contextualised along more appropriate and realistic lines (Selwyn, 2002, p. 179).

The educator who endeavors to rattle complacent cages, undoubtedly faces the treacherous ghosts of the other's fears and terrors, which in turn evoke one's own demons (Boler, 1999, p. 175).

The development of Web 2.0 technologies has been greeted with considerable interest by educators (Waycott & Sheard, 2011). These 'social technologies', encompassing a range of applications

DOI: 10.4018/978-1-4666-3649-1.ch006

such as blogs and wikis (Hanewald & White 2008; Terrell, Richardson & Hamilton, 2011), are seen as highly desirable as they have features designed to enable users to create content, share information and collaborate (Waycott & Sheard, 2011).

This enthusiasm for new technologies, what Selwyn (2002) refers to as a "technological evangelism" (p. 8), is common to education technology research. In early research, claims of 'possibilities' and 'potential' often associated with learning were made (Bigum, 2008; Groff & Mouza, 2011; Zhao, Pugh, Sheldon & Byers, 2002) as justification for their introduction of technologies. As Lankshear, Snyder and Green (2000) describe, "the history of the new information and communication technologies in Australian schools has been characterized by large quantities of faith, with returns that at best are difficult to identify"(p. 37). Technocentric views were commonly evidenced, in which the technology was focused on and the context downplayed or ignored (Harris, 2005). Often this introduction was underpinned by binaristic thinking, in which the new technology was pitted against the old (Lankshear, et al, 2000; Snyder, 1993). For example: the new was seen as superior to the old; the new seen as providing solutions to perceived problems with the old (Zhao & Rop 2001) and therefore needing to replace it. There was little consideration that both the old and the new could co-exist.

Alongside techno-centric approaches, there was generally little acknowledgement that teacher adoption is complex, and that changing practice takes time, is gradual and differs from individual to individual (Hall, 2010). Change models, such as Roger's (2003) theory of Diffusion of Innovations, were commonly used by education departments and government to guide teacher professional learning (Lloyd, 2008; Wilson & Stacey, 2003). A difficulty with these models is that they assume teachers can change their practice by moving along a predetermined set path (Orlando, 2009). The reality in education contexts is somewhat different (Zhao, Pugh, Sheldon & Byers, 2002).

Research suggests that teachers are relatively slow to take on change (Brown & Warschauer, 2006) and purposively select technologies based upon whether they 'value add' to their current practice, rather than transform it (Becker, 1999; Tyack & Cuban, 2000).

More recently, numerous researchers have advocated a new research agenda (Harris, 2005; Selwyn, 2002), one which offers alternate narratives about the introduction of new technologies, and one which takes into consideration some of the complexities in both how and why technologies can be used in educational contexts. This chapter in part responds to this call. It aims: to examine how beginning teachers used Elluminate for professional learning; to explore their decisions and choices regarding features in this technology; to consider the possibilities, risks and benefits for learning and more specifically educational contexts. To do so, we draw upon Third Space theory to consider alternative conceptualizations of uptake and use, in particular, to explore how learners, bridge, navigate and/or transform learning in Web 2.0 environments.

BACKGROUND

Recently, educational technological research has suggested that technological tools, with features that enable interaction and collaboration, could be valuable in supporting professional learning, in particular for beginning teachers (Schuck, 2003). For some time now, researchers here in Australia and overseas have agreed that beginning teachers face difficulties when they enter the profession, as well as the sometime related issue of high rates of attrition (Darling-Hammond, 1990; De Wert, Babinski & Jones, 2003; Maxwell, Harrington & Smith, 2010; Schuck, 2003). Herrington, Herrington Kervin & Ferry (2006) suggest that in Australia around a quarter of beginning teachers leave within five years, and that in the United States, this figure is higher, with around a third leaving within their first five years of teaching. Many countries including Australia have induction programs (Schuck, 2003) or mentoring programs that aim to provide a supportive environment for beginning teachers. Research tends to suggest however that despite good intentions, many of these programs are limited in their effectiveness (Schuck, 2003). There is consensus, here and elsewhere that more needs to be done to support beginning teachers.

As part of its efforts to support beginning teachers (those in their first year of teaching) the Victorian Department of Education and Early Childhood Development (DEECD) introduced the Supporting New Teachers Practice (SNTP) program in 2010. A three year program costing over $1 million, it aims to capitalize on perceived benefits of face-to-face professional learning and teacher networks by using a blended learning design. The program begins with a two day face-to-face program, and is then followed by an extended online program of around 6 months. The face-to-face component aims to provide beginning teachers with opportunities to share their first year experiences as well as discuss some challenges to their practice. The online component essentially has two functions, to provide them with further knowledge about issues affecting their practice and to provide a space for them as a community to share experiences and develop shared practice (Wenger, 1998). Online coaches who were experienced teachers were assigned to support groups of beginning teachers when online.

Several Web 2.0 technologies are used to achieve these aims including Elluminate (version 9.7, now known as Blackboard Collaborate). Elluminate is a relatively new Web 2.0 technology, which enables participants to talk over the internet with full audio, and text chat, and as well to share video, whiteboards, multimedia files and other applications within a web browser interface. Thus the program can enable many participants to interact with the instructor and with one another through multimodal ways. Users subscribe to an Elluminate session thereby enabling professional learning to occur in a secure space. In choosing to use Elluminate, program developers were mindful that merely putting the technology into place would not automatically result in the intended outcomes and therefore, paid particular attention to pedagogical considerations (see Appendix A for examples and further explanation).

Research around Elluminate is not extensive, and as has often happened in the past, tends to focus on case studies and participant perceptions of the technology. Fuller (2009) used Elluminate to enhance the teaching and learning experience of Bachelor of Business students while Murphy and Ciszewska-Carr (2007) reported on instructors' perceptions of using this technology. In this chapter, we extend this research by exploring the potential benefits and challenges offered by Elluminate in a professional learning program.

RESEARCH METHODOLOGY

This chapter focuses on one Elluminate session which was delivered as part of the beginning teachers program. This session was purposively selected as our focus as we felt that it best enabled us to explore the concept of Third Space. In this session 26 beginning teachers, three online coaches (experienced teachers), two moderators and one instructor/facilitator (university lecturer) participated in this session (initials of the beginning teachers were used to maintain anonymity). Audio capacity was enabled, but confined to a selection of beginning teachers who had volunteered for this role, to enable ease in communication. The Elluminate session was recorded, resulting in three sources of data: the PowerPoint presentation which had been uploaded into the window by the instructor; the transcript of all audio from the instructor presentation and beginning teachers' questions and responses; and the chat transcript of what participants wrote. These three sources of data were then read and focal points for possible in-depth analysis were identified. Focal points were defined as particular episodes in the Elluminate session in which interaction involved multiple participants and multiple spaces. Here we choose to use the term interaction broadly as that involving a two way interaction between persons or content (Anderson, 2003).

Our approach to content analysis of the Elluminate session is somewhat atypical, as content analysis usually involves the coding of the whole transcript, using a particular classification scheme or taxonomy. Various schemes have been developed to do so including Henri's (1992) model used in other studies such as those by Hara, Bonk and Angeli (2000) and McKenzie and Murphy (2000), as well as other schemes by Gunawardena, Lowe and Anderson (1997), and Garrison, Anderson and Archer (2000). We were concerned that this conventional approach would not suit our purpose. As well we were mindful of issues around reliability and validity that have been well documented in the literature (Enriquez, 2009; Rourke, Anderson, Garrison & Archer, 2001). We decided to take Stacey and Gerbric's (2003) advice and adopt "a pragmatic but systematic approach" (p. 496) and select episodes as our message unit to be analysed to more effectively capture interaction in multiple spaces. We then selected three episodes for detailed analysis, those which we felt best illustrated Third Space characteristics of building bridges from one space to another, navigating across spaces, and transforming spaces.

This chapter isn't about proving that Elluminate offers a better way of learning or instruction, when compared to older ways, nor that particular features within it should be used to remedy shortcomings or problems in instruction. Rather we are more interested in 'opening up' conversations, around the complexity, messiness and possible discomfort involved when introducing new Web 2.0 technologies and draw upon third space to provide a way of recognizing the dynamic and maybe contradictorily spaces that Web 2.0 technologies may take us.

THIRD SPACE THEORY

Third Space theory is utilized by researchers to explore and understand the spaces 'in between' two or more discourses, conceptualizations or binaries (Bhabha, 1994). Soja (1996) explains this through a triad where Firstspace refers to the material spaces whereas Secondspace encompasses mental spaces (Danaher, Danaher, & Moriarty, 2003). Third space then, becomes a space where *"everything comes together"* (Soja, 1996, p. 56, original emphasis) by bringing together Firstspace and Secondspace, but also by extending beyond these spaces to intermesh the binaries that characterize the spaces.

For the purposes of this chapter, we associate conventional notions of face-to-face instruction with first space. Often the goal of face-to-face learning is the delivery of learning from one (the instructor) to many (the learners), where learning is instructional, where the role of the facilitator is as expert, and the role of the participant is as passive recipient of knowledge. The use of PowerPoint in Elluminate, which is essentially used to deliver content to beginning teachers, is therefore seen as synonymous with face-to-face learning and first space. We associate computer-mediated communication technologies with second space. By using synchronous and asynchronous communications technology the goal for learning is often one (learner) to many (other learners), where learning is collaborative, the role of the teacher is as facilitator, and the role of the learner is as active co-constructor of learning. The use of the synchronous chat window, as well as asynchronous functionality is characteristic of second space. In our conceptualisation, drawing on Third Space theory, first and second spaces coexist within Elluminate. However, even though Elluminate has characteristics of both, we also believe that it evokes a third which "gives rise to something different, something new and unrecognisable, a new area of negotiation, meaning and representation" (Bhabha 1992, p. 211).

We are drawn to third space as it emphasizes the complexities that arise with the introduction of Web 2.0 technologies and acknowledges the possible tensions and dilemmas associated with change or negotiating "unfamiliar terrain" (Skillet, 2010, p. 78). Indeed as Hulme, Cracknell and Owens (2009) highlights, the interweaving of binaries and boundary crossing should not imply an unproblematic joining or the "production of harmonious, uncontested relationship" (Hulme et al., 2009, p. 541). Thus, for our research Third Space theory enables us to draw attention to the ways in which Elluminate technology destabilizes and challenges our usual ways of learning, but to also examine the multiple possibilities and constraints which may lead to enriched learning experiences and/or unresolved discomfort tensions and dilemmas (Gutiérrez, 2008) - or as we would argue, elements of both.

In this chapter, the concept of Third Space has been adapted to refer to the possibility of imagining (and inhabiting) an alternative space. Within this theory there is the scope to apply to professional learning contexts and highlight how users/learners/participants can bridge and navigate competing spaces and challenge, reshape and/or transform spaces. But this theory also allows our research to examine the possible destabilizing nature of third spaces and the uncertainties, conflict and discomfort that may arise through the use of Elluminate in a professional learning program. Specifically we question: how did the Elluminate technology empower participants to make connections that bridge their own experiences or practices? How did the beginning teachers attempt to shape, control or transform the original intent of the presentation? How did the voice and text transactions lead to the production of new ways of talking, thinking and interacting? In what ways did beginning teachers interact with one another, and with the instructor, learner and content? What possibilities, constraints, uniqueness and tensions may arise in third spaces within learning environments?

THIRD SPACES WITHIN ELLUMINATE

Episode 1: Interaction in Elluminate

Within Elluminate there is scope to allow multiple levels of interaction. This can be seen in the first analysis point which occurs midway through the session (Table 1).

In this episode the instructor is connecting the research on feedback with beginning teachers' practice. The instructor uses a PowerPoint slide to present a research quote about the connection between feedback and classroom management. Then using the audio function, she poses a reflective question "who got your feedback today and who missed out on your feedback?" inviting an audio response from beginning teacher participants. Three beginning teachers explicitly reply with two commenting that they usually give feedback to the "louder kids". At the same time four beginning teachers use the chat tool to explicitly interact to both the instructor's question and to the other beginning teachers' audio responses. The instructor using audio then responds to the chat discussion by reinforcing the appropriateness of a particular beginning teacher's response. In this episode there is evidence of chat interaction between beginning teachers; chat discussion in response to presentation/content; instructor response to what was written in the chat; and beginning teachers audio interaction in response to instructor. These are important for our research into how third spaces may be created.

Episode 2: Who is the Expert?

The second analysis point occurs at the beginning of the session as the instructor explores what feedback is and some of the ineffective ways in which feedback is provided to students in schools (Table 2).

Table 1. Analysis point 1

Beginning teacher chat	PowerPoint presentation	Instructor audio
CF: I don't believe that feedback is given enough to the 'gifted' students to extend them. CN::) E SS: I agree CN. Thinking back to today's lesson that's exactly what I did- especially because they were slightly unsettled. CN: trial and error N EH: Haha CN. Did you think what I said was too harsh? CN: Its just the first thing we do Stacey, is pick up on those who are in our faces CN: Not at all E SS: agreed EH: That's okay, CN. Thanks for clearing that up:)	Research '… the quality of teacher-student relationships is the keystone for all other aspects of classroom management. In fact, our meta-analysis indicates that on average, teachers who had high-quality relationships with their students had 31 percent fewer discipline problems, rule violations, and related problems over a year's time than did teachers who did not have high-quality relationships with their students.' (Mazarno, 2003)	It is worthwhile just pausing for a minute and asking yourself just who got your feedback today and who missed out on your feedback today. If anyone's brave and wants to respond to one of those "who got your feedback today and who missed out on your feedback?", I'd be happy for you to put your hand up and have a go. CN: I know I'm really guilty of giving the feedback to the louder kids (in your face and doing that obvious stuff) compared to the quieter kids who are quietly doing their work. KR: That's pretty much what I was going to say as well. It's always the loud kids that get your attention, so you go to them first. . . NB: I've spent a long time during the last break writing up feedback for all my year 10s and linking it altogether and today was the day I sat down to provide that back to them. . . CN made a really interesting comment on the chat that often not enough feedback is given to the gifted students to extend them.

Table 2. Analysis point 2

Beginning teacher chat	PowerPoint slide	Instructor audio
VK: a tick is really just saying "yes, I have opened your book to this page..." DS: i think it would be a great idea CN: we do that in many of our classes at school, but all day NL: tick or tape? CN: tape NM: wow NL: Cool EH: the taping idea is good EH: I'd be scared of what i might see though haha JM: Love the taping idea NB: What if it's a maths problem? What can we find that is original or unique about 2x2=4? CN: I suppose commenting on their working out?? VK: well with maths it's more important to give feedback based on their misconceptions and what they have gotten incorrect. CF: how they go there	Research Emptiness of a tick	My interest in feedback came from some research I was doing. . . . What came back from students is they like some of that individualism, they like that they can actually understand you've read their work and know them, know their work and given feedback based on that. I learnt to find something unique or original about their work if I was going to give a tick. But there were a lot of things that my peers tried to make feedback more effective. . . such as devising oral feedback and taping it so they could revisit the feedback that we'd given them orally.

At this time, the instructor activates a PowerPoint slide with the phrase 'emptiness of a tick' to convey a key argument that the use of ticks have little value. Using the audio function, the instructor draws on her own experience from interviewing and surveying learners and outlines a number of strategies that were tried. At the same time in the chat window, some nine beginning teachers interact with the content presented. VC engages explicitly with the focus being explored by the instructor and on the PowerPoint slide, and comments that "a tick is really just saying 'yes' I have opened your book to this page". Other beginning teachers continue this line of conversation, until NL poses the question 'tick or tape', which turns the conversation specifically onto taping as a means of providing feedback. The instructor then talks about giving specific and original feedback to students, with several beginning teachers supporting this idea, until NB, a maths teacher, questions whether this strategy is appropriate in all discipline areas, posting, "What can we find that is original or unique about 2X2=4?" Other beginning teachers join in this conversation and provide advice about how this might be achieved, and peer feedback is given including this comment that, "well with maths it's more important to give feedback based on their misconceptions and what they have gotten incorrect"(VK).

This second episode demonstrates how beginning teachers are able to navigate in online spaces, enabling them to share their own ideas and experiences, ultimately taking control of this space, if for a while.

Episode 3: Who Controls Space?

This third episode occurs towards the beginning of the session (Table 3).

The instructor uploads a PowerPoint screen with a model of different types of feedback. As part of discussion of this model, the instructor draws attention to how goal setting can be an important part of feedback and operates at four different levels. The instructor then illustrates this point by linking back to an earlier example, and then moves on to another point. The beginning teachers respond specifically to a small part of what the instructor has just said and turn discussion explicitly onto goal setting. Some forty interactions then result involving 14 beginning teachers, over half of the 26 participants in the session. This third episode highlights how these beginning teachers use chat to respond to both the instructor and other beginning teachers.

DISCUSSION

The first episode exemplifies a four minute episode within Elluminate when many of the functions are activated. It suggests that interaction in Elluminate, when text, whiteboard and audio tools are used, can occur in multiple spaces which interweave, intersect and rebound off each other. Initially, the instructor's behaviour as she delivers content is typical of what we associate with face-to-face instruction or first space. However, beginning teachers were then able to use the complexity designed in the Elluminate software to chat (second space) about their responses with other people and post their thinking and reflection which may or may not be encouraged in face-to-face environments. The audio response by beginning teachers to her question can be seen as typical of the spontaneous interaction which occur in synchronous environments, or second spaces. Thus, these interactions suggest that beginning teachers are coexisting within first and second spaces.

In the second episode, Elluminate is used as a navigational space or bridge in which beginning teachers are able to cross over or disrupt the boundaries around the expert/novice binary. For example, conventional lectures or first spaces are based on the notion of control of content by the instructor and limited interaction with participants. However, in this episode the participants both challenge the instructor and provide peer feedback rather than waiting for the 'expert' response or clarification. The initial interactions of the instructor are representative of this notion of first space, a formal space controlled by the instructor. The later interactions between the beginning teachers demonstrate third space interactions, ones in which the beginning teachers work together, question each other, and share ideas without the traditional instructor correction. Ultimately these beginning teachers take ownership of the interaction as they engage in high level reflection, bringing in their own context and concerns, and challenging what counts as important. It suggests that when in this third space beginning teachers can challenge and reshape what counts as knowledge. It also suggests that traditional notions of power between the instructor and participants can be shifted.

Within the third episode, participants are able to navigate both the first space and second space, introducing a third, one which they control and shape to suit their learning interests and needs.

Table 3. Analysis point 3

Beginning teacher chat	PowerPoint slide excerpt	Instructor audio
LMW: I agree F, sometimes you just give a positive or negative response and thats it TH: yes some students tend to call you more, and then there are the quiet ones who need the attention but aren't as vocal about it NM: agreed increasing individual interest in feedback is difficult NL: I tried developing a proforma indicate different levels in each criteria then wrote short comment to save time EH: Some students at my main school are writing their own rubrics. EH: for assessment-they've written them as a class. NM: that is a great way for students to understand topics EH: it's personal to them. LMW: Then they will always understand the feedback SS: they also take a lot more pride in their work NM::) great TH: good idea E EH: Cheers. I thought it was good when I saw it. LB: yes, it gives meaning and encourages them to be more active/ responsible for their own learning EH: that's right, and they're marked accordingly. RB: I know even with the preps we tell them what the goals for the week are so they can work towards them. I developmental one is to use teacher feedback. NL 1: Can I save this table? EH 1: I've seen prep classes with even really simple goals. They keep them on their desks to remind them. Moderator: The powerpoint will be up on Blackboard tomorrow EH 1: thanks NL: Ta Moderator: The slides will be available to everyone on the Blackboard after this session, so you can access this material there NL: Thank you RO: Fantastic!! RB: They are big on the wall for my students. EH: that's great too EH: I think each year level could use the goals listed somewhere. Them seeing it all time makes them not want to give up. VK: my class has goals in our 'time capsule' hanging from the roof so whenever they see it they are reminded of what their goals are, yet others don't have to see. DB: You could get them to record our feedback, we could discuss it with the students and then have them revisit it before the sybmit the next task? DB: oops submit EH: Oh wow, a time capsule, what a great idea! MY: we try to praise the effort not the result:) CN: im guilty of that VK: yeah thanks erin, we opened it today and they looked at how they had been going, and adjusted it for the last term NL: Hillbricks? Hillbrix? EH: I might have to pinch that idea, V:) DB: How do you spell Hilbricks? NL: Thanks DB: thanks SS: thats a very good idea V VK: wow, S and E, thanks for the praise:) DS: i might steal that idea too for my class EH: it's just so original	Effective feedback answers three questions: Where am I going (the goals)? How am I going? Where to next? (Hattie & Timperley, 2007)	But if you think about it, when you're setting your criteria's or your rubrics up, in answering "where am I going?" they have to include something about the task, the process, how they can self monitor and regulate their actions, as well as how they might personally evaluate how they are going. So, if we think about that tart that we showed at the very start, some of that feedback I might say is "the tart was very well presented on the plate, you did an excellent job with the decoration". That's very much that task level of feedback.

For instance, at the start of this episode, first space behaviours are evident, a formal environment has been created, the instructor is controlling the space, and the beginning teachers await knowledge to be imparted. But within several minutes, the instructor who continues to remain in this first space is deposed and there is a shift in the power relationships and a new space emerges, a third space navigated by the beginning teachers. Drawing upon Gutiérrez (2008), in this episode the "teacher and student scripts" have shifted and there may be a more "authentic interaction" and a challenge around what "counts as knowledge" (p. 152). In this space, beginning teachers take control of the content, readily shaping it by drawing on their own experiences aided by the pedagogical decision by organisers to take a non-interventionist approach to the session. Therefore the chat was not brought 'back on track' or in line with the presentation which may have happened in other communication environments. Indeed, within a face-to-face setting this amount of 'chat' may become a behaviour management issue. Interestingly, the participants at times interrupt the 'unofficial' chat discussion and refer back to the 'official' instructor content or audio (e.g. "How do you spell Hilbricks?" is a question in relation to some feedback strategies by Hillbricks (2004) being discussed by the instructor), so there is a sense that the participants were still listening and interacting on some level with the first space content. In this space, beginning teachers were empowered to destabilize what counts as official knowledge.

However, in destabilizing what counts as knowledge and 'official' roles and conventions, it is an important part of Third Space theory to acknowledge that this may also cause discomfort and tension. In acknowledging this, it does raise some interesting dilemmas and questions. The first - do we want third spaces? More specifically, drawing upon Boler (1999) what fears, terrors and demons may educators face within third space? How might educators perceive and react to a

change in roles and expectations? What does learning in third spaces mean for existing educational theory, curriculum and modes of delivery? Who and under what conditions and for what purposes do users/learners choose to bridge or navigate? What are the implications for transforming spaces? Who is valued in third space constructs? Who and how do we tell the story of those who didn't take up third space possibilities, whose experience may remain distanced and faceless because they don't feature in interaction? How does disruption through third space fit within the 'value add' model of technology adoption? Even though technology affordances allow third spaces, are we ready for third spaces in educational settings?

FUTURE RESEARCH

As seen in the previous section, this small-scale exploratory study reported in this chapter raises more questions than answers. It provides a useful way of reimagining the introduction of new technologies and as providing another story, but does not seek to offer prescriptive recommendations. Rather it seeks to encourage us to move the research agenda forward. In relation to educational technology research generally, it recommends that we continue the conversation around reimagining how research into technology can be constructed and reconstructed. This includes examining how users can move in and out of spaces, bridge from one space to another, navigate across spaces and in doing so create third spaces. Research could also consider alternative questions which focus more on the how and why of technologies within particular contexts rather than the what of technologies themselves. In this way, researchers could then, open up more complex conceptualizations that move away from an overreliance on techno-centric and binaristic discourses.

As well in relation to research around Ellumi-nate specifically, there is a need for further study, both small scale in-depth studies as well as longitudinal studies that explore a variety of contexts such as higher education and distance education, to better our understanding of the possibilities of this technology, to consider complexity in use and conditions under which it can be used. For example: How do users such as educators, and learners, operating in particular learning contexts (higher education, school education, open learning, distance learning, blended learning) negotiate this multimodal space? Which features do users choose to use (given that all or only some are enabled), when do they choose them, under what conditions and for what purposes? Do educators and learners in similar contexts choose different tools for the same purposes? Further research could aim to look at how users have possible control (depending upon what affordances are enabled) that may move the research agenda forward, away from a techno-centric space to one in which there is greater recognition of human agency. In this way, new conceptualizations of technology as mediating learning rather than determining learning have possibility. We have been mindful to not assume that educators will want to use Elluminate as part of a learning reform agenda. However the education landscape is continually changing and Elluminate could have a role to play in these changing times, and specific research could investigate these possibilities.

CONCLUSION

This chapter has reported on the ways that 26 beginning teachers and an instructor, along with 3 online coaches and 2 moderators interacted in one Elluminate session as part of a much larger professional learning program. The Supporting New Teachers Program aims to provide support for beginning teachers as they face the challenges of being new to the profession. Funded by DEECD, it is a three year program which will involve up to 600 beginning teachers from across the state in a blended professional learning program. Elluminate was one of the technologies used within the online component.

Often in the past when a new technology is introduced a dominant narrative is told: various claims are made in support of the new technology and assumptions based on techno-centric views, binary thinking and simplistic notions of how we can adopt technology are then made. Throughout this chapter we have suggested that this dominant discourse needs to be questioned and that alternative discourses need to be considered. Furthermore, it has suggested that Third Space theory can provide a useful lens to enable this re-imagining to occur and in so doing move the educational technology research forward.

Using an analysis of three episodes in one Elluminate session, we suggest that beginning teachers were able to navigate, bridge and transform spaces: first spaces associated with face-to-face instruction, second spaces associated with one media synchronous and asynchronous technologies, so as to create and take up hybrid or third spaces. When in this third space, beginning teachers were able to take control of this space, shaping it to suit their own needs. Thus, they were able to disrupt first and second spaces and ultimately challenge who controls the interactions and the space.

In this chapter we do not seek to make large claims about this small-scale study but rather wish to use it as a way of opening up further discussion about how we can introduce new technologies. For example: what are some of the risks and benefits for learners interacting within third spaces? How can educators scaffold the third space experience? How do we research interaction and learning within this rapidly developing online environment? The questions evoked from this research highlight that interaction within Web 2.0 technologies such as Elluminate may provide a space where learners' experiences are taken up in productive ways and used to inform, enrich or transform their professional learning; but at the same time, can also be seen as an opportunity to relish the possibility of uncertainty.

REFERENCES

Anderson, T. (2003). Getting the mix right again: An updated and theoretical rationale for interaction. *International Review of Research in Open and Distance Learning, 4*(2). Retrieved from http://www.irrodl.org/index.php/irrodl/article/view/149/230

Becker, J. H. (1999). *Internet use by teachers: Conditions of professional use and teacher-directed student use.* Retrieved from http://www.eric.ed.gov/ERICWebPortal/search/detailmini.jsp?_nfpb=true&_&ERICExtSearch_SearchValue_0=ED429564&ERICExtSearch_SearchType_0=no&accno=ED429564

Bhabha, H. (1992). The third space: Interview with Homi Bhabha. In Rutherford, J. (Ed.), *Identity: Community, culture, difference* (pp. 207–221). London, UK: Lawrence and Wishart.

Bhabha, H. (1994). *The location of culture.* London, UK: Routledge.

Bigum, C. (1998). Boundaries, barriers and borders: Teaching science in a wired world. *Australian Science Teachers Journal, 44*(1), 13–24.

Boler, M. (1999). *Feeling power: Emotions and education.* London, UK: Routledge.

Brown, D., & Warschauer, M. (2006). From the university to the elementary classroom: Students' experiences in learning to integrate technology in instruction. *Journal of Technology and Teacher Education, 14*(3), 599–621.

Danaher, P. A., Danaher, G. R., & Moriarty, B. J. (2003). Space invaders and pedagogical innovators: Regional educational understandings from Australian occupational travellers. *Journal of Research in Rural Education, 18*(3), 164–169.

Darling-Hammond, L. (1990). *Teacher supply, demand and quality.* Washington, DC: National Board for Professional Standards.

De Wert, M. H., Babinski, L. M., & Jones, B. D. (2003). Safe passages: Providing online support to beginning teachers. *Journal of Teacher Education, 54*(4), 311–320. doi:10.1177/0022487103255008

Enriquez, J. G. (2009). Discontent with content analysis of online transcripts. *Association for Learning Technology Journal, 17*(2), 101–113. doi:10.1080/09687760903033066

Fuller, J. (2009). Engaging students in large classes using Elluminate. In T. Robinson, T. Tang and A. Fletcher (Eds.), *Proceedings of Australasian Teaching Economics Conference*, School of Economics and Finance, Queensland University of Technology, Brisbane, Queensland, (pp. 84-97).

Garrison, D. R., Anderson, T., & Archer, W. (2000). Critical inquiry in a text-based environment: Computer conferencing in higher education. *The Internet and Higher Education, 2*(2-3), 87–105. doi:10.1016/S1096-7516(00)00016-6

Groff, J., & Mouza, C. (2008). A framework for addressing challenges to classroom technology use. *Association for the Advancement of Computing in Education Journal, 16*(1), 21–46.

Gunawardena, C. N., Lowe, C. A., & Anderson, T. (1997). Analysis of a global online debate and the development of an interactive analysis model for examining social construction of knowledge in computer conferencing. *Journal of Educational Computing Research, 17*(4), 397–431. doi:10.2190/7MQV-X9UJ-C7Q3-NRAG

Gutiérrez, K. D. (2008). Developing a sociocritical literacy in the third space. *Reading Research Quarterly, 43*(2), 148–164. doi:10.1598/RRQ.43.2.3

Gutiérrez, K. D., Baquedano-Lopez, P., & Turner, M. G. (1997). Putting language back into language arts: When the radical middle meets the third space. *Language Arts, 75*(5), 368–378.

Hall, G. E. (2010). Technology's Achilles heel: Achieving high-quality implementation. *Journal of Research on Technology in Education, 42*(3), 231–253.

Hanewald, R., & White, P. (2008). What, how and why Web 2.0? *Australian Educational Computing, 23*(2), 3–6.

Hara, N., Bonk, C., & Angeli, C. (2000). Content analysis of on-line discussion in an applied educational psychology course. *Instructional Science, 28*(2), 115–152. doi:10.1023/A:1003764722829

Harris, J. (2005). Our agenda for technology integration: It's time to choose. *Contemporary Issues in Technology & Teacher Education, 5*(2). Retrieved from http://www.citejournal.org/vol5/iss2/editorial/article1.cfm

Hatti, J., & Timperley, H. (2007). The power of feedback. *Review of Educational Research, 77*(1), 81–112. doi:10.3102/003465430298487

Henri, F. (1992). Computer conferencing and content analysis. In Kaye, A. R. (Ed.), *Collaborative learning through computer conferencing: The Najaden papers* (pp. 117–136). Berlin, Germany: Springer-Verlag. doi:10.1007/978-3-642-77684-7_8

Herrington, A., Herrington, J., Kervin, L., & Ferry, B. (2006). The design of an online community of practice for beginning teachers. *Contemporary Issues in Technology & Teacher Education, 6*(10), 120–132.

Hillbrick, A. (2004). *Tuning in with task cards: Middle primary*. Carlton, Australia: Curriculum Corporation.

Hulme, R., Cracknell, D., & Owens, A. (2009). Learning in third spaces: Developing trans-professional understanding through practitioner enquiry. *Educational Action Research, 17*(4), 537–550. doi:10.1080/09650790903309391

Khan, S. (2000). *Muslim women: Crafting a North American identity*. Gainesville, FL: University Press of Florida.

Lankshear, C., Snyder, I., & Green, B. (2000). *Teachers and techno-literacy: Managing literacy, technology and learning in schools*. St Leonards, Australia: Allen and Unwin.

Lloyd, M. (2008). Finding the 'on' switch: Being a digital teacher in the 21st century. In Millwater, J., & Beutel, D. (Eds.), *Transitioning to the real world of education* (pp. 97–119). Sydney, Australia: Pearson.

Marzano, R. J., Marzano, J. S., & Pickering, D. J. (2003). *Classroom management that works*. Alexandria, VA: ASCD.

Maxwell, T. W., Harrington, I., & Smith, H. J. (2010). Supporting primary and secondary beginning teachers online: Key findings of the education alumni support project. *Australian Journal of Teacher Education, 35*(1), 42–58.

McKenzie, W., & Murphy, D. (2000). "I hope this goes somewhere": Evaluation of an online discussion group. *Australian Journal of Educational Technology, 16*(3), 239–257.

Moje, E., Ciechanowski, K., Kramer, K., Ellis, L., Carrillo, R., & Collazo, T. (2004). Working toward third space in content area literacy: An examination of everyday funds of knowledge and discourse. *Reading Research Quarterly, 39*(1), 38–70. doi:10.1598/RRQ.39.1.4

Murphy, E., & Ciszewska-Carr, J. (2007). Instructor's experiences of web based synchronous communication using two way audio and direct messaging. *Australasian Journal of Educational Technology, 23*(1), 68–86.

Orlando, J. (2009). Understanding changes in teachers' ICT practices: A longitudinal perspective. *Technology, Pedagogy and Education, 18*(1), 33–44. doi:10.1080/14759390802704030

Rogers, E. M. (2003). *Diffusion of innovations* (5th ed.). New York, NY: The Free Press.

Rourke, L., Anderson, T., Garrison, D. R., & Archer, W. (2001). Methodological issues in the content analysis of computer conference transcripts. *International Journal of Artificial Intelligence in Education, 12*(1), 8–22.

Schuck, S. (2003). Getting help from the outside: Developing a support network for beginning teachers. *Journal of Educational Enquiry, 4*(1), 49–67.

Selwyn, N. (2002). *Telling tales on technology: Qualitative studies of technology and education.* Hampshire, UK: Ashgate Publishing Limited.

Skerrett, A. (2010). Lolita, facebook, and the third space of literacy teacher education. *Educational Studies, 46*(1), 67–84.

Snyder, I. (1993). Writing with word processors: A research overview. *Educational Research, 35*(1), 49–68. doi:10.1080/0013188930350103

Soja, E. W. (1996). *Thirdspace: Journeys to Los Angeles and other real and imagined places.* Malden, MA: Blackwell.

Stacey, E., & Gerbic, P. (2008). Success factors for blended learning. In R. Atkinson & C. McBeath (Eds.), *Hello! Where are you in the landscape of educational technology? Proceedings Australasian Society for Computers in Learning in Tertiary Education (ASCILITE) Conference,* Melbourne 2008.

Terrell, J., Richardson, J., & Hamilton, M. (2011). Using Web 2.0 to teach Web 2.0: A case study in aligning teaching, learning and assessment with professional practice. *Australasian Journal of Educational Technology, 27*(special issue, 5), 846-862.

Tyack, D., & Cuban, L. (2000). Teaching by machine. In Pea, R. D. (Ed.), *Jossey-Bass reader on technology and learning* (pp. 247–254). San Francisco, CA: Jossey-Bass.

Waycott, J., & Sheard, J. (2011). Editorial: Preface to the special issue. *Australasian Journal of Educational Technology, 27*(Special issue, 5), iii-ix. Retrieved from http://www.ascilite.org.au/ajet/ajet27/editorial27-5.html

Wenger, E. (1998). *Communities of practice: Learning, meaning and identity.* Cambridge, UK: Cambridge University Press.

Wilson, G., & Stacey, E. (2004). Online interaction impacts on learning: Teaching the teachers to teach online. *Australasian Journal of Educational Technology, 20*(1), 33-48. Retrieved from http://www.ascilite.org.au/ajet/ajet20/wilson.html

Zhao, Y., Pugh, K., Sheldon, S., & Byers, J. L. (2002). Conditions for classroom technology innovations. *Teachers College Record, 104*(3), 482–515. doi:10.1111/1467-9620.00170

Zhao, Y., & Rop, S. (2001). A critical review of the literature on electronic networks as reflective discourse communities for inservice teachers. *Education and Information Technologies, 6*(2), 81–94. doi:10.1023/A:1012363715212

APPENDIX

Use of Interactive Elements of the Technology

To facilitate greater participation, the poll function was used as well as icons (hand clapping, and smiley faces) to gauge reactions or opinions to a question (example provided in Figure 1). These were used to invite involvements from the participants, but to also validate their experience. Polls were often used as a way to introduce a session, gauge background knowledge and to enable the facilitator to differentiate learning if necessary.

Figure 1. Poll in Elluminate PowerPoint slide example

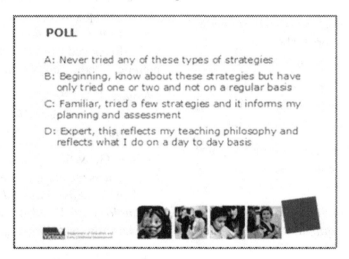

Providing Social Networking Opportunities

Participants in the SNTP program came from a broad range of teaching contexts, including primary, secondary, specialist positions (e.g. visual arts, physical education teacher), and Special Development and English Development schools. The break-out room function was used to provide a more intimate and directed discussion space for cognate groups. When participants were asked to consider or apply some of the theoretical content to their own classroom context, break out rooms were used to enable a social and more collaborative approach.

Provocative, Reflective Questioning

Throughout the Elluminate session the facilitator asked a number of complex open questions for deeper interaction. In these instances, responses were either given in the form of audio and/or chat depending on the timing and access to technology. These questions were designed to evoke a response as they were often debatable, contestable or reflective in nature. An example is provided in Figure 2.

Figure 2. Key questions PowerPoint slide example

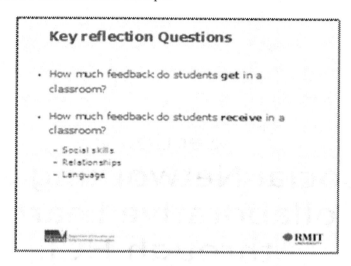

Metaphors, Stories, and Research

Metaphors were used to facilitate navigation, increase interest and enable participants to connect to big ideas. Throughout the Elluminate session multiple metaphors were used including shopping centres (used to explore differentiated curriculum), The Biggest Loser TV program (to look at the value of evidence in the feedback process), post mortems (to illustrate the complexities of summative feedback) and food (to explore assessment criteria). This was a deliberate practice designed to engage with content and introduce theoretical concepts. The use of personal stories and the practioner research of the facilitator were also included as a way of illustrating theories but also as a mechanism to make the participants feel more comfortable to also share their narratives, which they may have felt awkward doing via online mediums.

Participation and Connection to Other Online Spaces

Throughout the Elluminate session, program designers wanted to encourage discussion and reflection on practice. For instance, participants audited their current practices, suggested ways to move forward and encouraged to revisit these through reporting back to an online community connected to the program or their school context. For example, participants were often asked to share key learning to the online community space and develop the conversation further.

Section 2
Social Networking and Collaborative Learning through HCI:
Synchronous and Asynchronous Learning

Chapter 7
Bringing Web 2.0 into the Learning Environment

Saman Shahryari Monfared
Simon Fraser University, Canada

Peyman Ajabi-Naeini
Simon Fraser University, Canada

Drew Parker
Simon Fraser University, Canada

ABSTRACT

Social Networking, or the so-called Web 2.0 phenomenon, is changing the way we use the Internet. In turn, the way we use the Internet is changing the way we work, learn, communicate, and research. This chapter outlines a series of issues, tools, techniques, and pedagogy that may lie behind the process to bring social media into a learning environment. It then concludes with a four-year experience bringing these concepts into a senior undergraduate seminar, and offers observations and conclusions about the efficacy of our approach. Social networking has brought the Web into a conversation. Similarly, the chasm between synchronous and asynchronous learning is closing as the classroom becomes one part of a larger, continuous learning experience.

BACKGROUND

Web 2.0

There are numerous definitions of the concept of the Web 2.0 since Tim O'Reilley (2005) coined the phrase. The basic premise is that the Web itself underwent a fundamental transformation from a one-way broadcast medium to an interactive one. The concept is straightforward, but its impact is extensive. Web 1.0 has been described as a broadcast, and Web 2.0 as a conversation (See, for example, Tingling, Gemino and Parker, 2011). Corporate Web pages and online catalogues have given way to product and seller ratings alongside product offerings and more personalized discussions. Tools like static Web pages and email have taken from the forefront of the Internet to a place

DOI: 10.4018/978-1-4666-3649-1.ch007

alongside Facebook, Twitter, Blogs, Flickr and all things Google. Similarly, the educational process is evolving at a rate faster than ever.

The adoption of social networking is a result of evolutions of both product and process (Tingling, Gemino & Parker, 2011). Faster, richer and ubiquitous Internet access enabled users to work with rich media virtually anywhere, and portable devices such as tablets and smartphones moved this communication off the desktop and into a pocket. The resulting forms of communication have also evolved.

The genesis was the emergence of cellular devices and interactive Websites. Such advancements have not only impacted our personal and educational life, but have also changed the commercial world (See, for example. Personal Websites such as Facebook and Twitter in addition to resources such as Google, Yammer, and course management platforms such as Blackboard (http://www.blackboard.com/) and Moodle (http://moodle.org/) have changed the way we live our daily lives. Engagement is key. See, for example, Deloitte Australia for a discussion of how such a tool changes a level of corporate interaction.

In this chapter we are suggesting that our teaching and learning strategies should keep pace with current technology. To this end we describe our notion of the 'teach 2.0' concept to set the context for looking at how particular human-computer interaction (HCI) works in post secondary seminars. Because this territory is new, we analyze the environment and suggest strategies for dealing with the Web 2.0/teach 2.0 dilemma and then provide an overview of a 'case study' where we propose to practice what we preach.

INTRODUCTION

Teach 2.0

The first characteristic of communication in the Web 2.0 environment is 'participation.' While Web 1.0 was a way to provide communication through Websites, Web 2.0 moves to a more active two-way dialogue. To use an everyday business metaphor, one could suggest that the general Internet-storefront had inventory to offer in the Web 1.0 world. Yet the concept of the Web 2.0 has brought more than just product description. The digital goods on offer include: dialogue about the products offered; information and support; and introduced the ability to articulate and influence a seller's reputation. Sellers on eBay, for example, have a reputation that can be quickly measured by the amount of feedback received, and the percentage of that feedback that was rated 'positive'. Yet, with such a reputation comes trust. Other business offerings with the advent of the Web 2.0, the techno-tools now offer the ability to rate a product, and customers can share their experiences with a store, and with its offerings. This is empowering to both the vendors and to the customers. A tool such as 'shop savvy' (http://shopsavvy.mobi/), for example, allows a consumer to scan a bar code and receive reviews of the product, online and nearby prices, and choose to purchase online instead of at the location where the product was scanned.

Another attribute of social media is that of engagement. Tapscott and Williams (2008) coined the term 'prosumer' to describe the new consumer as someone who simultaneously produces content while they consume products. A prosumer in an educational setting offers the opportunity to greatly expand roles. It also offers the challenge of blurring the line between 'teacher' and 'learner'. In a subsequent book, Tapscott and Williams (2010) expanded on the notion of collaboration in the learning environment, suggesting collaboration impacts both inter-institutional relations and the role of the student. In discussing his experiences with a communications course, Howard Rheingold (http://www.rheingold.com/) suggested in his 'social media classroom' (http://socialmediaclassroom.com/) that there were typically students in his classes that knew more than him than about a specific element of discussion. His job, he suggested, was to find them and draw them out. If an educator can accept this fact, which we allege is reasonable in a postsecondary setting. Therefore the notion of 'engagement' becomes critical. Newer information gathering practices, such as 'crowdsourcing' and 'collaboration', move into the educational pedagogy.

HCI AND POSTSECONDARY SEMINARS

Much of the interaction among students and teachers is becoming computer-facilitated, even in face-to-face meetings, and computer-based at other times. There exists some debate regarding electronic devices in classrooms (Parry, 2012) an unofficial poll suggests the majority of teachers are in favor of allowing this phenomenon and supporting it (http://www.helium.com/). Students in an upper division seminar, for example, at the authors' home institution, regularly bring tablets, notebook computers, and smart phones to the point of saturation where electronic devices outnumber attendees. The mere existence of these devices has led to numerous pedagogical changes. Firstly, students are available for fact-checking and real-time research, simply by pointing and asking for someone to look something up. Secondly, polls are frequently taken, either by the teacher or students about attitudes as simple as when they want a break to issues that arise such as alternate dates for an exam.

Backchannel discussions, where a topic is being discussed but students are also tweeting and collaborating online in real time as well as the face to face interaction are frequent, for better or worse. Students collaborate on questions to pose, or comment on activities or speakers as they happen. HCI also takes the seminar outside of the time and space of the classroom. Students can easily relate to Facebook-like interactions using either a course management tool or a business collaboration tool like Yammer (yammer.com). Extending the example earlier, students work on multimedia presentations for course topics, and

then store them on a private course wiki in 'rich media form', where subsequent classes have the benefit of accessing past research work.

In the example course we use as a case study and discussed later in the chapter, this wiki has now replaced a textbook, and is enhanced exclusively by readings available on the Web. The topic lends itself to very current information, but a core 'body of knowledge' (the students' term) is emerging from term projects and presentations. The original idea for a wiki was proposed by students who expressed an interest in accessing one another's materials for reference. Since the idea was to create a 'paper' for grading, but subsequently for use as student reference material. The original document was produced by the group to be submitted for a grade. The material, however, was left on a wiki that allowed current and past students to read, modify, and update it in 'typical' wiki form, such as Wikipedia (Wikipedia.org). Similar to Wikipedia, material can be corrected and updated, but students are advised and encouraged to check specific references for validity.

CONSIDERING STRATEGIES TO ANALYZE THE ENVIRONMENT

The Web 2.0 phenomenon can be a disruptive technology with respect to educational pedagogy. Opportunities for interaction outside of the classroom, and even beyond the traditional course offering, can be a mixed blessing.

Disadvantages

Reading is the key to the critical thinking development, and as a result, the amount of out of class reading during school years has been suggested is a good predictor of critical thinking skills (Terenzini and Springer 1995). This might be because books are considered 'hard' medium, requiring mental effort to analyze and understand (Salomon 1984). According to the study conducted at the

University of California, Los Angeles (UCLA) by Patricia Greenfield, she analyzed more than 50 studies on learning and technology, including research on the Internet and video games. Technological advancements have strengthened the visual spatial intelligence; however, they have significantly weakened the inductive problem solving and critical thinking abilities of the new generation (Greenfield, 2009). As a result, people who have graduated over the past few decades are allegedly less capable of independent critical thought compared to previous generations, a phenomenon coined by Nicholas Carr as the 'Google effect' (Carr, 2008).

Convincing all students to participate in the Web 2.0 environments can be another challenge. Although at first blush, one might assume that engaging students in an online learning environment is easy, this may not always be the case. Undoubtedly, there are ways to motivate learners to contribute, but pushing students to participate will not guarantee the quality nor equality of participation. It is crucial to make students realize that the Web environment is not only about social networking, entertaining, or reading interesting materials. Instead it is also about collaborating, contributing, and learning. Therefore, changing the learning culture is vital to the success of the Web 2.0 movements in educational facilities.

Beyond textbooks, Wikis and blogs are good sources of general information; however, many university instructors discourage their students from using the information available on such platforms as Wikipedia. The trouble is that any individual has the ability to somewhat anonymously make comments or make changes, and therefore discredit the posted materials.

Advantages of Social Media as a Learning Enhancement

Unlike a more traditional setting, where the teacher acts as the storyteller and the student acts as the listener, in the Web 2.0 environment we have observed:

- Those students, who may be quiet and shy about speaking out, participate in the learning environment, ultimately improving the quality of their educational process (Parker and Rossner-Merrill, 1998), The teacher is presented with the opportunity to expand more on the topics, as the discussions are not restricted to the classroom's time limit.

- The teacher keeps themself up to date and learns with the students, as the conversations do not end with one quick answer similar to the classroom, and as they always have to be ready to answer unanticipated or complicated questions that the students might ask outside of the class in a wiki or forum.

- The teacher adapts to the needs and learning styles of students. In the traditional setting, the teacher designs a guideline for the course and might use the same outline year after year. In the Web 2.0 environments, however, the needs of the classroom are shaped based on the capabilities of learners and the changing environment, and the direction of the course usually changes as new teaching technologies emerge and as students enhance their learning abilities because of the technological advances.

Think and Act New

Implementing Web 2.0 into an educational facility requires changes at various levels. In general there are three segments that must be reconsidered when making such changes: The role of the educational institution, the role of the teacher and the role of the student.

Rethink the Role of the Educational Institution

The world of business, teaching, government, and learning has changed as Web 2.0 technologies have emerged (Tapscott and Williams, 2010), whereas some educational institutions have failed to adapt to fully embrace these changes to date (Berrett, 2012). Schools need to change the ways they approach the concept of education in order to continue to contribute value to the society. More 'traditional' schools are physical entities where groups of students gather to learn from learned figures. Although the current system is functional, this traditional approach is not yet fully utilizing the opportunities offered by rich media (Tapscott and Williams, 2010, p. 139-156).

Rethink the Role of Teachers

Conventional teaching methods required instructors to act as information filters, facilitators and as researchers. Within the Web 2.0 world, however, a teacher is no longer just going through a set curriculum and performing a fixed set of tasks. To succeed, we allege they must be adaptable to the tech-savvy students and be willing to try new methods of teaching (Couros, 2011). The new role consists of being a community leader, a concierge assisting students with finding their ways and a curator for putting together new teaching approaches.

In an experimental Management Information Systems course taught first in the Fall of 2008 at Simon Fraser University (SFU) of Canada, where students were given the option to suggest a guideline for the class, pick their own group projects based on their interests, and choose the method that they wanted to submit their projects. The students decided to submit wikis instead of term papers and communicate through blogs and/ or other social media platforms. The environment was somewhat democratized, but resulted in several distinct benefits. Firstly, the students are creating a legacy archive of their work for other students to follow. Secondly, the experience moves out of the classroom and into a real-time format. Thirdly, the students can continue to use these tools to communicate with their network of peers after completion of the course, and even after graduation.

Rethink the Role of Students

While today's students still perceive faculty knowledge and personnel as the primary source of learning, an EDUCASE survey stated that students want teachers and faculty members to use technology in order to communicate that knowledge more efficiently (Kvavik & Caruso, 2005). Remarkably, over 40% of the students surveyed preferred instructors to make moderate use of information technology while just fewer than 30% wanted extensive use.

With effective use of beneficial technologies and methods availed through Web 2.0, one would hope this ratio continues to point toward effective utilization of HCI to facilitate the educational process. (Kvavik & Caruso 2005).

Be Open to Suggestions, Think Outside the Box, and Try New Technologies

In the Web 2.0 environment, teachers and students lose their traditional roles and become part of a learning team. For the instructors, the goal is to improve the overall teaching skills, and act more as a coordinator than an educator. The teacher does not go to the class or post notes online to simply cover a certain topic; he or she opens the door for the discussion among students and then acts as the facilitator in the conversation. Instead of giving instructions to students, the educator tries to introduce the topic and motivate the students to use Web 2.0 technologies such as wikis and blogs to expand on the subject. In the current settings, the instructor defines the rules of the class, and students follow the prepared guideline. In the new environment, on the other hand, students get the chance to shape the course by giving suggestions to the teacher, who is now no longer the owner, but the coordinator of the course.

Suitable Web 2.0 Applications

Wikis are Web-based services that allow users to create, edit and link pages, and that provide an "organized and socially constructed repository for knowledge" (Crook, Fisher, Graber, Harrison, and Lewin, 2008: 22). Wikipedia is perhaps the most accepted wiki service used around the world. However, smaller special-purpose wikis such as the one used in our case study, is discussed later in the chapter, may also a valuable potential resource.

Many teachers are excited about the opportunities offered by wikis. In a report generated by Crook, Fisher, Graber, Harrison, & Lewin, a former UK government agency, which is now disbanded after a massive British government spending cut (BBC, 2010), was leading the national drive to ensure the effective and innovative use of technology throughout learning, 46% of teachers believed that students should have the experience of building their own wiki encyclopedia and over 70% reported using a wiki themselves (Crook, Fisher, Graber, Harrison, & Lewin, 2008).

Forums and discussion boards are the virtual or online versions of bulletin boards, in which users post notes. Forums usually have a set topic while discussion boards are generally more open-ended in content. Instant messaging and chat rooms enable real-time conversations between distinct users. Some users incorporate avatars or voice links into these arenas (Crook, Fisher, Graber, Harrison, & Lewin, 2008).

If correctly implemented and monitored, it was found (op. cit.) that discussion forums are perceived by a number of teachers to have significant potential for learning. More specifically, discussion forums provided the means for supporting weaker students through closer monitoring and additional assistant and higher-ability students through additional activities. According to Crook, Fisher, Graber, Harrison, & Lewin, nearly 50% of teachers felt competent or very competent with using discussion forums in their classes.

Social Networking sites are websites that structure social interaction among members who form sub-groups of friends (Wikipedia, 2011). Examples of popular social networking sites among learners and teachers include: Facebook; Orkut; and potentially, Google Plus in the near future. Many of the more commercially successful sites incorporate extensive functionalities such as: facilities for private messaging; blogs; uploading of photo; video and audio content; commenting capabilities; multiplayer games and quizzes.

Although 74% of students have accounts on social networking sites such as Facebook or Twitter, the use of such tools for learning is uncommon. Only 7.3% of teachers reported having used a social networking site in lessons or lesson planning (Crook, Fisher, Graber, Harrison, & Lewin, 2008).

CASE STUDY

Teach 2.0 in Action

An example of a Web 2.0 formatted course was originally motivated by the concept of 'reverse mentoring' (Carter, 2004). Newly hired graduates are given access to senior executives in order to teach the older managers the impact and application of social media. Executive interest in social media is high, but knowledge of the nuances of this phenomenon are generally best understood by the 'millenials' who have grown up with the Internet as part of their regular communication. In the summer of 2008, a new course was designed at SFU of Canada, to target the relatively novel application of social media, and Web 2.0 in general, in business administration. The Web 2.0 was starting to be recognized as a 'business' phenomenon, moving from a youthful adoption for such 'personal' applications as MySpace and Facebook, toward marketing, business intelligence, and communication throughout the ultimate supply chain.

Since the initial offering of the course, lessons learned have evolved, mainly because, to teach Web 2.0, one has to adopt the notion of Web 2.0, such as crowd sourced information and decisions, interactive media, and new media tools integrated into the learning experience itself. The roles of 'student' and 'teacher' are redefined and blurred. There are many new changes resulting from adoption of social media in the classroom, of which key elements are discussed in the following section.

An Example: Web-Based Business

In 2008, the Faculty of Business Administration at SFU decided to redesign a series of Management Information Systems (MIS) courses to modernize the curriculum and draw students back into the area after dismal enrolments post dot-com bomb, Y2K, and weak corporate technology spending and recruiting (Aiken, Garner, Ghosh & Vanjani, 2008). Internet technology and applications had been part of an upper division undergraduate seminar since the early 1990's, and the reverse-mentoring opportunity bode well for a focus on how some organizations were embracing social media through new business graduates. This course also involves looking at how others could potentially use this phenomenon as a marketing, business-to-consumer, and internal communication medium.

The idea to build and recruit students for a Business Web 2.0 course posed several challenges. Firstly, the impact of the participation had to be explored, understood, and articulated. Secondly, it had to be accommodated in the format of the course itself. The 'normal' approach to notifying students of a new course was to put a course outline on a portal, then send a mass email stating that outlines for forthcoming courses were now available for perusal online. At best, it was a Web 1.0 approach. This created a novel challenge, in that the delivery of the new material predicated a new delivery format at the same time. Offering a course about social media and advertising it with a paper-based course outline missed the point, as

did lecturing about participation as a new communication standard. Therefore, a novel approach was required.

Two courses had been redesigned with the objective of highlighting the forecast shortage of information and communications technology (ICT) professionals in the forthcoming decade, and attempting to convince students that these new courses were current and interesting. Further, one of the faculty members teaching the 'Web in business' course was returning from a leave and the students did not know who this person was, or what they planned to teach.

In order to 'get the word out,' a video was created for the 'Web in business' course with the teacher explaining who they were, what the new course was about, how it would be delivered, and assuring the students this was a course they should consider. It was posted on YouTube, but still the seed had yet to be planted to get this information to the desired audience. The faculty member had a group of past students as Facebook friends, so he posted a link on his wall asking for feedback about the new course format. Since most of these professor's student Facebook friends had already taken this course in an earlier incarnation, they were not the target audience, but their Facebook friends were. Given the viral nature of Facebook comments, and the need to emphasize the currency of this new course, it was hoped the post would invoke further comment. The 'guerilla marketing' attempt started to work when one former student complained they wanted to take this new course, but it was not available since it was listed as an update rather than a completely new course.

Other potential students, the 'friends of friends,' saw the post and started to comment and ask about the new course, which launched the desired viral marketing approach. Friends, and their friends, and so on, quickly saw the posted wall comments.

The next day, the second teacher posted a YouTube video. The first had been a pretty straightforward attempt to get information to the students. The second was more 'tongue-in-cheek', with the instructor morphing into a 'Zorro' costume and challenging the students to 'be brave' and take the 'Business Intelligence' course. Views of the two videos went into the hundreds within days, leading to a series of competitive, and more playful videos between the two instructors, involving motorcycles and lame threats, classes of students participating, and costumes including 'Zorro' being challenged by 'Marvin the Martian' who threatened to blow up the campus. The videos had the desired effect, filling both classes to capacity, while making the 'top ten' weekly category for YouTube educational videos in both Canada and Hong Kong. A final episode was recorded with the two being 'interrogated' where the statistics about the technology professional shortage was highlighted. The challenge was to deliver the interactive content that was now rather highly expected.

The course design was intended for a smaller group to start, yet the larger (35) format actually proved helpful. The course was designed using a business bestseller, Tapscott and Williams (2008), as a core reading, and weekly Internet-based articles and news reports. A wiki was designed for the course, where students could provide input about housekeeping things such as formation of teams to handle presentations based on common interests, and choices of presentation dates.

The course was initially structured to cover lecture material formally for the first three weeks, then one or two student groups would offer in-depth presentations on a mutually acceptable topic surrounding social media applications in business. The topics were left to the students, with the caveat that the instructor had to approve the idea. Students were then motivated to participate in the course wiki by going to a schedule page and signing up for a presentation date on a first-come first-served basis. This offered the start of the first of the Web 2.0 phenomenon entering the course.

Students quickly started creating pages on the course wiki to discuss matters pertaining to their presentations. These postings weren't a required part of the course, but they were a medium already familiar to the students. The class started to democratize, such as students seeking to renegotiate a date to write the final exam, 'deciding' that the final exam should be written in a computer-laboratory rather than a lecture hall, and spending countless amounts of time trying to 'decide' if the computers should have Internet access. The course evolution was observed to be much like the evolution of the Internet itself, which had been the topic of first week's lecture material. Participation in the activities of the course was nearly 100%, and the students started to assume a sense of ownership of the course.

In the fourth week, discussions were well underway about restructuring the course, and the first presentation took place. The presentation facility had high speed Internet, projection, and sound, so multimedia was encouraged. The presentations were not timed, and evolved into a combination of slides, YouTube demonstrations, and illustrations of hardware and software applications as suitable. They lasted from 45 minutes to over an hour, and subsequent term papers were written to codify the presentation material.

As the end of the first offering of the course neared, students decided they wanted to share their contributions so papers and presentation materials were voluntarily posted on the course wiki. The course wiki had been created specifically for that instance of the seminar, with the intention of creating a new wiki each time the course was offered.

The course progressed, with negotiations with the course instructor settling the final exam issues, where the course was written in an Internet-connected lab and all materials except live communication were allowed as resources. The final exam was a case illustrating a real organization that was not using social media to the extent the class would deem appropriate, seeking the student to devise a plan to bring the organization 'up to speed.' The exam reflects a real organization struggling with embracing social media, and the students build on their experiences through the term by applying the concepts to the case opportunity.

The course has evolved from its 2008 start. A legacy wiki, named by the students as the 'body of knowledge' for the course now exists with all the presentation/report topics posted as multimedia documents. The students make the rules, and have agreed that past, present, and future students in this course have exclusive access to it. It has been viewed by past students post-graduation prior to interviews for social media-type jobs, and remains a living document longitudinally connecting versions of the course. New applications are being tried, such as backchannel chats during presentations and a Yammer-page where current and past students regularly interact in a professionally-focused Facebook-like experience driven mostly by the students currently enrolled.

The professor has stated that delivering this course after a lengthy professorial career has completely changed the way he thinks about teaching, learning, and the classroom experience. Overall evaluative scores of the papers is higher than an earlier incarnation, and subjective quality evaluation metrics suggest this learning environment is more tightly bunched at a higher level, and continues to be a popular success.

As an endnote, the authors are two 'survivors' of the course, and the professor who originally proposed and designed it. The course is scheduled to run again, and has a waiting list.

REFERENCES

Aiken, M., Garner, B., Ghosh, K., & Vanjani, M. (2008). Dot.com boom and bust effects on MIS college enrollments: 1995-2006. *Communications of the IIMA, 8*(1), 31–42.

Arsham, H. (2002). Impact of the internet on learning and teaching. *USDLA Journal, 6*(3).

BBC. (2010). *George Osborne outlines detail of £6.2bn spending cuts.* Retrieved from http://news.bbc.co.uk/2/hi/uk_news/politics/8699522.stm

Berrett, C. (2012, February 5). Harvard conference seeks to jolt university teaching. *The Chronicle of Higher Education.*

Carr, N. (2008, July/August). Is Google making us stupid?' *Atlantic Magazine.*

Carter, T. (2004). Recipe for growth. *ABA Journal.* Retrieved from http://www.abajournal.com/magazine/article/recipe_for_growth/

Courus, G. (2011). Why social media can and is changing education. *Connected Principals.* Retrieved from http://www.connectedprincipals.com/archives/3024

Crook, C., Fisher, T., Graber, R., Harrison, C., & Lewin, C. (2008, September). *Implementing Web 2.0 in secondary schools: Impacts, barriers and issues.* Retrieved from http://decra.ioe.ac.uk/148/

Greenfield, P. (2009). Technology and informal education: What is taught, what is learned. *Science Magazine*, 323-69.

Helium.com. (2011). *Debate: Is the use of laptops in the classroom beneficial or a distraction?* Retrieved from http://www.helium.com/debates/180273-is-the-use-of-laptops-in-the-classroom-beneficial-or-a-distraction

Kvavik, R. B., & Caruso, J. B. (2005). ECAR study of students and information technology. *Convenience, Connection, Control, and Learning.* Boulder, CO: EDUCAUSE. Retrieved from http://www.educause.edu/ir/library/pdf/ers0506/rs/ERS0506w.pdf

Latham, T. (2011, July 16). The Google effect: Is our reliance on the internet making us dumber? *Psychology Today, Blogs.*

O'Reiley, T. (2005). *What is Web 2.0?* Retrieved from http://oreilly.com/Web2/archive/what-is-Web-20.html

Parker, D., & Rossner-Merill, V. (1998). *Socialization of distance education: The web as enabler.* WebNet '98, Association for the Advancement of Computing in Education, Orlando, Florida, Nov. 7-12.

Parry, M. (2012, March 7). Could many universities follow borders bookstores into oblivion? *The Chronicle of Higher Education.* Retrieved from http://chronicle.com/blogs/wiredcampus/could-many-universities-follow-borders-bookstores-into-oblivion/35711?utm_source=twitterfeedandutm_medium=twitter

Rheingold, H. (2008). Invitation to the social media classroom and collabatory. *Social Media Classroom.* Retrieved from http://socialmedi-aclassroom.com/

Rheingold, H. (2012 April). *Howard home.* Retrieved from http://rheingold.com

Salomon, G. J. (1984). *Education Psychology, 76,* 647. doi:10.1037/0022-0663.76.4.647

Tapscott, D., & Williams, A. D. (2008). *Wikinomics: How mass collaboration changes everything (expanded edition).* Penguin.

Tapscott, D., & Williams, A. D. (2010). *Macrowikinomics: Rebooting business and the world.* Penguin.

Terenzini, P., Springer, L., Pascarella, E. T., & Nora, A. (1995). *Research in Higher Education, 36,* 23. doi:10.1007/BF02207765

Tingling, P., Gemino, A., & Parker, D. (2011). Changing channels: The impact of web 2.0 on supply chain management. *Production and Inventory Management Journal, 47*(2), 31–44.

Chapter 8
Networked Learning and Teaching for International Work Integrated Learning

Jennifer Martin
RMIT University, Australia

ABSTRACT

This chapter explores the use of information communications technology (ICT) to support international work integrated learning to provide more understanding of Web-mediated communities. The findings of a study of ICT use by students enrolled in a student mobility course on campuses in Australia and Vietnam reveal that students used a range of university provided commercial software as well as freely available ICT services and tools, particularly social networking sites, during their studies. A major challenge for universities is to provide access to the latest technologies at a cost that is affordable to the institution and its students, which provides the necessary level of reliability, availability, accessibility, functionality, and security. An online central management system or base camp can assist students to navigate the complex technical, social, cultural, and knowledge building opportunities that work integrated learning abroad offers.

INTRODUCTION

Universities today are reliant upon efficient and effective information communications technology (ICT) systems as education and administration tools. Most modern universities these days have an ICT platform that is available for students to communicate with each other and staff members, as well as providing access to the learning materials and instructional resources. Generally speaking, ICT does not determine the educational experience, however ICT tools do provide opportunities to explore the interplay of technical, discursive social and cultural factors when developing new

DOI: 10.4018/978-1-4666-3649-1.ch008

curricula (Facer & Stanford, 2010). Increasingly, online learning environments are being used in higher education due to demands from students for courses that are delivered flexibly (Harris, 2009). ICT driven educational systems can be costly to implement and are eventually superseded due to the constant evolution of technology that spawns newer and more effective applications. A major challenge for universities is therefore to provide access to the latest technologies at a cost that is affordable to the institution itself and its' students. This chapter considers internationalisation of the curriculum, through student mobility and work integrated learning (WIL), and the use of ICT tools and services to support and enhance the student learning experience. A case study explores the use of ICT during a WIL course delivered at dual campuses in Melbourne, Australia and Ho Chi Minh City, Vietnam.

INTERNATIONALISING THE CURRICULUM

Internationalising the curriculum is an important and strategic initiative of universities today. An internationalised curriculum has the potential to enrich the educational experiences of local and international students by providing a range of opportunities for study and cultural exchange. Caruana and Hanstock (2003) identify student mobility as a main international activity. Student mobility is supported in university-led study tours, student exchange and field education overseas.

The cognitive approach to teaching and learning is often used with student mobility issues, and was the approach used in the WIL projects discussed in this chapter. This approach to education was developed in the latter half of the 20th Century with an emphasis on the active processes learners use to solve problems and construct new knowledge. It is also known as problem based learning. The two main instructional architectures that are used with the cognitive approach are the 'guided discovery' and the 'exploratory' (McKay,

2008). The guided discovery architecture uses real world problems or scenarios to drive the learning process. Students typically access various sources of data to resolve problems with instructional support available to help them. While the exploratory architecture offers high levels of learner control. The instruction is designed to provide a rich set of learning resources that include: learning content; examples; demonstrations; and knowledge/skills building exercises; complete with the means to navigate these materials. Educational instructional architectures of this type are frequently used for online courseware (Anderson, 2008).

Different approaches to teaching and learning create considerable challenges for mobility students with them often left to adapt to the new learning environment as part of the experience of studying in a different culture (Ward, Bochner & Furnham, 2001). Hofstede (1986) however contends however that, '"the burden of adaptation should be primarily on the teachers" and not the students (p. 301). Part of this adaptation includes the teacher taking responsibility for informing students of the approach taken to teaching and learning and how best to learn in this new environment. This involves recognition by the teacher of different levels and types of intellectual and social engagement, required by the student to participate effectively. Opportunities need to be provided to support and develop participation in a range of activities including listening, reading, speaking and writing (Northedge, 2003).

An internationalised curriculum requires assessment tasks and strategies that are "socially and culturally responsive" (MacKinnon & Manathunga 2003, p.133). Work produced by mobility students will reflect the level of course engagement and this needs to be reflected in assessment. Northedge (2003) stresses the importance of "teachers tolerating variant understandings provided there are clear signs of constructive engagement with the specialist discourse" (p. 5). Group work has been found to be effective for encouraging participation and the sharing of ideas and experiences between local and mobility students. However when it becomes a form of assessment outcomes are often found to be less successful, particularly for those deemed to be from minority groups (Strauss & Alice, 2007).

Student Mobility through Work Integrated Learning

Work Integrated Learning (WIL) is a central component of the commitment of universities worldwide to internationalizing the curriculum. Initially focused on the health and social sciences disciplines, in the past decade WIL has been offered to students in broad ranging multi-disciplinary project teams operating within an international context (Boyle, Nackerud & Kilpatrick,1997; Hawkins & Pattanayak, 2009; Rai, 2004). An extensive literature exists on the educational, psychological and social needs of students, with a range of international field practicum/WIL models developed (Pettys, Panos, Cox, & Oosthuysen, 2005; Razack, 2002; Tesoriero & Rajaratnam, 2001). Increasingly consideration is being given to the most appropriate use of technology to support these different models of international WIL and in particular cross cultural communication and teamwork in virtual spaces (Ahanchian & McCormick, 2009; Hawkins & Pattanayak, 2009).

Guldberg and Mackness (2009) stress the importance of ensuring that participants understand online community norms with this clearly articulated in induction materials and processes. In their study of online discussion groups De Wever, Van Keer, Schellens, & Valcke (2009) found that the assignment of roles, including the management of team building and communications early on in their learning programme, resulted in higher levels of social knowledge construction. Surprisingly however, in their review of 102 mobile learning projects Frohberg, Goth, and Schwabe (2009) found that few projects included a socializing context. They found that while most of these student mobility projects supported novices the greatest potential was with more advanced learners.

Networked Learning: ICT Services and Tools

The case study presented in this chapter focuses on the various ICT services and tools (ICT-ST) used for WIL, including: freeware and free ICT services; commercial software and ICT services. Freeware and free ICT services are complementary as in the case of electronic mail (email) (Martin & Tan, 2010). Email is a service provided to users for the purpose of communicating through the electronic/digital medium. However, actual communications are facilitated through software such as Microsoft 'Outlook' and various Web-browsers. While there are advantages with using a free ICT service, there are also many drawbacks. Like commercial services, the viability of these free services is dependent on funding, sourced invariably through donations or advertising. The security of information passing through external systems is not always secure as seen in security breaches on networking sites such as Facebook. The existence of malicious Web-sites that mimic legitimate ones also pose a significant risk to information security. Furthermore the technical support of these systems is variable, with it non-existent for some open source computer software (Grodzinsky & Wolf 2008; Reilly 2004; Thing 2002).

Commercial software and ICT services are usually available to individuals or corporations for a license fee with conditions of use protected by copyright. Invariably universities provide commercial email services and eLearning systems. At the university where the case study was conducted, this eLearning system is Blackboard. There are numerous free open source equivalent systems to Blackboard such as Moodle and Claroline. The primary focus of the following case study is on how Australian mobility students utilized ICT resources, to support their mobility studies abroad. A focus is on the purpose, methods and targets of ICT use and ICT usability.

CASE STUDY: THE USE OF ICT TO SUPPORT WORK INTEGRATED LEARNING ON DUAL CAMPUSES IN AUSTRALIA AND VIETNAM

Two WIL projects were conducted at an orphanage and a hospital in Vietnam. A cognitive approach to teaching and learning was adopted using problem based learning with guided discovery and exploratory architectures. Students were enrolled in undergraduate degree programs in business and marketing, project management, logistics, social work, psychology, social science and international studies. Students in both the orphanage and hospital groups allocated roles and responsibilities amongst themselves for the conduct of the project with one of these roles, ICT manager.

Orphanage Project

The orphanage was located in the south of Vietnam and run by a Buddhist monk who cares for approximately 160 children aged between six and 18 years. A donor established a water bottling plant at the orphanage in an endeavour to generate revenue. At the time of the WIL project the orphanage was producing bottled water, yet had not established this as a viable enterprise. The only means of distribution of the water was on a motorbike. The goal of the WIL project was to develop an achievable business and marketing plan for the water bottling plant at the orphanage.

This WIL project brought together a total of 30 undergraduate students in six multidisciplinary groups of five students from the university's dual campuses in Australia and Vietnam. All of the preliminary work was done by students in their home country location. Students in Vietnam visited the orphanage and communicated to the Australian students the main issues arising for the project. Chat rooms were established on Blackboard to facilitate this communication, with students also encouraged to use student email.

Prior to departing for Vietnam, the Australian students attended two intensive preparatory classes on Vietnamese cultural, social and economic issues. A focus was on organizational issues for the orphanage; in particular the shift from charity organization to business operator. In addition to these classes introductory sessions were also conducted on group work for the Melbourne based students. The Australian students travelled to Vietnam, accompanied by academic staff from Australia, and worked in their project groups for a two week period. On completion of the project students were required to present a coherent business plan to the management of the orphanage.

Hospital Project

The second project was located at a hospital in central Vietnam. This hospital was in the process of relocating a number of its departments to a new purpose built hospital. The oncology and paediatrics departments were to be expanded and remain in the original hospital building with funds committed to this project from a donor agency. The students' WIL project was to liaise with medical staff in the paediatrics department to assist in the redesign and refurbishment of the expanded wards. Specialist input was provided to the students by medical staff and a consultant, involved in the hospital redevelopment project.

The old paediatric wards consisted of 160 beds, most of which were shared beds with as many as three patients per bed, leading to an overall occupancy rate of around 350. The demand on beds had made it difficult to group patients according to their health needs such as gastroenterology, respiratory and neo-natal. Overcrowding was exacerbated by the presence of parents in the ward who provided meals, basic cleaning (bathing) and attended to the general needs of their children during their stay in the hospital.

The same cognitive problem-based teaching and learning model that was used in the orphanage project was applied to the hospital project, with

30 students from Vietnam and Australia working together in small multidisciplinary groups. These students were also reliant on ICT for communications with each other in the early stages of the project. Consequently the Vietnamese students conducted a site visit of the hospital and provided relevant information to the students in Australia through ICT-ST. This activity was followed by a joint site visit, conducted by the Vietnamese and Australian students. Upon the completion of the site visit, the students finalized their report and provided their recommendations to local hospital staff.

METHOD

The aim of this study was to gain a greater understanding of how students used ICT to support their WIL studies, and in particular for communications between Australia and Vietnam. Students communicated using technology over a period of approximately 10 weeks prior to departure from Australia, followed by a two week joint site visit on location in Vietnam to implement their plans. The online communication was a unique aspect of this course. In the past, such university-led study tours and multidisciplinary projects have been conducted between the Australian and Vietnam university campuses. These projects included 'environmental issues for water and waste management systems', and an 'architects without frontier's project' to design a building for homeless youth. These previous activities, for the most part, have been reliant upon the academic staff being on location in Vietnam with the students and their ICT tools used predominantly for administrative purposes.

Preliminary interviews were conducted with staff members in Melbourne who had experience using ICT resources at the Vietnam campuses. This material provided an overview of the range and functionality of the available ICT tools. Information gathered from these interviews was used to construct four student surveys. Three surveys were administered to all Melbourne-based students (MBS) at the beginning, middle and end of the WIL course, respectively with the fourth survey administered on location to all of the Vietnam students. A total of 29, 23 and 32 MBS responded to the first, second and third surveys, respectively. Twelve VBS participated in the fourth survey. The response rate for all surveys varied between 80 to 100 per cent.

The first survey identified proficiency levels with different types of ICT, what ICT resources students planned to use for WIL and the intended purpose. Usability of the ICT was measured according to the four criteria of; reliability, accessibility, availability and functionality as shown in Figure 1.

A second survey looked at specific ICT tools that students used while in Melbourne and how effective these tools were, relative to the above criterion. The third survey of Melbourne students was a replica of the second survey, yet from the perspective of ICT tools used within Vietnam. A fourth survey was carried out with Vietnam-based students (VBS) to provide a baseline data comparison with Melbourne-based students (MBS). This survey was a combination of the first- and the last-survey given to the Melbourne students.

Additional information was collected from contextual interviews and observations of MBS while they worked on their projects. The data was analysed by deriving a 'mean opinion score' (MOS) for each of these criteria based on the five point ordinal scale. Throughout the study, the use of ICT was monitored noting tools used for specific purposes. Observations of this communication by the research team assisted in developing an understanding of what technologies worked best for; facilitating relationship and team building, cultural knowledge and understanding and successful task completion.

A limitation of the study was different semester configurations on the Melbourne and Vietnam campuses. This reduced the study period as course-

Figure 1. Information communication technology-services/tools usability measurement criteria

Reliability - *Are ICT tools/services reliable?*
- *Bad* – Extremely slow. Continuous failures (eg. connection drop-outs, system down, etc).
- *Poor* – Very slow service. Frequent failures.
- *Adequate* – Mediocre service (e.g. some delays). Periodic failures.
- *Good* – Almost no failure. Rarely any delays in service.
- *Excellent* – Never experienced any failure. Instantaneous service.

Availability - *Are ICT tools available to all or are they restricted for specific purposes?*
- *Bad* – Close to zero availability. Strictly reserved for specific courses only. (eg. restricted to specific personnel on specific projects only).
- *Poor* – Very limited availability. Strictly for use with coursework only (any course).
- *Adequate* – Conditional availability. For any coursework and limited recreational purposes.
- *Good* – Readily available. For any coursework and most recreational purposes.
- *Excellent* – Available to anyone for any purpose.

Accessibility – *Are there geographical restrictions with regard to accessing the ICT tools (eg. campus access only, wired and/or wireless access)?*
Bad – Near ironclad restrictions (eg. access through specific laboratories only).
Poor – Highly limited access (eg. access through university campuses only).
Adequate – Access with some limitations (eg. within urban areas having appropriate ICT infrastructure coverage).
Good – Access with very few limitations (eg. mobile access within urban areas).
Excellent – Access with almost no limitations (eg. mobile access outside urban areas).

Functionality – *Do ICT tools provide necessary and sufficient functionality to facilitate communication? Is it user friendly?*
Bad – Rudimentary functions are absent. Difficult and cumbersome to use.
Poor – Lacking many basic functions. Quite complex to operate.
Adequate – Missing some basic functions. Not particularly complex to use.
Good – Covers almost all (if not all) basic functions. Easy to use and master.
Excellent – Has all basic functions plus additional features. Used with minimal learning effort.

work and exam periods were not synchronised. The available bandwidth for use of ICT at the Vietnam campus was also recognised as a limitation prior to the study. The primary focus on MBS was also a limitation of the study.

FINDINGS

The study findings present student levels of proficiency with ICT tools at the commencement of the student mobility WIL projects, methods and targets of ICT use and student usability ratings.

Proficiency in ICT

Both groups of students from Melbourne and Vietnam had adequate ICT proficiency skills. The majority of MBS considered themselves advanced in their use of email, networking sites, eLearning tools and mobile telephone. However most were

beginners when it came to video conferencing. The majority of the VBS also considered themselves advanced in the use of email and mobile telephone. In contrast to the MBS, however, most of the VBS considered themselves as being advanced in video conferencing. Interestingly, video conferencing was also the most frequent response recorded for VBS in the beginner category. VBS saw themselves for the most part adapting to using social networking sites and eLearning tools during their studies.

Purpose

As illustrated in Figure 2, MBS used ICT resources for accessing course related materials and information (89%), communication with VBS (89%) and submission of assignments (86%). They also used ICT-ST for staff consultations (79%) and discussions with other MBS (75%). In comparison, VBS used less ICT than MBS with a 10% decline

Figure 2. ICT-ST proficiency levels for Melbourne (left) and Vietnam (right) based students

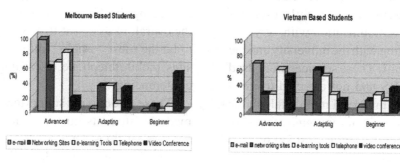

in most categories. The most notable differences were for staff consultation and local communication between students.

Type of ICT and Target

The information collected on type of ICT and target identifies what ICT resources were used with targets indicating who students communicated with. This was separated into pre- and post-departure with the former looking at Melbourne based communications and the latter ICT usage on location in Vietnam. During the pre-departure stage, students relied mostly on emails, networking sites and eLearning tools as seen in Figure 3.

When in Vietnam, the preferred ICT-ST students mostly used were: emails; networking sites; and mobile telephone services, with less use of eLearning tools. The networking site Facebook was predominantly used for communication between students. Contact with university staff was consistent with pre-departure levels. However, communication with the academic agency staff through ICT-ST was far less frequent on location in Vietnam. An additional communication target measured while students were in Vietnam was 'family and friends', with contact maintained through mobile telephone (80%), networking sites (75%) and email (60%).

A closer look at ICT-ST usage during pre-departure and post-departure periods, provides details of several popular networking sites and

different forms of mobile telephone services used. During the pre-departure stage, electronic messaging services (EMS) carried most of the volume of email communications with a small proportion (10%), coming from external email services. While Blackboard was the only eLearning tool available to MBS within the university's ICT infrastructure, a small number of students used external eLearning tools. The main networking site (NS), frequented by most students was Facebook (90%) with other NS recording lower levels of use. Mobile telephones were mostly used for sending smart messenger service (SMS)

Figure 3. Purpose of ICT utilisation, measured in percentage of student population, for Melbourne Based Students (MBS) and Vietnam Based Students (VBS). Categories: Course Material Acquisition (CMA), e.g. lecture notes; Assessment: Assignment submission (A-AS); Staff Consultations (SC); Discussions with Students in Melbourne (D-MBS); Discussion with Students in Vietnam – (D-VBS); Student Feedback Survey (SFS); Others (OTH).

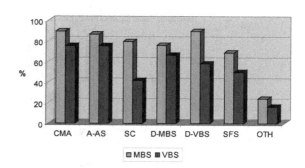

(50%) with slightly less use of voice calls (45%). Networking sites were predominantly used for student to student communication with very low use for communicating with the university and the academic agency staff. These services were used locally between MBS and not directed towards VBS. Skype was the preferred mobile telephone service for MBS (35%) when communicating with their Vietnam counterparts with most Skype calls conducted off-campus.

On location in Vietnam, the use of emails (-12%), networking sites and eLearning tools (-30%) decreased. This was associated with an increased use of mobile telephone services through voice calls (+28%) and SMS (+20%).

The ICT utilisation habits of VBS were similar to those of MBS post-departure. VBS were less reliant on EMS, phone calls and SMS. However, they were more partial to Yahoo Messenger and Skype. The main ICT-ST used by VBS were: EMS; Blackboard; Facebook; phone calls; SMS; Skype and Yahoo Messenger.

Usability

Figure 4 provides details of the general reliability, accessibility, availability and functionality of the different types of ICT-ST used throughout the projects, from the perspective of MBS. Usability was quantified by applying a 'mean opinion score' (MOS) to each criteria. With the exception of video conferencing, all ICT-ST, were found to have

adequate to good MOS ratings for every criteria. Averaging the MOS of all four criteria provides the overall usability of ICT-ST with email found to be the most "usable" followed by networking sites, mobile telephone, eLearning tools and video conferencing.

These findings are supported in the comments made by students during contextual interviews and observations. On completion of the projects, students commented on the desirability of having what they referred to as a 'base camp':

It would have been good to have a 'base camp' project management software/tool to communicate with other students and staff during the project.

Whilst email was found to have greatest usability student comments indicated increased functionality was desired:

The university email system lacks functionality. It should be upgraded to have better searching capabilities and have similar features as gmail.

The Blackboard system, the primary eLearning tool that was made available to students, had adequate reliability and functionality. However, a small, but noticeable proportion of students (20%) felt dissatisfied with the system, considering its functionality poor or bad as illustrated in the following student comments:

Figure 4. Methods and targets of communication for MBS pre-departure and post-departure

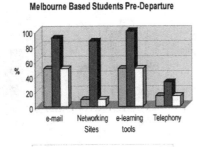

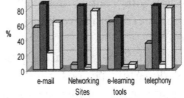

Blackboard has limited features, e.g., no alert, no automatic/live update of data/information, no discussion thread control. Files can only be uploaded one at time with no folders for file exchange; and

Blackboard is not as intuitive and flexible as it could be. It is difficult and clumsy to use. The disorganised structure makes it very tedious to navigate.

Furthermore, lengthy discussions with multiple project members and discussion threads proved difficult to keep track of as described in the following student comment:

Blackboard is an inadequate tool for communication. The Blackboard discussion board is chunky and outdated. I prefer to use email.

The functionality of Blackboard improved post-departure. A functionality that students desired was an 'instant messaging service' whereby group discussions could take place instantaneously. Some students used Facebook, Yahoo Messenger or MSN (Windows Live) Messenger, more so than the university-provided email and Blackboard for communications. Facebook was used for socialization, cultural exchange and project communications. From the commencement of the WIL course students in Melbourne and Vietnam communicated using Facebook to introduce one another, establish effective working relationships and for project communications. There was very low participation by university and agency staff in this medium of communication. For the purpose of short and instant communication, mobile telephone calls and SMS were found to be good in both reliability and functionality as illustrated in the following student comment:

Instant messaging services are better than Blackboard and email because of the message threads with instant responses.

The MBS were interested in using Skype. However, this system often suffered from synchronisation problems between the audio and video streams. Audio drop-outs occurred occasionally, though not as frequently as video drop-outs. These drop-out problems were intrinsically linked to the bandwidth capacity of the communication network. Just under half of MBS (45%) believed that the reliability of this system was poor or bad. In one particular observation where a Skype call was made between Melbourne and Vietnam, the video connection was practically non-existent while the audio aspect suffered from severe synchronisation problems. These problems were so severe that the meeting was switched to a mobile telephone audio conference call. However students reported that Skype functioned well during private communications conducted off campus. Staff interviewed at the commencement of the study, reported similar experiences. They also reverted to mobile telephone audio conferences on-campus, finding internet more accessible from venues (such as hotels) outside of the university. Staff attributed this problem to the limited bandwidth available on campus.

The lack of functional video conferencing facilities between the university campuses was an ongoing issue throughout the study as it was found to be the least usable ICT-ST. Students also expressed frustration with limitations in file exchange for image data. This dilemma was particularly an issue for the hospital group who were working on a building design with a student commenting:

Planning for building/architectural recommendations ideally should have video conferencing available for discussion with Vietnam students. ICT should be able to handle image data, building plans, floor plans, etc. Auto CAD and Photoshop were missing on computers (on campus) in Vietnam.

DISCUSSION OF FINDINGS

The problem-based cognitive approach to teaching and learning using, guided discovery and exploratory architecture, may be well suited to international student mobility WIL projects due to the high level of learner control. However clarity is required concerning the learning and assessment tasks with regular staff communication and feedback, with students experiencing cognitive difficulties needing additional support and guidance. The recommendation by students for the use of central project management, software, that they referred to as 'base camp', is consistent with recommendations in the literature (Hofstede, 1986; Northedge, 2003) that it is the responsibility of educators to provide the necessary structure for optimum student engagement and learning to occur. An online project management tool would also assist with important induction processes and information on cross cultural online community norms stressed by Guldberg and Mackness (2009). As well, it could provide students with a rich set of learning resources that include: learning content; examples; demonstrations; knowledge/skills building exercises (cross cultural and project related), complete with the means to navigate these.

The assignment of roles by both the hospital and orphanage groups, including ICT manager, assisted with socialisation, cultural knowledge exchange and the management of the projects. This finding is consistent with the De Wever et al. (2009) benefits of the early assignment of roles. All of the students in the projects were undergraduates with little or no international experience. These students benefited immensely from the WIL international student mobility experience challenging the assertion by Frohberg et. al (2009) that the greatest potential for student mobility projects is with the more advanced learners. These study findings suggest that both the level of experience of the students, the size of the mobility group and support that is provided, will influence learning experiences and outcomes.

Irrespective of geographical location in Melbourne or Vietnam, most of the ICT resources that students used during the WIL course were readily accessible through any internet connection. These ICT-ST (email, networking sites, eLearning tool) typically only required a functional Web-browser with a network connection to operate. The slightly higher use of ICT by the MBS overall throughout the study, particularly for the academic staff consultation and communication between students, suggests that these occurred in person more often throughout the duration of the course for the VBS than for the MBS. The considerably lower use of eLearning tools and mobile telephone by Melbourne students on location in Vietnam, for communications with the VBS and agency-staff is not surprising. The nature of the two week on-site visit for the projects meant that most communications between students and staff, previously facilitated through ICT, now occurred in person. Thus, the inefficient discussion board on the Blackboard system, previously used to when conducting group meetings, was replaced with face-to-face meetings. Therefore, the perceived usability of Blackboard, minus the associated discussion board, improved accordingly. Furthermore, when on location in the agencies, a lack of access to internet would have potentially limited or terminated the use of ICT-ST such as EMS, Blackboard and networking sites.

The SNS Facebook was found to be as reliable as EMS with greater functionality due to instant messaging services. While Facebook, and other external ICT services, provided additional functionality they may also pose security threats due to information transfer and repository that passes through, or remains in external systems. For general information this is not an issue. However, for sensitive data such as identity details and confidential project information this may be a problem. The technical support of these systems varies with some open source software not having any technical support. In the WIL study Facebook was predominantly used for student to student communication with very low staff and agency communication. This raises the question of to what extent staff should incorporate SNS such as Facebook in formal education programs. Should students continue to use Facebook for communication between themselves unofficially, or should it become more formalised? Is there a more formalised approach contrary to the intended and seemingly preferred use of SNS by undergraduate students? What are the implications of an increased use of freeware for study puroposes? This begs the question of the use of SNS and the intended informal nature of usage amongst friends as well as potential security threats if sensitive data is transmitted.

When in Vietnam, ICT tools provide the only convenient means of contact between students and their family and friends in Melbourne (See Figure 4). The effectiveness of different types of ICT-ST varied according to the different requirements of the project. The Blackboard system functioned well with its basic feature of distributing lecture notes and course materials, submitting reports and assignments, and broadcasting announcements, etc. However, students desired supplementary ICT-ST that supported real-time audio and visual communication. This is particularly important for facilitating constructive engagement for cultural exchange and project work for distance based projects, where meetings and discussions can only be conducted remotely. The study findings support the importance of group work for effective participation and sharing of ideas between mobility students (Northedge, 2003; Strauss & Alice, 2007), and the importance of ICT tools that support constructive engagement and meaningful exchange.

Students found that email and Blackboard were inefficient for conducting group discussions between the Vietnam and Melbourne campuses. This may be because the structure of discussions is organized in threads and it is often quite tedious to keep track of all of these. The preferred method for inter-campus discussions was video conferencing. Unfortunately however video conferencing technology, while commercially available

for many years, has limited scope of application and does not enjoy the same degree of proliferation and accessibility as other types of ICT such as emails, mobile telephones and social networking sites. The high reliability of Facebook made this a preferred means of communication. The greater reliability of software off campus raises the question of cost shifting as students are reliant upon their own, rather than university provided ICT resources. Issues of access and equity arise in terms of affordability for some students.

Data collected on proficiency levels with ICT, indicate that both MBS and VBS were adept with all of the ICT-ST used in the projects. However given less exposure to video conferencing technology, the MBS were unfamiliar with operating these tools/services. Proficiency data collected at the commencement of the study found the majority of MBS beginners were adapting to this technology. This was in contrast to the VBS who were advanced in their use of video conferencing, yet they still encountered considerable difficulties when attempting to use this technology on campus. Video conferencing services require considerable infrastructure investment, in terms of equipment and dedicated communication bandwidth, to operate effectively (See Figures 5-7).

Figure 5. ICT-ST usage for pre-departure (MBS). email: EMS (E1); others (E2). Networking sites: Facebook (N1); Myspace (N2); MSN (N3); Yahoo Messenger (N4); Others (N5). eLearning tools: Blackboard (L1); Others (L2). Telephony: phone calls (T1); SMS (T2); MMS (T3); Skype (T4); others (T5)

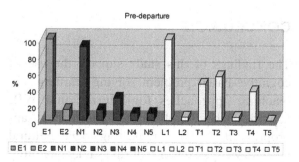

Figure 6. ICT-ST usage for post-departure (MBS). email: EMS (E1); others (E2). Networking sites: Facebook (N1); Myspace (N2); MSN (N3); Yahoo Messenger (N4); Others (N5). eLearning tools: Blackboard (L1); Others (L2). Telephony: phone calls (T1); SMS (T2); MMS (T3); Skype (T4); others (T5)

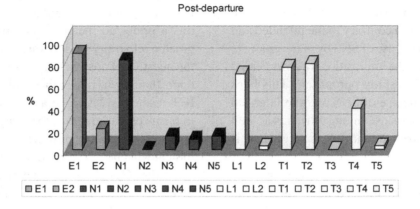

Figure 7. General reliability, accessibility, availability and functionality of different types of ICT-ST relative to the perspective of MBS

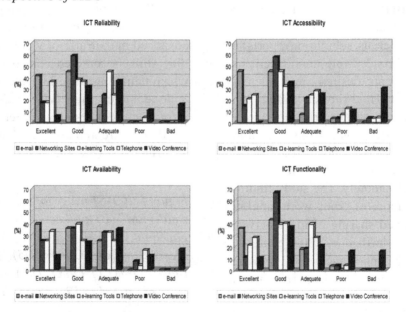

CONCLUSION

The findings of this study support the use of cognitive-based problem solving learning and teaching approaches for international WIL activities. They highlight the importance of appropriate ICT-ST for supporting social, cultural and knowledge exchange during student mobility abroad. ICT is particularly suited to coordinating the active, learner directed approaches to teaching and learning frequently used in student mobility projects abroad. Throughout the study, student choices of ICT tools of use were influenced by the purpose of the communication alongside: availability functionality; reliability; and accessibility. The study found that university-provided internal ICT services (EMS and Blackboard) were adequate in supporting WIL students. However, the primary concern with ICT resources for WIL, was the functionality of the Blackboard eLearning tool, provided by the university, predominantly the discussion board, and document handling and exchange functions. Facebook, which is an external ICT-ST, was considered more useful than the university's internal ICT systems. Audio visual communication was a preferred ICT for inter-campus communication, however reliability was limited. An ongoing challenge for universities is the decision making around the type and level of ICT to provide internally and what external ICT services and tools to include, when developing new curricula. Ultimately the reliability, availability, accessibility, functionality, security and appropriateness of these systems will have a major impact upon the quality of the learning and teaching experience. An online central management system or 'base camp' can assist students to navigate the complex technical, social, cultural and knowledge building opportunities that work integrated learning abroad offers.

ACKNOWLEDGMENT

Sincere thanks are expressed to the students involved the WIL projects in Melbourne and Vietnam for their generous participation in this study. Thanks also to Damian Tan, Julie Roberts, Jose Roberto Guevara, Phillip Dare, and Sarah Cunnian for their significant contribution. This project was funded by a Learning and Teaching Innovation Fund grant from RMIT University.

REFERENCES

Ahanchian, M. R., & McCormick, J. (2009). Culture and the processes of virtual teaming for training. *Journal of Computer Assisted Learning*, 25(4), 386–396. doi:10.1111/j.1365-2729.2009.00314.x

Anderson, T., & Elloumi, F. (Eds.). (2004). *Theory and practice of online learning*. Athabasca University.

Boyle, D., Nackerud, L., & Kilpatrick, A. (1997). The road less traveled: Cross-cultural, international experiential learning. *International Social Work*, 42(2), 201–214. doi:10.1177/002087289904200208

Caruana, V., & Hanstock, J. (2003). *Internationalising the curriculum: From policy to practice*. Retrieved from www.edu.salford.ac.uk/her/proceedings/papers/vc

De Wever, B., Van Keer, H., Schellens, T., & Valcke, M. (2009). Structuring asynchronous discussion groups: The impact of role assignment and self-assessment on students' levels of knowledge construction through social negotiation. *Journal of Computer Assisted Learning*, 25(2), 177–188. doi:10.1111/j.1365-2729.2008.00292.x

Facer, K., & Sandford, R. (2009). The next 25 years? Future scenarios and future directions for education and technology. *Journal of Computer Assisted Learning*, 26, 74–93. doi:10.1111/j.1365-2729.2009.00337.x

Frohberg, D., Goth, C., & Schwabe, G. (2009). Mobile learning projects: A critical analysis of the state of the art. *Journal of Computer Assisted Learning*, 25(4), 307–331. doi:10.1111/j.1365-2729.2009.00315.x

Grodzinsky, F. S., & Wolf, M. J. (2008). Ethical interest in free and pen source software. In Himma, K. E., & Tavani, H. T. (Eds.), *The handbook of information and computer ethics*. New Jersey: John Wiley & Sons. doi:10.1002/9780470281819.ch10

Guldberg, K., & Mackness, J. (2009). Foundations of communities of practice: Enablers and barriers to participation. *Journal of Computer Assisted Learning*, 25(6), 528–538. doi:10.1111/j.1365-2729.2009.00327.x

Harris, L. (2009). Electronic classroom, electronic community: Designing elearning environments to foster virtual social networks and student learning. In Martin, J., & Hawkins, L. (Eds.), *Information communication technologies for human services education and delivery: Concepts and cases* (pp. 87–104). Hershey, PA: IGI Global. doi:10.4018/978-1-60566-735-5.ch006

Hawkins, L., & Pattanayak, S. (2009). Virtual communication for field education placements in a global context. In Martin, J., & Hawkins, L. (Eds.), *Information communication technologies for human services education and delivery: Concepts and cases* (pp. 133–151). Hershey, PA: IGI Global. doi:10.4018/978-1-60566-735-5.ch009

MacKinnon, D., & Manathunga, C. (2003). Going global with assessment: What to do when the dominant culture's literacy drives assessment. *Higher Education Research & Development*, 22(2), 131–144. doi:10.1080/07294360304110

Martin, J., & McKay, E. (2009). Developing information communication technologies for the human services: Mental health and employment. In Martin, J., & Hawkins, L. (Eds.), *Information communication technologies for human services education and delivery: Concepts and cases* (pp. 152–166). Hershey, PA: IGI Global. doi:10.4018/978-1-60566-735-5.ch010

Martin, J., & Tan, D. (2010). Freeware solutions and international work integrated learning in higher education. In Burton Browning, J. (Ed.), *Open-source solutions in education: Theory and practice*. California, USA: Informing Science Press.

McKay, E. (2008). Human-dimensions of human-computer interaction: Balancing the HCI equation. In Balacheff, J. B. N. (Ed.), *The future of learning series* (*Vol. 3*). Amsterdam, The Netherlands: IOS Press.

Northedge, A. (2003). Rethinking teaching in the context of diversity. *Teaching in Higher Education*, 8(1), 17–32. doi:10.1080/1356251032000052302

Pettys, G., Panos, P., Cox, S., & Oosthuysen, K. (2005). Four models of international field placement. *International Social Work*, 48(3), 277–288. doi:10.1177/0020872805051705

Rai, G. (2004). International fieldwork experience: A survey of US schools. *International Social Work*, 47(2), 213–226. doi:10.1177/0020872804034138

Razack, N. (2002). A critical examination of international student exchanges. *International Social Work*, 45(2), 251–265.

Tesoriero, F., & Rajaratnam, A. (2001). Partnership in education. An Australian school of social work and a South Indian primary health care project. *International Social Work*, 44(1), 31–41. doi:10.1177/002087280104400104

Section 3

ePedagogy and Students' Use of HCI Interactive Learning Environments:

Performance Measurement Issues– How Can We Tell that People Have Learned Anything?

Chapter 9
Wiki–Mediated Peer Review Process:
Participation and Interaction

Long V. Nguyen
The University of Danang, Vietnam

ABSTRACT

The focus of this chapter is to explore if the collaborative potential offered by wikis translates into actual practice. The study examines the peer review process of 20 groups of English as a foreign language (EFL) students from two classes, i.e. a paper-based class and a wiki class, of a Bachelor of Arts (BA) in a Teaching English as a Foreign Language (TEFL) programme in a large university in Central Vietnam. Data analysis shows that the user-friendly wikis afford learning opportunities in two levels of analysis, namely participation and interaction, which lead to a high degree of information synthesis in the collaborative learning process. In terms of quantity, the multi-way nature of wiki-based exchanges confirms its characteristic of an architecture of participation. Likewise, the quality of the online peer review process is confidently affirmed in all three themes of collaborative interaction, i.e., socioaffective, organizational, and sociocognitive. It is concluded that the online platform of wikis turns the peer review process into a networking of both the academic and the social, and that wikis support a non-linear nature of collaborative learning.

INTRODUCTION

Different from traditional pedagogy where learning is a transmission of information from the teacher to learners, collaboration is a learning method that considers social interaction as a means of knowledge construction. Three critical attributes used to measure a collaborative learning process, as identified by Ingram and Hathorn (2004), are participation, interaction, and idea synthesis. While participation is important since collaboration cannot occur without roughly

DOI: 10.4018/978-1-4666-3649-1.ch009

extensive and equal participation among the participants, intensive participation per se is not enough. Even more important is the nature of interaction and synthesis of ideas among the group. Whether it is online or face-to-face (FTF), without these three characteristics, group work may be many things, but it cannot be called collaboration. Previous research (e.g., DiGiovanni & Nagaswami, 2001; Lee, 2010; Mawlawi Diab, 2010) consistently demonstrates that peer review (sometimes termed peer response, peer feedback, or peer editing) not only enhances a sense of audience and raises learners' awareness of their own strengths and weaknesses but also encourages collaborative learning in relation to idea synthesis among group members. This study aims to discuss the impact of computer-based technology, wikis in this case, on learner-learner interaction in an EFL collaborative task.

REVIEW OF LITERATURE

Theoretically, collaborative learning and peer review originate from sociocultural theory (SCT) which has become the focus of much research interest in recent years. While the psycholinguistic view of cognition construes the language learning process within the individual mind and emphases the significance of final products as a single measure to evaluate a learner's language proficiency (Ortega, 2009), SCT views language cognition as occurring first between individual minds and then within the individual mind during the internalization process. The learning process is therefore best understood in the social, cultural, historical, and institutional context where a learner is embedded. As a result, both product- and process-oriented learning styles are equally important and should be treated in an equal manner.

SCT highlights the significance of collaboration in language development through the zone of proximal development (ZPD), one of the most important constructs of the theory (Vygotsky,

1981). In the field of language education, ZPD is defined as the distance between the actual developmental level and the level of potential development through language, produced collaboratively with a teacher or peer (Ohta, 2001). Another outstanding construct of SCT is the concept of mediation. SCT stresses the central role of social interaction for learning as: all human learning is mediated through, or shaped by, interaction with others; and this shaping does not take place in a vacuum but through mediational tools. These tools include: language; cultural assumptions; social institutions; software or hardware; and time structure (Lamy & Hampel, 2007). Lantolf and Thorne (2007) even argue mediation is the principle construct that unites all varieties of SCT and is rooted in the observation that humans do not act directly on the world; rather their cognitive and material activities are mediated by symbolic (language, numeracy, concepts, etc.) and material (technology) artifacts. This concept paves the road for technology to enter into pedagogical approaches of collaborative learning and peer review.

Computer-mediated peer review can be considered an important aspect of collaborative learning (Arnold, Ducate and Kost, 2009; Liang, 2010; Nguyen, 2008; Ware & O'Dowd, 2008), as it enhances the process of evaluating and editing drafts, leading to the synthesis of information in the final product, as suggested in the work of Honeycutt (2001) and Liu and Sadler (2003). Honeycutt, for instance, compared the two classical text-based forms of computer-mediated communication (CMC) (email and chat) to study their effectiveness in the process of grammatical peer response. The results showed that synchronous conferencing and email could aid in the acquisition of collaborative peer review competence in different, yet complementary, ways. Liu and Saddler investigated the effect and affect of peer review in electronic, such as MOO (MOO stands for 'MUD object-oriented', and MUD stands for 'multi-user domain') and Microsoft Word, versus traditional modes on second language (L2) writing. The study found that, in terms of participation, the CMC students had a much larger percentage of editing and comments than the traditional peer response group. However, the results also revealed FTF communication was more effective than online exchanges due to the nonverbal interaction features in a peer review process. Another related study, by Ho and Savignon (2007), comparing computer-mediated peer review (email and Microsoft Word) and FTF peer review concluded that online peer review offered more flexibility, more comfort and less pressure than did the traditional method, thereby generating a high level of motivation.

Wiki has recently become known as a computer-based resource to facilitate collaborative learning (Coniam & Lee, 2008; Kessler, 2009; Kessler & Bikowski, 2010). One of the defining features of wiki The wiki-based Web space also offers a hyperlinked revision history of the writing where users can go back and track the development and base modifications on a previous version. These features of wikis strongly support collaborative communities of practices (Wheeler, Yeomans and Wheeler, 2008). Above all, what makes a wiki different from other forms of online interaction, according to Lund (2008), lies in its open architecture. The structure of a wiki "is not imposed or pre-determined [...] but emerges as a result of participation" (Lund, 2008, p. 41). By the same token, Warschauer (2010) asserted that wikis has turned conventional CMC activity around from informal, author-centric, personal exchanges found in email or chat to more formal, topic-centric, depersonalized interactions. One recent study was conducted by Lee (2010), who investigated the affordances and constraints of using wikis for collaborative writing in an elementary Spanish class. Lee concluded that most students were satisfied with and motivated by wiki-based task types that fostered creativity and interactivity while at the same time encouraging attention to form; but that they felt unsecure or uncomfortable correcting each other's work due to their low language proficiency. Another wiki-based study conducted

by Arnold et al., (2009) in three different universities involved 54 undergraduates of German. The authors concluded that wikis were evidently an effective educational tool to foster collaborative writing skills and revision behaviors and that this online tool seems to solve issues concerning equal contribution of work.

THE CURRENT STUDY

Keeping in mind the current scarcity of research on wikis in language teaching and learning (Warschauer, 2010), this chapter aims to explore various collaborative potentials that wikis may bring about in language education. Within the theoretical framework of SCT in collaborative learning and peer review, the study focuses on the level and nature of Vietnamese EFL students' participation and interaction in the process of collaborative exchanges via wikis. The research seeks to complement findings from other studies on the use of wikis in foreign language education by presenting a unique way of examining the types of feedback exchanges among learners. Following are the research questions that were addressed in the study:

1. What is the level and nature of Vietnamese EFL learners' participation in the wiki-mediated process of peer review, compared with traditional pen-and-paper peer exchanges?
2. What are the features of the learners' interaction in the wiki-mediated process of peer review, compared with traditional pen-and-paper peer exchanges?

Participants and Activity

Sixty students from two BA in TEFL classes were invited to participate in the project while they were taking a compulsory course of 'American Culture' in their sixth semester out of the eight-semester programme. The study was conducted at the College of Foreign Languages (CFL) of a large university in Central Vietnam, where, as in many other universities and colleges in Vietnam, the use of technology was still quite limited, both at the managerial level and in relation to application to teaching and learning (Nguyen, 2010). One of the classes (n=30) was designated the paper-based class while the other (n=30), the wiki class.

According to a survey conducted to determine their educational backgrounds and computer technology skills, the average age of these teacher trainees (55 female and 5 male) was 21.5 years. They were quite confident in grammar, vocabulary, and reading with the mean score of 3.83, 3.12, and 3.12 respectively in the 5-point scale, with 5 indicating the strongest (Nguyen & White, 2011). The survey conversely indicated that they were rather weak in writing, speaking, and listening. Also reported in the questionnaire was their computer literacy. Only 50% of the students owned a computer at home; and 40% had used computers for less than a year. More specifically, 15 students in the wiki class self-reported that their computer skills as poor, while 14 considered good, and only one student feeling very good. Once a week for two hours, the paper-based class studied with the teacher in their normal classroom, while the wiki class learned in the technology-rich classroom.

As part of the course requirements, the students worked in groups of three each to compose an essay about at least three similarities and/or differences between American and Vietnamese culture. The students formed groups themselves and worked together throughout the task. After discussing with each other about topic selection, idea development, and task division, group members wrote their first drafts which were exchanged with others for peer editing, based on a peer review sheet previously provided by the teacher (See Box 1 in Appendix 1). They then revised their work accordingly. The final product was a process of merging individual drafts together into a single essay. The whole process of peer review

lasted for three weeks and was out-of-class time. Groups were required to submit all their work to the teacher/researcher. For the paper-based class, these included first and second drafts, peer review sheets, and the final essays. The wiki groups had also to submit similar items. However, instead of collecting their work on paper, the teacher was able to view all their peer review process online. Written consent was obtained for the collection, analysis, and quotation of the data.

Use of Technology

Wiki has been known as a recent computer-based resource to facilitate collaborative learning (Coniam & Lee, 2008; Kessler & Bikowski, 2010; Lee, 2010; Richardson, 2006). The name wiki is Hawaiian for quick or super-fast and the defining feature of the technology is the ease with which pages can be created and updated by several users at the same time. In general, any users can modify any documents and there is no prior review before modifications are accepted, and most wikis are theoretically open to the general public - or at least anyone who has access to the wiki server. Once in a site on the wiki system, users are immediately presented with the most recent writing. This piece of writing can be altered, edited, and resubmitted. The wiki-based Web space also offers a hyperlinked revision history of the writing where users can go back and track development and base modifications on a previous version. These features of wiki strongly support a collaborative 'communities of practice' (Wheeler, et al., 2008). Above all, what makes a wiki different from other forms of online communication, according to Lund (2008), lies in its open architecture. The structure of a wiki "is not imposed or pre-determined … but emerges as a result of participation" (Lund, 2008, p. 41).

There were several options to choose which wiki platform to use for the current study. These included Writeboard, Wikispaces, and PBWorks among many others. While these platforms share many common characteristics, consisting of a sharable, Web-based text documents that let users save any edits, roll back to any versions, and easily compare changes, they are different in some minor aspects.

Writeboard, being the easiest one, lets users register directly on the frontpage; but this platform does not have much security capacity. Wikispaces, on the other hand, despite being quite popular, was not selected for the current study because the comment feature, named Discussion, is not quite user-friendly. Users must click on the 'discussion button', taking them away from the main page, in order to give comments.

PBWorks is different. In addition to being easy to use, it has the comment function located right at the bottom of the main page, making it convenient for users to leave their feedback right below the writing, together with the page history utility that helps users to conveniently compare between versions. In addition, the workspace security is high in PBWorks, where the owner of a site can choose who will be able to view only, who will be able to edit, and who will have the same rights as the owner's. Another feature of PBWorks is that site members are almost immediately informed of any edits, comments, feedback, and changes through email. So, it was convenient for the researcher, who just checked his regular email to see if any modifications had been made in any groups. PBWorks was hence selected. Ten PBWorks sites in total were created and a basic instruction of how to use this platform was prepared and placed on the front page of each group site (http://americancultures.pbworks.com/). The three students in a particular group could view, edit, and give comments on their own group sites only. The purpose of this was to help wiki students feel securely private within their group, and also to make it similar to the paper-based situation. All the sites, however, were open to public view by the end of the course when all assignments had been completed so that the whole class could learn from each other.

Data Collection and Analysis

Sixty drafts together with corresponding peer review sheets were collected: 30 pen-and-papers and 30 wiki pages. All comments were entered into NVivo 8.0 to make them ready for coding. While comments on the wiki pages were copied and pasted to the NVivo windows, paper-based comments were typed verbatim from the students' papers. The coding was based on sentential meaningful units (Liu & Sadler, 2003). An entry could consist of several sentence-level comments. A comment may be as short as just one word, like 'Good!'; or as long as a compound and/or complex sentence, such as "[i]n the paragraph about the Valentine day, it will be more interesting if Tuan make clear about how romantic and interesting Valentine day is, which I think there should be more information in this point". All comments were first analyzed in terms of the number of comments made by each group, and then the number of comments contributed by each member in a group. In order to analyze the level of contribution, the number of comments per person was used to calculate the participation percentage per member, which was then used to calculate the Gini coefficients (Fitze, 2006; Warschauer, 1996) of inequality for each mode of peer exchange. The Gini coefficient presents values from 0 to 1, in which the smaller Gini coefficients correspond to greater equality.

Comments were then classified in accordance with their general focus into three broad themes, i.e. socioaffective, organizational, and sociocognitive, identified by Mangenot and Nissen (2006), which were then recoded into emergent subcategories according to their focus and purpose in each theme (See Table 3 in Appendix 2). Furthermore, comments in the sociocognitive theme were coded into global versus local areas. While the global comments include those with regard to idea development, essay structure and organization, and audience and purpose, the local feedback covers those relating to grammar structure, wording, punctuation and spelling.

All the comments in the sociocognitive theme were then classified into various types, such as" clarification; explanation; suggestion; request; evaluation; addition; deletion; and alteration (Liu & Sadler, 2003). Evaluation comments were also coded as complimentary or critical (Liou & Peng, 2009). This classification of types helped to decide the revision-oriented nature versus the non-revision-oriented nature of comments. In addition, qualitative information from informal interviews and the researcher's observations was used to support the discussion.

In order to check the reliability of the coding process, a PhD candidate was requested to help with the coding. Guidelines were prepared stating clearly what constituted an entry and a sentential meaningful unit; and the three collaborative themes as well as emerging subcategories were formulated; and were introduced to the student. The two coders worked together, coding a sample peer review sheet until they both felt satisfied with the criteria. Then, all the entries from a randomly selected group of each mode were selected and coded independently by the two coders. The themes and subcategories from the two sets of coding attained 90% agreement. Discussions between the two coders resolved all disagreements.

RESULTS

Participation

The quantitative data revealed that the peer review by the wiki groups produced a total of 1,117 comments, considerably more than double those made by the paper-based groups of 476 comments. More specifically, the number of comments ranged from as few as 31 to 82 in the paper-based class (See Table 4 in Appendix 3). Meanwhile, the wiki class produced a much higher number of comments, varying from 61 to 135, not to mention group W10, who had the extraordinary total of 250 comments contributed by the three

members (See Table 5 in Appendix 4). As far as participation of individual students was concerned, the comment number ranged from only 5 to 39 in the paper-based groups; and up to 66 in the wiki groups, again not including the exceptional number of 133 comments made by Phuong (all names are pseudonyms) in the wiki group W10. In general, it can be concluded from Table 1 that the number of comments by groups in the wiki class (Mean: 101.50, SD: 52.36) is significantly higher than those in the paper-based class (Mean: 47.40, SD: 15.95) at .01 level of significance. Similarly, wiki members produced a significantly higher number of comments per individual (Mean: 33.83, SD: 23.84) than those contributed by the paper-based members (Mean: 15.80, SD: 9.49) at the .01 level of significance. Finally, of interest was the Gini coefficient figure. Though there was no statistically significant difference between the two classes regarding the measurement of participation inequality, contribution (in terms of the number of comments) among members in the wiki groups tended to be more equal than in the paper-mode groups as the mean Gini coefficient was higher in the latter (.19 versus .28)

These substantial differences can be explained by the learning situation in which the paper-based groups used pen and paper to give feedback on their peers' drafts. This traditional mode partly impeded learners from easily editing drafts and interacting with other group members. The paper-based students had three weeks to do this in their own, out-of-class time. How much time was spent by each student to read and/or give comments on drafts was unknown by the teacher. The wiki groups, on the other hand, conducted the same required task on the wikis. With the same period of their own, out-of-class time, they could log in to their group wiki sites to read and/or comment on their peers' drafts as many times as they wanted to. Their login times, observed by the teacher, ranged from 10 to 102, making a mean of 45 times per student during this peer comment process. This reveals the effectiveness of the wiki on the learn-

Table 1. Pen-and-paper versus wiki peer comments: T-test analysis

	Paper-based class (n=10)		Wiki class (n=10)			
	Mean	S. D.	Mean	S. D.	t	$p*$
Total words by groups	434.40	184.44	997.60	469.86	3.53	.004
Total comments by groups	47.40	15.95	101.50	52.36	3.13	.006
Gini coefficients	.28	.15	.19	.10	.96	.086
	Paper-based members (n=30)		Wiki members (n=30)			
	Mean	S. D.	Mean	S. D.	t	p*
Comments by members	15.80	9.49	33.83	23.84	3.85	.000

* Significant at $p < .01$

ers' motivation and involvement in this instance, reflected in the quantity of comments and the tendency of more equal participation. Moreover, in addition to following the peer review guideline provided by the teacher and correcting directly on the peers' draft, as did the paper-based groups, wiki students could also edit their own draft as well as the final essay. It is therefore no wonder that there were a considerably larger number of comments in the wiki groups compared to the paper-based mode.

Interaction

The analysis reveals that comments coded into the sociocognitive theme dominated in both modes of learning with 795 comments found in the wiki groups and 458 obtained from the paper-based groups. On average, the wiki class produced 80 sociocognitive comments per group, nearly double the mean of 45 made by a paper-based group. This indicated that the groups in both classes stayed focused on the assigned task, especially the paper-based groups, who in contrast had a minimal number of comments related to the other themes: socioaffective and organizational. Regarding these two themes, the wiki groups sketched a different picture with a roughly equal, and comparatively high, number of comments (Table 2).

The online groups turned the wiki platform into a collective environment for their supplement of chatting, making jokes, and expressing emotions, besides the main sociocognitive duty of giving corrective comments on each other's drafts. They made use of the various functions of the wiki to make the peer review process more than just giving and receiving feedback but also an online community of learning and interaction. The nature of these comments will be discussed below.

Socioaffective Comments

Emergent subcategories under the socioaffective theme included comments relating to (1) intersubjectivity, (2) personal exchanges, (3) emotional

Table 2. Comments coded into themes

	Paper-based Peer Comments		Wiki Peer Comments	
	No	%	No	%
Socioaffective	16	3.4%	173	15.5%
Organizational	2	.4%	149	13.3%
Sociocognitive	458	96.2%	795	71.2%
Total	476	100%	1,117	100%

expression, (4) social cohesion, and (5) the use of first language, i.e. Vietnamese. Even though these social and affective elements were not part of the required task in the peer review process, the convenience of the wiki encouraged the wiki groups to produce a huge number of 173 socioaffective comments in comparison with only 16 made by the paper-based groups (Figure 1).

Most of the socioaffective comments were categorized into the intersubjectivity subcategory, defined as consisting of sentences encouraging, acknowledging, seeking agreement, and agreeing or rejecting general ideas. Nga's and Loc's entries below (all examples are cited verbatim) show how wiki group W04 expressed their acknowledgements after their drafts were commented on by other group members. All of this group's socioaffective exchanges were in the intersubjectivity subcategory.

Nga, W04: *Ok, I see. Thanks for your feedback. They are really useful. I will revise the topic sentence and rewrite it when we make a whole essay.*

Loc, W04: *I agree with your comment, i'll combine 2 sentences of the para.*

In addition, intersubjectivity was experienced when Phuong in group W10, the most contributing member, continuously gave support to Chuyen on her draft, from encouragement, "This's interesting. [...] Good job 🌑" to seeking consensus, "I hope my comment is useful to for you. [...] Let me know your idea" after giving some advice on Chuyen's piece of writing.

The number of comments concerning emotional expression and personal exchanges were also high and roughly equal in the wiki groups while the whole 10 paper-based groups wrote only one or two sentences on these subcategories. In addition, the use of paper-based comments proved that no social cohesion, such as greeting, introducing, and farewell, was needed in this editing procedure whilst the wiki groups had 11 comments of this

type. Similarly, the use of Vietnamese, mainly to express various personal feelings, was also observed throughout the wiki sites, whereas no instance of the first language use was found in the traditional version. M. Hang in W10 had the most comments, using Vietnamese to show her interest and curiosity for learning with the wiki for the first time. Notably, the use of half English and half Vietnamese like M. Hang's second example below are quite frequent among these Vietnamese students of English.

M. Hang, W10: *woa, we se lam an j here? Kaka (Translated: Wow, what will we do with this? Kaka)*

M. Hang, W10: *xong dat your page day^^ (Translated: Glad to be the first footer in your page^^)*

To sum up, socioaffective exchanges did, without a doubt, appear on the wiki sites throughout the online groups to a various extent. The wiki environment, by nature, facilitated socially and affectively oriented collaborative interaction. The students made use of various functions in the wiki to exchange their emotional expressions, intersubjectivity, personal exchanges, and social cohesion as part their reviewing process.

These comments, as a supplement to the sociocognitive theme, helped to build a collaborative community of learning, in which members

Figure 1. Socioaffective comments coded into emergent subcategories

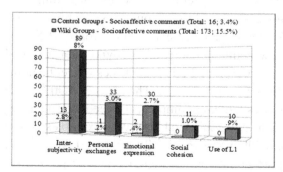

used various techniques, such as encouragement, seeking agreement, self-disclosure, and first language use among many other social and affective means, in order to attain and maintain a shared understanding and interdependency.

Organizational Comments

Comments in the organizational theme are sub-coded into (1) feedback management, (2) teacher involvement, (3) group management, and (4) technical management according to their focus and purpose (Figure 2). There were 87 organizational comments in the wiki groups coded as feedback management. Second in the rank as regards the organizational theme were entries made by the teacher, whose comments during the peer review procedure were mainly to control and to remind students to participate. Also in the wiki-based data, 18 comments were coded under the group management subcategory, consisting of comments expressing the finishing of the peer review process and the group work time management, while only 7 comments were found regarding the technical management. The paper-based groups had only two comments in the organizational theme, produced by N. Phuong, the class monitor and also the leader of group P01, and coded as feedback management.

All of the wiki groups to various extents made use of the wiki environment to control the group feedback process. By reminding the other members to contribute, Nguyen in W06, for example, directly helped increase the quantity of entries and the quality of peer review in this wiki group. She alone wrote up to 24, out of 32, comments on feedback management of this group. The page view count statistics on the wiki later revealed that Nguyen had 102 login times while the number for Anh was 8 and Thoa was 30. Other wiki groups did have comments on feedback management, but considerably fewer. Examples below show how she repeatedly prompted Anh to add more comments on their work. The second reminder was three days after the first one:

Figure 2. Organizational comments coded into emergent subcategories

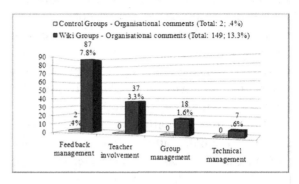

Nguyen, W06: *Anh! Why u don't comment our writing? I think it's useful for our writing. We must write the final essay, so, u hurry up.*
Nguyen, W06: *Anh! Plz add your comment on final essay!*

The two other subcategories, which had a modest number of comments, were group management and technical management. The two examples below are representatives of the 18 comments coded as group management, generated exclusively by the wiki groups. One indicated the finishing phase of the peer review process, "ok, if you have not any comment, I'll edit again and send to our teacher!" (H. Phuong, W02), while the other expressed a concern about the due time, "Be quick please. The due date is coming..." (Nghia, W07). Regarding the technical management, the general low number of comments of this subcategory demonstrates the fact that the groups were able to function effectively within the online asynchronous learning setting; and that the use of wiki, as a learning environment, was not so challenging for these groups of learners, whose computer skills were reported to be rather limited. Similar to those in the group management category, comments coded as technical issues are clearly generated by the online groups only.

In general, it is easy to understand that there were hardly any entries by the paper-based groups coded as organizational because this was not required in the peer review task, and because the traditional pen-and-paper peer review method did not encourage them to add any comments other than those were directly related to the requirements. The wiki groups, on the other hand, made use of the wiki platform to manage group dynamics.

Sociocognitive Comments

The wiki groups had nearly 75% more sociocognitive comments than those produced by the paper-based groups (795 versus 458). This correlates with findings by Liu and Sadler (2003). Nevertheless, comments in this theme covered up to 96.2% in the paper-based mode, compared to only 71.2% in the wiki modality, due to the latter groups' considerable percentage of comments allocated to the two other themes. Revealed below are the types, the areas, and the nature of sociocognitive comments.

As illustrated in Figure 3 presenting a variety of types according to their focuses, the first and most outstanding of all were those comments categorized into the 'alteration' type which accounted for 26.7% of all comments made by the wiki groups (298 out of 1,117). As mentioned previously, the traditional use of pen-and-paper limited the number of this type. However, these comments were still outnumbered in the paper-based groups as it seemed to be the easiest way to give feedback

Figure 3. Sociocognitive comments coded into emergent types

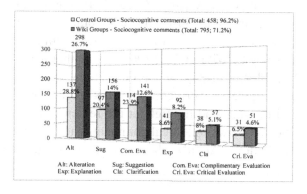

as compared with other more global and abstract components. Alteration comments covered 28.8% of all comments made by the paper-based groups (137 out of 476). Other than just underlining and correcting on the side of the paper, the wiki groups used various tools provided by the wiki platform to add, delete, and replace text directly on the wiki space. The snapshot in Figure 4 shows how the wiki group W05 members corrected one of their peer's drafts, by underlining, bolding, coloring, capitalizing, bracketing, inserting, deleting and so on. It is noted that there is not a spelling and grammar check function, like Microsoft Word's, on PBWork.

The second big difference in number between the two modes of peer review was in comments concerning explanation. This type of comment usually followed what was evaluated, suggested, and/or responding to others' request for clarification. As shown in the example below, Nghia (W07) started her entry with some complimenting evaluations, followed up with an explanation for the appraisal, indicating it facilitated correction, "Your writing has a clear topic sentence which is easy to understand and the tone is very smooth. You don't make so many grammatical errors. Therefore, it is easier for me to recommend correction…"

Explanations responding to clarification requests were, however, exclusive in the wiki groups due to the nature of the multi-way interaction of the wiki-based exchanges. An example of this type of explanation was found in group W10 when Chuyen, on reviewing the final essay, found out that there was an introduction part missing, "no introduction or [yo]u leave it later?" Phuong, who was in charge of compiling the final essay, explained to Chuyen two days later, "I didn't know how to write the introduction in an effective way, so I leave it blank, Chuyen." Especially, explanation comments may trigger instances of negotiation and challenge. Thoa in group W06, for example, rejected Anh's comments suggesting that she should add more detail in the general organization of the draft. One day later, Thoa replied:

Figure 4. A snapshot captured and pasted from the W05's wiki site

Anh, W06: *I think that your topic sentence is not good enough! It's should be more general! The best thing is that you showed the reason why the view of cohabitation are quite different between US and VN. In my opinion, you should add more information about the result of this life style; and*

Thoa, W06: *Thanks for your comments. However, my paragraph only focus on comparison 'the social attitudes toward cohabitation in US and VN' so i think the results is not necessary. And my topic sentence is the first sentence, the last sentence is to summarize for my paragraph.*

These exchanges, while hardly seen in the paper-based groups due to the paper-based nature of their comments, were scattered on the 10 wiki sites. The chains of evaluation-explanation, suggestion-explanation, and especially clarification-explanation made the online peer review much more efficient than the traditional method so far as the collaborative community of learning was concerned. These chains, or cycles, of negotiation

and scaffolding transferred the intermental plane of social interaction to the intramental plane of thinking in terms of Vygotsky's ZPD (1981).

Both classes had a comparatively low number of clarification comments, with the exceptions of P04 (9 comments) and W09 (10 comments), indicating the high and shared level of English. Finally, of consideration was the discrepancy in the number of comments concerning complimenting evaluation and critical evaluation in both classes. The wiki groups had 141 complimenting comments, nearly three times as many as those of critical feedback of only 51. Similarly, all 10 paper-based groups had only 31 critical comments, compared to the large number of 114 complimenting remarks. Group W10 stands out with as many as 30 instances of praising their peers' work, while only one critical comment was found. Wiki group W06, on the other hand, had 14 (out of 35) critical evaluations. Nguyen alone made eight critical comments in this group; and these spread throughout the review period. Shown below are critical comments she gave on Anh's draft. At first, she requested more ideas in the writing as "it is not enough". The second comment, which came 10 days after the first one when Anh had modified on her writing accordingly, suggested more coherence:

Nguyen, W06: *I think your writting has good ideal but it is not enough; and*

Nguyen, W06: *Your writing has a clear topic sentence which is easy to understand for us. That"s good. However, your writing has not coherence.*

As for areas of comments, it is revealed in Figure 5 that there were a relatively similar number of comments on global (230) and local (228) areas in the paper-based groups.

In the wiki groups, a difference, though small, was observed in respect of these two areas, in which there were more local comments than global comments. This discrepancy in the wiki groups was mainly contributed to by the large quantity of comments coded as alteration type as presented previously. Overall, the wiki groups exceeded the paper-based groups in both areas. These findings justly reflected the nature of the peer review procedure based on the review guidelines, in which the students were asked to cover both local grammatical errors and global essay organization, together with their evaluation towards the piece of writing. A clearer discrepancy is seen in the local comments, the average number

Figure 5. Sociocognitive comments coded into areas and nature

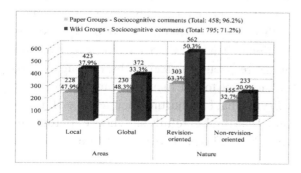

per group of which was 42 in the online class, nearly double the 23 comments per group in the paper-based version. Individually, Nghia in W07 created the highest of 47 local comments, while the record of 28 global comments was keyed in by Phuong in W10. Both of these students were in the wiki modality.

The last criterion for the classification of the sociocognitive comments was their orientation, i.e. nature of comments. The sociocognitive comments were divided into two groups. The revision-oriented group included comments categorized as alteration, suggestion, and critical evaluation, while the non-revision-oriented group consists of those comments coded as clarification, explanation, and complimenting evaluation. Both modes of the peer review process produced a considerably higher number of revision-oriented comments than non-revision-oriented (See Figure 5). More clearly, there were 2.5 times as many revision-oriented comments as non-revision-oriented in the wiki groups, while this ratio in the paper-based groups was under 2.0. This signified that the wiki-based peer review was more effective than the traditional method in terms of proportionately more revision-initiated comments.

A comparison between the two modes within each category reveals that there was a slight difference between the wiki groups (233) and the paper-based groups (155) in non-revision-oriented sociocognitive comments. Nevertheless, the number of revision-oriented comments by the wiki groups was nearly double that of the paper-based groups, with 562 versus 303 respectively. On looking at the presentation of the comment types, it can be inferred that the evidently high quantity of revision-oriented comments in the wiki groups was due to the large number of alteration comments made by these online members.

In summary, online comments substantially outnumbered those generated in the traditional method of peer review in all three themes of collaborative learning. While there was a dearth of comments related to the socioaffective and organizational themes in the 10 paper-based groups, these social, emotional, and logistical exchanges accounted for a considerable proportion throughout the 10 wiki-based groups. Hence, the two modes of peer review illustrated a high concentration on task, reflected in the dominant percentage of sociocognitive comments. Still, there were significantly more cognitive comments produced by the online groups than the paper-based version in all three criteria, namely: types; areas; and nature. Above all, the multi-way interactive feature of wikis facilitated a large number of comments that were rarely seen in the paper-based version of peer review.

SUMMARY AND DISCUSSION

The initial inference is that the wikis, as a mediational tool for interaction, afforded the students opportunities to work collaboratively. More specifically, in this peer review process, the user-friendly wiki platform, which is termed an 'architecture of participation' by Wheeler et al. (2008), facilitated student contribution, reflected in the huge number of comments generated, in comparison to the paper-based groups. This open architecture was perceived by many online students. Similar to Lee's (2010) students who expressed their satisfaction and motivation while learning in the wiki-mediated environment, Tam (W02), for example, shared her views in an interview with the researcher that "working on the wiki was more motivating. We could have many more comments on wiki. I gave comments to others, then the others gave feedback on mine; then I commented again ... continuously. It was hard to do this on paper". This was thanks to the fact that peer exchanges on the wikis could be done independently of space and time. Another reason might also be due to the novelty of using wikis in the classroom. Moreover, the number of online comments was multiplied by the multi-way

nature of wiki-based exchanges, based on which a considerable number of interactive and negotiable comments were generated. In sum, by increasing, and tending to equalize, the level of contribution, wiki seems to fulfill the first requirement, i.e. participation, of collaborative learning, according to Ingram and Hathorn (2004)

Furthermore, the task requirement and the traditional nature of peer feedback made the paper-based groups orientate their comments mostly to sociocognitive components. Beyond these, the wiki groups also had a considerable number of comments related to socioaffective and organizational themes, which were found to be minimal in the paper-based feedback. These two comment themes evidently had their own significant roles in creating learning opportunities within the ZPD. While the traditional mode of commenting reflected a one-way interaction, in which there was hardly counter-feedback and/ or explanation, the wiki mode of peer review, by nature, supported the two, if not multi, way of interaction, as one of the outstanding characteristics of Web 2.0 (Wheeler, et al., 2008), based on which not just and mostly the cognitive level of learning, indicating a high degree of commitment to task, but also the socioaffective and organizational levels of collaboration can be attained. The wiki groups by and large furthered the peer review process beyond the designated task with a range of socioaffective and organizational comments to a networking of both academic and social aspects.

Regarding the socioaffective theme that captured all of the students' social and emotional exchanges, the five subcategories coded under this theme reflected collaborative effectiveness by illustrating how the online groups express their emotional behaviors, social cohesiveness, and mutual respect, as perceived by Phuong (W10), "... I feel free to give them my comments without worrying that I am hurting their feelings. It is because I can think carefully and choose appropriate words before I type them down. More than that, I can delete previous comments and replace them with more suitable ones". While all of the five subcategories were seen throughout the online groups' peer review process, intersubjectivity turns out to be the most outstanding element. From the Vygotskian view of cognitive development, intersubjectivity is considered a significant byproduct of collaborative discourse (Darhower, 2002). Intersubjectivity assists in establishing a shared perspective between group members during the process of problem solving. Rather than just experience and reflection on the world, the concept consists of an engagement with the social context. The various intersubjectivity comments constructed a social and cognitive space facilitating participants' mutual support and indicated cycles of negotiation and challenge, leading to a higher degree of autonomy, the efficacy of collaborative peer review procedures, and a potential level of information synthesis. Obviously, the platform made learners more committed to and prepared to invest more effort in the collaborative process. For M. Hang (W10), the wiki was certainly not only a cognitive environment for learning and collaboration, but also a social platform for sharing emotion, "Wiki does encourage us to leave comments on our partners' writings. Furthermore, this is also a good place for us to share things happening in our daily lives, which are now gradually reduced to meet the study requirements. I myself feel so close to my group thanks to wiki. Thanks so much for this helpful website, teacher".

Similarly, the four subcategories in the organizational theme also played significant roles in building up and maintaining the peer review process. Feedback management comments were comparatively copious, indicating the high level of autonomy across the 10 wiki groups and thereof affording the occurrence of ZPD. In essence, most of the organizational comments, similar to those in the socioaffective theme, were generated in order to construct, maintain, and enhance the collaborative community of learning. Obviously,

this member of Web 2.0 and social software tools facilitate the notions of participation and productivity (McLoughlin & Lee, 2008) in the learning process of the networked society.

The analysis of the sociocognitive comments aiming to explore the peer review process's affordances revealed that comments in the wiki groups outnumbered those made by the paper-based groups with regard to types, areas, and nature. Of the six types of comments coded, alteration comments in the wiki groups were more prominent in number and were more than double those of the paper-based groups. This finding is endorsed by Liu and Saddler (2003), who, in their study, concluded that the major difference in comment types made by two groups was to do with alteration comments. This was obviously on account of the user-friendly aspects of the wiki platform, as a social and artifact mediator (Lantolf, 2000) during the peer review process. The result is also correlated with studies by Kessler (2009) and Lee (2010), who claimed that their students were more attentive to form within the collaborative construction of a wiki. In addition, of interest were explanation comments, the second significant difference in number between the two methods of peer exchange. A range of comments regarding explanation and counter-explanation facilitated the cycle of negotiated interaction and challenge in the online peer review process, making this mode of learning more efficient in terms of collaboration and highlighting opportunities for learners' potential language development through working with peers. Moreover, the number of online comments was also higher than paper-based comments with regard to areas, in which the difference between the two modalities was clearer in local comments, mainly because there were a larger number of alterations from the wiki groups. This larger quantity of alteration comments also resulted in the much higher number of comments coded as revision-oriented in the wiki groups as compared with the paper-based groups. Therefore, if the success of the peer review process is measured by the number of revision-oriented comments (Liou & Peng, 2009), then the online wiki-based peer feedback in the current study proved more successful than the paper-based version.

By tradition, Vietnamese learners tend to praise other people's work rather than criticize them, with the aim of keeping group harmony and unity. These Confucian-heritage collaborative practices were experienced in this study. There were a larger number of comments providing complimenting evaluation than critical evaluation in both modes of peer review. However, the ratio of critical comments per complimenting comments in the paper-based groups was (31/114 = .26) lower than the similar ratio in the online groups (51/141 = .36). Apparently, the wiki-based peer review process proportionately generated more critical comments than did the paper-based groups. This indicates that online peer review tended to be more analytical and revision-oriented than the traditional method of giving feedback. It is therefore concluded that these Vietnamese students with their particular traditional group work practices tended to either offer mellifluous words rather than criticize each other's contribution or mollify the criticism with laudatory comments. Though the online mode did help reduce the ratio of complimenting versus critical comments, as compared to that of the paper-based groups, there were still more compliments than critics. It can be inferred from this conclusion that, similar to other CMC tools, such as email and Microsoft Word (Ho & Savignon, 2007), wikis provide a more comfortable and less pressing mediational environment, in which learners felt more critical in their exchanges.

The logistics of the traditional class appeared to make collaborative writing a linear process: ideas were first generated and discussed; drafts were written by individuals and then corrected by other members; final products were compiled and submitted. Meanwhile, learning on the wikis did more than the sequential process of writing by allowing for discussion and negotiation at any stage of the collaborative process. Furthermore, this process can be observed and monitored by the teacher. In particular, written products on a wiki are never fixed, but rather, "function as resources for expansion, reconfiguration, and new synthesis" (Lund, 2008, p. 50). It is therefore argued that the interactive manner of the wiki-based peer exchanges led to a positive level of information synthesis. In other words, the application of wikis to this academic setting facilitated a format for the collaborative creation of knowledge, or "wisdom of crowds" (McLoughlin & Lee, 2008: 19). Above all, if the degree of learners' satisfaction in online learning is, as Swan (2002) suggests, based on the quantity and quality of interaction and negotiation, then the wiki peer review process did fulfill the mission. The use of wikis in this particular social and academic context is considered successful as they did facilitate students' collaborative generation and synthesis of knowledge within a sharable and freely accessible space.

By the same token, while the pen-and-paper version of exchange requires multiple logistical procedures, wiki-based style just needs one website address that stores all of the information. This indicates that information display (Dillenbourg, 2005) is more persistent online than in the conventional paper-based version. Wikis save information online that can be accessed anywhere and anytime. It is this persistency of information display that generates a shared working memory among group members. It helps increase the level of communication and common understanding, and therefore involves more commitment to and investment in the collaborative learning process from learners. It is concluded that paper-based writing may be quite useful for expression and dialogue, but less so for collaboration and idea synthesis among group members due to its nature of slowness and logistical complexity. Arguably, the persistence of information display and interactive features in the wiki-based composition makes the online communication a powerful tool for peer review and collaboration.

CONCLUSION

Obviously, wikis are certainly a remarkably influential digital mediator for collaborative learning and collective construction of knowledge. The current study shows that the online students appeared to have a more constructive attitude toward group work. Motivation from the wiki-based peer review process encouraged the students to become more cogitative and active. Moreover, reflective learning which is believed to lead to a successful learner-centred learning environment (White, 2007), was more evident in this wiki-mediated exchanges. The multi-way interaction pattern of the wiki-based peer review seemed to be exclusive to online. While the paper-based mode of peer feedback was in a linear sequence, the wiki-based method of the review process was truly interactive and thereby more reflective. Various instances of challenge and negotiation were observed in these wiki-based asynchronous exchanges. This contributes to the interpretation that the social-oriented development of Web 2.0 technology encourages creative and reflective learning practices. In short, the motivational and favourable features of this social-oriented technology per se can encourage a learning-oriented process of peer review; and this type of 'learning-in-progress' is significant in light of SCT perspectives: Group, or inter-psychological, learning as a rule paves the way for individual, or intra-psychological, learning. A pedagogical reform is called for in order to naturally transfer the language teaching and learning methodologies from a confined focus on individual learning and final products toward a more process-emphasised conceptual approach to language development.

The present research limited its analysis to the quantitative and qualitative examination of the feedback generated by the students. A further direction of future research is recommended to investigate how much learners consider and make use of comments by group members in their revision (Liu & Sadler, 2003; Zeng & Takatsuka, 2009). The level of wiki-based revisions can then be compared with previous studies in the literature in order to examine the social oriented potential of wikis to revision. Another limitation is that this study does not touch on teacher feedback, which is suggested by previous studies to be more powerful than peer feedback, whatever the modality. An investigation into the sociotechnical affordances of wikis in particular and of Web 2.0 in general is another direction for future research. Future research may intensively and extensively examine the sociotechnical affordances provided by wikis, as a principal member of the Web 2.0 family. If a future study investigates wikis in terms of peer review like the current one, then how peer exchanges on this socially oriented platform are different from those made with traditional CMC tools, such as email or other learning management systems, is an interesting avenue of investigation. Wikis are of course not only used for peer review; they can be used for other research studies on collaborative learning. For example, explorations of the sociotechnical affordances of wikis can be directed to other areas of second language acquisition and collaborative learning, such as attention to meaning (Kessler & Bikowski, 2010), and focus on form (Kessler, 2009), among many others.

REFERENCES

Arnold, N., Ducate, L., & Kost, C. (2009). Collaborative writing in wikis: Insights from culture projects in German classes. In Lomicka, L., & Lord, G. (Eds.), *The next generation: Social networking and online collaboration in foreign language learning* (pp. 115–144). San Marcos, TX: Computer Assisted Language Instruction Consortium.

Coniam, D., & Lee, M. (2008). Incorporating wikis into the teaching of English writing. *Hong Kong Teachers'. Centre Journal, 7,* 52–67.

Darhower, M. (2002). Interactional factors of synchronous computer-mediated communication in the intermediate L2 class: A sociocultural case study. *CALICO Journal*, *19*(2), 249–277.

DiGiovanni, E., & Nagaswami, G. (2001). Online peer review: An alternative to face-to-face? *ELT Journal*, *55*(3), 263–272. doi:10.1093/elt/55.3.263

Dillenbourg, P. (2005). Designing biases that augment socio-cognitive interactions. In Bromme, R., Hesse, W., & Spada, H. (Eds.), *Barriers and biases in computer-mediated knowledge communication - and how they may be overcome* (pp. 243–264). Dordrecht, The Netherlands: Kluwer. doi:10.1007/0-387-24319-4_11

Fitze, M. (2006). Discourse and participation in ESL face-to-face and written electronic conferences. *Language Learning & Technology*, *10*(1), 67–86.

Ho, M., & Savignon, S. (2007). Face-to-face and computer-mediated peer review in EFL writing. *CALICO Journal*, *24*(2), 269–290.

Honeycutt, L. (2001). Comparing e-mail and synchronous conferencing in online peer response. *Written Communication*, *18*(1), 26–60. doi:10.1177/0741088301018001002

Ingram, A. L., & Hathorn, L. G. (2004). Methods for analyzing collaboration in online communications. In Roberts, T. S. (Ed.), *Online collaborative learning: Theory and practice* (pp. 215–241). Hershey, PA: Information Science Publishing.

Kessler, G. (2009). Student-initiated attention to form in wiki-based collaborative writing. *Language Learning & Technology*, *13*(1), 79–95.

Kessler, G., & Bikowski, D. (2010). Developing collaborative autonomous learning abilities in computer-mediated language learning: Attention to meaning among students in wiki space. *Computer Assisted Language Learning*, *23*(1), 41–58. doi:10.1080/09588220903467335

Lamy, M. N., & Hampel, R. (2007). *Online communication in language learning and teaching*. Palgrave Macmillan. doi:10.1057/9780230592681

Lantolf, J. P. (2000). Introducing sociocultural theory. In Lantolf, P. J. (Ed.), *Sociocultural theory and second language learning* (pp. 1–26). Oxford, UK: Oxford University Press.

Lantolf, J. P., & Thorne, S. L. (2007). Sociocultural theory and second language learning. In VanPatten, B., & Williams, J. (Eds.), *Theories in second language acquisition: An introduction* (pp. 197–221). Mahwah, NJ: Lawrence Erlbaum Associates.

Lee, L. (2010). Exploring wiki-mediated collaborative writing: A case study in an elementary Spanish course. *CALICO Journal*, *27*(2), 260–276.

Liang, M. Y. (2010). Using synchronous online peer review response groups in EFL writing: Revision-related discourse. *Language Learning & Technology*, *14*(1), 45–64.

Liou, H.-C., & Peng, Z.-Y. (2009). Training effects on computer-mediated peer review. *System*, *37*(3), 514–525. doi:10.1016/j.system.2009.01.005

Liu, J., & Sadler, R. W. (2003). The effect and affect of peer review in electronic versus traditional modes on L2 writing. *Journal of English for Academic Purposes*, *2*(3), 193–227. doi:10.1016/S1475-1585(03)00025-0

Lund, A. (2008). Wikis: A collective approach to language production. *ReCALL*, *20*(01), 35–54. doi:10.1017/S0958344008000414

Mangenot, F., & Nissen, E. (2006). Collective activity and tutor involvement in e-learning environments for language teachers and learners. *CALICO Journal*, *23*(3), 601–621.

Mawlawi Diab, N. (2010). Effects of peer- versus self-editing on students' revision of language errors in revised drafts. *System, 38*(1), 85–95. doi:10.1016/j.system.2009.12.008

McLoughlin, C., & Lee, M. J. W. (2008). The three p's of pedagogy for the networked society: Personalization, participation, and productivity. *International Journal of Teaching and Learning in Higher Education, 20*(1), 10–27.

Nguyen, L. V. (2008). Computer mediated communication and foreign language education: Pedagogical features. *International Journal of Instructional Technology and Distance Learning, 5*(12), 23–44.

Nguyen, L. V. (2010). Computer mediated collaborative learning within a communicative language teaching approach: A sociocultural perspective. *The Asian EFL Journal Quarterly, 12*(1), 202–233.

Nguyen, L. V., & White, C. (2011). The nature of 'talk' in synchronous computer-mediated communication in a Vietnamese tertiary EFL context. *International Journal of Computer-Assisted Language Learning and Teaching, 1*(3), 14–36. doi:10.4018/ijcallt.2011070102

Ohta, A. S. (2001). *Second language acquisition processes in the classroom: Learning Japanese.* Mahwah, NJ: Lawrence Erlbaum Associates.

Ortega, L. (2009). *Understanding second language acquisition.* London, UK: A Hodder Arnold Publication.

Richardson, W. (2006). *Blogs, wikis, podcasts, and other powerful web tools for classrooms.* Thousand Oaks, CA: Corwin Press.

Swan, K. (2002). Building learning communities in online courses: The importance of interaction. *Education Communication and Information, 2*(1), 23–49. doi:10.1080/1463631022000005016

Vygotsky, L. S. (1981). The instrumental method in psychology. In Wertsch, J. (Ed.), *The concept of activity in Soviet psychology* (pp. 143–184). Armonk, NY: M.E. Sharpe.

Ware, P. D., & O'Dowd, R. (2008). Peer feedback on language form in telecollaboration. *Language Learning & Technology, 12*(1), 43–63.

Warschauer, M. (1996). Comparing face-to-face and electronic discussion in the second language classroom. *CALICO Journal, 13*(2), 7–26.

Warschauer, M. (2010). Invited commentary: New tools for teaching writing. *Language Learning & Technology, 14*(1), 3–8.

Wheeler, S., Yeomans, P., & Wheeler, D. (2008). The good, the bad and the wiki: Evaluating student-generated content for collaborative learning. *British Journal of Educational Technology, 39*(6), 987–995. doi:10.1111/j.1467-8535.2007.00799.x

White, C. (2007). Focus on the language learner in an era of globalization: Tensions, positions and practices in technology-mediated language teaching. *Language Teaching, 40*(4), 321–326. doi:10.1017/S026144480700451X

Zeng, G., & Takatsuka, S. (2009). Text-based peer-peer collaborative dialogue in a computer-mediated learning environment in the EFL context. *System, 37*(3), 434–446. doi:10.1016/j.system.2009.01.003

APPENDIX 1

Box 1. Peer review sheet

<table>
<tr><td>

PEER REVIEW SHEET

Your name: …………………………………….. Group: ………………….
Author's name: ………………………………….

Please answer the following questions, keeping in mind that the purpose of peer response is to help each other write better.

1. Can you find the topic sentence? [ ] Yes   [ ] No   [ ] I don't know
2. Explain your answer: ……………………………………………………….
3. ……………………………………………………………………………….

4. Please underline what you think is the topic sentence.

5. Read the paragraph carefully. Underline everything that you don't understand.

6. What do you like best about this essay?
    ………………………………………………………………………………
    ………………………………………………………………………………
    ………………………………………………………………………………

7. What questions, comments, and/or suggestions do you have for the author?
    ………………………………………………………………………………
    ………………………………………………………………………………
    ………………………………………………………………………………

</td></tr>
</table>

APPENDIX 2

Table 3. Coding scheme for peer comments

Theme	Subcategory	Definition
Socioaffective	Intersubjectivity	Comments regarding encouragement, acknowledgement, seeking agreement, and agreeing or rejecting ideas
	Personal exchanges	Comments asking and responding to ideas not related to task
	Emotional expression	Comments regarding humour, self-disclosure, and use of emoticons
	Social cohesion	Comments referring to greeting, introducing, closing, and farewell
	Use of L1	Comments in Vietnamese

continued on following page

Table 3. Continued

Theme	Subcategory	Definition
Organisational	Feedback management	Comments (1) indicating to other members that some entries have been entered, (2) indicating to other members that drafts have been revised, and (3) reminding others to add comments
	Group management	Comments expressing the finishing of the peer review process and group work time management
	Technical management	Comments regarding the use of wiki as a platform
	Teacher involvement	Comments added by the teacher
Sociocognitive	Alteration	Any addition, deletion, and replacement on text
	Suggestion	Comments suggesting others to modify drafts (both local and global areas)
	Evaluation	Comments evaluating drafts (either critical or complimentary/both local and global areas)
	Explanation	Comments following what was evaluated, suggested, and/or responding to others' request for clarification (both local and global areas)
	Clarification	Comments asking others to clarify confusing points in drafts (both local and global areas)

APPENDIX 3

Table 4. Contribution in the peer review process: paper-based groups

Group	Member	Socioaffective comments		Organizational comments		Sociocognitive comments		Total		Gini
		N	%	N	%	N	%	N	%	
P01	Quy	0	.0	0	.0	5	8.6	5	8.6	
	Trang	0	.0	0	.0	17	29.3	17	29.3	
	N. Phuong*	5	8.6	2	3.4	29	50.0	36	62.1	
	Total	5	8.6	2	3.4	51	87.9	58		.35
P02	Anh	1	3.0	0	.0	4	12.1	5	15.2	
	Chau*	0	.0	0	.0	6	18.2	6	18.2	
	P. Thanh	3	9.1	0	.0	19	57.6	22	66.7	
	Total	4	12.1	0	.0	29	87.9	33		.35
P03	Huong	0	.0	0	.0	9	18.0	9	18.0	
	Duong	1	2.0	0	.0	9	18.0	10	20.0	
	Nhuan*	0	.0	0	.0	31	62.0	31	62.0	
	Total	1	2.0	0	.0	49	98.0	50		.29
P04	Hoa	0	.0	0	.0	14	29.2	14	29.2	
	Cuc*	0	.0	0	.0	16	33.3	16	33.3	
	Nga	0	.0	0	.0	18	37.5	18	37.5	
	Total	0	.0	0	.0	48	100	48		.06
P05	Thuy*	0	.0	0	.0	6	19.4	6	19.4	
	Thao	0	.0	0	.0	8	25.8	8	25.8	

continued on following page

Table 4. Continued

Group	Member	Socioaffective comments		Organizational comments		Sociocognitive comments		Total		Gini
		N	%	N	%	N	%	N	%	
P05	Trang	2	6.5	0	.0	15	48.4	17	54.8	
	Total	2	6.5	0	.0	29	93.5	31		.24
P06	Quynh	0	.0	0	.0	6	10.5	6	10.5	
	Duyen*	2	3.5	0	.0	22	38.6	24	42.1	
	Toan	0	.0	0	.0	27	47.4	27	47.4	
	Total	2	3.5	0	.0	55	96.5	57		.24
P07	Van	0	.0	0	.0	6	12.0	6	12.0	
	Quyen	1	2.0	0	.0	20	40.0	21	42.0	
	Ngan*	0	.0	0	.0	23	46.0	23	46.0	
	Total	1	2.0	0	.0	49	98.0	50		.23
P08	Thom	1	1.2	0	.0	12	14.5	13	15.7	
	Tram*	0	.0	0	.0	31	37.3	31	37.3	
	Th. Anh	0	.0	0	.0	39	47.0	39	47.0	
	Total	1	1.2	0	.0	82	98.8	83		.20
P09	T. Anh	0	.0	0	.0	10	29.4	10	29.4	
	Kieu*	0	.0	0	.0	10	29.4	10	29.4	
	Uyen	0	.0	0	.0	14	41.2	14	41.2	
	Total	0	.0	0	.0	34	100	34		.08
P10	Hieu	0	.0	0	.0	7	21.9	7	21.9	
	Loan	0	.0	0	.0	10	31.3	10	31.3	
	Thanh*	0	.0	0	.0	15	46.9	15	46.0	
	Total	0	.0	0	.0	32	100	32		.17

Note: Members who (*) were group leaders.

APPENDIX 4

Table 5. Contribution in the peer review process: Wiki Groups

Group	Member	Socioaffective comments		Organizational comments		Sociocognitive comments		Total		Gini
		N	%	N	%	N	%	N	%	
W01	Suong	1	1.2	5	6.1	16	19.5	22	26.8	
	T. Huong	0	.0	0	.0	26	31.7	26	31.7	
	Hang*	1	1.2	0	.0	33	40.2	34	41.5	
	Total	2	2.4	5	6.1	75	91.5	82		.09
W02	Tuan	3	3.4	0	.0	13	14.6	16	18.0	

continued on following page

Table 5. Continued

Group	Member	Socioaffective comments		Organizational comments		Sociocognitive comments		Total		Gini
		N	%	N	%	N	%	N	%	
W02	H. Phuong*	4	4.5	13	14.6	10	11.2	27	30.3	
	Tam	8	9.0	6	6.7	32	36.0	46	51.7	
	Total	15	16.9	19	21.3	55	61.8	89		.23
W03	Yen	2	2.6	4	5.2	5	6.5	11	14.3	
	Binh*	3	3.9	7	9.1	14	18.2	24	31.2	
	Ngan	7	9.1	11	14.3	24	31.2	42	54.5	
	Total	12	15.6	22	28.6	43	55.8	77		.27
W04	Thi	1	1.6	0	.0	11	17.2	12	18.8	
	Loc	5	7.8	0	.0	10	15.6	15	23.4	
	Nga*	6	9.4	1	1.6	30	46.9	37	57.8	
	Total	12	18.8	1	1.6	51	79.7	64		.26
W05	Hanh*	6	4.6	0	.0	24	18.5	30	23.1	
	Hoa	0	.0	0	.0	44	33.8	44	33.8	
	Viet	6	4.6	0	.0	50	38.5	56	43.1	
	Total	12	9.2	0	.0	118	90.8	130		.13
W06	Anh	2	1.3	2	1.3	30	18.8	34	21.3	
	Thoa	6	3.8	4	2.5	32	20.0	42	26.3	
	Nguyen*	9	5.6	31	19.4	44	27.5	84	52.5	
	Total	17	10.6	37	23.1	106	66.3	160		.21
W07	Thuy	2	2.0	1	1.0	10	9.8	13	12.7	
	Dao	0	.0	0	.0	15	14.7	15	14.7	
	Nghia*	0	.0	5	4.9	69	67.6	74	72.5	
	Total	2	2.0	6	5.9	94	92.2	102		.39
W08	Thang*	5	5.7	3	3.4	18	20.7	26	29.9	
	Nhung	4	4.6	4	4.6	22	25.3	30	34.5	
	V. Hang	1	1.1	0	.0	30	34.5	31	35.6	
	Total	10	11.5	7	8.0	70	80.5	87		.04
W09	Huong	0	.0	1	1.3	17	22.4	18	23.7	
	Thao	0	.0	0	.0	25	32.9	25	32.9	
	Dzung*	0	.0	0	.0	33	43.4	33	43.4	
	Total	0	.0	1	1.3	75	98.7	76		.12
W10	Chuyen	20	8.0	9	3.6	21	8.4	50	20.0	
	M. Hang*	16	6.4	10	4.0	41	16.4	67	26.8	
	Phuong	55	22.0	32	12.8	46	18.4	133	53.2	
	Total	91	36.4	51	20.4	108	43.2	250		.22

Note: Members who (*) were group leaders.

Chapter 10
E–Citizenship Skills Online:
A Case Study of Faculty Use of Web 2.0 Tools to Increase Active Participation and Learning

Sultana Lubna Alam
University of Canberra, Australia

Catherine McLoughlin
Australian Catholic University, Australia

ABSTRACT

With Web 2.0 technologies becoming increasingly integrated into all facets of higher education and society, it is vital to use the digital communicative tools and digital media so that students develop appropriate digital literacy and human-computer interaction (HCI) skills to enable them to become participatory citizens in our future society. In this case study, Web 2.0 tools and scenarios for learning are used in learning tasks to connect learners, share ideas, communicate, and co-create content within a university learning environment. The context for the study is social informatics – a composite class comprising 25-30 postgraduate and 3rd year undergraduate students within the Faculty of Information Sciences and Engineering.The study of social informatics examines the impact of technology upon social processes and learning. In order for students to gain a more comprehensive understanding of the topic, they engaged in range of tasks that enabled them to engage in collaborative dialogue and knowledge creation. In this case study, a Moodle mashup (the integration of information from different sources into one Website) is used to amalgamate information from the class and external sources such as blogs, wikis, and Twitter. The integration of HCI and Web 2.0 technologies into the learning process is examined, highlighting how social media tools can improve student engagement, collaboration, and digital literacy and e-citizenship skills.

DOI: 10.4018/978-1-4666-3649-1.ch010

INTRODUCTION

The rising popularity of social media tools (for example Weblogs, wikis, Twitter) is the result of the qualities that characterise Web 2.0 software. Such digital tools are easy-to-operate, user-generated, personalisable and allow for content creation and modification. In addition, they can be 'meeting places' for socialisation, sharing and collaboration. It does not come as a surprise then that using Web 2.0 tools to facilitate the learning process is encouraged in the educational literature (McLoughlin & Lee, 2008). In this networked age, the transmissive model of teaching is being replaced with constructivist, blended eLearning approaches, while the need to make the curriculum more relevant and engaging is imperative (Tapscott, 2009). A number of researchers refer to the changing landscape as 'pedagogy 2.0' and 'learning 2.0' (McLoughlin & Lee, 2009; Downes, 2006) and signal greater use of the affordances of social media to enable connectivity, communication, participation, and the development of dynamic communities of learning.

For many years, mechanical factory models of teaching and learning have been at war with participatory and interactive education. Currently, the affordances of Web 2.0 – sharing, collaboration, customization, personalisation have given rise to a number of alternative paradigms of learning e.g. personal learning environments (Atwell, 2007) and heutagogy, both of which are focused on development of self-regulatory skills among students (Conole & Oliver, 2007). In many fields, "the life of knowledge is now measured in months and years" (Siemens, 2005, para. 2). Thus, pedagogical methods used for years and considered instructionally sound have been brought into question and are becoming outdated as students adapt their learning to the networked world. Although more formal forms of instruction eLearning will persist, it is becoming increasingly important to integrate informal teaching strategies and blended learning approaches The recent emergence of pedagogies that are based on self-determination and networked learning such as heutagogy (Phelps, Hase, & Ellis, 2005) and connectivism (Siemens, 2005) help us understand learning as making connections with ideas, facts, people and global communities.

Goals of Education in the Networked World

For decades, the chief aim of education has been the development of democratically oriented global citizens. Today's learners need to be equipped with skills to survive in future digital participatory global world (Council of Europe, 2010; Dewey, 1938).

Desirable features of a democratically oriented citizen are:

- Knows how to interact with others and share views;
- Has the capacity to develop lifelong learning skills and attitudes;
- Is open to new ideas and alternative perspectives;
- Listens to others and is able to incorporate their views within their own understandings;
- Wants to share knowledge; and
- Does not strive to control others.

To prepare students as global citizens, it is essential for teachers to adopt learning designs that foster inquiry, meta-learning and learning-to-learn skills. Use of information and communications technologies is also essential in supporting networked, dialogic learning, and the addition of, emerging digital tools (Twitter, blogs, wikis, Flickr) also enable rapid communication, collaboration and engagement with government, commerce and society (Richards 2010). Social identity processes and the means, by which people formulate their outlook and relationship with the world, have changed. The skills and dispositions of digital citizenship are relevant learning outcomes in this digital age. For example, young people may feel a greater desire to embrace issues that are connected to lifestyle values rather than conventional civic participation and voting activities. Currently, social networks and digital media are increasingly oriented towards social and participatory activities (Lara & Naval, 2009; Bryant, 2006). With information technology people gain new abilities and ways to participate and express themselves in a networked society –often called 'digital empowerment'. Such participation increases the competence of individuals and communities to act as influential participants in the information society (Makinen, 2006). Active citizens will engage, communicate, collaborate, vote, and access communication services and thus participate in civic activities using digital tools as governments around the world embrace Web 2.0 (aka government 2.0) (Gibson et al, 2009; Government 2.0 Taskforce Report, 2009; Chang & Kannan, 2008;Tapscott, Williams & Herman, 2007). The raft of tools now available on Web 2.0 enables the development of social and citizenship competencies among students while also developing digital literacy skills (Moll & Krug, 2009). The communicative power of social software tools offers a means for individuals and groups to address matters of political or global concern and, thus, contribute to an online democratic commons (Moll & Krug, 2009, p.133).

This chapter presents a case study where Web 2.0 tools and scenarios for learning are used in learning tasks to connect learners, share ideas, communicate and co-create content within a university learning environment. The context for the study is 'social informatics' – a composite class comprising 25-30 postgraduate and 3rd year undergraduate students within the Faculty of Information Sciences and Engineering.The study of social informatics examines the impact of technology upon social behaviour. In order for students to gain a more comprehensive understanding of the topic, it is highly beneficial

to develop the skills and knowledge to question and understand the value of these tools in a social context, by actually using them. In this case study, a Moodle mashup (the integration of information from different sources into one Website) is used to amalgamate information from really simple syndication (RSS) feeds from the class and external blogs, wikis and Twitter. The integration of Web 2.0 technologies into the learning process is examined, highlighting how this can improve student engagement, collaboration, digital literacy and e-citizenship skills.

DIGITAL CITIZENSHIP AND CITIZENSHIP 2.0

'Digital citizenship' in the simplest terms it refers to the ability to participate in society online and to use technology appropriately. Digital citizenship represents the capacity, sense of belonging, and the potential for political and economic engagement in society in the information age (O'Brien, 2008). Digital citizens practice conscientious use of technology, demonstrate responsible use of information, and maintains a good attitude for learning with technology (ISTE 2007). For example, the aim of the Dutch e-Government policy is to improve information exchange, service delivery and interactive participation by introducing a new partnership between citizen and government. This is to be achieved by giving more responsibility and choice to citizens. Social communication technologies like Web 2.0 offer new channels for contacting officials, discussing issues, and mobilizing, then the network externalities or the benefits of bringing people together online exceed the satisfaction gained by the individual participants - creating what economists call 'positive externalities' or spill over benefits.

Westheimer and Kahne (2004) propose that citizens can be categorized as: (1) responsible; (2) participatory; and (3) justice-oriented. The personally responsible citizen*s* acts responsibly in his/her community by, for example, picking up litter, giving blood, recycling, volunteering, paying taxes and staying out of debt. A participatory citizen actively participates in the civic affairs and the social life of the community at local, state and national levels. Participatory citizens need to understand how government and community organizations work, and they need to understand how to plan and lead meetings. The justice oriented citizen is one who pursues social justice, does not simply respond to a problem, and instead works to find a solution to the cause of it. They question and change established systems and structures when they reproduce patterns of injustice over time (Westheimer & Kahne, 2004, p.240-242). The typologies are not mutually exclusive, and one person may encapsulate all qualities.

The set of participatory and pro-active activities around civic engagement (aka citizenship 2.0) as demonstrated through initiatives like 'FixMyStreet' (citizens reporting on problems in their neighbourhood), '10 Downingstreet' (UK PM's effort to create citizen petitions), mySociety.org (facilitating public civic movement), 'TheyworkForYou' (enlisting public servants and grants expenditure), 'Patient.co.uk', which patients can use to record their experiences and rate health services are changing the way we perceive and engage with government, making services more open, transparent and participatory. In addition, the informal, citizen journalism is creating content for publication as individual citizens emerge as authors, content creators, thought leaders, filmmakers, blog diaries etc (Carnaby, 2009). As the potential of Web 2.0 tools becomes more evident in networked digital environment, it is equally important to prepare students with the skills needed to understand Web-based communication platforms, and how to become collaborators rather than mere information disseminators, along with the need for civic engagement in a community of like minded peers (Lave & Wenger, 1991).

DIGITAL CITIZENSHIP, SOCIAL TECHNOLOGY, AND INSTRUCTIONAL STRATEGIES

Social media integrated underpinned by constructivist pedagogy has been demonstrated by a number of studies that use digital tools to connect learners in communities in order to engage them as global citizens (Richards, 2010; Lara & Naval, 2009; Bennett, Wells & Rank, 2008; O'Brien, 2008; Westheimer & Kahne, 2004). Richards (2010) has devised instructional activities for enabling the three types of digital citizenship using Web 2.0 tools in learning environments. Similarly, Lara and Naval (2009) have articulated a framework for gaining civic and social competences using power and the participatory potential of Web 2.0 tools. Building on the work of Lara and Naval, (2009) and Bennett, Wells and Rank, (2008), we identify the social and civic competencies of citizen 2.0 and align these skills with Web 2.0 tools that have the affordances to support pedagogies and instructional strategies to support development of these skills (see Figure 1). This framework includes a new dimension to Lara and Naval's (2009) model – 'Civic learning styles' which are preferred methods of learning for actualising citizens (Bennett et al, 2008). For example, a wiki can be used for a project-based learning activity using instructional strategies such as collaborative work and project management to build knowledge and comprehension for digital citizenship.

CONTEXT OF THE STUDY

The context of the present study is a university level unit on social informatics which explores the impact of informatics on society in areas such as: e-government, eLearning and e-law and deals with the social, cultural, philosophical, ethical, legal, public policy and economic issues relating to information technologies. The unit offers students

Figure 1. The four dimensions: Web 2.0 applications and instructional strategies to promote of the social and citizenship competence in teaching and learning

Web 2.0 Applications

Blogs   Wikis   RSS /Content aggregators   Microblogs
Social bookmarking   Social Networks
Documents sharing   Multimedia sharing
Idea generation & voting   Professional networking

Social and citizenship competence

Conceptual (knowledge & understanding)
- Knowledge and comprehension
- Critical reflection
-Receiving & producing information

Procedural (skills):
- technical skills improvement
Communicating
- Accepting and practicing social rules
-widening social networks

Attitudinal (values & dispositions):
- Considering of a set of values
- Respectful behaviour with the environment,
-cultural and natural patrimony and the sustainable
-Development of a new course of action

Four Dimensions

Instructional Strategies

Project management
Peer teaching
Case solving
peer-2-peer learning
WebQuest
Work-integrated learning
Collaborative learning
Collective Intelligence
Leaner centred instruction
Student generated content
Blended learning
Informal learning
Mobile learning
Personalisation
Community of learning
Self-regulated learning
Distributed intelligence
Experiential learning

Civic learning styles

interactive project-based
peer-to-peer networked information sharing
participatory media creation
preference for democratic environments
content creation
Assess credibility /peer assessment

a unique opportunity to use the affordances of social software tool in innovative ways to generate knowledge for the emerging domain of social technology impact on society, in particular government. Through the study of social informatics learners examine the impact of technology upon social behaviour. In order for students to gain a more comprehensive understanding of the topic, it is highly beneficial to develop the skills and knowledge to question and understand the value of these tools in a social context, by actually using them. The four dimensions of promoting digital citizenship (See Figure 1) was used with a suite of Web 2.0 tools, a set of pedagogy 2.0 principles (McLoughlin & Lee, 2009) and a set of project based activities that suits civic learning styles. Detailed pedagogy principles have been reported in Alam and McLoughlin (2010) and McLoughlin and Alam (2011).

The present research study was conducted on a social informatics course which comprised a composite class of 25 postgraduate and 3rd year undergraduate students within the Faculty of

Information Sciences and Engineering. There were mostly male students (77%) and majority was aged between 22-25 years (66%).

In the following sections, the integration of Web 2.0 technologies into the learning process is examined, highlighting the activities that can improve student engagement, collaboration, digital literacy and e-citizenship skills. Outcomes of learning achieved through use of each Web 2.0 tool are evaluated based on student reflections and feedback.

The Moodle Mashup

Based on the four dimensions of teaching digital citizenship, in designing the learning environment for this unit, multiple digital social tools were incorporated that allowed students to share ideas and co-create content to enable them to engage fully in experiential learning while developing digital literacy skills. In this case study, a Moodle 'mashup' (the integration of information from different sources into one Website) is used to amalgamate information from RSS feeds from the class and external blogs, wikis and Twitter (See Figure 2). In this way, different activities that students conduct in each technology can be summarized and highlighted on one Webpage, making it easier for students to assimilate information. This is depicted in the following picture. More details about the mashup and Web 2.0 tools descriptions can be found in learning to teach an online case study (McIntyre, 2011).

In this model, students are active, creative learners who constantly engage in two-way communication with their peers and with information networks and communities to generate new ideas and contribute micro-content to the course curriculum wiki. To enable this, students will use the affordances of social software and a dynamic set of Web 2.0 applications leveraging the network power of the Web. The idea is to use technology e.g. a suite of tools rather than a particular technology giving learners choice to engage in mean-

Figure 2. Integration of wiki, blog feeds, and Twitter feeds in Moodle

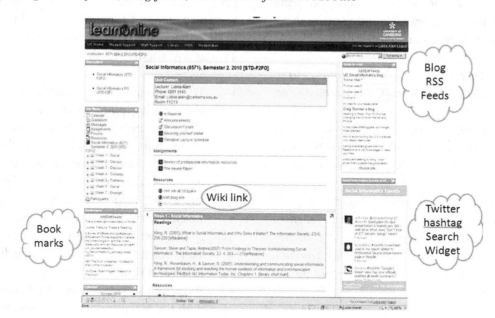

ingful tasks using multiple media types in order to achieve relevance and clarity. Using technology innovatively can pave the way for creating content within a peer-to-peer formal and informal learning environments (Dron, 2007; Boettcher, 2006), and the unit *Social informatics* is based on this model.

In this learning design environment, teachers facilitate learning by providing personalised learning with a suite of Web 2.0 tools integrated within institutional learning management system (LMS) (e.g. Moodle) and by scaffolding, collaborating and coaching students as needed. There are strategies and tools adopted to teach digital literacy skills i.e. self-regulated learning, community of practice, and experiential learning. Students generate content in pairs or groups to produce micro-content, podcasts and vodcasts to share topics and ideas from the course schedule to peers. This approach of two-way interaction: peer-to-peer (Frydenberg, 2006) and the outside world serve many purposes such as:

- Students are given an opportunity to demonstrate their understanding of the course topics through production of micro-content for their peers.
- Students develop knowledge in an emerging field such as government 2.0 and create a knowledge repository for future students in this course and external information networks.
- Students in this process will gain necessary skills to engage in civic activities using dynamic digital tools to become participatory and justice oriented citizens.

This integration of Web 2.0 tools with existing LMS resulted in positive feedback and has contributed to learning new skills that they may use in their personal lives - "It's a new way of teaching by introducing wiki, Twitter, blogs. I never used them before but because of this unit these Social networking sites have become part of my daily life. It's quite interesting unit." Students also enjoyed the flexibility and ability to communicate and carry out assessment task online using these tools. Some comments are quoted below:

Use of social networking tools which allows us to do tutorial work and other stuff whenever we want.

I am enjoying all the tools we are exposed to i.e. Twitter-Wordpress, and also the various Websites we had to work around with for our vodcasts.

A great unit. Was a bit reluctant at first to take up this unit as it's a new unit but got to learn so many things and I'll keep on using my Twitter account and Wordpress as well, as for YouTube and Animoto, i already have my account. Great tools and great unit.

I would strongly prefer social media to be used in other units.

Twitter Use and Learning Outcomes

Twitter is a micro-blog and offers users the capacity to send short messages (tweets). Twitter can be a valuable tool for exchanging ideas and for professional development, connect with other professionals, and even host an online book club. Recently, Twitter has grown into a powerful tool for business, communication, and education. While many institutions are just starting to be aware of the educational benefits possible with Twitter, there is evidence that Twitter has grown into a powerful tool for business, communication, and education. The use of twitter was based on the need for students to question, share ideas and provide feedback to each other on new and emerging topics as they arose during the unit, and to appreciate the role of Twitter in practices of civic engagement. Twitter was used in the unit in multiple ways. Students were asked to follow, and post to the #socinfo hashtag so that everyone in the class could see and contribute to the conversation. One of the advantages of using Twitter was the ability to access a broad range of opinions from people outside of the university system. Students were also able to Twitter on their mobile devices to keep in touch with each other between classes. Twitter was used:

- To facilitate debates, comment on discussions taking place in the face-to-face tutorial (by projecting tweets onto the wall using third party Twitter utilities like tweetchat.com or visibletweets.com), asking questions of each other and the teacher, and giving feedback during presentations.
- To enable students to quickly and informally share information amongst themselves;
- To efficiently contribute outside links and internet resources to the class.
- As a quick way to communicate directly with the lecturer outside of class time.
- To follow hashtags such as #socinfo, #gov2au and #election2010. This allowed students to apply what they learned in class by contributing to conversations about current issues in the larger social context.

Students made over 1000 tweets during the semester. 80% of the tweets were made by 77% of the Tweeters, demonstrating good participation by most students. Among the Web 2.0 tools introduced, Twitter was most popular. The following student comments highlight some of the reasons of why they preferred Twitter:

Twitter helped me to post what i wanted to show to the class n [and] also helped me to see other comments made by students.

Twitter because of the ability to interact with others without having to bother about the time and distance. Further, it is such a great tool that I can find anything jobs, news....etc.

Twitter- buzz [because] until i started this unit i never used twitter but its cool chatting about the topics that are interesting!!!

Twitter, I like reading the posts for people I follow. I enjoyed the immediacy of it.

However caution needs to be used for Twitter use as echoed in following student comments:

Twitter was easy to use once I got used to it - short and sharp. Though you had to keep on top of it to retain the context of tweets.

The twitter stream was overwhelming at times - it would be good to have a pause button sometimes. I got frustrated that getting context of a tweet was difficult if you had missed previous tweets.

A lot of people put out links to lots of articles via Twitter but these were only useful if a person had an immediate interest in the topic, difficult to find later.

The other issue with Twitter was that tweets are transient that is tweets eventually disappear from Twitter. This became a problem as tweets were used to make class announcements and to share links and readings. Students hardly check tweets every day. So there was a need to somehow archive them so students could access a whole week's tweets. To archive #socinfo tweets (the hashtag the class used to make sure everyone could follow the Twitter conversation), we needed to create a permanent record and blog was used as a vehicle for archiving Twitter feeds. Future implementations can explore other microblogging tools such as Yammer which archives micro-content. In addition, the search widget that brings in RSS feeds in Moodle often did not work for unknown reasons.

Wiki Use and Learning Outcomes

It is recognized that teaching young people how to use digital media to convey their public voices could enable exploration and social interaction with direct experiences of civic engagement (Rheingold, 2007). Learning to use blogs and podcasts

(as media of self-expression, with an emphasis on 'public voice', should be considered a pillar—not just a component—of the twenty-first-century civic curriculum. Participatory media that enable young people to create as well as consume media and engage in democratic decision making. Confluence (http://www.atlassian.com/software/confluence) was chosen as the class wiki because it was already securely hosted on the university servers. This assists with authentication and contributions are recognised with student identification. The wiki was used in the class as:

- A delivery mechanism for all of the class lectures. Students were also asked to add extra content and references to the existing lectures for the class, building upon the starting point offered by the teacher.
- Support for face-to-face tutorials. Students were able to build upon, edit and dispute the information provided by the teacher, summarize readings and provide extra resources.
- A resource for the class exam. Students were allowed to use the information in the wiki in their final exams. It was envisioned that it will create a high level of motivation for the class to work together ensuring that the information that was developed was analysed correctly, accurate and succinct.

Feedback on wiki use has been twofold. On the one hand, it was seen as useful "The unit wiki was good and the ability to add to it was good" but on the other hand, "it was not used often. I was OK adding references from my own work _where indicated by the lecturer_ but I would not feel comfortable adding my own material". Further concerns regarding the use of wiki was related to workload issues – "The request to continually update the wiki was potentially time-consuming - it would have been good if links to these portions could be co-located so that if we found something relevant well after the lecture we could easily find where to add the information." These comments point to usability issues with the organisation of the wiki page. This can be improved in future implementations by including both lectures and tutorials in wiki with a more firm structure around where contributions are sought.

Blog Use and Learning Outcomes

The instructional design of the unit was based on the pedagogic assumption that students should learn collaboratively in a social constructivist manner and to engage students in democratic decision making, expression of opinions and awareness of the power of media in enabling civic participation. Blogs were therefore employed as part of the learning experience in social informatics class in a number of ways:

- For tutorial exercises, peer review and students commenting on each other's work.
- To blog about (or write interpretations and responses to) subject matter from lectures.
- To archive #socinfo tweets (the hashtag the class used to make sure everyone could follow the Twitter conversation) so there was a permanent record, given that tweets eventually disappear from Twitter.
- Blogs in the public domain dedicated to relevant topics were also followed via their RSS feeds in Moodle.

Students however did not enjoy the blogging component of the unit as much as the other tools. A student said: "I could not edit the content once a post was published and I got a bit caught up in the formatting of the blog so that it was presentable for others." Another student said "The fact that tutorial and lecture material was kept on two different tools (wiki and blog) I found distracting as I couldn't easily connect the two." Essentially both the class blog and wiki had comment features. Based on the feedback received, it is obvious that either blog or wiki should be used for assessment

and participation. However it was still useful to bring in RSS feeds for external blogs that were relevant for the unit.

Many blogs are hosted on the open Web, which can carry security risks. Hence to ensure security and privacy for students, Wordpress.org (a version of wordpress.com that is designed to be installed locally) was installed on the university servers. This required an understanding of the installation process, so the support of the information technology (IT) department was required. However due to technical difficulty during the installation process, the multi-user installation was not possible. Hence students resorted to use the wordpress.com site (externally hosted) for their own blogging. This became a time consuming process as students were added to the social informatics blog space manually as blogroll. This has contributed to some dissatisfaction with students.

Other Web 2.0 Tools and Citizenship Scenarios

Many of the Web 2.0 tools were introduced to meet the learning outcome of this unit – that is to learn to use digital tools for civic engagement. Many digital tools can be used for civic activities such as contributing to a forum, voting on ideas, uploading a question on YouTube, tweet a question etc. Some of these tools were introduced in the unit coupled with e-citizenship scenarios. Other tools that were introduced as part of the suite of Web 2.0 tools are as follows:

- **Idea Generation and Voting:** Many government and civic sites now use idea generation and voting tools to explore issues or policy. It is based on the simple model of crowd sourcing. Students were asked to post an idea to their IdeaScale community via a blog. Each idea then can be expanded through comments by students. The ultimate measure of an idea is determined by a voting system. Students were asked to comment and vote on their presentations. This was a useful exercise, but requires careful scaffolding and guidance during tutorials.

- **Vodcast Presentation:** Students were asked to prepare multimedia presentations in the format of a vodcast that included pictures, video clips and audio. Students were introduced to many online tools for production such as Animoto, Screentoaster, windows movie maker etc and then sharing through tools such as Vimeo, YouTube, SlideShare etc. These are some of the tools currently being used by citizens to connect, share or talk to their constituents, government and social movements.
- **Bookmarking:** Bookmarking is way of organizing online Web page links with tags that is accessible through browsers. Tags can be sorted, organised and shared. Delicious was introduced in the unit as a way of sharing relevant links with other students and the course Moodle site. Students found this social bookmarking tool difficult to use. Rather, Twitter was used to share online links and content.

General Outcomes

Based on the end of the semester feedback from students, the views feedback showed that for most this was a novel and challenging experience, and one that contributed to their learning. The following conclusions can be derived that are of general nature but are of interest as a way of evaluating the benefits of the unit:

- For all students, this was their first unit that used a blended learning with Web 2.0 tools (100%).
- More than half of the students were not familiar with Web 2.0 tools (55%).
- 55% agreed that use of Web 2.0 has enhanced their learning in this unit.

- 66% also agreed that Web 2.0 has made it easy to collaborate with peers; however there was no agreement on whether it has actually increased peer interaction. This needs to be investigated further.
- 77% students agreed that interaction with instructor was greater than a regular face to face class.
- 66% agreed that Web 2.0 provided flexibility to the course.
- 55% of students wanted to take a future course that uses Web 2.0.
- Majority of the students agreed that the digital Web 2.0 tools used changed their perception of civic engagement and said they would use these tools to engage in civic activities.
- Overall, the majority of students were satisfied with the unit.

LESSONS LEARNED FROM FACULTY ABOUT USE OF WEB 2.0

Use of Web 2.0 tools requires careful planning and implementation. The innovative nature of social software means that it is in the early stages of development and there are likely to be ongoing implementation issues (Alam & Campbell, 2009). However, these problems largely relate to the initial learning processes surrounding the adoption of a new learning technology (Alam & Campbell, 2009). As noted earlier in the use and outcome of each tool, significant resources for system testing and general technical support are required to manage the technical and usability issues that surface.

Participation Issues

Students require training in using Web 2.0 tools even though they are familiar with some of these social networking tools. Not all students found it easy to use the technology right away. It is crucial to provide technical support for students in the form of a workshop or training session at the beginning of semester, and to also provide on-going access to help resources, and answering questions when they arise. Scaffold the students' use of the technology such that they begin by undertaking simple tasks, increasing in complexity (if required) as they build confidence. As one student commented "I was confused at starting of this unit but I think everything is well now. It just take me some time to understand how this all will work."

It is wise to only introduce a limited number of Web 2.0 tools when starting out, evaluating their impact thoroughly before moving onto new technologies. As one student negatively commented: "I have been introduced to too many social media tools (wiki, blog, twitter, delicious) and expected to use them all as part of the assessment. I haven't managed this."

Some students will only use tools and online discussion to satisfy the minimum requirements of the class, while others will embrace the technology and begin to use tools effectively in many aspects of their study. This is not necessary a bad thing, as much can be learnt by those students silently watching the online interaction taking place, or simply by reading and commenting on blog posting of others rather than generating their own (Abu & Fong, 2010).

Students were generally excited about the social tools being introduced into the unit. However in some instances, students were confused about which tool to use for different tasks. Students may not immediately understand the benefits of using Web 2.0 tools. Care needs to be taken at the outset in explaining to students why each tool is used, how it works, why it is relevant to their learning, and how it can benefit them. As part of the class, teach strategies on how to use the tools effectively, and explain what you are expecting students to achieve with them. One way this can be managed is to have different assessment tasks directly related to the use of one technology. Clearly state in the instructions for the task how the tool is to be used to achieve the learning outcomes. For example, some assignments required the use of Twitter, some the blogs, and others the wiki.

Workload Issues

Workload can increase for both teachers and students when Web 2.0 tools are used outside of class time. Given that this technology provides the ability to communicate at any time, there is likely to be some increase in workload for teachers and students. However, the added benefits it can bring can counterbalance this, if the tasks assigned to the technology are carefully considered such that they do not require the constant attention of the teacher. Maximise the potential of collaborative learning by encouraging students to help each other, understand how to access help information online and not always be reliant on the teacher. You need to set some ground rules such as any question posted using Twitter would be answered within 24 hours. How you spend time teaching may change when using Web 2.0 technology. It is necessary to plan to make time available at regular intervals through the week to look at questions coming from the Twitter feed, comments in blogs etc. This was to ensure that the benefits of immediacy the technology afforded were not lost because students were waiting a long time for a response

Risks

It is important for students to understand any risks associated with using online social media networks. The very first lecture of the class was dedicated to explaining to students how to make themselves secure online. This was reinforced each time a new tool was introduced. Although it is important to choose different passwords for different Web 2.0 tool account, students may find it difficult to remember these passwords. As one student said "I just have some problems in remembering lot of passwords as we have account on wordpress, twitter and delicious." There is no easy solution to this problem except to write them down somewhere (which is not a good practice) or follow good password creation guidelines that may also result in easy passwords for remembering.

Pedagogical Issues

Teaching and learning innovations are best implemented when informed by learning theory (Cochrane, 2006). This learning design followed established pedagogy 2.0 principles (McLoughlin & Lee, 2009; Downes, 2006). In addition, the following observations can be made about Web 2.0 tool use for instructors and teachers:

- Employ relevant pedagogical strategies for using the technology effectively. Be familiar with what each technology does well, and analyse your curriculum to see where the technology could benefit or enhance student learning. Examining case studies such as this one, speaking to experienced colleagues and reading literature on the topic can provide exemplars to guide your practice.

- Ensure that the technology you want to use in class actually works. Use it yourself and become familiar with its functions and limitations, and understand what can potentially go wrong. If the technology fails in class this will undermine student confidence. You also need to consider strategies to support students in their adoption of the technology, for example by modeling and demonstrating.

- Don't simply use the technology as an 'add-on' to the class. There must be an educational reason and purpose for the inclusion of any Web 2.0 tools. Integrating the technology appropriately into class activities and assessments to help students

achieve the learning outcomes is very important. Teachers need to make clear to students how the technology should be used to complete tasks.

- The pedagogies adopted to support and scaffold civic engagement favor interactive, networked activities often communicated through participatory media such as videos shared across online networks (Frydenberg, 2006). At the practical level, online environments may offer an expanded notion of civic behavior and thereby extend the interests of many students for whom citizenship holds little appeal. In this way, citizenship skills may be learned in conjunction with digital literacies that enable participation in global networks. For example, knowledge sharing, creative expressions, content creation, organization of resources and research skills have value as lifelong learning skills and as media literacy skills.

A Usability Approach for Designing Web 2.0 Based Learning Tasks

It is useful to think of piloting social Web 2.0 technologies from a systems perspective (Alam & Campbell, 2009; Alam, 2008). Each trial may be thought of as a small project. It is important to follow a quality process to produce a quality outcome. Based on an enhanced model of input-process-output model, quality needs to be achieved for process (e.g. teaching methods), product (the learning) and fit for task argument (e.g. was the technology fit for the task?). A usability approach can be followed to design learning tasks with Web 2.0 (adapted from Alam & Campbell, 2009).

Usability—can students use the tool to do the learning task?

- **Functionality:** Does the tools have the functionality required for the task to be carried out by students and marked by tutors?

- **Interface Issues:** Are there any navigation challenges and does the structure of the site support the way information is organized, accessed and shared among students and staff?
- **Reliability:** How reliable is the tool/platform e.g. downtime, upload issues, authentication etc?

Usable–does it support the learning task?

- **The 'Fit-for-Task' Argument:** Does the tool support the way the assessment task is set?
- **Context:** Can students use the tool to do the required task within given constraints including timeframe?

Usefulness–the business case

- **Pedagogical Benefits:** What are the pedagogical benefits from using the tool? Does it increase student learning and engagement?
- **Alignment:** Are the learning tasks and software tool use aligned with the learning outcomes of the subject?

CONCLUSION

In summary, the case study presented in this chapter resulted in noticeable increase in communication and collaboration amongst students both in class and online with external information networks. Students developed more independent digital learning skills and confidence and became co-producers of class knowledge and content. This model is useful for changing environment and emerging fields of research oriented courses. Students can easily follow current events and integrate them into their discussions and assignments, and instantly engage online with people involved in the topic area. This enables students to validate their learning in the wider context of what is happening in the world beyond the classroom.

Several key issues need to be considered for optimum implementation of Web 2.0 based learning environments. Teachers need to factor in technical support and training for students when introducing new technologies and test all of the technology thoroughly before using it in a class. Using too many tools at once may overwhelm students, and support and practice are essential. Web 2.0 technologies can enable students to continue networking and communicating in their own time and pace.

Faculty use of interactive, networked activities for teaching and learning enabled through participatory media such as Web 2.0 can enhance student participation, communication and collaboration. Web 2.0 based online environments may offer an expanded notion of civic participation and thereby extend students' citizenship skills, which may be learned in conjunction with digital literacies that enable participation in global networks. With respect to what kinds of engagement experiences are available online, it is clear that digital media and web networks offer great potential for reinvigorating authentic participation, peer-to-peer learning, e-research and higher order thinking (Iyengar & Jackman, 2003).

REFERENCES

Abu, Z. A., & Fong, S. F. (2010). *Lurking as learning in online discussions: A case study.* Paper presented at the Global Learn Asia Pacific 2010.

Alam, S. L. (2008). *To wiki or to blog: Piloting social software technologies for assessment in a large first year information systems class.* Paper presented at the 19th Australasian Conference on Information Systems, Christchurch.

Alam, S. L., & Campbell, J. (2009). Using social software to support assessment tasks in information systems: Trialing wiki and blog technologies. *Journal of Informatics Education Research, 11,* 1–28.

Alam, S. L., & McLoughlin, C. (2010). Using digital tools to connect learners: Present and future scenarios for citizenship 2.0. In C. H. Steel, M. J. Keppell, P. Gerbic, & S. Housego (Eds.), *Curriculum, Technology & Transformation for an Unknown Future: Proceedings ASCILITE Sydney 2010* (pp. 13-24). Retrieved from http://ascilite.org.au/conferences/sydney10/procs/Alam-full.pdf

Attwell, G. (2007). *Personal learning environments – The future of eLearning?* eLearning Papers, 2. Retrieved from http://www.elearningeuropa.info/files/media/media11561.pdf

Bennett, W. L., Wells, C., & Rank, A. (2008). *Young citizens and civic learning: Two paradigms of citizenship in the digital age.* Report from the Civic learning online project.

Boettcher, J. V. (2006, 28 February). The rise of student performance content. *Campus Technology.* Retrieved from http://campustechnology.com/articles/2006/02/the-rise-of-student-performance-content.aspx

Bryant, T. (2006). Social software in academia. *EDUCAUSE Quarterly, 29*(2), 61–64.

Carnaby, P. (2009). *Citizen-centric content, digital equity and the preservation of community memory.* World library and Information Congress:75th IFLA General Conference and Council, 23-27 August 2009, Milan, Italy. Retrieved from http://www.ifla.org/annual-conference/ifla75/index.htm

Chang, A., & Kannan, P. (2008). *Leveraging Web 2.0 in government.* Industry research paper. Retrieved from http://www.businessofgovernment.org/

Cogan, J., & Derricott, R. (1988). *Citizenship for the 21st century: An international perspective on education.*

Conole, G., & Oliver, M. (Eds.). (2007). *Contemporary perspectives in e-learning research: Themes, methods and impact on practice. The Open and Flexible Learning Series.* UK: Routledge.

Council of Europe. (2010). *Communication from the Commission: Europe 2020 – A strategy for smart, sustainable and inclusive growth.* COM(2010). Retrieved from http://ec.europa.eu/education/llp/doc/call12/part1_en.pdf

Dewey, J. (1938). *Experience and education.* New York, NY: Collier Books.

Downes, S. (2005, October). E-learning 2.0. *ELearn.* Retrieved from http://www.elearnmag.org/subpage.cfm?section=articles&article=29-1

Dron, J. (2007). Designing the undesignable: Social software and control. *Journal of Educational Technology & Society, 10*(3), 60–71.

Ebner, M., Lienhardt, C., Rohs, M., & Meyer, I. (2010). Microblogs in higher education- A chance to facilitate informal and process oriented education? *Computers & Education, 55,* 92–100. doi:10.1016/j.compedu.2009.12.006

Frydenberg, M. (2006). Principles and pedagogy: The two P's of podcasting in the information technology classroom. In D. Colton, W. J. Tastle, M. Hensel, & A. A. Abdullat (Eds.), *Proceedings of ISECON 2006,* Vol. 23 (Dallas) (§3354). Chicago, IL: AITP. Retrieved from http://proc.isecon.org/2006/3354/ISECON.2006.Frydenberg.pdf

Gibson, A., Courtney, N., Ward, A., Wilcox, D., & Holtham, C. (2009). *Social by social: A practical guide to using new technologies to deliver social impact.*

Government 2.0 Taskforce Report. (2009). *Engage: Getting on with Government 2.0.* Retrieved from http://www.finance.gov.au/publications/gov20taskforcereport/index.html

Grosseck, G. (2009). *To use or not to use Web 2.0 in higher education?* Procedia - Social and Behavioral. doi:10.1016/j.sbspro.2009.01.087

ISTE. (2007). *National educational technology standards and performance indicators for students*. Retrieved from http://www.iste.org/standards/nets-for-students/nets-student-standards-2007.aspx

Iyengar, S., & Jackman, S. (2003). *Technology and politics: Incentives for youth participation*. International Conference on Civic Education Research — 16-18 November, New Orleans.

JISC. (2009). *Higher education in a Web 2.0 world*. Retrieved from http://www.jisc.ac.uk/publications/documents/heWeb2.aspx

Junco, R., Heiberger, G., & Loken, E. (2010). The effect of Twitter on college student engagement and grades. *Journal of Computer Assisted Learning*, *27*(2). doi:doi:10.1111/j.1365-2729.2010.00387.x

Kessler, S. (2010, 5 November). Twitter increases student engagement. Mashable/Social Media blog. Retrieved from from http://www.mashable.com/2010/11/04/twitter-student-engagement//r:t

Lara, S., & Naval, C. (2009). Educative proposal of Web 2.0 for the encouragement of social and citizenship competence. In G. Siemens & C. Fulford (Eds.), *Proceedings of World Conference on Educational Multimedia, Hypermedia and Telecommunications 2009* (pp. 47-52). Chesapeake, VA: AACE.

Lave, J., & Wenger, E. (1991). *Situated learning: Legitimate peripheral participation*. Cambridge, UK: Cambridge University Press. doi:10.1017/CBO9780511815355

Lee, M. J. W., Chan, A., & McLoughlin, C. (2006). Students as producers: Second year students' experiences as podcasters of content for first year undergraduates. In *Proceedings of the 7th Conference on Information Technology Based Higher Education and Training* (pp. 832-841). Sydney, Australia: University of Technology, Sydney.

Lee, M. J. W., & McLoughlin, C. (Eds.). (2010). *Web 2.0-based e-learning: Applying social informatics for tertiary teaching*. Hershey, PA: Information Science Reference. doi:10.4018/978-1-60566-294-7

Lundy, K. (2010). *Open submission to the National Curriculum Consultation*. Retrieved from http://www.katelundy.com.au/2010/04/22/open-submission-to-the-national-curriculum-consultation/

Makinen, M. (2006). Digital empowerment as a process for enhancing citizens' participation. *E-learning*, *3*(3), 381–395. doi:10.2304/elea.2006.3.3.381

McIntyre, S. (2011). *Teaching with Web 2.0 technologies: Twitter, wikis & blogs-Case study*. Retrieved from http://online.cofa.unsw.edu.au/learning-to-teach-online/ltto-episodes?view=video&video=229

McLoughlin, C., & Alam, S. L. (2011). Digital literacy and e-citizenship skills: A case study in applying Web 2.0 tools. In T. Bastiaens & M. Ebner (Eds.), *Proceedings of World Conference on Educational Multimedia, Hypermedia and Telecommunications 2011* (pp. 3505-3510). Chesapeake, VA: AACE. Retrieved from http://www.editlib.org/p/38361

McLoughlin, C., & Lee, M. J. W. (2007). *Social software and participatory learning: Pedagogical choices with technology affordances in the Web 2.0 era*. Paper presented at the Ascilite 2007: ICT: Providing Choices for Learners and Learning.

McLoughlin, C., & Lee, M. J. W. (2009). Pedagogical responses to social software in universities. In Hatzipanagos, S., & Warburton, S. (Eds.), *Handbook of research on social software and developing community ontologies* (pp. 269–284). doi:10.4018/978-1-60566-208-4.ch023

Mejias, U. (2005). A nomad's guide to learning and social software. *The Knowledge Tree: An E-Journal of Learning Innovation, 7*. Retrieved from http://knowledgetree.flexiblelearning.net.au/edition07/download/la_mejias.pdf

Moll, R., & Krug, D. (2009). Using Web 2.0 for education programs on global citizenship: Addressing moral and ethical issues. Retrieved from http://www.policyalternatives.ca/sites/default/files/uploads/publications/Our_Schools_Ourselve/13_Moll_Krug_using_web_2.pdf

O' Reilly, T. (2009). Gov 2.0: Promise of innovation. In Gotze, J., & Pedersen, C. (Eds.), *State of the eUnion: Government 2.0 and onwards. 21Gov.net.*

O'Brien, J. (2008). *Are we preparing young people for 21st-century citizenship with 20th century thinking? A case for a virtual laboratory of democracy.* Contemporary Issues in Technology and Teacher.

Osimo, D. (2008). *Web 2.0 in government: Why and how*, vol. 23358. Institute for Prospective Technological Studies (IPTS), JRC, European Commission, EUR.

Paavola, S., & Hakkarainen, K. (2005). The knowledge creation metaphor – An emergent epistemological approach to learning. *Science and Education, 14,* 535–557. doi:10.1007/s11191-004-5157-0

Phelps, R., Hase, S., & Ellis, A. (2005). Competency, capability, complexity and computers: Exploring a new model for conceptualising end-user computer education. *British Journal of Educational Technology, 36*(1), 67–84. doi:10.1111/j.1467-8535.2005.00439.x

Punie, Y., & Cabrera, M. (2006). *The future of ICT and learning in the knowledge society.* Luxembourg: European Communities. Retrieved from http://www.eenet.org/upload/File/Vision%20 2015/Thefutureofictandlearningintheknowledgesociety.pdf

Rheingold, H. (2008). Using participatory media and public voice to encourage civic engagement. In W. L. Bennett (Ed.), *Civic life online: Learning how digital media can engage youth*, (pp. 97–118). The John D., & Catherine T. MacArthur Foundation Series on Digital Media and Learning. Cambridge, MA: The MIT Press.

Richards, R. (2010). Digital citizenship and Web 2.0 tools. *MERLOT Journal of Online Learning and Teaching, 6*(2).

Scardamalia, M., & Bereiter, C. (2003). Knowledge building. In Guthrie, J. W. (Ed.), *Encyclopaedia of education* (2nd ed., pp. 1370–1373). New York, NY: Macmillan.

Schroeder, A., Minocha, S., & Schneider, C. (2010). The strengths, weaknesses, opportunities and threats of using social software in higher and further education teaching and learning. *Journal of Computer Assisted Learning, 26*(3), 159–174. doi:10.1111/j.1365-2729.2010.00347.x

Siemens, G. (2005, January). Connectivism: A learning theory for the digital age. *International Journal of Instructional Technology & Distance Learning.* Retrieved from http://www.itdl.org/Journal/Jan_05/article01.htm

Smith, M. K. (2001). David A. Kolb on experiential learning. In *Encyclopaedia of informal education.* Retrieved from http://www.infed.org/encyclopaedia.htm

Tapscott, D. (2009). *Grown up digital: How the Web is changing your world.* McGraw Hill US.

Tapscott, D., Williams, A. D., & Herman, D. (2007). *Government 2.0: Transforming government and governance for the 21st century, new paradigm's government 2.0: Wikinomics, government and democracy program.*

Westheimer, J., & Kahne, J. (2004). What kind of citizen? The politics of educating for democracy. *American Educational Research Journal, 41*(2). doi:10.3102/00028312041002237

KEY TERMS AND DEFINITIONS

Digital Literacy: Digital literacy is the ability to locate, organize, understand, evaluate, and analyze information using digital technology. It involves a working knowledge of current technologies and social media, and an understanding of how it can be used. Digitally literate people can communicate effectively in Web based environments and have the knowledge and skills to use Web 2.0 for work and leisure.

E-Citizenship: E-citizenship involves broader and more active citizen participation enabled by the Internet, mobile communications, and other technologies in today's representative democracy, as well as through more participatory or direct forms of citizen involvement in addressing public challenges.

Pedagogy 2.0: Digital tools and applications, especially emanating from the Web 2.0 movement, require for a new conceptualization of teaching that is focused on participation in communities and networks for learning, personalization of learning tasks, and production of ideas and knowledge. Pedagogy 2.0 (McLoughlin & Lee, 2009) is a response to change. It consists of a set of approaches and strategies that differs from teaching as a practice of passing on information. Instead, it advocates a model of learning in which students are empowered to participate, communicate, create knowledge, and exercise a high level of agency and control over the learning process.

Social Networking: A social networking service is a platform, or site that focuses on building and reflecting of social networks or social relations among people, who, for example, share interests and/or activities and people with similar or somewhat similar interests, backgrounds and/or activities make their own communities. Most social network services are Web-based and provide means for users to interact over the Internet, such as e-mail and instant messaging. Social networking tools such as Bebo, Facebook and MySpace allow users to share ideas, activities, events, and interests within their individual networks.

Web 2.0: A term used to describe the second generation or improved form of the World Wide Web that emphasizes collaboration and sharing of knowledge and content among users. Characteristic of Web 2.0 are the socially-based tools and systems referred to collectively as social software (for example blogs and wikis).

Chapter 11
A Study on a Problem–Based Learning Method Using Facebook at a Vocational School

Shi-Jer Lou
National Pingtung University of Science and Technology, Taiwan

Min-Yeuan Lan
National Nei-Pu Senior Agricultural-Industrial Vocational High School, Taiwan

Hsiu-Ling Yen
Kaohsiung Municipal San-Min Home Economics & Commerce Vocational High School, Taiwan

ABSTRACT

This study used a single-group pre-test/post-test design for a quasi-experimental study to implement a 12-week teaching activity. The research tools included a learning achievement test, a learning attitude scale, a portfolio assessment scale, a response and observation record form on Facebook, and a teaching reflection log. Each tool helped to identify the effect of problem-based learning on students' learning effectiveness and attitude. The following statistical methods were used to analyze quantitative data: descriptive statistics, one-way analysis of variance (ANOVA), nonparametric tests, single sample t-tests, dependent sample t-tests, Pearson product moment correlations, and Kendall harmony coefficients. The research results are as follows: (1) the teaching model of problem-based Facebook learning has a significant effect on the learning effectiveness of some students and has a positive effect on learning attitude; (2) there is a significant difference in the effectiveness of problem-based Facebook learning among students with different Website hosting experiences and among those who used Facebook's message function to varying degrees; (3) the problem-based Facebook learning has a significant impact on the effectiveness of the learning portfolios for students with different Website hosting experiences and message function utilization; (4) the problem-based Facebook learning method used for plant identification has a significant effect on the learning attitude of students; and (5) there is a significant positive correlation among the problem-based Facebook teaching of plant identification, students' learning effectiveness, and learning attitude.

DOI: 10.4018/978-1-4666-3649-1.ch011

INTRODUCTION

Research Background and Motives

Currently, online interactive learning has been popularly applied in classroom settings, yet the solutions through the classroom use of multimedia have not been well-investigated. Therefore, the current study aims to explore the effectiveness of a problem-based learning method using Facebook to enhance the learning and attitude of sophomores studying agricultural at vocational high schools. Curriculum is an important means by which to achieve educational objectives, and teaching materials are important tools with which to put that curriculum's contents into practice. Because for certain subjects only a small number of students take elective courses, publishers are unwilling to edit or publish the relevant textbooks. As a result, the small academic departments that offer these courses cannot find suitable textbooks for those students. However, vocational schools, which often teach such subjects, play a very important role in the process of industrial development in Taiwan. The Department of Wildlife Conservation at the National Nei-Pu Senior Agricultural-Industrial Vocational High School is the only vocational high school where such a department exists in Taiwan. Plant identification is a fundamental course for the program, supported by comprehensive teaching materials and resources. There are approximately 800,000 to 1,000,000 species of plants around the world (Wei, Chen, & Chang, 1998). Various species of plants are distributed throughout the school roughly according to the distribution of plants in the world. Naturally, it is difficult for teachers to fit all of the world's plants into their teaching materials. Therefore, the department's teaching model has to be adjusted to achieve the best learning effectiveness.

Although there are abundant natural plants in the learning environment, it is impossible for students to confirm the accuracy of the information they read about plants. In addition, because there are too many plants in the learning environment, it is hard for students to absorb the knowledge in a short period of time. However, the cooperative method of group learning can help reduce learning burdens and improve effectiveness. Through cooperative learning teaching activities, students can use various electronic media, such as smart phones or laptops to conduct Internet searches, while teachers provide guidance, diverging from past teaching methods to enable students to actively observe and summarize plant-related information. Problem-based learning, which is different from the traditional teaching model, has been comprehensively implemented in many fields. Its main attribute is 'activeness', favoring student-centered and 'problem-solving' approaches in which teachers act as designers and guides. Students must independently collect and arrange relevant information and participate in discussion and knowledge sharing mainly based on group cooperative learning (Hong & Lin, 2006). In Taiwan, relevant studies (Chang Lai & Yang, 2006; Chiu, 2003; Chi & Chang, 2001) have indicated that problem-based learning is a teaching and learning strategy worthy of promotion.

At present, herbarium-based traditional teaching is used in almost all of the plant identification-related courses in Taiwan, and many newly developed courses are still under design. The integration of problem-based learning and a Web 2.0 platform is an innovative teaching model. The Web 2.0 platform transfers the learning environment from the traditional classroom setting to a Web platform that enables students to actively interact with plants. Therefore, learning is no longer restricted to books and classrooms. This study selected a functional and easy-to-operate learning platform, Facebook, to assist students in understanding forage plants. This study conducted a teaching experiment to understand how the problem-based Facebook method affected the learning effectiveness, learning attitude, and learning process of vocational high school students studying plant identification.

Research Purpose

- To develop a teaching model for problem-based Facebook learning for plant identification.
- To investigate the learning effectiveness of problem-based Facebook learning for plant identification.
- To investigate the effectiveness of portfolios used within a problem-based Facebook platform for plant identification.
- To investigate how the problem-based Facebook method for plant identification affects learning attitude.

LITERATURE REVIEW

Facebook

Web-based teaching technologies have become a popular option for digital learning. According to the Website CheckFacebook.com, there are approximately 600 million users of Facebook globally. In Taiwan, Facebook has become the most rapidly growing and comprehensively applied Web 2.0 tool. Facebook provides free applications that enable users to establish their own social networking Websites. What makes the platform educationally relevant is that the interactive space enables teachers to provide content and instruction without textbooks. In addition, students can enrich their learning through various media, appropriate cooperative learning, and sharing. The largest difference between Facebook and the Web 2.0 application is that the former is a highly integrated social platform. Its personal Webpage integrates the synchronous (chat room) and the asynchronous (graffiti wall, messaging, and discussion forum), image and video sharing, a community function, various applications, dynamic searching, really simple syndication (RSS), blogging, address book, and e-mail. Moreover, with the platform's two most important elements,

networking and friends, users can enjoy a unique network socialization experience. As opposed to other Web 2.0 platforms, Facebook can more effectively develop trends. Lai, Chang, and Liu (2009) noted that Facebook provides opportunities for interaction and contract.

International studies have indicated that the campus culture developed by Facebook will have an effect on the learning experiences of students in academia and other social fields. It is important for educators to understand how to cultivate this platform's potential for valuable learning experiences and meaningful student development (Eberhardt, 2007). Haverback (2009) suggested that Facebook could be a more effective platform for teacher-student discussion than simply for self-reflection. Susilo and Wang (2009) indicated that Facebook provides students with a social access, which further changes the original functions of learning. Anderson (2009) suggested that the effectiveness of Facebook-based learning is greater than that of face-to-face learning. Lai et al. (2009) suggested that the use of Facebook can reduce the time students devote to schoolwork. However, Facebook does significantly affect academic performance; the key factor is effective time management.

The Facebook Web platform enables teachers to experiment beyond textbook-based teaching. In addition, the Web-based interactions and learning opportunities allow students to explore other learning methods. Therefore, it is likely that Facebook will certainly reform future digital learning.

Problem-Based Learning

Problem-based learning originates from a progressive educational movement started by John Dewey, which decrees that teachers should tap into students' natural instinct for exploration and creation (Chou (trans), 2003). Barrows (1996) suggested that problem-based learning is student-centered. It is not only a method for organizing courses, but also a teaching strategy and learning process

(Barrows & Kelson, 1998; Torp & Sage, 1998). Wegner, Holloway and Crader (1998), suggesting that problem-based learning is one in which teachers make the students relate the course content to real world questions, and learners actively solve problems, arrange relevant information, establish learning objectives as required by those problems, and obtain the best explanation through proposing hypotheses, investigating and verifying research, and constantly evaluating and rearranging. The pioneer of problem-based learning, Barrows (1985), wrote that the process includes five stages: problem analysis, data collection, comprehensive summarization, and reflection.

The main purpose of problem-based learning is to solve problems in a real-life situation, using group cooperative learning to guide students in exploring, establishing teaching objectives, solving problems and further increasing their interest and motivation. Hiltz (1994) suggested that cooperative learning can help students understand different viewpoints and effectively increase their educational achievement, motivation, and effectiveness. Chi and Chang (2001) specified that the cooperative, problem-based learning model is one where teachers design or develop a question or assignment for student groups to solve or complete. During the problem-solving process, students construct their own knowledge and skills through cooperation with others. Students exhibit and witness different learning characteristics and patterns through their discussion of a problem with others. They then can record and reflect on what they have seen and heard to verify their understanding of the problem (Lin, 2002).

As for relevant studies, Kumar and David (2010) found that interactive video-based problem-based learning enhanced college students' knowledge and understanding of scientific problems. Rossiter, Petrulis, & Biggs, (2010) selected freshmen in the Department of Chemistry as subjects and found that under the instruction of problem-based teaching, students could better develop their own thinking and actively communicate with classmates about their ideas. Kuo (2009) compared problem-based teaching with traditional teaching, and found that the teaching effectiveness of problem-based teaching was significantly better than that of traditional lecture teaching. Chen (2011) investigated the effect of problem-based learning on students' deep learning strategies and found that it had a significantly positive impact on strategic time and resource control. Problem-based learning designs real-life questions and uses group cooperative learning to guide students in exploring, establishing teaching objectives, solving problems, and further increasing their interest and motivation. The theory is that problem-based learning is superior to traditional learning because students can more actively develop their own ideas and aggressively discuss and share them with peers. Therefore, their learning effectiveness and learning attitude are significantly improved.

Learning Portfolio

A learning portfolio collects students' assignments to reflect their learning process and self-growth. As early as the 1980s, scholars introduced the learning portfolio method to educational fields, defining them as "learning records attaching importance to students' works or their feelings about their works" (Chang & Chou, 2006). Tzou (2000) indicated that a learning portfolio could itself be an effective teacher, showing students how to construct objectives and plans. Tzou requested that scholars continuously and actively collect the learning portfolios of organizations to enable teachers to combine their own teaching objectives with an assessment strategy based on curriculum reflection, student work, and test materials. Yueh and Wang (2000) argued that learning portfolios enabled students to construct and verify their knowledge and skills. Gaide (2006) suggested that learning portfolios painted a more accurate picture of a student's ability, organizational skills and performance on school assignments. Besides being used as an assessment tool, the learning portfolio can also be used as a learning tool. The study conducted by Barak and Doppelt (2000) indicated that the learning portfolio can help students develop innovative thinking. During the learning process, students have to use a variety of intellectual strategies to complete their learning portfolios.

The Internet has changed the traditional face-to-face teaching model, as well as the learning portfolio. The ability of computer technologies to record and save learning portfolios, that is, the development of electronic learning portfolios, are solving the problems concerning data storage or management. Students can combine texts with images, videos, and sounds to create larger and more diversified portfolios (Williams, 2007). In teacher training institutions in the Unites States, eLearning portfolios have been indispensable teaching application tools (Chung, 2005). According to scholarly studies on eLearning portfolios (Chen, 2002; Tsai, 2001; Chang & Tung, 2000), the basic functions of the eLearning portfolio are as follows: it can store files in various formats (sound, image, text, and video); it enables students to actively participate in their own eLearning portfolios; it enables teachers, students, and parents to browse the eLearning portfolios more conveniently to guide and assess learning effectiveness; it provides students with a platform of cooperative learning, instantaneous exchange, and feedback, and it possesses a real-time update function.

In terms of relevant studies, You (2001) conducted hands-on research on the implementation of eLearning portfolios in natural science courses, revealing that file-sharing, peer-editing and feedback can positively affect learning achievements. Chen (2002) found that the eLearning portfolio system has a positive effect on the learning process. Tseng (2003) investigated learning portfolios, peer assessments, and cooperative learning and found that the eLearning portfolio system could help students organize their personal learning process, peer assessments, and cooperative learning. This in turn made the system management smoother for teachers or teaching assistants.

The computerization of learning portfolios facilitates the storage of various files and enables students to participate in learning more aggressively. Moreover, the records of peer interactions and cooperative learning also have a positive effect on the learning process.

Figure 1. Research framework

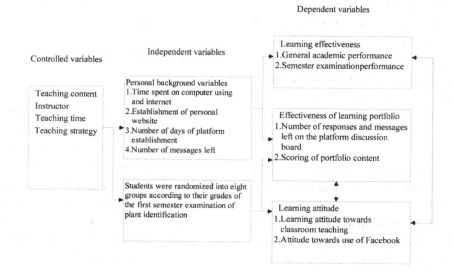

RESEARCH DESIGN AND IMPLEMENTATION

Research Structure and Design

The main purpose of this study is to construct a Facebook digital learning platform for a problem-based learning cooperative learning environment that provides students with information about basic plant structures. The research framework is shown in Figure 1.

Thirty-seven sophomores from a vocational high school in Pingtung County were selected as subjects. This study used S-shaped heterogeneous grouping to divide them into eight groups according to their pre-test scores. Problem-based Facebook learning was implemented, and Facebook was used as the platform for group discussion and information sharing with the aim of learning to identify plants. The teachers provided the students with feedback and guidance in a timely manner, enabling students to have their questions answered, divide the work, collect data, summarize their conclusions, and reflect on the finished works. The teaching experiment was conducted over 12 weeks, and three classes were given weekly for a total of 36 meetings. Before the teaching activity was implemented, a 'student learning attitude scale' was used to conduct a pre-test. After the completion of the pre-test, learning achievement and learning attitude scales were used to conduct the post-test, which involved 'plant identification'. During the teaching experiment, an observation method was used to record students' participation from the Facebook learning platform. After the teaching experiment was completed, a one-on-one, semi-structured interview was conducted with the subjects.

To achieve the maximum effectiveness from the Facebook-based learning of plant identification, the teaching model was divided into a preparation stage, an implementation stage, and a work completion stage. During the preparation stage, the teacher would gauge students' prior knowledge to determine the teaching content, establish the Facebook learning platform and become familiar with its functions, and instruct students in how to develop and reflect on their learning process. The implementation stage was divided into problem analysis, data collection, comprehensive summary, and reflection. For problem analysis, the teacher would post questions on the Facebook graffiti wall, and students would analyze the problems and confirm their solutions. For data collection, students would divide the work, and the teacher would provide them with the direction to search and interpret data. For the comprehensive summary, students would arrange the data and summarize the conclusion. Student groups would leave messages and respond to one another, and teachers would encourage students and provide feedback in a timely manner. As for reflection, students would assess themselves, assess one another, and reflect on their personal learning experiences, and the teacher would praise them, analyze their works, and complete the teaching log. For the completion stage, students would use group cooperative learning to help provide accurate information to each other and revise the portfolios of their works based on reflection and feedback. The teacher would make revisions, provide scores, and assess the quality and content of the students' work. The problem-based teaching model, including preparation and process, is shown in Figure 2.

Research Hypotheses

H-1: After the Facebook learning platform is established, there is a significant difference in plant identification learning achievement test scores among students with different personal background variables.

H-2: After the Facebook learning platform is established, there is a significant difference in the plant identification learning portfolio scores among students of different personal background variables.

Figure 2. Framework of PBL teaching model of Facebook for plant identification

Group	Portfolios on Facebook	Mean score	Work characteristics
Group 1		86.3	1. Clear images and explicit explanations of features. 2. Careful data arrangement and complete content framework. 3. Serious group discussion and detailed observation.
Group 2		77.3	1. Abundant data about plants were found. 2. The group earnestly observed plants on campus and explicitly specified the locations and names of plants.
Group 3		81.7	1. Detailed information 2. Photographed plants with detailed features.
Group 4		80.0	1. The group leader was sincere and responsible and completed most of the work. 2. The main features of plants were photographed, and the features were specified to enable browsers to understand them easily.
Group 5		83.7	1. Most of the photographs were taken by the students themselves. The students touched the detailed features of plants with their hands, which aided the independent learning process. 2. Explicit descriptions of plant features and highly cooperative group members.
Group 6		85.7	1. Simple and explicit descriptions of plant features. The learning objectives were properly managed by the students themselves. 2. Highly cooperative group members. Any mistake would be rapidly corrected after feedback was obtained. 3. The portfolios were completed during the teacher's lecture instruction.
Group	Portfolios on Facebook	Mean score	Work characteristics
Group 7		84.7	1. Highly cooperative group members. When the group leader was arranging data, the group members were responsible for dividing up plants. 2. The collected forage plants were arranged into a database.
Group 8		82.0	1. Simple and explicit descriptions of plant features. 2. The data collected were placed on the platform to discuss and share with other groups to achieve cooperative learning.

H-3: After the Facebook learning platform is established, there is a significant difference in the plant identification learning attitude scale scores.

H-4: After the Facebook learning platform is established, there is a significant positive correlation between plant identification, learning effectiveness, and learning attitude.

Research Tools

The research tools included the plant identification learning achievement test, the learning attitude scale, and the portfolio assessment scale. The plant identification learning achievement test was developed by the researcher according to the course curriculum with the goal of assessing the effectiveness of the Facebook problem- based learning platform. The validity of the learning attitude scale was tested after it was developed; namely, the advisor along with one off-site expert and one on-campus senior teacher were invited to revise the items on the scale. The scale items were eventually revised according to the comments from the expert and the teachers. The validity of the portfolio assessment scale was tested by inviting the advisor and two plant identification professional teachers to review the dimensions of the scale. The dimensions were then revised based on their comments. To increase the reliability of the portfolio assessment scale, the researcher and two plant identification professional teachers jointly assessed the scale. The Kendall harmony coefficients of the assessment results of three teachers were obtained, where W<0.793 and p<0.05, suggesting that the assessment results of the three teachers were significantly correlated and, thus, consistent.

Data Processing

Statistical methods such as descriptive statistics, one-way ANOVA, nonparametric tests, single sample t-tests, dependent sample t-tests, Pearson product moment correlations, and Kendall harmony coefficients were used to perform analyses on the quantitative data. The qualitative data included a 12-week teaching observation, including student records and reflections, a group discussion learning form, student learning portfolios, and interview records. The quantitative data and qualitative data analyses were verified to determine the effect of different background variables and groups on learning effectiveness, learning attitude, and learning portfolios of students in the Facebook PBL plant identification program.

RESULTS AND DISCUSSION

Students' Background Variables

Before the teaching experiment was conducted, students had an understanding of various plant organs and possessed basic computer skills. In terms of the average daily time spent on computer and Internet use, 11% spent less than 1 hour, 54% spent 1~3 hours, 27% spent 3~6 hours, and 8% spent more than 6 hours. Therefore, on average, students spent 1~3 hours on computer and Internet use. As for the results of the Website hosting survey, most students hosted Websites on Wretch, followed by Blogs and other Web 2.0 Websites or Websites in the 'none of the above' category.

During the course of the experiment, the weekly average number of days that the students hosted the Facebook learning platform was calculated. 16 students hosted the platform for 1 day, 10 hosted it for 2 days, 8 hosted it for 3 days, 2 hosted it for 4 days, and 1 hosted it for 7 days. Therefore, most of the students hosted the learning platform for 1~3 days weekly. The number of messages left weekly on the Facebook learning platform was also tallied. 10 of the students left 0 messages, 18 left 1 message, 4 left 2 messages, and 5 left 3 messages. Therefore, most of the students left 1 message per week. Most of the content on the Facebook learning platform was irrelevant to the course. The rest, in order of frequency, concerned course discussion and learning feedback, problems or difficulty with the material, sharing learning portfolios, mutual encouragement and support, and sharing general statuses. Most of the content on the Facebook learning platforms of other groups was also irrelevant to the course. The rest, in order of frequency, concerned problems and difficulty with the material, sharing learning portfolios, course discussion and learning feedback, mutual encouragement and support, and sharing general statuses.

Learning Effectiveness

Descriptive Statistics of Achievement Test Scores of Various Groups

The results of three achievements tests are shown in Table 1. The score of each group on the third achievement test was higher than that on the second one, and the score on the second test was higher than that on the first test for each group as well, suggesting that the mean score progressed every time.

Table 1. Descriptive statistics of learning achievement test scores of various groups

Group	Item	Number	Mean	Standard deviation	Standard error
Group 1	First Achievement Test	5	31.80	7.50	3.35
	Second Achievement Test	5	48.80	23.22	10.39
	Third Achievement Test	5	58.00	32.81	14.67
Group 2	First Achievement Test	5	32.60	4.34	1.94
	Second Achievement Test	5	48.00	14.70	6.57
	Third Achievement Test	5	63.80	23.57	10.54
Group 3	First Achievement Test	5	34.40	3.97	1.78
	Second Achievement Test	5	48.00	18.55	8.29
	Third Achievement Test	5	53.40	33.02	14.77
Group 4	First Achievement Test	5	29.20	9.52	4.26
	Second Achievement Test	5	40.80	18.20	8.14
	Third Achievement Test	5	54.80	30.99	13.86
Group 5	First Achievement Test	5	34.00	4.24	1.90
	Second Achievement Test	5	56.00	28.71	12.84
	Third Achievement Test	5	70.80	17.34	7.76
Group 6	First Achievement Test	4	34.00	4.69	2.35
	Second Achievement Test	4	60.00	12.65	6.32
	Third Achievement Test	4	66.75	20.52	10.26
Group 7	First Achievement Test	4	34.50	1.29	0.65
	Second Achievement Test	4	63.00	11.94	5.97
	Third Achievement Test	4	72.25	17.19	8.60
Group 8	First Achievement Test	4	33.75	3.77	1.89
	Second Achievement Test	4	47.00	34.16	17.08
	Third Achievement Test	4	69.25	14.73	7.36

Analysis of Students' Portfolios

The analysis of the portfolios of eight groups of students is shown in Table 2. According to the scores of the learning portfolios produced by each group, the more aggressively the group members participated in the portfolio production process, the higher the scores were.

Scores of Achievement Test and Portfolio Works Different Background Variables

1. Variance in the Time Spent on Computer Use and the Internet by Students

The difference in time spent on computer use and the Internet (F value=0.139, p=0.871>0.05) did not have a significant effect on achievement test scores. There was no significant difference in achievement test scores among students spending different amounts of time on computer use and the Internet. The difference in time spent on computer use and the Internet (F value=0.203,

Table 2. Scores and work characteristics of the portfolios of eight groups of students

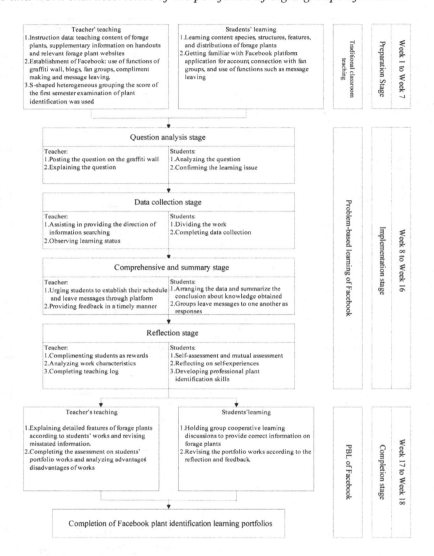

p=0.817>0.05) did not have a significant effect on portfolio scores either. There was no significant difference in portfolio scores among students spending different amounts of time on computer use and the Internet.

2. Variance Analysis on Students of Different Website Hosting Experiences

There was a more significant difference (F value=6.534, p=0.002<0.05) in the achievement test scores. The post hoc comparison showed that the achievement test scores of student who had hosted Websites on both Wretch and Blogs (M=79.42) was significantly higher than the scores of those who had only hosted Websites on Blogs (M=48.32) or Wretch (M=60.72). The achievement test scores of the groups with Website hosting experiences on both Websites was significantly higher than the scores of other groups. There was a significant difference in the portfolio scores among students with different Website hosting experiences (F value=6.128, p=0.002<0.05).

The post hoc comparison showed that the scores of the students who had hosted Websites on both Wretch and Blogs (M=96.26) were significantly higher than the scores of those who had only hosted Websites on Blogs (77.26), those who only hosted on Wretch (M=84.95), and those who had never hosted a Website (M=81.34). The scores of the student groups with Website hosting experiences at both Wretch and Blogs were significantly higher than other groups.

3. Variance Analysis on Students Hosting the Platform for Different Numbers of Days

The difference in number of days of platform hosting had a significant effect (F value=3.644, p=0.038<0.05) on the achievement test score. The post hoc comparison showed that the difference in number of days of platform hosting did not have a significant effect on the portfolio score (F value =2.734, p=0.081>0.05). There was no significant difference in the portfolio scores among students with different numbers of days of platform hosting.

4. Variance Analysis between Students with Different Numbers of Messages Left

The difference in number of Facebook messages left had a significant effect (F value=12.209, p=0.000<.05) on the achievement test score. The post hoc comparison showed that the scores of students who did not leave any messages online were significantly lower than those of other groups (M=46.35). This non-messaging group had achievement test scores that were significantly lower than those of other groups. The average number of messages left had a significant effect (F value=5.5, p=0.009<0.05) on the portfolio scores. The post hoc comparison showed that the scores of the students (M=89.95) who on average left 2~3 messages per week and those of the students (M=86.12) who on average left 1

message per week were significantly higher than the those of the students who never left any message online (M=77.33), The score of the student group with at least 1 message left per week was significantly higher than the group that didn't leave any messages.

Summary

The research results showed that the differences in students' Website hosting experience and the number of messages left had a significant effect on their achievement test and portfolio scores in the Facebook PBL for plant identification program. However, differences in the time spent on computer and Internet use and in the number of days of Website hosting did not have a significant effect on their achievement test and portfolio scores. H-1—"After the Facebook learning platform is established, there is a significant difference in the plant identification learning achievement test scores among students with different personal background variables"—was partially supported. In addition, H-2—"After the Facebook learning platform is established, there is a significant difference in the plant identification learning portfolio scores among students with different personal background variables"—was also partially supported. The results are consistent with the finding of Anderson (2009), which suggested that while Facebook could increase learning effectiveness, it would not significantly affect scores. Some of this study's results are consistent with the finding of Lai (2009), which suggested that while Facebook could reduce the time spent on schoolwork, it would not significantly affect scores.

It can be concluded that the Facebook PBL can improve learning effectiveness. However, the time spent on Facebook should be adequately controlled and students' levels of active participation enhanced to improve learning effectiveness.

Learning Attitude

Dependent Sample T-Test on Pre-Test/Post-Test of Learning Attitude

The dependent sample t-test analyzing students' pre-test vs post-test learning attitudes, cognitive attitudes, affective attitudes, and attitude skills suggested that there were significant difference in all comparisons ($p < 0.05$); the scores of the post-tests (138.41, 51.00, 44.24, and 43.16, respectively) were significantly higher than those of the pre-tests (132.14, 49.22, 41.26, and 41.30, respectively) in all comparisons. It can be concluded that the Facebook PBL can improve students' learning, cognitive, and affective attitudes as well as their attitude skills. Based on the above, the scores of the post-test in cognitive attitude, affective attitude, and attitude skills were significantly higher than those of the pre-test.

Correlation among Learning Achievement, Portfolio Score, and Learning Attitude

The post-test of students' achievement test and attitude scale showed that $r = 0.334$ and $p < 0.05$, suggesting that there was a significant difference. Additionally, this analysis showed that there was a significant positive correlation between students' learning achievement and learning attitude in Facebook PBL, suggesting that the higher the students' learning attitude score is, the higher their learning achievement will be. The post-test of students' portfolio scores and attitude scale showed that $r = .374$, $p < .05$, suggesting that there was a significant difference. There was a significant positive correlation between portfolio scores and learning attitude in Facebook PBL, suggesting that the higher the students' learning attitude score is, the higher their scores of portfolio works will be.

Summary

The research results showed that the post-test learning attitude, cognitive attitude, affective attitude, and attitude skills scores were significantly higher than the pre-test scores in Facebook PBL for plant identification, suggesting that the learning attitudes of students receiving such PBL can be improved. H-3—"After the Facebook learning platform is established, there is a significant difference in the plant identification learning attitude scale scores"—was supported. This result was consistent with the findings of Kuo (2009) and Chen (2011). Therefore, Facebook PBL can significantly improve students' learning attitude. There is a significant positive correlation between achievement test scores and learning attitude in the Facebook PBL, and there is also a significant positive correlation between portfolio scores and learning attitude. H-4—"After the Facebook learning platform is established, there is a significant positive correlation between plant identification learning effectiveness and learning attitude"—was supported. This result is consistent with the finding of Hsu (2008). It can be concluded that there is a positive correlation among students' learning achievements, portfolio scores, and learning attitudes in the Facebook PBL course. The higher the achievement test and portfolio scores are, the better the learning attitude will be.

Teaching Reflection

During the implementation of problem-based learning courses in this study, several problems arose. These included students playing various Facebook games, a lack of self-reflection and analysis, unfamiliarity with the Facebook interface, failure to assess the accuracy of data, lack of group discussion or messages on the platform, difficulty gathering a group to discuss topics concurrently, low participation, and the non-objectiveness of mutual assessment scores. By focusing on the teaching process, this study observed how students learn to diagnose their own learning problems, analyze them, and solve them. Although students were lacking in traditional textbook knowledge, they developed the ability to face and solve problems.

CONCLUSION AND SUGGESTIONS

Research Conclusions

Based on the findings, the conclusions of this study are as follows: (1) After the Facebook learning platform is established, there are significant differences in the plant identification learning achievement test scores among students with different background variables. The learning achievement scores of the students who hosted Websites and left weekly messages are significantly higher than the scores of those who have never hosted Websites and or left any messages. Other variables do not have a significant effect on the score; (2) After the Facebook learning platform is established, there is a significant difference on plant identification learning portfolio scores among students with different background variables. The scores of the students who have hosted Websites and left weekly messages are significantly higher than the scores of those who have neither hosted Websites nor left any messages. Other variables do not have a significant effect on the score; (3) After the Facebook learning platform is established, students' post-test leaning attitudes, cognitive attitudes, affective attitudes, and attitude skills scores are significantly higher than the pre-test scores; and (4) After the Facebook learning platform is established, there is a significant positive correlation between learning achievement and learning attitude in Facebook PBL. There is also a positive correlation between the learning portfolio score and the learning attitude in Facebook PBL.

Research Suggestions

The suggestions for future studies are as follows: (1) The application of Facebook problem-based learning in professional courses at vocational high schools can reduce the time of implementation, and problem-based learning course contents can be properly planned to improve students' learning effectiveness; (2) The operation of the Facebook platform requires long-term planning. Facebook can be used as the platform for after-class discussion or weekday homework submission to enable students to cultivate the skills to publish comments on Facebook. This habituation also reduces operation-related problems, which helps smooth the future implementation of problem-based learning; and (3) As for follow-up studies, this study recommends selecting subjects at different grade levels or applying the model to different professional courses. This teaching experiment had a relatively small sample size; increasing the sample size or adding a control group may produce different experimental results.

REFERENCES

Anderson, L. S., & Hildenbrand, E. K. (2009). Can Facebook replace face-to-face? *Learning and Leading with Technology, 37*(2), 8–9.

Barak, M., & Doppelt, Y. (2000). Using portfolio to enhance creative thinking. *The Journal of Technology Studies, 26*(2), 16–25.

Barrows, H., & Kelson, A. (1998). *Problem-based learning: A total approach to education.* Springfield, IL: SIU School of Medicine, Department of Medical Education Springfield.

Barrows, H. S. (1985). *How to design a problem-based curriculum for the preclinical years.* New York, NY: Springer Publishing Company.

Barrows, H. S. (1996). Problem-based learning in medicine and beyond: A brief overview. *New Directions for Teaching and Learning, 68*, 3–11. doi:10.1002/tl.37219966804

Chang, C. C., & Chou, P. N. (2006). Development, implementation and effect of a competency-based web learning system. *Chinese Journal of Science Education, 14*(2), 209–235.

Chang, C. C., & Tung, Y. H. (2000). Constructing an e-learning portfolio on World Wide Web. *Instructional Technology & Media, 51*, 37–45.

Chang Lai, M. L., & Yang, K. Y. (2006). *A study of biodiversity problem-based learning portfolio for college freshmen.* Paper presented at the 22nd Annual Conference of Science Education.

Chen, D. L. (2002). *Design and implementation of a web-based portfolio supporting system.* Unpublished Master's Thesis. National Sun Yat Sen University, Kaohsiung, Taiwan.

Chen, Y. C. (2011). *The influence of problem-based learning on primary school senior students' scientific attitude and learning strategy.* Unpublished Master's thesis. National Pingtung University of Education, Pingtung, Taiwan.

Chiu, H. D. (2003). *A comparative study of establishing the basic concepts in junior high school electromagnetism by subject-based learning and problem-based learning.* Unpublished Master's thesis. National Chiao Tung University, Hsinchu, Taiwan.

Chung, C. J., Rodriguez, M., & O'Hara, S. (2005). Building a community of practice in electronic portfolios. *Proceeding of SITE 2005—Society for Information. Technology & Teacher Education International Conference*, Phoenix, AZ, USA, (pp. 2188-2192).

Delisle, R. (2003). *How to use problem-based learning in the classroom* (Chou, T. S., Trans.). Taipei, Taiwan: Psychological.

Eberhardt, D. M. (2007). Facing up to Facebook. *About Campus, 12*(4), 18–26. doi:10.1002/abc.219

Gaide, S. (2006). E-portfolios supercharge performance-based student assessment. *Distance Education Report,* 4-6.

Guo, Z. Y. (2009). *A study on effectiveness of applying problem-based learning to electronics course for the electronic information department in vocational high schools.* Unpublished master's thesis. National Taiwan Normal University, Taipei, Taiwan.

Haverback, H. R. (2009). Facebook: Uncharted territory in a reading education classroom. *Reading Today, 27*(2), 34–34.

Hiltz, S. R. (1994). *The virtual classroom: Learning without limits via computer networks.* Norwood, NJ: Alex Publishing Corp.

Hong, J. J., & Lin, C. L. (2006). *Theory and practice of problem-based learning curriculum development.* Taipei, Taiwan: Shtabook.

Hsu, W. C. (2008). *A study of problem-based learning strategy on energy cognition and conservation for fourth graders.* Unpublished Master's thesis. National Taipei University of Education, Taipei, Taiwan.

Jih, H. J., & Chang, H. F. (2001). The instructional design model for problem-based learning. *Instructional Technology & Media, 55*, 17–30.

Kumar, D. D. (2010). Approaches to interactive video anchors in problem-based science learning. *Journal of Science Education and Technology, 19*(1), 13–19. doi:10.1007/s10956-009-9154-6

Lai, Y. C., Chang, Y. F., & Liu, Z. F. (2009). *Motives of using Facebook and its influence on making-friends and learning performance*. Paper presented at the International Conference of Web 2.0 and Education (ICWE 2009), Taoyuan, Taiwan.

Lin, L. J. (2002). Apply problem-based learning to Internet resource-based learning. *Instructional Technology & Media, 60,* 42–53.

Rossiter, D., Petrulis, R., & Biggs, C. A. (2010). A blended approach to problem-based learning in the freshman year. *Chemical Engineering Education, 44*(1), 23–29.

Torp, L., & Sage, S. M. (1998). *Problems as possibilities: Problem-based learning for K-12 education*. Virginia: Association for Supervision and Curriculum Development.

Tsai, M. F. (2001). *Designing an analysis system for e-learning portfolio*. Unpublished Master's thesis. National Sun Yat Sun University, Kaohsiung, Taiwan.

Tseng, C. H. (2003). *The implementation and evaluation of networked portfolio system for individual and group*. Unpublished master's thesis. National Chiao Tung University, Hsinchu, Taiwan.

Tzou, H. Y. (2000). Project-based learning for curriculum, teaching, and evaluation. *Journal of National Tainan Teachers College, 34,* 3–9.

Wang, S., & Susilo, A. (2009). Using Facebook to develop network learning communities. *Journal of Tianjin Radio & Television University, 13*(1), 17–18.

Wegner, S. B., Holloway, K., & Crader, A. (1998). *Utilizing a problem-based approach on the World Wide Web*. ERIC: ED414262.

Wei, D., Chen, C. S., & Chang, Y. Y. (1998). Statistics of biological species in Taiwan. *Accounting and Statistics Monthly Report, 85*(4), 20–53.

Williams, B. T. (2007). I'm ready for my close-up now: Electronic portfolios and how we read identity. *Journal of Adolescent & Adult Literacy, 50,* 500–504. doi:10.1598/JAAL.50.6.7

Wu, C. S., & Lin, T. Y. (2002). Creative-thinking teaching. *Journal of Educational Resources and Research, 60,* 46.

Yew, R. S. (2001). *An action research of electronic portfolio in six-grade science course*. Unpublished master's thesis. National Taichung University, Taichung, Taiwan.

Yueh, H. P., & Wang, Y. C. (2000). A study of students' attitudes toward the electronic portfolio practice. *Bulletin of Educational Psychology, 31*(2), 65–84.

Chapter 12
Web–Mediated Education and Training Environments:
A Review of Personalised Interactive eLearning

Eileen O'Donnell
Trinity College Dublin, Ireland & Dublin Institute of Technology, Ireland

Mary Sharp
Trinity College Dublin, Ireland

Catherine Mulwa
Trinity College Dublin, Ireland

Vincent P. Wade
Trinity College Dublin, Ireland

ABSTRACT

This chapter reviews the concept of personalised eLearning resources in relation to integrating interactivity into asynchronous learning. Personalised eLearning resources are learning resources which are selected to suit a specific student or trainee's individual learning requirements. The affordance of personalised eLearning would provide educators with the opportunity to shift away from eLearning content that is retrieved and move towards the provision of personalised interactive content to provide a form of asynchronous learning to suit students at different degree levels. A basic introduction to the concept of ePedagogy in online learning environments is explored and the impacts these systems have on students learning experiences are considered. Issues, controversies, and problems associated with the creation of personalised interactive eLearning resources are examined, and suggested solutions and recommendations to the identified issues, controversies, and problems are reviewed. Personalised interactive asynchronous learning resources could potentially improve students' learning experiences but more research on the human computer interface of these authoring tools is required before personalised eLearning resources are available for use by non-technical authors.

DOI: 10.4018/978-1-4666-3649-1.ch012

INTRODUCTION

This chapter provides a review of personalised interactive eLearning resources. Personalised eLearning resources are suitable for integrating interactivity into asynchronous learning. Asynchronous learning is the learning which takes place when a student has the opportunity to interact with learning resources and return at a later time to discuss or question the content with peers or lecturers. Alternatively, asynchronous eLearning refers to the learning which takes place through communication with other students or lecturers who are not necessarily online at the same time; this type of learning is facilitated by the use of: e-mails; discussion boards; blogs; and wikis.

Personalised eLearning resources refer to the creation of eLearning resources which have been specifically selected or tailored to suit the learning preferences of individual learners. Personalised interactive eLearning resources provide students and trainees with the opportunity to engage with interactive eLearning resources which have been specifically selected relevant to their individual requirements. The benefits to be achieved by enabling students to interact with personalised eLearning resources will be discussed. The objectives of this chapter are to provide the reader with a clear understanding of the concept of personalised eLearning resources and how these resources can integrate interactivity to form asynchronous learning. Also, to provide an overview of the issues, controversies and problems associated with the creation of personalised eLearning resources and some of the solutions to be considered to make personalised eLearning resources achievable.

BACKGROUND

Electronic learning (eLearning) has not impacted on education and training quite as much as expected. Educational environments refers to formal teaching environments which provide a broad range of instruction for students and also issue recognised standardised certification of awards at various levels of academic achievement. The potential use of technology in higher educational environments has not yet been fully realised (Donnelly & O'Rourke, 2007). Higher level educational Institutions provide tuition and examinations which lead to high level qualifications for successful students in: Bachelor; Master; or Doctoral degrees.

The reasons for the low adoption rate of eLearning or the use of learning management systems (LMS) are numerous; some reasons are mentioned in this chapter. LMSs are computer applications or systems which have been specifically developed to facilitate the use of technology by lecturers or trainers when instructing students or trainees. Over the years several lecturers have expressed concerns that engagement with eLearning would lead to redundancies and their active participation in the use of a LMS would lead to the demise of the lecturing profession (O'Donnell, 2010). Others were of the opinion that eLearning would weaken the branding of their educational environment (Sonwalkar, 2008). Some lecturers are afraid of putting all their work from over the years onto the world wide Web (www) for fear that it will be stolen by others (O'Donnell, 2008), copyright theft, that is: others who never took the time to create class handouts and learning resources of their own would use the online learning resources created by others as their own. Several observed that the pedagogical benefits to be achieved through the use of technology enhanced learning (TEL) had yet to be proven. TEL refers to the use of technological devices and communication mediums to augment the learning experience. Quite a few simply admitted that they would not have the time required to create eLearning resources and that no designated time table allocation of hours was allowed for the creation of TEL resources. Several lecturers admitted to lacking sufficient computer skills and knowledge of eLearning platforms to enable them to create eLearning activities (O'Donnell, 2010). Others admitted that they were not convinced that their pedagogical philosophies could be achieved through the use of eLearning, educators are ill prepared to make pedagogical connections between technology and knowledge content (Angeli & Valanides, 2009).

Traditional Learning Management Systems (LMS)

A LMS facilitates eLearning by providing a suitable online environment for educators to: store their learning resources; keep their students informed about course requirements; monitor students usage and progress through the learning resources provided; and so forth. eLearning to date has not yet impacted on the learning experience as expected and feared by some academics. Littlejohn (2009) suggested that LMS were predominantly used for e-administration and e-dissemination. E-administration would provide information to students regarding: course timetables; examination dates; continuous assessment due dates; calendar of activities for the academic year; and so forth. E-dissemination would enable lecturers to: offload the cost of printing notes to hand out to students in lectures by making the notes available online in electronic format for students to read on the screen or alternatively, print out if they so desired; or to provide links to other eLearning resources. Sonwalkar (2008) claims that online learning is ineffective; has not delivered on the expected benefits to be achieved through its use; and also adds to the existing work load of educators.

McGinnis, Bustard, Black and Charles (2008) surmised that there was insufficient attention paid by designers of eLearning resources to providing interactive content which was compelling and would meet the expectations of the net generation. The net generation refers to people who have grown up over the last 30 years or so who are more comfortable with the use of technology than the previous generation because of the prolific use of technology in their play, communication with their

peers and life in general. Students who grew up in the net generation are so familiar with interactive games run on gaming consoles, computers and mobile phones, that it is very difficult for an individual lecturer or trainer to create eLearning resources which could compete with students expectations of the personalised interactive eLearning experiences created. Hence, the requirement for institutions such as the National Digital Learning Repository (NDLR), based in Ireland, which provide lecturers with good quality, peer reviewed eLearning resources to engage their students. Lecturers engaging with personalised interactive eLearning could utilise resources deposited with the NDLR to enhance the eLearning experience of their students.

The information and communications technology (ICT) infrastructures of large corporations are generally extensive and complex; therefore there is a need for personalised training for staff in specialised areas. The content of these specialised learning resources should be compiled by experts in the field. Personalised interactive eLearning could be used to establish which eLearning resources are most suited to each staff members learning requirements. Problem based learning could be used if testing of trainees is required to guarantee that the trainee has interacted with the topics provided by the personalised system in sufficient depth.

While lecturing to postgraduate students who were working in the corporate sector and engaging in continuous professional development (CPD) training realisation dawned that they would possibly benefit from having access to personalised learning resources as they were all working in different areas of IT. No personalised interactive eLearning resources were available for use with that group of students but it would have been interesting from a research perspective to see if they would have benefitted from engaging with personalised eLearning resources. That is, each student could have been guided through the personalised interactive eLearning resources based on their prior experience, knowledge level and topics relevant to their area of work. Personalised interactive eLearning would enable students to engage with eLearning resources specifically selected to suit their individual learning requirements to facilitate asynchronous learning. Synchronous learning refers to the learning which takes place through communication with other students or lecturers who are online at the same time; this type of learning is facilitated by use of: videoconferencing and chat facilities.

Web 2.0 technologies would then provide users with a set of tools which enable synchronous eLearning: video conferencing and social networking sites, such as: Facebook; Flickr; You Tube; Bebo; Delicious; and Twitter, to broaden their understanding of the topics learned during engagement with the personalised interactive eLearning resources through discussion and feedback from peers who have studied topics relevant to the same subject area but particularly selected to suit their own personal work environment. Web-mediation refers to the use of the www to facilitate various activities, for example: e-commerce; online banking; engagement with and payment to service providers; dissemination of information; e-mail and Skype communication; webinars; video conferencing; and many more activities. Web-mediated education refers to the use of Web technologies to enrich and enhance the educational experience of students and trainees.

Training environments refers to courses which have been specifically set up to provide trainees with knowledge and understanding in specific areas, for example, mandatory compliance training i.e. manual handling or emergency response training. Web technologies can offer alternative training environments to traditional training environments. Sometimes due to cost and work commitments it is impossible to release workers for training all at the one time, personalised interactive eLearning would facilitate asynchronous eLearning to reduce the impact which training would have on the work environment by reducing disruption. Web technologies would facilitate engagement

with eLearning resources which are created by lecturers and topic experts who are intent on improving the learning experience of students by providing good quality learning resources available online. Okamoto (2003) recommends that the quality and effectiveness of eLearning resources should be evaluated to ensure that pedagogical considerations are met. Conducting regular evaluations of learning outcomes are very important to ensure that pedagogical standards are upheld in all teaching methodologies applied to provide education and training.

With the increased use of technological eLearning resources comes the need to ensure that pedagogical considerations are heeded when designing these resources. Okamoto (2004) suggests that new pedagogies are needed which suit the use of new technologies in the educational environment.

Lecturers or trainers may have to move from 'host on the post' standing on the lecturing platform or at the top of a training room to 'guide on the side' facilitated by e-mail, webinars, discussion boards, skype or chat facilities, all facilitated through the use of technology.

Personalised Interactive eLearning Resources

Personalised interactive eLearning resources are specifically created or selected to suit the learning requirements of individual students or trainees. Alternatively, they could be created or selected to suit the learning requirements of specific cohorts of students. For example, educators who have experience of teaching both undergraduate and postgraduate students may have perceived a differentiation between both cohorts of students in the students' level of awareness of their own learning capacity and requirements. Such educators may find it useful to tailor the learning resources at their disposal to suit the learning needs of students at different levels of achievement as well as focusing on the individual learning requirements of each individual student.

Sonwalkar (2008) suggests tailoring/adapting eLearning resources to suit individual students interests and needs would increase the effectiveness of the LMS used in educational environments. Settouti, Prié, Marty and Mille (2009) also recommend that there is a need for personalisation in eLearning applications. Although some agree that personalised eLearning would enhance the learning experience, personalised eLearning is not easily achievable and the benefits through adoption have not yet been proven.

Personalisation of learning resources would be achieved by using an adaptive application which would match suitable learning resources with individual students learning requirements. Adaptive eLearning resources are designed to adapt to suit individual learners learning requirements based on the criteria set for determining their learning needs. Sonwalkar (2008) suggests that an eLearning adaptive application should have the ability to generate suitable learning resources based on student information which has been inputted to the LMS or collected by the LMS. The problem here is how to physically collect this student information and when it has been collected how to use this information to provide the most relevant eLearning resources to each individual learner.

The proposed adaptive application is envisaged to run as an add-in to an existing LMS. The students' engagement with the LMS will be recorded and saved in a user profile which will be stored on the server which supports the LMS. The adaptive application will access the user profile to obtain information on individual students, the adaptation rules in the adaptive application will select appropriate learning resources based on this information. The creation of adaptive applications which enable lecturers or trainers to create educational experiences personalised to individual student needs may help to facilitate the widespread use of adaptive eLearning resources. But, such adaptive systems are expensive and complex to develop.

Student/Trainee User Profiling

Settouti et al. (2009) state that there is a requirement for personalised eLearning based on individual users' interaction with the TEL system. In order to realise personalised eLearning individual user profiles would be required (Brusilovsky, 2001) to identify the eLearning resources which would be most beneficial to each learner. User profiles for adaptive educational systems contain keywords and concepts which represent the user's interests (Brusilovsky & Millan, 2007). Lecturers or trainers would doubtfully have the time to gauge the learning requirement of every student or trainee, hence, the requirement to develop personalised eLearning authoring tools to harvest information on users to populate user profiles to facilitate the allocation of the necessary eLearning resources to students based on their user profiles.

Knauf, Sakurai, Takada and Tsuruta (2010) recommend that the creation of student profiles are necessary to match personalised learning plans with individual learners preferences and talents. Should a lecturer have in excess of a few hundred students during the course of a year the creation of student profiles for all would be a mammoth task, and possibly unachievable due to time pressures and lack of knowledge on how to set up user profiles which incorporate sufficient information to enable the personalised eLearning system generate suitable learning plans for each individual student.

Some insight can be established on user preferences by performing a trace of a learner's use of a computer system (Knauf et al., 2010). Settouti et al. (2009) also recommend users interactions with the computer application should be traced to enable the creation of individual student profiles for the purpose of enabling adaptation. Such traces would need to be particularly designed to ensure that the resulting data collected on user preferences are relevant to the learning outcomes they are expected to achieve and that these user preferences give a good indication of the eLearning resources which are most appropriate for each learner.

Electronic pre tests and post tests provide lecturers with a very effective and efficient way of gauging learners' knowledge levels of any specific topic. The provision of pre tests enables students to engage with a bank of online questions, the outcome of which will determine their level of competence in a specific topic.

Gauging this level of competence prior to the students' engagement with the eLearning resources will enable the lecturer to set the personalised software to deliver suitable training material to each student based on their individual learning requirements. The use of technology in higher education facilitates the creation of a variety of different teaching resources. In adaptive TEL, the learning process experienced by each individual student is tailored to suit their needs as a direct response to their previous actions in the system (Burgos et al., 2007). The educator or trainer using the adaptive/personalised eLearning tools must ensure that the pre-recorded actions in the system provide sufficient user information to enable the adaptive system to select the relevant learning resources to suit the learning needs of each student and that they are satisfied that the pedagogical requirements of the course are realised by students engaging with the personalised system.

The concept of adaptation in technology enhanced education has been explored for nearly three decades (Burgos et al., 2006). Despite all the time and money spent on the exploration of adaptation in TEL over the past 30 years creating personalised eLearning resources is as yet not easily realisable for general use. Brusilovsky (2004) surmises that a significant amount of research and co-operation will be required in order to realise the objective of bringing adaptive hypermedia into the common practice of eLearning. Seven years on and still adaptive hypermedia has not been incorporated into the common practice of eLearning. Hauger and Köck (2007) came to the conclusion that the vast amount of effort involved in creating and implementing adaptive courses cannot be justified. This would depend on the level of success of personalisation achieved.

Foss and Cristea (2009) suggest that improved functionality and usability of these tools is necessary to promote user acceptance. From the literature review undertaken on adaptive eLearning, it would appear at times that innovators in personalised eLearning authoring tools have possibly tried to incorporate too complex a toolset into one authoring tool without sufficient heed to the pedagogical benefits and how they could be achieved by educators using these tools.

Benefits of Creating Personalised Interactive eLearning Resources

Personalising eLearning resources empowers the learner (McGinnis et al., 2008) and encourages collaboration through the sharing of knowledge (Bellows & Jankowski, 2009). The whole concept of personalising eLearning resources would empower the learner to overcome obstacles to their success by providing personalised hints and tips along the way as the learner fails any online assessments or tests. Such personalised tuition could help by retaining students focus on their weak areas of the course and assist with student attrition. By tailoring eLearning resources to suit individual students needs information overload will be reduced (Arapi, Moumoutzis, Mylonakis & Christodoulakis, 2007). Information overload could be avoided for the students as the students would only gain access to the eLearning resources which have been selectively tailored to their individual needs. Lecturers could provide personalised interactive eLearning resources to suit each student's ability and learning requirements, hence, making the students learning experience much more personal. Personalisation of eLearning resources could facilitate the re-use of good quality eLearning resources as the same eLearning resources could be presented to many students in different formats and at various levels. Different formats and levels of concepts could be presented to undergraduate and postgraduate students based on their knowledge and learning requirements.

ELearning provides students with a flexible opportunity to learn when and where they choose (McGinnis et al., 2008). The ubiquitous nature of eLearning resources facilitates student interaction with good quality learning resources despite time and location. Muñoz-Merino, Kloos, Muñoz-Organero, Wolpers and Friedrich. (2010) suggest that personalised tests can be used by educators to assist students learning by targeting individual learners weaknesses in any specific topic, once learners individual weak points are identified, built in hints can guide them to achieving the correct learning outcomes.

Existing ePedagogical Strategies

Pedagogy is the art and skill of teaching or knowledge transfer. Kumar (2007) claims that pedagogy is concerned with the creation of effective context specific learning resources. Each lecturer would be responsible for ensuring that the pedagogical requirements of students are met in relation to every learner on every course. The pedagogical approach deemed to suit a particular course of study may not be relevant to another course of study; context would have to be considered when designing the personalised learning experiences of students. Postgraduate students may require a different pedagogical approach to undergraduate students. Okamoto (2004) recommends that new pedagogical strategies are required which have been created specifically to ensure that the quality of teaching online is as good as if not better than traditional teaching methods.

Computer Supported Collaborative Learning (CSCL)

The creation of personalised interactive eLearning resources would provide lecturers with an alternative asynchronous teaching methodology to enhance the learning experience of students.

Initially, students would be given the opportunity to engage with their personalised interactive eLearning resources. Subsequently, the students would be invited to join a discussion board, chat facility or video conference to discuss or question the concepts involved and to generally share opinions with peers and lecturers. Alternatively, students could be encouraged to engage with role playing through synchronous learning as this works well in TEL environments (Bender, 2005). Similar to games players liking for sharing gaming experiences with peers, learners also like to share and discuss learning experiences with their peers (McGinnis et al., 2008) and computer mediated interaction can improve learning (Alvino et al., 2009). The reason for encouraging students to engage with synchronous computer supported collaborative learning (CSCL) is to improve their understanding and hence their retention of knowledge learning as a result of engaging with the asynchronous personalised interactive eLearning resources.

ISSUES, CONTROVERSIES, AND PROBLEMS ASSOCIATED WITH THE CREATION OF PERSONALISED INTERACTIVE ELEARNING RESOURCES

Before one commences designing personalised interactive eLearning resources, one must consider what criteria the personalisation is to be based on: A student's level of achievement in this subject area to date; the prior experience of students; or the student's learning preferences. To seek to achieve all three criteria when aiming to design initial eLearning resources may be ambitious. To ensure that ePedagogy requirements are met, the creator should firstly have a very firm view of the learning outcomes expected and how best to use the medium of asynchronous personalised eLearning to achieve these objectives.

In order to measure students' level of achievement in a specific concept, the students could be subjected to an online assessment. From the results achieved in this assessment students could be directed to specific eLearning resources which could enhance their understanding of the specific concepts. Subsequent to engaging with the eLearning resources the students could be subjected to another online assessment to gauge if there is any improvement in the marks achieved in the previous assessment as a result of the students' interactivity with the selected personalised eLearning resources. To measure students' prior experience in a specific concept, factors like: level of qualifications achieved to date; former work experience; and projects completed could be weighed up and students presented with relevant personalised eLearning resources based on this information.

To gauge the most suitable personalised interactive eLearning resources to be selected for an individual based on their learning preferences may be the most difficult to quantify and therefore the most difficult to achieve in personalised/adaptive eLearning. Franzoni and Asar (2009) claimed that recent research had shown that students learn in different ways and prefer to learn through the use of different teaching resources. In the instance of matching suitable eLearning resources to students learning preferences, the lecturer would have to be sure that the learning preferences identified through click streaming (or whatever method is selected to capture information on the students learning preferences) are relevant to the students learning preferences for asynchronous or synchronous learning of examinable topics.

Knauf et al. (2010) suggest that learning plans which proved successful with previous students should be considered along with individual learner profiles, preferences and talents when designing learning content. Lecturers should build their personalised eLearning approach based on past successes, incorporating new approaches gradually to evaluate which approaches prove the most effective in improving the students learning experiences. Lecturers would be aware of the need to captivate their audience and hold their attention. Should any particular pedagogic approach fail, some lecturers will take this on board and move on to try other approaches to achieving personalised eLearning to evaluate with their students.

Chalfoun and Frasson (2011) suggest a smart 'learning system interface' for eLearning or intelligent tutoring systems should be able to match eLearning resources with students emotional and cognitive states. To match eLearning resources to individual student's emotional and cognitive states would be an ambitious project to undertake and could be a very interesting area for future research. Kumar (2007) emphasise the need to ensure that the quality of learning is maintained in eLearning environments. The quality of learning should also be maintained in personalised interactive eLearning environments.

Link, Schuster, Hoyer and Abeck (2008) observed that users have increased expectations for improvement in graphical user interfaces, human-computer interaction (HCI) and the reduction of the time required for software development in general. Potential users of asynchronous eLearning resources would expect the 'learning system interface' of these resources to be as user friendly as possible. Padda, Mudur, Seffah and Joshi (2008) express the important contribution that visual comprehension has on human cognition of information. When developing personalised eLearning resources authors should consider the visualisation of the presented information and how this may impact on learners understanding and grasp of concepts. McGinnis et al. (2008) recommend employing some of the design strategies used in computer games to encourage students to interact with eLearning resources. Some of the design strategies used in games and computer applications have been so effective that some people are now addicted to using computers for various reasons which can have an adverse impact on their daily lives and relationships. To identify the design strategies which have proved most successful in maintaining users interest while interacting with eLearning applications would be an interesting topic for future research.

Should students have the opportunity to select the eLearning resources which they believe suit their learning needs? It is up to the individual lecturer to enable students to select their own eLearning resources or to only allow students access to the eLearning resources which the lecturers have directed the system to select to suit each individual students learning requirements based on the user information contained in the student user profile. Different approaches may be taken for undergraduate and postgraduate students.

Issues

Students are increasingly expecting LMS to cater for their personal learning requirements by providing tailored learning resources (Shank, 2008, p. 247). Providing tailored learning resources for each individual student is not an easy task to accomplish. Time, resources, training and commitment on behalf of the lecturers are required to create tailored learning resources. In addition, pedagogical requirements must be met to ensure that tailored/personalised learning resources provide the students with adequate material to fulfil the course requirements and adequately cover the syllabi.

The ability to create relevant user profiles is paramount to the realisation of personalisation (Paireekreng & Wong, 2010). The creation of effective user profiles is no easy task even to designers who are proficient in the area of personalisation; this task may be unachievable to other lecturers and trainers. Capuano (2009) suggests that personalised eLearning resources should be dynamically created to suit individual learners needs based on their previously recorded behaviour. How many lecturers would be sufficiently qualified to record students' behaviour? This issue would need to be addressed before

personalised eLearning resources could be dynamically created. Liang, Zhao and Zeng (2007) propose a solution for determining user's interest in topics in eLearning systems by analysing their behaviour when reading, the results of which could be included in the user profile for personalised eLearning systems. To analyse user's interest in topics by their online reading habits would not be easily achieved. Some benchmarking process would need to be developed to establish a way of recording and analysing user behaviour to provide data to populate user profiles before personalised interactive eLearning resources are realisable.

One significant issue to be addressed in user profiling is to identify the most appropriate solution to harvesting data on abilities and preferences. In the creation of student user profiles for the purpose of providing personalised interactive eLearning resources for students use, the students should be made aware of the monitoring methods which will be applied to harvest data to populate the user profiles. In addition, agreement with the individual students should be obtained prior to the harvesting of data and the students interaction with the personalised eLearning resources (McGinnis et al., 2008). In recent years significant cases have been reported regarding breaches of data protection and the privacy of users. Some prior knowledge of users is necessary to populate user profiles (Paireekreng & Wong, 2010). Another issue to be addressed is how to effectively gather information on users prior knowledge, what metrics should be used to quantify and analyse this data and how to feed this data into the user profiles. Another important consideration is how to collect data on student ability and preferences to store in a personalised learning environment. One more significant issue to consider is the safe storage of the personal user information gathered in the user profiles, who will have access to this information, and who exactly will be responsible for ensuring the access controls to this information are enforced.

Concerns

Some lecturers claim that there is no designated time table allocation for the creation of TEL resources (O'Donnell, 2008) not to mention personalised eLearning resources which would take more time, computer skills, and commitment to create as previously mentioned. There is also the concern regarding copyright; some lecturers are afraid of putting all their work from over the years onto the www for fear it will be stolen by others. Harvesting data on students and data protection considerations would have to be taken into consideration; what types of data are educators allowed to harvest regarding their students and subsequently concerns with respect to the correct and secure storage of this collected data. In addition, lecturers may have concerns regarding whether or not the students will receive the most appropriate combination of learning resources to enhance their personal learning experience. Also, how can anyone be sure that the system developed to deliver a personalised interactive eLearning experience for students will work effectively? There is always the possibility that personalised eLearning resources may impact negatively on the students learning experience and some students may feel that they were not given the opportunity to engage with all the interactive learning resources available to the class group and failure could ensue if the course material was not adequately presented to all participants.

Controversies

Some academics at top research universities expressed concerns that the use of TEL may negatively impact on the quality of the students' university experience (McKay & Merrill, 2003). From experience some students have complained that all lecturers are not using LMS to provide eLearning resources equally. Some lecturers use LMS profusely while others do not use them at all. These concerns should be addressed by university management respectively.

Obstacles

There are several obstacles to the creation of personalised interactive eLearning resources which must be overcome before the use of personalised interactive eLearning resources will be achievable by non-technical authors. The cost of production is a major obstacle. Even if the LMS and the add-in application for achieving personalised learning resources are freely available open source software; there would still be a requirement to engage the services of a service provider to manage the integration of the LMS and the add-in application if sufficient technical expertise was not available in-house. The overall cost of running high-level LMS tools would be dependent on: the number of authors; number of students engaging with these personalised learning resources; server requirements; type and level of services to be provided; training costs; and whatever other services are required.

The time commitment required to develop personalised interactive eLearning resources would be another impeding factor (Chiu & Yu, 2002). The complexity involved in the creation of personalised interactive eLearning resources would be sufficient to turn off even the most enthusiastic lecturer. The technical support which would be required in setting up personalised interactive eLearning resources would need to be one to one for technically challenged lecturers. Sonwalkar (2008) argues that the struggle to create a pedagogically sound adaptive eLearning application has gone on for some time now, and suggests that even if such an application is realised the resulting impact on learning may be minimal.

Problems

Hauger and Köck (2007) suggest that providing the same user profile for all learners is a problem of most LMS implentations? This may well be a problem relating to most LMS sites, but the provision of personalised eLearning systems and the harvesting of the user data which is necessary to

197

populate the user profiles required to enable these systems to function correctly, could pose an even bigger problem.

Sonwalkar (2008) expressed concern that there are no pedagogical strategies available for educators to follow to ensure that their efforts to provide worthwhile eLearning resources will be realised and also that such learning resources will be effective in enhancing the learning experience of students. There is no incentive for lecturers to engage with the creation of personalised eLearning systems at present. When, and if personalised eLearning systems have shown that significant benefits can be achieved by developing these systems, then and only then will some of the general populace of lectures consider using personalised eLearning systems?

Law et al. (2010) mention the fact that some developers of software applications do not abide by user-centred design guidelines and end up developing products that users are unable to understand or use. This point should be heeded by anyone considering designing an authoring tool to facilitate the creation of personalised interactive eLearning resources. The application should be frequently evaluated during the development stages to ensure that potential users understand; the functionality of the authoring tool; how to effectively use the authoring tool; and the eLearning resources which can be created by using the authoring tool. The question of ePedagogy should also be a major consideration in the development of these systems.

Settouti et al. (2009) claim that hard work is required to make sense of the data collected by traces on individual students before any attempt can be made to select particular eLearning resources which would meet any students personal learning requirements. All the hard work required on the behalf of lectures in collecting user data and creating personalised eLearning resources would also be viewed as a problem to lecturers who even now feel over stretched in their duties.

SOLUTIONS AND RECOMMENDATIONS

Personalised eLearning for all will only be achieved when sufficient numbers of educators get involved in the process of evaluating appropriate authoring tools to facilitate the creation of personalised learning experiences. In addition, the sharing and reuse of personalised learning resources would be paramount to the success of this aim due to the high costs and extensive time commitment involved in the creation of these learning resources. As with eLearning, through trial and error, educators will realise what approaches to achieving personalised eLearning experiences work, the approaches which need more refinement to work, or which approaches do not work at all, and for what reasons. A substantial amount of the findings from research into the realisation of personalised learning resources are presented at specialised computer science conferences and specialised publications. The purpose of this chapter is to bring the concept of the personalisation of learning resources to the attention of a broader audience of educators.

Følstad and Knutsen (2010) recommend that the early involvement of users in the design of HCI is one of the key factors leading to the successful development of software solutions. Therefore, lecturers' and trainers' views on the use of personalised eLearning resources in their education/training approach should be collected and analysed. In addition, the views of potential users should also be analysed to identify the front end learning system's interface requirements of authoring tools which are developed to facilitate the creation of personalised eLearning resources by non-technical authors. Such systems could then be designed to suit the HCI requirements recommended by potential users.

Potential users could also suggest ways in which personalised eLearning resources could be utilised to ensure that they are used to achieve the best educational benefits from this teaching method.

Evaluations

The outcome of evaluations of personalised solutions should be considered with a view to implementing changes to existing systems to enhance and encourage engagement with the creation of personalised interactive eLearning resources. Educators who are interested in the provision of personalised eLearning will have to consider this teaching method worthwhile in order to achieve realisation of this teaching method in the classroom. Parrish (2009) claims that the learning experience will only reach its full potential when learners consider it worthwhile and thought provoking. A sufficient number of educators would have to be convinced of the benefits to be realised from using personalised eLearning resources before personalised eLearning will be generally accepted and utilised. Additionally, lecturers/trainers should also be involved in the design of personalised eLearning systems to ensure the ambitious aspirations of computer programmers are kept in check and that the solutions created perform as expected by potential users: lecturers; trainers; students; and trainees. Through engagement in an iterative process of evaluations of personalised eLearning resources, the recommendations made by potential users will be fed back into the loop to instantiate improvements in future development and designs and bring the possibility of providing personalised eLearning for all closer to realisation.

User Profiles

Settouti et al. (2009) recommend that mechanisms are required to assist users in determining which traces to apply and how; when trying to understand individual user learning preferences and requirements.

A tracking cookie could be used to trace and capture a user's interaction with the Web or an application; the generated data would then be stored in a user profile. One tracking method which can be applied to indicate user preferences is click streaming. Click streaming refers to the recording of users' navigational clicks when using an application or the Web. Each click the user makes is recorded and subsequently analysed to ascertain the user preferences. Clarification is needed on what traces can be applied to student behaviour to avoid infringing on their privacy rights. Guidance would be required on how to interpret information collected on students learning preferences and how best to apply this to assigning personalised interactive eLearning resources to each individual student. Lectures would require institutional policies regarding secure storage of personal data collected on students.

FUTURE RESEARCH DIRECTIONS

The objective of this research is to encourage more educators outside of the discipline of Computer Science to consider the possibilities which personalised eLearning could bring to their students learning experience. In addition, to encourage educators to consider the functionality which they would require in an authoring tool which would enable the creation of personalised learning resources. This research is ongoing; the ideal toolset which will enable non-technical authors to create personalised learning resources has not yet been identified. Chalfoun and Frasson (2011) suggest a smart learning system's interface or intelligent tutoring system should be able to match eLearning resources with students emotional and cognitive states. To match eLearning resources to individual students emotional and cognitive states would be a very interesting area for future research as matching eLearning resources to emotional and cognitive states lies outside the scope of this chapter.

McGinnis et al. (2008) recommend employing some of the design strategies used in computer games to encourage students to engage with eLearning resources. To identify the design strategies which have proved most successful in maintaining users interest when interacting with systems would be an interesting topic for future research. In addition to test how these designs could be applied to encourage lecturers and trainers to interact with authoring tools for creating personalised interactive eLearning resources. An evaluation of the design strategies employed in the development of authoring tools for the creation of personalised eLearning resources would be beneficial to the identification of the ideal toolset functionality expected in such a tool.

Personalised eLearning resources for all learners will never be achievable if the concept is not considered in great detail by many educators. Suitable solutions will only be identified as a result of the analysis of data collected on what functionality non-technical users expect to see in such authoring tools.

CONCLUSION

This chapter reviews the use of personalised eLearning. The objective in creating personalised interactive eLearning resources is an attempt at moving away from learning content which is retrieved to learning content which can be experienced. The provision of learning activities which could be experienced by the learner through interaction with Web-mediated personalised interactive learning resources may improve understanding and possibly retention and therefore empower the learner, but the pedagogical merits of personalised eLearning have yet to be proven. It is envisioned that personalised interactive eLearning resources would be integrated into existing LMS for ease of use by lecturers and trainers. The issues, concerns and obstacles to the creation of personalised interactive eLearning resources were discussed and in conclusion personalised eLearning resources are not easily achieved. The privacy rights of students and trainees would have to be considered and resolved before traces can

be put on their online activities to build up appropriate personal information to populate their user profiles. Web-mediated education has not impacted on the learning experience as much as expected, the realisation of personalised interactive eLearning may impact positively on the learning experience of students and trainees, but this has yet to be proven. The concepts of adaptive eLearning and personalisation of eLearning resources has been explored for more than 30 years, yet these Web-mediated educational resources are still not available for use by mainstream educators and trainers. Personalised eLearning resources are promising but there are as yet a vast number of issues, controversies and problems to be resolved before widespread application can be realised.

ACKNOWLEDGMENT

This research is in part funded by Trinity College Dublin and Dublin Institute of Technology. In addition, this research is in part based on works supported by Science Foundation Ireland (Grant Number 07/CE/I1142) as part of the Centre for Next Generation Localisation (www.cngl.ie).

REFERENCES

Alvino, S., Asensio-Perez, J. I., Dimitriadis, Y., & Hernandez-Leo, D. (2009). Supporting the reuse of effective CSCL learning designs through social structure representations. *Distance Education, 30*(2), 239–258. doi:10.1080/01587910903023215

Angeli, C., & Valanides, N. (2009). Epistemological and methodological issues for the conceptualization, development, and assessment of ECT-TPCK: Advances in technological pedagogical content knowledge (TPCK). *Computers & Education, 52*, 154–168. doi:10.1016/j.compedu.2008.07.006

Arapi, P., Moumoutzis, N., Mylonakis, M., & Christodoulakis, S. (2007). *A pedagogy-driven personalization framework to support adaptive learning experiences.* Paper presented at the IEEE International Conference on Advanced Learning Technologies, ICALT 2007., Niigata, Japan.

Bellows, S., & Jankowski, J. (2009). Live and learn. *Contract (New York, N.Y.), 50*(2), 32–33.

Bender, T. (2005). *Role playing in online education: A teaching tool to enhance student engagement and sustained learning.* Retrieved from http://www.innovateonline.info/index.php?view=article&id=57

Brusilovsky, P. (2001). Adaptive hypermedia. *User Modeling and User-Adapted Interaction, 11,* 87–110. doi:10.1023/A:1011143116306

Brusilovsky, P. (2004). *Knowledge tree: A distributed architecture for adaptive e-learning.* Paper presented at the International World Wide Web Conference - Proceedings of the 13th international www conference - Session: Adaptive e-learning systems, New York.

Brusilovsky, P., & Millan, E. (2007). User models for adaptive hypermedia and adaptive educational systems. In Brusilovsky, P., Kobsa, A., & Nejdl, W. (Eds.), *The adaptive Web.* Berlin, Germany: Springer. doi:10.1007/978-3-540-72079-9_1

Burgos, D., Tattersall, C., & Koper, R. (2006). *Representing adaptive eLearning strategies in IMS learning design.* Paper presented at the Workshop Learning Networks for Lifelong Competence Development, Sofia, Bulgaria.

Burgos, D., Tattersall, C., & Koper, R. (2007). How to represent adaptation in e-learning with IMS learning design. *Interactive Learning Environments, 15*(2), 161–170. doi:10.1080/10494820701343736

Capauno, N., Miranda, S., & Ritrovato, P. (2009). *Creation and delivery of complex learning experiences: the ELeGI approach.* Paper presented at the Internation Conference on Complex, Intelligent and Software Intensive Systems, Japan.

Chalfoun, P., & Frasson, C. (2011). Subliminal cues while teaching: HCI techniques for enhanced learning. *Advances in Human-Computer Interaction.* doi:10.1155/2011/968753

Chiu, B., & Yu, Y. (2002). Promoting the use of information technology in education via lightweight authoring tools. *Proceedings of the International Conference on Computers in Education* (ICCE '02), Auckland, New Zealand.

Donnelly, R., & O'Rourke, K. (2007). What now? Evaluating e-learning CPD practice in Irish third-level education. *Journal of Further and Higher Education, 31*(1), 31–40. doi:10.1080/03098770601167864

Følstad, A., & Knutsen, J. (2010). Online user feedback in early phases of the design process: Lessons learnt from four design cases. *Advances in Human-Computer Interaction, 9.* Retrieved from doi:10.1155/2010/956918

Foss, J., & Cristea, A. (2009). *Adaptive hypermedia content authoring using MOT3.0.* Paper presented at the 7th International Workshop on Authoring of Adaptive and Adaptable Hypermedia, Nice, France.

Franzoni, A., & Asar, S. (2009). Student learning styles adaptation method based on teaching strategies and electronic media. *Journal of Educational Technology & Society, 12*(4), 15–29.

Hauger, D., & Köck, M. (2007). *State of the art of adaptivity in e-learning platforms.* Paper presented at the 15th Workshop on Adaptivity and User Modeling in Interactive Systems, Halle/Saale, Germany.

Knauf, R., Sakurai, Y., Takada, K., & Tsuruta, S. (2010). *Personalised learning processes by data mining*. Paper presented at the 10th IEEE International Conference on Advanced Learning Technologies (ICALT 2010), Sousse, Tunisia.

Kumar, V. (2007, July 18-20). *Innovations in e-pedagogy*. Paper presented at the Seventh IEEE International Conference on Advanced Learning Technologies (ICALT 2007), Niigata, Japan.

Law, C., Jaeger, P., & McKay, E. (2010). User-centred design in universal design resources? *Universal Access in the Information Society, 9*(4), 327–335. doi:10.1007/s10209-009-0182-z

Liang, Y., Zhao, Z., & Zeng, Q. (2007). *Mining user's interest from reading behavior in e-learning system*. Paper presented at the Eighth ACIS International Conference on Software Engineering, Artificial Intelligence, Networking, and Parallel/Distributed Computing, Qingdao, China.

Link, S., Schuster, T., Hoyer, P., & Abeck, S. (2008). *Focusing graphical user interfaces in model-driven software development*. Paper presented at the First International Conference on Advances in Computer-Human Interaction, Sainte Luce, Martinique.

Littlejohn, A. (2009). Key issues in the design and delivery of technology-enhanced learning. In Lockyer, L., Bennett, S., Agostinho, S., & Harper, B. (Eds.), *Handbook of research on learning design and learning objects: Issues, applications, and technologies* (pp. 1–1018). Hershey, PA: IGI Global.

McGinnis, T., Bustard, D., Black, M., & Charles, D. (2008). *Enhancing e-learning engagement using design patterns from computer games*. Paper presented at the First International Conference on Advances in Computer-Human Interaction, Sainte Luce, Martinique.

McKay, E., & Merrill, M. D. (2003). Cognitive skill and web-based educational systems. Paper presented at the *eLearning Conference on Design and Development: Instructional Design - Applying first principles of instruction*. Informit Library: Australasian Publications. Retrieved from http://www.informit.com.au/library/

Muñoz-Merino, P., Kloos, C., Muñoz-Organero, M., Wolpers, M., & Friedrich, M. (2010). *An approach for the personalization of exercises based on contextualized attention metadata and semantic Web technologies*. Paper presented at the 10th IEEE International Conference on Advanced Learning Technologies, Athens, Greece.

NDLR (National Digital Learning Repository). (n.d.). Retrieved from http://www.ndlr.ie/

O'Donnell, E. (2008). *Can e-learning be used to further improve the learning experience to better prepare students for work in industry*. Masters in Information Systems for Managers, Dublin City University, Dublin. Retrieved from http://arrow.dit.ie/buschmanoth/1

O'Donnell, E. (2010). *E-learning can improve learning: Preparing students for work*. Saarbrücken, Germany: Lambert Academic Publishing AG & Co. KG.

Okamoto, T. (2003). *E-collaborative learning technologies and e-pedagogy*. Paper presented at the The 3rd IEEE International Conference on Advanced Learning Technologies (ICALT '03), Athens, Greece.

Okamoto, T. (2004, August 30 - September 1). *Collaborative technology and new e-pedagogy*. Paper presented at the IEEE International Conference on Advanced Learning Technologies (ICALT '04), Joensuu, Finland.

Padda, H., Mudur, S., Seffah, A., & Joshi, Y. (2008). *Comprehension of visualization systems - Towards quantitative assessment.* Paper presented at the First International Conference on Advances in Computer-Human Interaction, Sainte Luce, Martinique.

Paireekreng, W., & Wong, K. W. (2010). *Mobile content personalisation using intelligent user profile approach.* Paper presented at the Third International Conference on Knowledge Discovery and Data Mining.

Parrish, P. E. (2009). Aesthetic principles for instructional design. *Educational Technology Research and Development, 57,* 511–528. doi:10.1007/s11423-007-9060-7

Settouti, L., Prié, Y., Marty, J., & Mille, A. (2009, July 15-17). *A trace-based system for technology-enhanced learning systems personalisation.* Paper presented at the Ninth IEEE International Conference on Advanced Learning Technologies, Riga.

Shank, P. (2008). Web 2.0 and beyond: The changing needs of learners, new tools, and ways to learn. In Carliner, S., & Shank, P. (Eds.), *The e-learning handbook: Past promises, present challenges. Pfeiffer - Essential resources for training and HR professionals* (pp. 241–278). San Francisco, CA: Pfeiffer.

Sonwalkar, N. (2008). Adaptive individualization: The next generation of online education. *Horizon, 16*(1), 44–47. doi:10.1108/10748120810853345

ADDITIONAL READING

Aroyo, L., De Bra, P., Houben, G., & Vdovjak, R. (2004). Embedding information retrieval in adaptive hypermedia: IR meets AHA! *New Review of Hypermedia and Multimedia, 10*(1), 53–76. doi: 10.1080/13614560410001728146

Bajraktarevic, N., Hall, W., & Fullick, P. (2003, May 20). *Incorporating learning styles in hypermedia environments: Empirical evaluation.* Paper presented at the Workshop on Adaptive Hypermedia and Adaptive Web-Based Systems, Budapest, Hungary.

Bennet, A., & Bennet, D. (2008). e-learning as energetic learning. *The Journal of Information and Knowledge Management Systems, 38*(2), 206–220.

Bos, N., & Shami, N. (2006). Adapting a face-to-face role-playing simulation for online play. [Article]. *Educational Technology Research and Development, 54*(5), 493–521. doi:10.1007/s11423-006-0130-z

Bovey, N. S., & Dunand, N. (2006). *Seamless production of interoperable e-learning units: Stakes and pitfalls.* Paper presented at the Workshop Learning Networks for Lifelong Competence Development.

Brusilovksy, P., Karagiannidis, C., & Sampson, D. (2004). Layered evaluation of adaptive learning systems. *International Journal of Continuing Engineering Education and Lifelong Learning, 14*(4/5), 402–421. doi:10.1504/IJCEELL.2004.005729

Brusilovsky, P., & Nijhawan, H. (2002). *A framework for adaptive e-learning based on distributed re-usable learning activities.* Paper presented at the AACE Proceedings of World Conference on e-Learning, E-Learn 2002, Montreal, Canada.

Brusilovsky, P., Sosnovsky, S., Lee, D., Yudelson, M., Zadorozhny, V., & Zhou, X. (2008, June 30 – July 2). *An open integrated exploratorium for database courses.* Paper presented at the ITiCSE '08, Madrid Spain.

Clapper, T. C. (2010). Role play and simulation. *Education Digest, 75*(8), 39–43.

Dagger, D., Wade, V., & Conlan, O. (2004). Developing active learning experiences for adaptive personalised e-learning. In Nejdl, W., & De Bra, P. (Eds.), *AH 2004* (*Vol. 3137*). Lecture Notes in Computer Science Berlin, Germany: Springer-Verlag.

De Bra, P., Aroyo, L., & Cristea, A. (2004). Adaptive Web-based educational hypermedia. In Levene, M., & Poulovassilis, A. (Eds.), *Web dynamics, adaptive to change in content, size, topology and use* (pp. 387–410). Springer.

Donovan, M., & Bransford, J. (Eds.). (2005). *How students learn: History, mathematics, and science in the classroom*. Washington, DC: National Academic Press.

Eirinaki, M., & Vazirgiannis, M. (2003). Web mining for Web personalization. *ACM Transactions on Internet Technology*, *8*(1), 1–27. doi:10.1145/643477.643478

Exeter, D., Ameratunga, S., Ratima, M., Morton, S., Dickson, M., & Hsu, D. (2010). Student engagement in very large classes: The teachers' perspective. *Studies in Higher Education*, *35*(7), 761–775. doi:10.1080/03075070903545058

Felder, R. M., & Soloman, B. A. (2009). *Learning styles and strategies*. Retrieved from http://www4.ncsu.edu/unity/lockers/users/f/felder/public/ILSdir/styles.htm

Frick, T. W., Chadha, R., Watson, C., Wang, Y., & Green, P. (2009). College student perceptions of teaching and learning quality. *Educational Technology Research and Development*, *57*, 705–720. doi:10.1007/s11423-007-9079-9

Gena, C., & Weibelzahl, S. (2007). Usability engineering for the adaptive Web. In Brusilovsky, P., Kobsa, A., & Nejdl, W. (Eds.), *The adaptive web* (pp. 720–762). Berlin, Germany: Springer-Verlag. doi:10.1007/978-3-540-72079-9_24

Granic, A., Mifsud, C., & Cukusic, M. (2009). Design, implementation and validation of a Europe-wide pedagogical framework for e-learning. *Computers & Education*, *53*, 1052–1081. doi:10.1016/j.compedu.2009.05.018

Griffiths, D., Beauvoir, P., Liber, O., & Barrett-Baxendale, M. (2009). From reload to recourse: Learning from IMS learning design implementations. *Distance Education*, *30*(2), 201–222. doi:10.1080/01587910903023199

Griffiths, D., & Blat, J. (2005). The role of teachers in editing and authoring units of learning using IMS Learning Design. *Advanced Technology for Learning*, *2*(4), 1–9.

Hannafin, M., Hannafin, K., & Gabbitas, B. (2009). Re-examining cognition during student-centered, web-based learning. *Educational Technology Research and Development*, *57*, 767–785. doi:10.1007/s11423-009-9117-x

Harrigan, M., Kravcik, M., Steiner, C., & Wade, V. (2009). *What do academic users really want from an adaptive learning system?* Paper presented at the 17th International Conference on User Modeling, Adaptation, and Personalization; formerly UM and AH.

Harrigan, M., & Wade, V. (2009, June 29 - July 1). *Towards a conceptual and service-based adaptation model*. Paper presented at the International Workshop on Dynamic and Adaptive Hypertext: Generic Frameworks, Approaches and Techniques. DAH '09., Torino, Italy.

Hendrix, M., De Bra, P., Pechenizkiy, M., Smits, D., & Cristea, A. (2008). *Deffining adaptation in a generic multi layer model: CAM: The GRAPPLE conceptual adaptation model*. Paper presented at the 3rd European Conference on Technology-Enhanced Learning EC-TEL., Maastricht, The Netherlands.

Herder, E., Koesling, A., Olmedilla, D., Hummel, H., & Schoonenboom, J. (2006). *European lifelong competence development: Requirements and technologies for its realisation.* Paper presented at the Workshop Learning Networks for Lifelong Competence Development.

Herington, C., & Weaven, S. (2008). Action research and reflection on student approaches to learning in large first year university classes. *Australian Educational Researcher, 35*(3), 111–134. doi:10.1007/BF03246292

Hockemeyer, C., & Albert, D. (2003). Adaptive e-learning and the learning grid. In S. S. M. G. E. P. Ritrovato (Ed.), *1st LEGE-WG International Workshop on Educational Models for GRID Based Services.* Lausanne, Switzerland: British Computer Society (electronic publication, 3 pages).

Holohan, E., Melia, M., McMullen, D., & Pahl, C. (2006). *The generation of e-learning exercise problems from subject ontologies.* Paper presented at the Sixth International Conference on Advanced Learning Technologies (ICALT'06), Kerkrade, The Netherlands.

Jelfs, A., & Kelly, P. (2007). Evaluating electronic resources: Personal development planning resources at the Open University, a case study. *Assessment & Evaluation in Higher Education, 32*(5), 515–526. doi:10.1080/02602930601116755

Karampiperis, P., Lin, T., & Sampson, D., & Kinshuk. (2006). Adaptive cognitive-based selection of learning objects. *Innovations in Education and Teaching International, 43*(2), 121–135. doi:10.1080/14703290600650392

Karetsos, S., & Haralambopoulos, D. (2009). *An ontology to support authoring tools for sustainable energy education.* Paper presented at the International Conference on Complex, Intelligent and Software Intensive Systems, Fukuoka Institute of Technology (FIT), Japan.

Katuk, N., Sarrafzadeh, A., & Dadgostar, F. (2009). *Effective ways of encouraging teachers to design and use ITS: Feature analysis of Intelligent Tutoring Systems authoring tools.* Paper presented at the Proceedings of the 6th international conference on Innovations in information technology, AI-Ain, United Arab Emirates.

Knutov, E., De Bra, P., & Pechenizkiy, M. (2009). AH 12 years later: A comprehensive survey of adaptive hypermedia methods and techniques. *New Review of Hypermedia and Multimedia, 15*(1), 5–38. doi:10.1080/13614560902801608

Marchiori, E., Torrente, J., Blanco, A., Martínez-Ortiz, I., & Fernández-Manjón, B. (2010). *Extending a game authoring tool for ubiquitous education.* Paper presented at the Ubi-media Computing (U-Media), 2010 3rd IEEE International Conference, Jinhua.

Mulryan-Kyne, C. (2010). Teaching large classes at college and university level: Challenges and opportunities. *Teaching in Higher Education, 15*(2), 175–185. doi:10.1080/13562511003620001

Murray, T. (2003). An overview of intelligent tutoring sytems authoring tools: Updated analysis of the state of the art. In Murray, T., Blessing, S., & Ainsworth, S. (Eds.), *Authoring tools for advanced technology learning environments.* Dordrecht, The Netherlands: Kluwer Academic Publishers.

Nikoukaran, J., Hlupic, V., & Paul, R. (1998). *Criteria for simulation software evaluation.* Paper presented at the 1998 Winter Simulation Conference, Washington DC, USA.

Nikoukaran, J., Hlupic, V., & Paul, R. (1999). A hierarchical framework for evaluating simulation software. *Simulation Practice and Theory, 7,* 219–231. doi:10.1016/S0928-4869(98)00028-7

Ocak, M. (2010). Why are faculty members not teaching blended courses? Insights from faculty members. *Computers & Education, 56*(3), 689–699. doi:10.1016/j.compedu.2010.10.011

Oliver, M., & Carr, D. (2009). Learning in virtual worlds: Using communities of practice to explain how people learn from play. *British Journal of Educational Technology, 40*(3), 444–457. doi:10.1111/j.1467-8535.2009.00948.x

Oliver, R. (2006). Exploring a technology-facilitated solution to cater for advanced students in large undergraduate classes. *Journal of Computer Assisted Learning, 22*(1), 1–12. doi:10.1111/j.1365-2729.2006.00155.x

Peirce, N., Conlan, O., & Wade, V. (2008). *Adaptive educational games: Providing non-invasive personalised learning experiences*. Paper presented at the Second IEEE International Conference on Digital Games and Intelligent Toy Enhanced Learning.

Peterson, M. (2010). Computerized games and simulations in computer-assisted language learning: A meta-analysis of research. *Simulation & Gaming, 41*(1), 72–93. doi:10.1177/1046878109355684

Rani, S., Ashok, M., & Palanivel, K. (2009). *Adaptive content for personalized e-learning using Web service and semantic Web*. Paper presented at the IEEE International Conference on Intelligent Agent & Multi-Agent Systems (IAMA).

Raybourn, E., Deagle, E., Mendini, K., & Heneghan, J. (2005, November 28 - December 1). *Adaptive thinking & leadership simulation game training for special force officers*. Paper presented at the Interservice/Industry Training, Simulation and Education Conference Proceedings, Orlando, Florida, USA.

Romero, C., Ventura, S., Zafra, A., & De Bra, P. (2009). Applying Web usage mining for personalizing hyperlinks in Web-based adaptive educational systems. *Computers & Education, 53*(3), 828–840. doi:10.1016/j.compedu.2009.05.003

Rousseau, B., Jouve, W., & Berti-Equille, L. (2005). *Enriching multimedia content description for broadcast environments: From a unified metadata model to a new generation of authoringn tool*. Paper presented at the Seventh IEEE Symposium on Multimedia (ISM '05), Irvine, California.

Tai, Y., & Yu-Liang, T. (2007). *Authoring tools in e-learning: A case study*. Paper presented at the Seventh IEEE International Conference on Advanced Learning Technologies.

Vassileva, D., Bontchev, B., Chavkova, B., & Mitev, V. (2009). *Software construction of an authoring tool for adaptive e-learning platforms*. Paper presented at the 2009 Fourth Balkan Conference in Informatics.

Vogten, H., Martens, H., Nadokski, R., Tattersall, C., Van Rosmalen, P., & Koper, R. (2007). CopperCore service integration. *Interactive Learning Environments, 15*(2), 171–180. doi:10.1080/10494820701343827

KEY TERMS AND DEFINITIONS

Adaptive eLearning Resources: eLearning resources which adapt to suit individual learners learning requirements based on the criteria set for determining their learning needs.

Asynchronous eLearning: Student learning through communication with other students or lecturers who are not necessarily online at the same time, this type of learning is facilitated by the use of: e-mails, discussion boards, blogs, and wikis.

Educational Environments: Formal teaching environments which provide a broad range of instruction for students and also issue recognised standardised certification of awards at various levels of academic achievement.

eLearning: The provision of online learning resources.

Higher Education: Institutions which provide tuition and examinations which lead to high level qualifications for successful students in: Bachelor; Master; or Doctoral degrees.

Learning Management Systems: Applications specifically developed to facilitate the use of technology by lecturers or trainers when instructing students or trainees.

Net Generation: People who have grown up over the last 30 years or so who are more comfortable with the use of technology than the previous generation because of the prolific use of technology in their play, communication with their peers, and life in general.

Pedagogy: The art and skill of teaching or knowledge transfer.

Personalised eLearning Resources: Refers to the creation of eLearning resources which have been specifically selected or tailored to suit the learning preferences of individual learners.

Synchronous Learning: Student learning through communication with other students or lecturers who are online at the same time, this type of learning is facilitated by use of: video-conferencing and chat facilities.

Technology Enhanced Learning: The use of technological devices and communication mediums to augment the learning experience.

Training Environments: Courses specifically set up to provide trainees with knowledge and understanding in specific areas, for example, mandatory compliance training i.e. manual handling or emergency response training.

Section 4
Rich Internet Applications and HCI in Educational Practice– Educational and Training Design:
Support Systems, Models, Case Studies, etc.

Chapter 13
The Use of HCI Approaches into Distributed CSCL Activities Applied to Software Engineering Courses

Fáber D. Giraldo
University of Quindío, Colombia

María Lilí Villegas
University of Quindío, Colombia

César A. Collazos
University of Cauca, Colombia

ABSTRACT

This chapter is written as one method to supply the necessary support systems for educational and training design. As such, the authors propose their global development software (GDS) methodology emerges as a revolutionary discipline. It is based on the externalization of software development between geographically distant places in order to reduce development costs. Traditional educational and training process in software engineering must be advocated to consider (or enhance) this new trend, with its respective challenges and necessary skills (multicultural interaction, effective communication, distributed software project management), into curriculums. GDS therefore demands the presence of supporting systems to provide permanent user interaction and enhanced communication tasks. The presence of such interactions is a key aspect to promote the performance and knowledge acquisition processes among globally distributed software development teams. The main goal of such interactions into platforms that support distributed contexts is to reduce the impact generated by the tyranny of distance. This work exposes some human-computer interaction (HCI) principles applied by the authors' research team in order to structure a supporting user interface environment that reflects the distributed computer supported collaborative learning (CSCL) practice in software engineering. The chapter describes several services that are provided for managing the interaction between participants, such as synchronous interactions through Microsoft © LiveMeeting and Adobe © Connect, and asynchronous interactions such as Moodle forums. In this way, the authors implement effective HCI into educational professional practice scenarios for a distributed CSCL within the specialized domain of software engineering.

DOI: 10.4018/978-1-4666-3649-1.ch013

INTRODUCTION

Since 2008, we have created a consortium of Latin American universities with the purpose of applying distributed computer supported collaborative learning (CSCL) experiences in software engineering courses supported by high speed academicals networks of Latin America. This consortium is called Latin American colaboratory of eXperimental software engineering research (LACXSER) (http://www.lacxser.org/). The consortium of Latin American universities involved in this project has proposed a collaborative model to support the distributed teaching learning software engineering process called: collaborative distributed learning activity (CODILA) (Collazos et al., 2010).

This experimented instructional environment proposes to include learning activities through collaborative work. To this end, the structure and dynamics of the model try to involve participants, who are geographically dispersed, so that the development of their activities can be achieved in an effective manner. Also, the model promotes the active participation of members of the workgroups. This technology provides academies with high speed networks of each Latin American country (such as the videoconference from RENATA http://www.renata.edu.co/ - offering low cost, custom software solutions for various educational organizations, in Colombia for example), and developed by research from open source initiatives such as Moodle and Jommla.

In this chapter we will provide a background to set the context for our approach for the use of HCI as the means to implement distributed CSCL activities as they apply to 'software engineering' courses. These distributed interactions are then further explained showing how CSCL works well. Central to our HCI approach is the importance of including developmental strategies that involve usability accessibility; we provide a more detailed description of how we conducted our study to evaluate our newly developed tool. This description includes: the information architecture; the interaction design; the usability tests; and the technological platforms that were used to support the CSCL.

BACKGROUND

Collaborative learning is a pedagogical framework that has been interested in the study and reflection of the real dynamic of learning (Johnson & Johnson, 1986). It can inquire about the educational interactions because it is supported by cognitive theories: situations in which the protagonists (or users) are acting and interacting simultaneously in particular contexts about a specific task or the learning content, in order to achieve more or less defined goals. The teaching/learning process is determined by communication and the features of the educational context and interpersonal contact in the development of teaching. We propose that the CSCL is characterized by the equality that each individual must have in the process, and mutuality (connection, depth and scope bi-directionality that reach the experience), this variable is a function of an existing competitive level, which involves the distribution of responsibilities, joint planning and exchange of roles (Stahl, 2010).

This educational interaction is a prominent feature of collaborative distributed teaching in software engineering, as it seeks out how to provide spaces in which it is possible to develop individual and group skills from the discussions and interactions among the students when they explore new concepts. Each student is responsible for their own learning, generating discussions among themselves when they explore concepts for elucidating, or troublesome situations to be solved. Therefore, looking for the combination of situations and social interactions may contribute to personal and significant group learning.

In a modern software engineering teaching and learning process, students cannot learn alone: the auto-structuring activity of the subject is mediated by the influence of others. Therefore, learning is a reconstruction activity of knowledge of one culture and the historical moment (Barriga & Hernández, 2002). Collaboration in the teaching/learning process of software engineering has the ability for enriching and reflecting over the objects of knowledge, increasing the perspectives of analysis and application, ensuring the development of students and teachers as human beings continually in cognitive, social and emotional developing.

Software engineering is largely based on group work (in a local or distributed way). Reflecting this is the emphasis of teamwork and the formation of groups for projects within the usual educational process for software construction learning. Focusing on teams is a mechanism that allows students to gain experience in building medium-large scaled software, for critical business process and industrial environments. Experience in teamwork should be complemented with contemporary trends imposed by the software industry. It has become one of the sectors most affected by the phenomenon of globalization and subsequent emerging markets, as well as the geographical distribution of customers. The resultant growth results in early industrialization related to the building of software, and the internationalization of best practices, such as standards, information architectures and technological platforms (Giraldo & Collazos, 2011). We are therefore proposing in this chapter that it is necessary to strengthen local education in software engineering, by providing a global experience in building software applications as collective effort, rather than how it is applied in the more traditional methods for teaching/learning software engineering. These distributed interactions are now explained to reveal, in our opinion, how CSCL works better than the more traditional approaches.

INTERACTIONS AS SUPPORT IN CSCL DISTRIBUTED ACTIVITIES

In the globalization of the software industry, this activity highlights the fact that distance as a critical factor that directly affects the distributed execution of software development projects. This feature is subdivided according to the identified manifestations that include: temporal distances that may create communication problems, such as reducing hours of collaboration; difficulties in synchronous meetings; and delays in obtaining responses (Ågerfalk et al, 2005). As a result, the processes of coordination in a globalized process are significantly affected (Ågerfalk & Fitzgerald, 2006). Geographical distance makes communication difficult due to the decreased ability to keep face-to-face meetings (Abrahamsson, Salo, Ronkainen & Warsta, 2002). The absence of these meetings reduces informal contact and this can lead to issues such as: a loss of awareness of critical tasks; lack of cohesion in the team; and reduced confidence (Abrahamsson et al, 2002; Moe & Šmite, 2008). Therefore, a fundamental problem in implementing software engineering projects in a globalized context may account for the absence or interruption of the functions of coordination of work in a co-located environment (Krishna, Sahay and Walsham, 2004). The socio-cultural distances may create problems with inconsistent working practices, such as: different perceptions of authority and lack of mechanisms for the creation of shared knowledge; avoiding misunderstandings; and reducing cooperation (Paasivaara, Durasiewicz & Lassenius, 2008; Carmel, 2009). Different models and frameworks to implement globalization strategies in software projects are reported in works like (Hossain, Babar & Paik, 2009; Ågerfalk & Fitzgerald, 2006; Hossain, 2009). These works are oriented towards the implementation strategies and specific practices of development processes, for example in practices based on 'agile methods'. The term 'agile methods' relates to a software project management approach that is based on the delivery of artifacts through a fast interactive and incremental process; for more information about 'agile methods' and principles see http://agilemethodology.org/ and http://martinfowler.com/articles/newMethodology.html. However, these models do not focus on collaborative training for members who belong to distributed teams and do not report the support offered by media platforms to counter the presence of the distance during the execution of globalized software projects.

Instead, distributed software development requires proper technological support, with a sufficient level of interaction between members of a software team project, to counteract the effects of the presence of distance as a critical factor in group cohesion. In the case of distributed-collaborative practices developed in our project, the infrastructure of high-speed academic networks provide services that promote interaction between the 'distributed actors', seeking to increase the quality of their audio/video in order to obtain a higher level of awareness. We are proposing that interaction design becomes an important consideration when formulating collaborative experiments; moreover, that an improper use of the interaction platforms may alter the execution of the experience.

Currently, the development platforms for the software industry evolve to address the collaboration between members of development teams, highlighting initiatives, such as: IBM Jazz; Visual Studio Team Foundation Server; and GForge. These collaborative environments for software development offer Web scenarios that contain control tools, such as: task lists; bug tracking; document management; forums; mailing lists; access to change control repositories, among others. Consequently, they support the relationship among the participants, which modify collaborative entities, such as: the development of an idea; creating a design; and the performance of a shared goal. In general, collaboration technologies are strategies designed to capture the efforts of many participants into a managed content environment.

In a more collaborative context, it is necessary and essential to understand the differences in human interactions, in order to ensure the use of appropriate technology to meet the needs of the interaction. In our project this interaction occurs through 'virtual environments' supported by the Web and its communicational tools.

Therefore, the collaborative-distributed experiences performed in our project have prioritized the interactions among students as a fundamental factor that must be manifested in its most natural form, without the distortion or noise generated by the technological platform used. The surveys submitted by the participant-students of our project belonged to universities that included: Colombia; Chile; Argentina; Panamá; and Costa Rica. They reported on the use of platforms of interaction based on common information and communications technology (ICT) tools that afford for example: instant messaging and social networks. However, it is necessary to provide an additional platform to support both the administration of technical artifacts generated in the development of our experiment and the influence of learning styles and report abnormalities.

We can say that the design of interaction is a permanent issue in the application of collaboration strategies over distributed learning environments. Research works as (Ma, Wang & Sun, 2009) are highlighted, as having the ability to communicate with others, which is essential to the achievement of objectives in life, as it is in presenting the same situation in networked learning situations. The interaction through the Web portal of our project's video conference services were by Microsoft © LiveMeeting; while the communication services included: Skype; Windows Live Messenger; Googletalk; and Facebook.

As such, they facilitated appropriately to the learners for their cooperation with other colleagues and the achievement of their learning tasks. In Yoshitaka et al. (2009), it is proposed that a framework to handle misunderstandings may be generated among participants in an interactive process that is supported by CSCL remote web platforms. While in Monasor, Vizcaino and Piattini (2010), they present a simulator that helps to train students to face global software development practices, through interaction with 'virtual agents'. These 'agents' are characterized according to a particular culture, that place learners in globalized scenarios, specifically designed to improve the interaction capabilities with respect to the cultural differences and the language level.

Consequently, we propose that our approach to HCI demonstrates the importance of including developmental strategies to enhance the usability and accessibility. To this end therefore, next we provide a more detailed description of how we conducted our study to evaluate our newly developed tool. This description includes: the information architecture; the interaction design; the usability tests; and the technological platforms that were used to support the CSCL.

USABILITY/ACCESSIBILITY HCI

Effective collaboration requires agreement on a structured development process model. Even for smaller projects, when teams are tiny and individuals fill multiple roles, tackling the right challenges at the right time is critical to success (Morville & Rosenfeld, 2007). Without a process or model of collaboration, students may focus on completing assignments using job splitting strategies by employing 'divide and conquer' activities (for example), in which they fail to learn and develop the collaborative skills that they may have obtained if there had been a real collaboration. Students may focus on the 'task', forgetting the added values that may be obtained with more collaborative work. We maintain that collaborative learning processes must therefore promote interactive discussions between students that are focused on relevant topics.

Interaction and collaboration are cognitive activities requiring willing people to think and share ideas about problems and opportunities

that determine the best course of action (Hudson, 2011). For this reason, the real purpose of any collaborative tool is to nurture the group learning, and their decision making through their collaboration processes. However, creating an effective collaborative work environment requires more than just codifying knowledge, storing it in information systems and developing access and distribution (Owen, 2001). It is also a matter of facilitating contact, communication, mutual understanding and sharing. As a consequence, contributing with and using knowledge is an important communication process among an organization's employees (actors).

We can say that, as a communication process, the transfer of knowledge among these 'actors' can only be effective if there is a common interpretive of focus and context, where they can understand each other and communicate (Brézillon & Araujo, 2005).

With this purpose in mind, we applied an HCI approach that involved the 'information architecture' and 'interaction design', in order to structure an effective CSCL environment to encourage the interactions among the LATAM distributed students (see http://www.lacxser.org/ for a further description of this software environment). Accordingly, to perform the activities related to collaborative distributed learning, we required tools that support the interaction of participants involved in these processes. For our project, we designed and built a collaborative learning environment called LACXSER that used several platforms to support the interaction, such as: Moodle; Microsoft © LiveMeeting; and RENATA Virtual Office, powered by Adobe © Connect (See Figure 1). These services are provided by high speed academic networks implemented in Latin American countries, such as RENATA in Colombia, and RedCLARA in South America. See the discussion at the end of this chapter for further details relating to how Moodle, RENATA Virutal Office and Microsoft LiveMeeting were implemented for our project.

Figure 1. Main page of LACXSER collaborative learning environment

LACXSER is the formal platform for our project. It is divided into two sections, one of which is Moodle-based. LACXSER was designed in 'Joomla', which is a highly extensible content management tool that allows for building tasks quickly and easily through a configuration of software 'plugins' for supporting typical and advanced Web-site operations, such as: forums; chats; templates for Web-based forms; news. Being a completely free tool (no cost), it also presents a series of utilities that helped us to create other features.

Information Architecture

Distributed practices of our project demanded an adequate technological support, with a sufficient level of interaction, to counteract the effects of the presence of distance as a critical factor in the cohesion and functioning of groups of students. We suspected that improper use of the interaction platforms, together with the large amount of information that we intended to show, may affect the execution of collaborative experiences.

For this reason, it was necessary to design an effective 'information architecture' to involved the organization of the visual elements in the graphical user interfaces, to that ensure a high level of interactivity of students with their technological platforms. Therefore, we devised a comprehensive 'information architecture' for the LACXSER environment that invokes: labeling; organization; and navigation. The 'label system' was designed for the both the information, navigation, and the search systems according to Morville and Rosenfeld (2007). We devised a comprehensive 'information architecture' that involves: labeling; organization; and navigation.

Labeling

The classification realized for our LACXSER platform is based in two labels that are mentioned in Morville and Rosenfeld (2007), as 'contextual links' and 'headings'. Our classification of information takes into account the results obtained to bring forth both the required user activities and our analysis of their tasks. In general, for all the users, the requested information was labeled in categories defined according to the kind of project and the content type, as shown below:

- General information of the project (e.g.: mission, vision and the objectives)
- Contact information
- Practices and experiments

- Partners
- Universities and participant research
- CSCL distributed experiences

Organization

The information which the platform provides, is organized based on several organization schemes that are both exact as well as ambiguous (Morville & Rosenfeld, 2007). To provide a top-down structure to our LACXSER system and as such, the 'topics scheme' was considered as the main organization scheme, with the 'task scheme' as a secondary scheme. In addition, the system provides a bottom-up structure that is supported by the system's 'search component'. In order to guarantee an enhanced information organization, we used successful 'design patterns' and their features are described in the 'patterns' subsection below.

Navigation

As is shown in (Morville & Rosenfeld, 2007), there are three main navigational systems: global, local and the context. Although it is normally required, we consider that treating them separately is not good enough. Hence, our design of the LACXSER platform consideres these three systems separately, which provides flexibility, and helps the users to

be aware of the context to understand where they are in the system and know where they can go. Figure 2 presents the three kinds of graphical user interaction (GUI) navigation.

In defining our 'information architecture', it was necessary to define and implement a 'searching system'. This component provides access to a large volume of information related to collaborative learning experiences and its participants. Our 'search system' was therefore implemented as an additional support component to the 'navigation system' so that users (of the platform) have another optional mechanism to locate the information they may wish to find. Since search engines have become in a mechanism that must be provided by default, Web-site users do expect to find this searching tool (Morville & Rosenfeld, 2007). Search engines also have a positive impact on user experience, as the system designers generally make the interfaces consistent with similar interfaces the users have known previously. Consequently, the users can feel the sensation of freedom, because they can separate themselves from the technical aspects of the navigation scheme installed. There is also the possibility with these tools, to optimize the time spent by the users to find their information. The failure to provide this type of mechanism may generate a negative impact on user satisfaction.

Figure 2. LACXSER GUI with global menu, local menu and context menu

Interaction Design

Our interaction features aim to define the way a user will interact with the tools provided by the system. For example, how to launch the functionality option for setting up the details of the tasks (Shneiderman & Plaisant, 2005; Preece, Rogers & Sharp, 2002). Interactive learning environments promise to enrich the students' experience, allowing them to explore information under their own intrinsic motivation and to use what they discover to construct knowledge in their own words. This construction of knowledge occurs primarily through interaction in working groups. This type of computer-supported interactive tools empower groups to construct a form of group cognition that may exceed what possibly could be achieved by the group members as individuals. Clearly, the technology that supports effective communication networks should allow as much group interaction as possible in one place, or the same for geographically dispersed working groups (Stahl, 2006).

The main goal of our 'interaction design' is to support a further analysis related to the measurement of the effective collaboration, interaction and learning. The actual analysis process itself is beyond the scope of our current project.

According to previous work exposed in Bratitsis and Dimitracopoulou (2006) and in Duque, Rodriguez, Visitacion Hurtado, Bravo and Rodriguez-Dominguez (2012), the analysis of the tasks that users perform in their work environment, presents clear benefits with regards to understanding users' behavior as well as evaluating the use of the system. It also contributes useful information and methods for providing information that enables members of a workgroup to become 'aware' of the shared (digital) objects, as well as the evolution of the shared workspace and cooperative activities in collaborative software systems.

Collaboration and interaction analysis is an instrument for representing and studying users' work within a collaborative software system. This type of analysis is conducted to meet different purposes including to support researchers in ethnographic studies provide advice to their students. This methodology is pparticularly vital to the CSCL research community, as it is important to measure the level of learning of the students who participate in the classroom-based distributed CSCL experiences. Ideally, the collaboration and interaction variables should be closely related to the effectiveness of the cognitive process that may be developing in the students.

Moreover, computer-supported interaction analysis tools and methods have the potential to leverage research and practice in CSCL. The work carried out by Martínez-Monés, Harrer and Dimitriadis (2011), provides a systematic analysis of the problems that may be found when trying to apply interaction analysis tools to CSCL settings. As such, they outline the path for possible solutions for facing these problems. However, there are still many problems to solve at the design and the application and architecture levels. For instance, that computers can store large amounts of interaction data which may be analyzed by automatic or semi-automatic means.

The challenge of analyzing such data obtained from such interaction analysis tools, is even stronger in CSCL scenarios. This is because of the complex and multimodal interactions among participants that are totally or partially mediated by computers; and thus, are not directly observable by traditional means in the remote scenarios (Martínez-Monés et al., 2011). Often, the collaborative experiences data saved does not provide substantive evidence of how the interactions between students have flowed. If the data collection instruments are very specialized, students may become too afraid to report how their interactions really were carried out.

The process of the interaction design involves:

- The identification of needs and the establishing of requirements.
- The development of alternative designs that meet these requirements.

- The building of interactive versions of the designs, so they can be communicated and valued.
- The assessment of what is being built through the process.

Analysis of Users and Tasks

To achieve a good interface design, it is necessary to understand different aspects related to the users who use the system to be built, including: their characteristics; work environment; and their needs regarding what the system should provide, among others (Hackos & Redish, 1998). According to these considerations during the development of our project, the team performed activities, such as: identification of general needs; identification of user profiles for the LACXSER platform.

Therefore, the definition of the information that it should provide involves:

- A Web-site where the people who belong to the project find all the information about the project itself, and also it must show what is being done.
- A space in which it is possible to conduct group practices.

Moreover, in each practice where a number of students are involved, where each one is assigned to a group that is usually geographically distributed, the platform must:

- Support the communication between students.
- Present tasks previously assigned.
- Display the content that teachers have prepared to execute and practice.

In addition, the research team identified the following relevant aspects that are also related to usability and user experience that ought to be considered during the design of the platform.

Usability Issues

- Effectiveness
- Learnable
- Recordable
- Usefulness

User Experience Issues

- Satisfaction
- Usefulness
- Motivation
- Aesthetically appealing

Once we identified the needs of the users, the information requirements that the system should cover were established. Then, the team designed the interfaces that would provide this functionality according to the following steps:

- The design of the way the users were to access to the different systems' functionalities.
- The definition of (digital) objects with which the user should interact, and the way these objects may be manipulated by the users.
- To design the dialogue forms that are necessary to obtain the required user information for offering a service.

Access to the System Functionalities

The navigation is performed by user interaction with conventional devices, such as a keyboard and a mouse. The research team considered that the navigation system be defined in the 'information architecture' and the 'classification of information' be defined in the user and tasks analysis. We therefore, implemented a 'linear-menu' we define here as a 'pattern' (Morville & Rosenfeld, 2007). In other words, in the first-level of the menu, there is the general project information; like: start; what is LACXSER?; News; Vision; etc. Therefore, in order to visually capture this menu we used the 'pattern' known as 'tabs' (Tidwell, 2006).

The second-level menu is defined by the 'labels' assigned to offer the CSCL distributed experiences performed in the project, as:

- *Participant universities*
- *Sponsors*
- *Industry*
- *Instructions for accessing the Moodle platform*
- *Moodle login*
- *Publications*

Capturing User Data

When the users 'click' on the 'login option', it registers them as participants in the collaborative practices, forums and information requests through the 'contacts link'. To capture this information, system-generated forms are used. These forms comply with design patterns as mentioned in the 'patterns' section below.

Collaboration Description

As collaboration tools, all of them are considered as those which may allow interaction between two or more users of the platform, whether to provide services or to communicate with them. Since our LACXSER system can be used from any computer connected to the Internet or high speed academic network, the collaboration may be performed geographically distributed. LACXSER is therefore based on the Moodle platform, which provides asynchronous collaboration tools such as: Forum; Messaging, Tasks Assignment and Surveys.

Patterns

The organization of information in our system is made based on these 'patterns' (Tidwell, 2006), such as:

- **Extras on Demand:** That show the most important content up front, yet hide the rest.and let the user reach it via a single, simple gesture.
- **Closable Panels:** That put sections of content onto separate panels, and let the user open and close each of them separately from the others.
- **Right/Left Align:** When designing a form or table of two columns, right-aligned labels go to the left and left-aligned items go to the right (See Figure 3).

The patterns used for the design of the navigation system (Tidwell, 2006) involve:

- **Global Navigation:** That use a small section of every Web-page, and show a consistent set of hyper-links or buttons that take the user to key sections of the site or application.
- **Breadcrumbs:** That appear on each page when occurring in a hierarchy mode, and there is a map of all the 'parent' Web-pages one would need to navigate back to reach the 'main' or home-page.

To capture the user data we took into account the following 'patterns' as described by Tidwell (2006), as:

- **Good Defaults:** That wherever appropriate, the pre-fill form fields with 'your best guesses' at the values the user wants to see.

Figure 3. Example of application of right/left alignment patterns

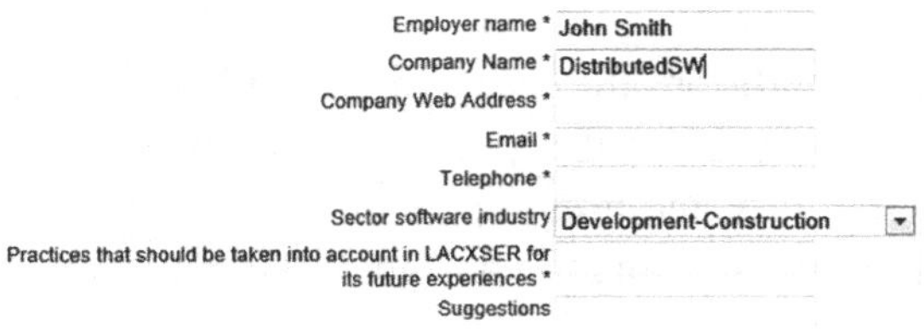

- **Prominent 'Done' Button:** That is located to complete the transaction at the end of the visual flow; its size should be appropriate and well labeled.

Having completed our discussion of the 'interaction design' our attention turns to the 'usability testing' that underpins our research.

Usability Tests

Our 'heuristic (rule-based) test' was conducted to evaluate the Web-based portal in a general way that enabled the research team to concentrate on the 'usability and accessibility' issues. We also applied a test using the usability evaluation, based on a 'managed discussion' approach. There were some elements of our 'heuristic test' that were extracted from a Microsoft © Excel template that was provided by the GRIHO research group (University of Lleida, Spain). Moreover, the original 'Excel template' we used is available from http://www.grihohcitools.udl.cat/mpiua/software.htm.

Heuristic Evaluation

This rule-based test took into account of several aspects that widely encompass 'usability and accessibility' of a Web-based portal. The evaluated features involved:

- **Clarity of Objectives:** Where the interface should immediately communicate its purpose, objective and functions.
- **Visibility of System Status:** Where the system should always keep users informed of the system status with appropriate feedback within reasonable time.
- **Adaptation to the World and the Mental Objects of the User/Logic of the Information:** The site/application is adapted to the real world of users, their language, knowledge, and so on.

- **Control and User Freedom:** Where the users often choose system functions by mistake and sometimes they need a clearly marked emergency exit that is leaving the unwanted state without having to go through an extended dialogue. It is important to have undo and redo.
- **Consistency and Standards:** Where the users have to ask whether different words, situations or actions mean the same thing. They generally follow the rules and conventions of the platform on which the system is implemented.
- **Prevent Errors:** Where it is more important to prevent the occurrence of errors that generate good error messages.
- **Recognition Rather than Memory:** Where the Web-site/'interactive system' is based on recognition rather than recall, which allows the user to interact with the site easily and productively.
- **Flexibility and Efficiency of Use:** Where the interface facilitates and optimizes access to users regardless of their characteristics.
- **Aesthetic Dialogues and Minimalist Design:** Where the Web-site/'interactive system' avoids any irrelevant information or graphics and includes only the necessary information.
- **Help and Documentation:** Where although it is best if the system can be used without documentation, it may be necessary to provide help and documentation. This should be easy to find, centered with the user's tasks, to get information about the steps to perform, and not being very extensive.
- **Search:** Where this heuristic applies if there is a 'search engine interface' (usually for Web-interfaces).

- **News**: Where this 'heuristic' is applied to those interfaces that include a special section for news.
- **Information Architecture:** For the organization of the information on the Web-site or interactive system.

Usability Evaluation with a Managed Discussion Approach

An evaluation of the logic and format of the information and interface design for our LACXSER Web-site was performed. The research team met a group of users (students) to discuss in a period of approximately two hours about topics of interest, under the coordination of a member of the project.

During this session, we took some photos and video recordings that were used for academic purposes. The topics of interest during the discussion were: the logic of information, the format of information and the interface design. For each of these issues involved, people put forward a number of questions, which met the objectives of the discussion.

Results

A series of changes to the platform were applied based on both tests in order to improve the 'usability and accessibility' of the Web-site. Each of the heuristics (rules) give a base point where the design of the Web-site could generate problems; we used the heuristics where the ratings were less favorable. Particularly in the managed discussion, the evaluation team concluded that the Web-site had a better acceptance by users, and it was necessary to include more detailed information and pictures.

Having completed the discussion on our usability testing, we shall now provide a brief description of the software platforms that were implemented to support our CSCL.

Technological Platforms Used to Support CSCL

Moodle

The platform on which the activities were performed among the students took place is Moodle (http://www.moodle.org). This is a virtual educational environment that allowed us to meet our project needs. In addition, it can be widely extensible and it is a free tool. Moodle provides collaboration tools such as forums for asynchronous communication between students and teachers. It allows the group settings; scheduling and also supporting upload content and news from teachers in order to inform students. With the extension called 'Joomdle'; it was possible to have a very clear transition between the two platforms (front end Joomla and the learning management system (LMS) Moodle), to be easier for the users, so they can access the main page of LACXSER and through this, enter Moodle without leaving the portal.

RENATA Virtual Office

This platform (built on the Adobe Connect facility), let us share files, such as a PowerPoint slides, JPG Images and others, so that the participants in a virtual meeting could see them simultaneously. Often it is used as a support tool for the interaction of participants in collaborative practice as shown in Figure 4. The Adobe Connect is running as a tool invoked from the browser. It supports transmission of video and sound, and coordination between participants.

Microsoft LiveMeeting

The Microsoft LiveMeeting (https://www103. livemeeting.com) was the most important tool used by the research team, due to its notable high simplicity to transmit audio and video and share files. A negative factor found was that this tool

Figure 4. Collaborative interaction through RENATA virtual office

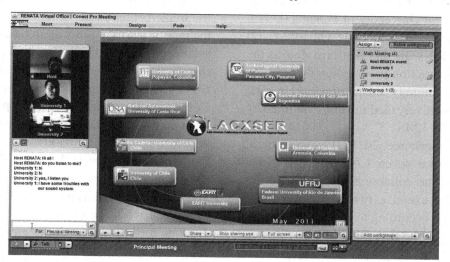

can only have one video simultaneously. For this reason, if there are a number of attendees, you can only watch one video (usually the video shows who is participating at the moment). The same as the 'RENATA virtual office' tool, for our project; it was used as a support tool for the interaction of participants in collaborative practice.

Preliminary Results

In the collaborative experiences performed by the research group we conducted a 'survey' in order to measure, among other things, the satisfaction level of the 'technological platform' that was used between the distributed students. Table 1 exposes our results. 'Technology' satisfaction was measured using a range from 0 to 5. Collaborative

experiences are according with the collaborative distributed learning activity (CODILA) model proposed (Collazos et al, 2010; Giraldo, Collazos, Ocoa, Xapata & Torres de Clune, 2010).

Our results are explained as follows: although the collaborative experiments began in 2008, it was only during 2009 that the research team used a technological platform for supporting the interactions.

Therefore, the first platform was a LMS system provided by the Technological University of Panamá (UTP). However, the score obtained in the survey applied to students was low, due to problems of interaction and usability of this platform. In the 'Experience 2010 I' experiment, the participant-students from two universities worked collaboratively, using the same technological

Table 1. Results of satisfaction with technology used in our LACXSER collaborative environment

	Experience 2009 – Source: Aballay (2011)	Experience 2010 I		Experience 2010 II		Experience 2011
Modality	Global	UQ Students	UTP Students	Distributed Track 1	Distributed Track 2	Distributed
Satisfaction with Technology	2,8545	2,47	3,64	3,5	3,475	4,0797

platform based in a proprietary LMS offered by the Technological University of Panama (UTP). Students from the University of Quindío (UQ) were dissatisfied with this platform due to the low level of interaction provided by these LMS, whereas the technology satisfaction level in UTP students was relatively medium due to familiarity of them with the LMS.

In the 'Experience 2010 II' experiment, the students from seven LATAM universities participated in the collaborative distributed experience. In this exercise, two distributed tracks were conformed according to a heuristic group's formation. It was the first time that the research group used the LACXSER platform applying the results obtained in the 'heuristic test' made by the usability experts based on elicited requirements.

In the 'Experience 2011' experiment, the distributed students who interacted with our LACXSER platform version 2 participated. This new version has been included the results and feedback obtained in the 'usability test' with 'managed discussion approach'.

CONCLUSION AND FUTURE RESEARCH DIRECTIONS

We propose that from these findings, a central aspect for the effective implementation of collaborative learning is the construction of the learning task itself (Barkley et al., 2005). When CSCL approaches are applied, although students are charged with the responsibility for their own learning, the responsibility for defining and structuring their learning tasks, is assigned to the instructor. Whereas, in a collaborative learning environment, teachers structure a learning situation, so that the students then take control of the learning process. We can also say that there are two more critical elements in building collaborative learning situations that involve: the design of the appropriate learning tasks; and the structuring of

procedures for students to participate actively in the implementation of these tasks. Therefore, if the task of learning is not appropriate, or it is not sufficiently understood by the student: the activities are delayed; students lose attention; and the frustration will appear in the group interaction. Consequently, students may complain and the team may fail to obtain the benefits of interaction with their peers. This previous scenario highlights the importance of properly designing a technical environment that supports effective interaction and learning within a specific CSCL process.

In this work we exposed the main considerations for building a CSCL environment that support the interactions in a distributed teaching/learning process for 'software engineering' deployed by LATAM researchers under an HCI and usability approach. These environments are conformed by Web-based portals and videoconference tools, that provide high speed academic networks. Our effort was therefore oriented to resolve: how the student groups apply critical thinking skills; express different opinions; deal with conflict; negotiate outcomes and coordinate its activities in productive ways, inside a collaborative 'software engineering' teaching/learning process.

The use of patterns and heuristic evaluations of user interfaces for our project, allowed us to identify problems that may interfere with the operation of the collaborative platforms and expose an initial diagnosis, to provide feedback on how to generate new optimized versions of our project's user-interfaces.

The application of our 'usability and Web-enabled accessibility' approach, which involved the implementation of interaction tools to support collaborative practices, was performed by distributed participants. This was to help to address the 'interaction design principles' as being consistent to: the interpretation of user behavior (consistency of both platforms such as the internal consistency of the information); the balance of the platforms with respect to the user needs; and the anticipation of operations to be executed by the users. We propose that the deployed environment to support collaborative practices provides the students and researchers with the tools to make their searches confidently, for information required in any instant of the collaborative experience. The used strategies allowed ranking and structuring the information from the user needs as identified by the researchers involved.

The results of the qualification of the technological dimension, obtained from students shows an increase in satisfaction from the use of technological tools deployed by the team to manage the interaction among the participants, in their distributed collaborative experiences. As future work, and when considering that the number of interactions between team members represent a important step to interpret the effective implementation of collaboration and group knowledge, the research team now has the challenge of obtaining and evaluating the interactions performed by other students during their collaborative practices, through social networks as a natural mechanism for interaction among students. It is necessary therefore, to evaluate the effectiveness of these platforms in the consolidation of learning and performance of these other student groups.

ACKNOWLEDGMENT

This work has been partially funded by the project entitled 'Red Latinoamericana de Investigación Aplicada en Ingeniería de Software Experimental', Grant IF-007-09 CINTEL Colciencias RENATA Colombia (Call Colciencias 487 - RENATA 2009). Authors also thank to LACCIR for partial funding of this work through the grant R1209LAC003 and RedCLARA through ComCLARA 2010 call. Authors thank the students, instructors and researchers of the LACXSER project, who made possible the distributed collaborative experiences.

REFERENCES

Aballay, L. (2011). *A model for the teaching of usability from a collaborative perspective. Final work for obtaining the Bachelor of Science in Information*. National University of San Juan Argentina.

Abrahamsson, P., Salo, O., Ronkainen, J., & Warsta, J. (2002). *Agile software development methods: Review and analysis*. Technical Report # 408. Espoo, Finland: VTT Publications.

Ågerfalk, P. J., & Fitzgerald, B. (2006). Flexible and distributed software processes: OLD petunias in new bowls? *Communications of the ACM, 49*(10), 27–34.

Ågerfalk, P. J., Fitzgerald, B., Holmström, H., Lings, B., Lundell, B., & O'Conchuir. (2005). A framework for considering opportunities and threats in distributed software development. In *International Workshop on Distributed Software Development 2005,* (pp. 47–61).

Arceo, F. D. B., & Rojas, G. H. (2002). *Estrategias docentes para un aprendizaje significativo: Una interpretación constructivista*. Mc Graw Hill.

Bareisa, E., Karciauskas, E., Macikenas, E., & Motiejunas, K. (2007). Research and development of teaching software engineering processes. *Proceedings of the 2007 International Conference on Computer Systems and Technologies,* (p. 75). ACM Press.

Barkley, E., Cross, K., & Major, C. H. (2005). *Collaborative learning techniques - A handbook for college faculty*. The Jossey-Bass Higher and Adult Education Series.

Bratitsis, T., & Dimitracopoulou, A. (2006). Monitoring and analysing group interactions in asynchronous discussions with the DIAS system. In *Proceedings of the 12th International Workshop on Groupware, GRIWG' 2006, in: Lecture Notes in Computer Science, vol. 4154,* (pp. 54–61). Berlin, Germany: Springer.

Brézillon, P., & Araujo, R. M. D. (2005). Reinforcing shared context to improve collaboration. In *Proceedings of Revue d'Intelligence Artificielle* (pp. 537-556).

Carmel, E. (2009). *Global software teams: Collaborating across borders and time zones*. NJ: Prentice-Hall.

Collazos, C., Giraldo, F., Zapata, S., Ochoa, S., Lund, M., Aballay, L., & Clunie, G. (2010). *CODILA: A collaborative and distributed learning activity applied to software engineering courses in Latin American Universities*. International Conference on Collaborative Computing COLLABORATECOM.

Damian, D., & Zowghi, D. (2003). Requirements engineering challenges in multi-site software development organizations. *Requirements Engineering Journal*, 8(1), 149–160. doi:10.1007/s00766-003-0173-1

Fáber, F. D., & César, C. A. (2011). *Red latinoamericana de investigación aplicada en ingeniería de software experimental: Un esfuerzo de integración latinoamericano para la investigación y cooperación en ingeniería de software*. Editorial Universidad del Quindío.

Giraldo, F. D., Collazos, C. A., Ochoa, S. F., Zapata, S., & Torres de Clunie, G. (2010). Teaching software engineering from a collaborative perspective: Some Latin-American experiences. *Proceedings of DEXA Workshops, 2010*, 97–101.

Hackos, J. T., & Redish, J. C. (1998). *User and task analysis for interface design*. John Wiley & Sons, Inc.

Herbsleb, J., & Grinter, R. (1999). Coordination, and distance: Conway's law and beyond. *IEEE Software*, 16(5), 63–70. doi:10.1109/52.795103

Holmstrom, H., Fitzgerald, B., Agerfalk, P. J., & Conchuir, E. O. (2006). Agile practices reduce distance in global software development. *Information Systems Management*, 7–26. doi:10.1201/1078.10580530/46108.23.3.20060601/93703.2

Hossain, E., Babar, A. M., & Paik, H. (2009). Using Scrum in global software development: A systematic literature review. *Proceedings of ICGSE, 2009*, 175–184.

Hossain, E., Babar, A. M., Paik, H., & Verner, J. (2009). Risk identification and mitigation processes for using Scrum in global software development: A conceptual framework. In *Proceeding of the Asia Pacific Software Engineering Conference, APSEC 2009*, (pp. 457–464).

Hossain, E., Babar, M. A., & Verner, J. (2009). How can agile practices minimize global software development co-ordination risks? In O'Connor, R. V., Baddoo, N., Cuadrago Gallego, J., Rejas Muslera, R., Smolander, K., & Messnarz, R. (Eds.), *EuroSPI 2009: Communications in Computer and Information Science* (*Vol. 42*, pp. 81–92). Heidelberg, Germany: Springer. doi:10.1007/978-3-642-04133-4_7

Hossain, E., Bannerman, P., & Jeffery, D. (2011). Scrum practices in global software development: A research framework. In Caivano, D. (Eds.), *Product-focused software process improvement* (pp. 88–102). Berlin, Germany: Springer. doi:10.1007/978-3-642-21843-9_9

Hudson, A. (2011). *Grouputer report: Five ways to improve work group collaboration in virtual meetings*. Technical Report. Retrieved from http://www.grouputer.com/papers/5_ways_to_improve_work_group_collaboration.pdf

Jimenez, M., Piattini, M., & Vizcaino, A. (2009). Challenges and improvements in distributed software development: A systematic review. *Advances in Software Engineering*, 1–14. doi:10.1155/2009/710971

Johnson, D., & Johnson, R. (1986). *Circles of learning: Cooperation in the classroom*. Edina, MN: Interaction Book Company.

Krishna, S., Sahay, S., & Walsham, G. (2004). Managing cross-cultural issues in global software outsourcing. *Communications of the ACM, 47*(4), 44–47. doi:10.1145/975817.975818

Kussmaul, C., Jack, R., & Sponsler, B. (2004). Outsourcing and offshoring with agility: A case study. In *Proceedings of XP* (pp. 147–154). Agile Universe. doi:10.1007/978-3-540-27777-4_15

Ma, L., Wang, Y.-S., & Sun, H.-Y. (2009). Construction and practice for interaction in networked learning situation. International Forum on Information Technology and Applications, Vol. 1, (pp. 447-452).

Mackenzie, O. J. (2001). Tacit knowledge in action: basic notions of knowledge sharing in computer supported work environments. In M. Jacovi, A. Ribak & A. Woodcock (Eds.), *Proceedings of the European CSCW Workshop on Managing Tacit Knowledge*, Bonn.

Martínez-Monés, A., Harrer, A., & Dimitriadis, Y. (2011). An interaction-aware design process for the integration of interaction analysis into mainstream CSCL practices. In Puntambekar, S., Erkens, G., & Hmelo-Silver, C. (Eds.), *Analyzing interactions in CSCL* (pp. 269–291). Springer, US. doi:10.1007/978-1-4419-7710-6_13

Moe, N. B., & Šmite, D. (2008). Understanding a lack of trust in global software teams: A multiple case study. *Software Process Improvement and Practice, 13*(3), 217–231. doi:10.1002/spip.378

Monasor, M. J., Vizcaíno, A., & Piattini, M. (2010). An educational environment for training skills for global software development. In *Proceedings of the 2010 10th IEEE International Conference on Advanced Learning Technologies* (ICALT '10), (pp. 99-101). Washington, DC: IEEE Computer Society. DOI=10.1109/ICALT.2010.35

Morville, P., & Rosenfeld, L. (2007). *Information architecture for the World Wide Web*, 3rd ed. O' Reilly.

Paasivaara, M., Durasiewicz, S., & Lassenius, C. (2008). Distributed agile development: Using Scrum in a large project. *Software Process Improvement and Practice, 13*(6), 527–544. doi:10.1002/spip.402

Preece, J., Rogers, Y., & Sharp, H. (2002). *Interaction design: Beyond human computer interaction*. John Wiley & Sons, Inc.

Rafael, D., Rodríguez, M. L., Hurtado, M. V., Bravo, C., & Rodríguez-Domínguez, C. (2012). Integration of collaboration and interaction analysis mechanisms in a concern-based architecture for groupware systems. *Science of Computer Programming, 77*(1), 29-45. ISSN 0167-6423

Shneiderman, B., & Plaisant, C. (2005). *Designing the user interface - Strategies for effective human computer interaction* (4th ed.). Pearson Education.

Simmons, D. B. (2006). Software engineering education in the new millennium. *Proceedings of the 30th Annual International Computer Software and Applications Conference* (COMPSAC'06). IEEE Press.

Stahl, G. (2006). *Group cognition: Computer support for building collaborative knowledge*. MIT Press. ISBN 0-2-19539-9

Stahl, G. (2010). *Global introduction to CSCL*. Philadelphia, PA: Gerry Stahl at Lulu.

Tidwell, J. (2006). *Designing interfaces*. O' Reilly.

Wellington, C. A., Briggs, T., & Girard, C. D. (2005). Examining team cohesion as an effect of software engineering methodology. *Proceedings of the 2005 Workshop on Human and Social Factors of Software Engineering,* (pp. 1- 5). ACM Press.

Yoshitaka, S. Kinshuk, Graf, S., Zarypolla, A., Takada, K., & Tsuruta, S. (2009). Enriching web based computer supported collaborative learning systems by considering misunderstandings among learners during interactions. *ICALT, Ninth IEEE International Conference on Advanced Learning Technologies,* (pp. 306-310).

KEY TERMS AND DEFINITIONS

RedCLARA: Acronym for the 'Latin American Cooperation of Advanced Networks (Cooperación Latino Americana de Redes Avanzadas in spanish)'. RedCLARA is a Latin American system of collaboration through advanced telecommunications networks for the research, innovation and education. More information available in http://www.redclara.net/.

RENATA: Acronym of 'National Academic Network of Advaced Technology (Red Nacional Académica de Tecnología Avanzada in spanish)'. This facility is a high speed network that connects the universities in Colombia, in order to share academic and research contents. More information available in http://www.renata.edu.co/.

Chapter 14
A Case Study of Designing Experiential Learning Activities in Virtual Worlds

C. Candace Chou
University of St. Thomas, USA

Rama Kaye Hart
University of St. Thomas, USA

ABSTRACT

This chapter aims at examining, through a case study, student perceptions of interactive learning activities based on the experiential learning model in Second Life (SL). Undergraduate students in an Honors Program reflected on their learning experiences in a blended learning course that took place both in person and in SL for four weeks. Student reflections on two main learning tasks: discussion about assigned readings and SL field trips which include simulating and gaming, were recorded in weekly journals. Sixty journal entries were the data source for coding. Student experiences of the learning tasks are predominately positive with some challenges. Positive views include: excitement, enhanced confidence, motivation for learning, and increased knowledge. Challenges were mostly due to technical issues. Instructor interventions, including ground rules for online conversation and tech support, were important in minimizing barriers to student learning in virtual worlds.

INTRODUCTION

The affordances of the 3D virtual worlds have attracted an increasing number of higher education institutions to establish presences in Second Life (SL), the most popular virtual world for training and learning activities (Michels, 2008). Virtual worlds refer to three-dimensional learning environments that allow participants to represent themselves with an avatar, interact with other avatars, and offer opportunities to create authentic learning contexts (Chou & Hart, 2012). An

DOI: 10.4018/978-1-4666-3649-1.ch014

avatar is a persona representing a user that can walk, move, gesture, and communicate with other avatars. SL is a virtual world that was developed by Linden Labs and launched in 2003. SL is accessible from the Internet through a free SL client or other compatible client. The affordances refer to the capabilities that allow participants to communicate through voice and text chat, to embody social presence through 3D avatars, to engage in simulation and immersive learning through virtual campuses, and to establish learning communities from anywhere and anytime (Jarmon, 2007). The typical learning activities in virtual worlds, also known as 3D immersive learning, include: 3D demonstrations; simulations; virtual meetings. In addition there are communities of practice in a wide range of disciplines, including: science; medicine; education; arts; literature; business; music; humanities; and engineering (Chou & Hart, 2012). Studies in virtual worlds have shown that students appreciate the opportunities to learn in virtual worlds but are also frustrated with the technical difficulties and learning functionalities of SL (Leong, Joseph, & Boulay, 2010; Sanchez, 2009).

Most studies have focused on the general perceptions of student adaptation to activities in SL. What is little known are the specific student learning experiences associated with various learning activities. Student learning in virtual worlds can take many forms, which can include but are not limited to: scavenger hunts, project galleries, role playing, language learning, field trips, dialogues, public speaking; lectures; presentations; art design; science experiments; leadership training; team-building; game-based learning; project-based learning; and manipulation and creation of objects. This chapter explores student perceptions of different types of learning tasks by describing the results of a case study and highlighting interventions employed to minimize the barriers to learning.

LITERATURE REVIEW

Experiential Learning in Virtual Worlds

Kolb (1984) defines experiential learning theory (ELT) as "the process whereby knowledge is created through the transformation of experience. Knowledge results from the combination of grasping and transforming experience" (p. 41). The ELT model captures two modes of acquiring experience, through concrete experience (CE) and abstract conceptualization (AC). The ELT model also describes two ways of transforming experience, through reflective observation (RO) and active experimentation (AE). As shown in Figure 1, the four-stage learning cycle depicts how people learn through various ways of transforming experiences into knowledge. The emphasis on 'experiences' differentiates ELT from cognitive learning theories, which place more emphasis on cognition over affect, and behavioral learning theories, that pay little attention to experience in the learning process. According to Kolb, Boyatzis, and Mainemelis (2009), concrete experience serves as the base of observations and reflections, which are incorporated into abstract concepts. Abstract conceptualization provides the ideas for action.

Figure 1. Kolb's experiential learning cycle (adapted from Kolb, 2009)

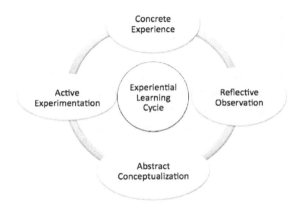

Learners experience various stages of learning in the cycle depending on the learning context and personal learning styles. In acquiring experience, some rely on concrete and tangible products or immerse themselves in concrete reality. Others take in information through "symbolic representation or abstract conceptualization" (Kolb, Boyatzis, & Mainemelis, 2009, p. 194). In transforming experience, some rely on observation of others or reflections on an event, while others need to learn by doing and experimenting. Each learner will choose various stages of grasping and transforming experience in the learning process.

ELT lays the foundation for the design of virtual world learning activities. The learner-centered approach encourages learner engagement and immersion in the virtual world to solve real-world problems with active participation. In a survey of learning theories applied to courses conducted in SL, the most active virtual world environment, Anderson (2010) found that 73% of educators applied ELT to the SL learning projects, 52% applied social learning, and 63% incorporated collaborative learning theory in the learning activities (multiple responses were allowed). The strong emphasis on experiential and collaborative learning matches well with the affordances of virtual worlds. Learners can use their avatars to be in the same 3D space to: meet; discuss; travel; build objects; make plans; reflect; and collaborate together. With the right pedagogy, educators can fully utilize the characteristics of virtual worlds to provide students with the learning opportunity based on Kolb's four-step cycle: experiencing; reflecting; generalizing; and applying.

Mason (2007) suggested the following guidelines to incorporate experiential activities into learning in SL which can be applied to all virtual world environments:

1. **Have SL Relevance:** Utilizing the unique qualities that SL has to offer, for example, avatar interaction.

2. **Involve Students in Experience Design:** Requiring learners to research and reflect while constructing an item or repurposing existing content into a new experience that teaches others.

3. **Require Collaboration:** Encouraging synchronous and asynchronous work together.

4. **Leverage the SL Community:** Reaching out to various online communities to enrich student learning experiences.

5. **Provide the Opportunity to Reflect in both New and Traditional Media:** Giving students opportunities to use tools inside and outside to present information.

In a case study of student experience in working on virtual world projects, Mason (2007) found students expressing more enthusiasm and spending more hours in virtual world projects than in traditional course work. The study also found that students stay online longer and move around less when other students are present at the same time since most work requires collaboration.

Studies on experiential learning in virtual worlds have focused largely on the design, pedagogy, and general student experiences (Mason, 2007; Warburton, 2009). Leong, Joseph, and Boulay (2010) found three categories emerged from student experiences in virtual worlds: "a) frustrations with technical issues and learning functionalities of SL, b) need for socialization and sense of presence, and c) appreciation for the potential of SL for teaching and learning" (p. 16). Chou and Hart (2012) identified six themes of student perceptions of learning activities in virtual worlds: challenge; engagement; activity types; transformation; collaborative and democratic participation; and new opportunities. The common themes in these studies are technical issues and the educational potential of the 3D learning environment. Technological challenges lead to frustration at the initial stage and yet the innovative aspect of virtual worlds often motivates students to continue with their exploration.

Dieterle and Clarke (in press) examined the use of virtual worlds for teaching and summarized that virtual worlds have been used in education for: (1) creating online communities for teacher education (Bull, Bull & Kaider, 2004; Ried, Bronack, & Tashner, 2005; Schlager, Fusco, & Schank, 2002); (2) engaging science-based activities with socially responsive behavior (Kafai, 2006); (3) experiencing historical and political events (Squire & Jenkins, 2003); (4) enhancing social and moral development through cultures of enrichment (Barab, Thomas, Dodge, Carteaux, & Tuzun, 2005); (5) exploring new mathematical concepts (Elliott, 2005); and (6) participating in scientific inquiry (Clarke, Dede, Ketelhut, & Nelson, 2006; Ketelhut, Dede, Clarke, Nelson, & Bowman, in press). The essence of virtual worlds for learning lies on the capabilities that allow participants to use the avatars to take part in problem-solving of issues that are similar to those in a real world context (Dede, Nelson, Ketelhut, Clarke, & Browman, 2004).

Simulation and Games in Virtual Worlds

3D virtual learning environments have gained acceptance and can be seen in business, government, non-profit, and education. For higher education and workplace learning, 3D virtual worlds are commonly used for 3D demonstration, simulation, virtual meetings, and communities of practice (Chou & Hart, 2012). An example of the 3D demonstration can be seen in the Palomar West Hospital SL site which provided a prototype of a hospital for visitors to take a tour of the hospital before its actual opening. Visitors can use their avatars to freely move through featured facilities to learn about the services the hospitality has to offer. Examples of simulation are often demonstrated in role plays. Take the performance-based training by General Electric (GE) for example, trainees participated in a role-playing strategy game in

which they have to interact with peers and learn about the protocols and software tools in a timely manner to prevent a power plant shutdown.

3D virtual worlds have also provided new venues for virtual conferences and meetings. Many professional organizations in the United States such as Association for Education and Communication Technology (AECT), International Society of Technology for Education (ISTE), and American Educational Research Association (AERA) have held regular member meetings in virtual worlds. A community of practice is defined as a group of people to interact regularly to advance themselves based on common interests (Wenger, 1998). Examples of communities of practices can be seen in highly organized professional organizations or loosely structured special interest groups. According to Galarneau (2005), self-grouping in a structure-free massively multiplayer online gaming environment (MMOG) can be observed as an example of the latter.

Simulations provide the opportunity to prepare learners for skill practice such as CPR prior to actual practice on real patients or through experiencing situations that may not occurs often such as a Tsunami simulation to learn about nature disasters. An increasing number of simulation examples in virtual worlds have proved to be effective in improving learning. For example, students participating in a border interview simulation in SL at Loyalist College performed 28% better than the students without the SL simulation in the previous year in passing the Canadian custom officer exam (Heiphetz & Woodill, 2010). Michelin Group utilized scenario-based learning in SL to train the trainers about IT system in its global network. An internal study indicated improved understanding of the topics and increased interest in mastering the skills (Heiphetz & Woodill, 2010).

In testing a simulation game to teach about electromagnetic forces, Squire, Barnett, Grant, and Higginbotham (2004) found that students who played a game to learn the content outperformed students who learned via interactive lectures. Reports of games as effective ways of learning are usually found in isolated lab settings or as a single module in the school curriculum. Most learning at school emphasizes memorizing facts and asking students questions about the facts. Shaffer, Squire, Halverson, and Gee (2005) argued that:

To know is a verb before it becomes a noun in knowledge. We learn by doing – not just by doing any old thing, but by doing something as part of a larger community of people who share common goals and ways of achieving these goals. We learn by becoming part of a community of practice and thus developing that community's ways of knowing, acting, being, and caring – the community's situated understandings, effective social practices, powerful identities, and shared values (p. 107).

Examples of games that embody these characteristics of hands-on learning, community of practices, and shared values can be found in what Shaffer et al., (2005) has coined 'epistemic games.' Knowledge can be acquired from a form of activity and experience in which learners are doing something within a community of practice. Facts and information will eventually come when learners are immersed in activities that utilize these facts for plans, goals, and purposes within a knowledge domain. Epistemic games emphasize 'initiation' and 'transformation'. Through proper initiation, learners have the opportunity to learn about the world through meaningful activities that are well aligned with the essential life skills of a society. Take 'Madison 2200', a city design game using interactive geographic information system. For example, students worked together to design a downtown pedestrian mall at Madison, Wisconsin. The learners became knowledgeable about community issues such as: city budget; revenue; jobs; waste; and so on, as a result of immersing in the game. Learners developed their understanding of the ecology and were able to apply it to urban issues. In addition to initiating

learners into learning scenarios, epistemic games emphasize transforming learning by providing novices with expert suggestions and representations of professional knowledge at critical moments of 'expectation failure'.

Through the lenses of experienced professionals, learners will be able to develop strategies to tackle key problems. Epistemic games allow "players the freedom to act within the norms of a valued community of practice ...To work successfully within the norms of a community, players necessarily learn to think as members of the community" (Shaffer et al., 2005, p. 109).

Simulation and game-based learning are popular learning designs in virtual worlds. The interactive features of virtual worlds make simulation and game-based learning more accessible for developers and learners alike. Aldrich (2009) summarized succinctly the connection among games, simulation, and virtual worlds. According to Aldrich (2009), games use fun and engaging activities to provide entertainment and assist people in learning specific ideas or skills. Simulations which share some characteristics of games often come with rigorously structured scenarios to help people develop specific competencies that can be applied to the real world. Virtual worlds often allow multiple players in three-dimensional social learning environments which can house games and simulations. A stand-alone virtual world environment itself does not teach but the platform offers great potential to integrate with games and simulations. Virtual worlds offer the context which needs content to make the learning in them worthwhile. Playing games such as 'SimCity' alone will not make someone a great mayor. Likewise, some players of 'World of Warcraft' may learn transferrable or measurable leadership skills, yet not all players will. Aldrich (2009) argued that careful design and structure must be integrated to invoke specific competencies or transferrable skills. Games, simulations, and virtual worlds can be integrated well to provide highly interactive learning environments for learners. Aldrich (2009) emphasized three commonalities across games, simulations, and virtual worlds: an introductory structure; a community; and active learning.

Firstly, an introductory structure offers asynchronous self-paced learning to allow participants to become familiar with the required competencies in manipulation, navigation, and communication before moving to the real activities. For example, a scavenger hunt or field trip in SL will provide the necessary training for participants to become familiar with the basic movements and features of the virtual environments. Secondly, tools to establish a community can be built into virtual worlds using chat or other features. Participants will become more engaged when there are other people working together or providing support. Thirdly, participants should be actively doing things, not just listening to lectures in virtual worlds. Instructors can design activities to encourage learners to achieve specific goals through active participation in simulations and games. Assessment, coaching, and mentoring techniques can all encourage active learning. In short, integrating games and simulation in virtual worlds can provide "a natural way for people to learn by nurturing an instinctive progression from experiencing to playing to learning" (Aldrich, 2009, p. 3-4).

Human-Computer Interaction (HCI) in Virtual Worlds

When it comes to designing simulations and games in virtual worlds, it is important to take into consideration the characteristics of virtual worlds that facilitate interaction. Human-computer interaction (HCI) refers to the discipline and research that emphasizes the design, evaluation, and implementation of interactive computing system for human (Hewett et al., 1996). A good HCI user interface helps to "reduce anxiety and fear of computer usage, assist the graceful transition for novice users, provide direct manipulation of objects, offer input devices and online assistance, and allow information exploration through easy navigation"

(Shneiderman, 1998, pp. 29-30). Romiszowski (1981) summarized Bruner's (1966) theory on three levels of learning: enactive level (direct manipulation), iconic level (visual and mental image process), and symbolic level (manipulation of symbols via language). People learn through all three levels of interaction. Virtual worlds have the capability to allow user direct manipulation, to provide excellent visualization of artifacts, and to encourage symbolic interaction through language exchanges or online search.

Lucke and Zender (2011) observed three levels of user interaction in virtual worlds:

- **Passive:** Participants are present in a virtual world (e.g., walk, fly, sit) without influencing the environment. They may be participating a meeting or reading text on a bulletin board or projector.
- **Active:** Participants are actively shaping the environment according to their view. For example, they may be presenting via a projector, giving a talk, or creating objects for modeling or simulation.
- **Interactive:** Participants are interacting with other members (using text or voice) or objects in virtual worlds or external environments.

Many of the HCI features in virtual worlds have made it possible to implement highly interactive activities. The complexity of the highly interactive environments can also be intimidating for novice learners. Conducting learning activities in virtual worlds to accommodate both novice and experienced learners can be challenging. In reviewing the literature regarding 'experiential learning', simulations, games, and HCI, some commonalities can be observed. Firstly, all of them have a component that encourages learning in doing something or direct manipulation of objects. Secondly, frequent interactions among learners are strongly supported. Thirdly, community of practice is essential to sustain learning. Table 1

Table 1. HCI features of virtual worlds that support experiential learning

Experiential Learning Elements	HCI Tools	Instructional Activities
Experiencing	Avatar animation, teleport self or friends	Field trips, scavenger hunt, orientation, games
Reflecting	Text and Voice Chat, avatar gestures	Synchronous discussion, lecture discussion, research, brainstorming, small group activities
Generalizing	Navigation in various virtual worlds, grouping, presentation tools	Team work, jigsaw activities, simulation, team-meetings, training, public speech
Applying	Object manipulation, slide presentation, building, engineering, scripting	Language exchanges, project gallery, role-play, debates, artifact design, global project-based learning, inquiry-based learning

outlines how HCI tools in virtual worlds can be utilized to support instructional activities under the experiential learning framework.

Instructional strategies are utilized to support student learning. In addition to improving user interface, researchers or designers also need to understand student experiences in various virtual world learning activities so that these activities can be improved to maximize student learning. In the next section, we will explore student perceptions of experiential learning in virtual worlds through a case study.

COURSE BACKGROUND

This case study focuses on a blended learning course that was conducted over four weeks with three virtual sessions in SL and four face-to-face sessions in a computer lab with SL installed in 2011. Several activities based on Kolb's learning cycle were implemented to address these four aspects of learning as shown in Table 2.

The two consistent weekly activities were conversation starters and SL field trips. The purposes of the field trips were to improve student proficiency in SL navigation and experience the affordances and diversity that SL has to offer. The conversation starter was designed to encourage student interaction and deepen their understanding of the readings. Online conversation can support student learning and affect student over-

all perceptions of a course (Berge, 1999). Research reviews by Jin and Ingram (2008) have found ample evidence that online conversations play a key role in the success of a technology-mediated or online learning environment, including community building, knowledge construction, and student satisfaction of learning. Jenlink and Carr (1996) summed up three general purposes of conversation: (1) *transacting*: conducted for the purpose of negotiation or exchange within an existing problem setting; (2) *transforming*: conducted when individuals suspend their own personal opinions or assumptions and their judgment of others' viewpoints; and (3) *transcendent:* where the purpose is to move beyond or "leap out" of existing mindsets (pp. 31–32). The online conversation activity in this course also fit well with the framework of Kolb's Experiential Learning in which students took a broader view of the theories in a real-world context and shared experiences to deepen their understanding of the topics.

Students were divided into five groups of three members. One group was in charge of leading a conversation starter and a field trip in each session. In the 'conversation starter', the facilitating group would summarize the required readings and prepare questions to facilitate the class discussion. Students were encouraged to use a combination of text, voice, and the avatar gestures to communication with each other. In the field trip, the leading group would take the whole class to three to five

Table 2. Learning activities based on Kolb's experiential learning model

Experiential Learning Elements	Learning Activities	Purpose
Experiencing	SL field trips SL Scavenger hunt Presentation in SL	To become proficient in navigating in SL and learn about various SL sites for educational and training purposes
Reflecting	Weekly reflection journals	To reflect on their observation of learning activities and learning experiences in virtual worlds
Generalizing	Conversation Starter	To gain a broader understanding of the impact of virtual worlds in society, groups and interpersonal interaction
Applying	Case Studies	To apply course materials to develop strategies of best practice in virtual worlds

interesting SL sites. Students primarily used the voice chat to interact with each other. In addition to SL, Facebook, a wiki, and Blackboard were also utilized for the purposes of information sharing and community building.

RESEARCH METHODS AND QUESTIONS

This is an explorative case study on student perceptions toward interactive learning tasks in 3D virtual worlds. The use of a case study method is appropriate for this study when sample size is small and no clear outcomes are in sight. The qualitative approach can provide a holistic account of the phenomenon under investigation (Yin, 2003). The course in this study, an Honors course entitled 'Virtual Worlds and Society' in a mid-size university in the Midwestern U.S., consisted of 15 students who gave consent to provide anonymous data for research purposes. The participants included seven males and eight females. The course was conducted over four weeks of intensive sessions through blended learning with three virtual sessions in SL and four face-to-face sessions in a computer lab in 2011. The two consistent weekly activities were a student-led conversation starter and an SL field trip. Students were divided into five groups of three members for both activities. The two authors are also the course instructors who team-taught the course. The data came from the weekly reflection journals and the final anonymous course evaluations. The reflection journal consists of the following main questions:

1. How would you characterize your learning experiences so far?
2. What are the three important things you have learn from today's session or this week's activities?
3. How would you characterize your team experience?
4. Based on your experience in the class, what has worked for you so far?
5. Based on your experience in the class, what has not worked for you?
6. Additional comments.

The research questions are:

1. What are student perceptions of virtual world interactive learning tasks such as the conversation starter and SL field trip?
2. What interventions can be implemented to minimize the barriers to excel in the learning tasks?

DATA ANALYSIS

Sixty entries of weekly reflection journals were entered into the qualitative data analysis program NVivo for coding. When students made references to either the conversation starters or the field trip, the learning experience was coded as engaging, neutral, or challenging based on students comments. Comments were coded as positive when students remarked on engaging or enhanced learning experiences. Comments were coded as neutral when students mentioned a task without positive or negative expressions. Comments were coded as challenging when students associated a task with difficult learning scenarios such as technical issues. The data indicate that 67% of comments related to the conversation starter and the field trips were positive. Only 13% of the conversation starter, or 12% of field trips comments were coded as challenging experiences as shown in Table 3.

The second data source, the course evaluation, has also shown consistent results. More than 80% of students have indicated that the field trips and the conversation starters were the most popular class activities. The following sections will discuss the positive and challenging experiences of both activities in details.

Field Trip

The data showed that every student had positive comments of the field trip with occasional negative experiences. The students prepared three to five SL sites to guide their fellow classmates to tour these sites. Each group prepared a slide show to introduce these sites based on the framework of the six Ps:

1. **Purpose:** What is this site for, e.g., commercial, e-government, professional development, higher education, K-12 education, virtual services, organizational learning, or other?

Table 3. Student comments on tasks

Task types	Conversation	Field trips
Challenging	13%	12%
Neutral	20%	21%
Positive	67%	67%
Subtotals	100%	100%

2. **Place:** Where is the location, i.e., the SLURL?
3. **Population:** What is the intended target population?
4. **Platform:** What are the unique features of this site? What kind of learning activities are employed, e.g., simulation, community of practice, role-play, demonstration, etc.?
5. **Profit Model:** How does a virtual world supports itself, through registration fee, fee per use, subscription fee, advertising fee, pay as you go, sales of ancillary products, or grant funding?
6. **Prospect:** How do you envision this site can be further adopted for organization learning and development? (The six Ps are adopted from the typology of virtual worlds developed by Messinger, P. R., Stroulia, E., & Lyons, K, July 2008).

Through this activity, students learned to conduct a PowerPoint presentation inside SL and acquired the skills to navigate around various sites.

Positive Experiences

The positive experiences of the field trips can be summarized into the following themes:

1. **Excitement:** Student expressed enjoying seeing new possibilities of what SL can offer to extend educational and community-based activities. Here are a few excerpts of student comments: "I enjoyed the field trips. Traveling to a new location exposes us to a new experience"; "I like the field trip. ... I did not feel like it was a 3-hour class at all".
2. **Increased Confidence:** Students gained confidence in SL movements, navigation, site managements, and search. The new found confidence has made learning in SL more interesting and comfortable. Selected comments include: "I felt much more adept

at using second life."; " It helped me to become more comfortable with navigating the spaces on my own".

3. **Motivated to Learn:** Students expressed strong interest in learning about the purposes of various SL sites and would go back to explore more on their own. For example, students commented that "the field trips engaged me and made it much easier to learn " or "the field trips are where I believe I learned the most".

4. **Increased Knowledge:** Students learned the real-world applications of virtual worlds in the fields of education, government, business, and non-profit agencies. For example, students commented that: "I expanded my knowledge of the vast offerings of Second Life. This was most evident in the field trip presentations".

5. **Enhanced Team Experiences:** Field trips also provided an opportunity for student collaboration. Student commented that: "my group worked very well together. ... We were in constant communication with each other through multiple mediums" or "I feel that this part of the team experience was important because it involved using class material for actually life tasks".

Challenging Experiences

Student comments on challenging experiences can be summarized into the following two categories:

1. **Lost in Time and Space:** In a large group tour, there were always one or two participants getting left behind due to technical or personal issues as indicated in the comments here: "I could no longer hear.., so I was left behind" or "while I do enjoy the field trips, we always end up losing people".

2. **Technical Glitches:** This is the major factor that made the field trips challenging for some participants as indicated by the following comments: "My teammate got kicked out

of second life and my microphone did not work for the first half of the class" or "I also found the first couple field trips to be a little hectic, granted the majority of the problems were just technical difficulties".

Conversation Starter

Students also demonstrated strong interest in the conversation starters. The conversation starter assignment involved asking students to assemble in pairs or trios and take responsibility for facilitating a conversation centered on the readings associated with the course, which included topics such as: community; identity; social interaction; and teamwork. The facilitator teams were also expected to craft a 'conversation starter,' a brief reflection (1/2-1 page) highlighting two to three key concepts in the reading that were intriguing or confusing, along with two to three questions related to their inquiry/discovery to generate conversation during the class session. Students distributed these documents prior to the class session.

During the first session, the students were asked to use the text chat to conduct the conversation starter discussion. However, some students found it difficult to scroll through a large amount of the text chat log during a live conversation. After the instructor suggested ground rules for participating in a conversation, the discussions went much smoother. The rules included the option of the voice chat and the use of a text gesture to express 'I have an idea' to inform the moderator when one is ready to speak.

The idea is similar to students raising hands to signal the desire to speak in a face-to-face classroom. The comments can be summarized into the categories in the following sections.

Positive Comments

1. **Active Participation:** Students took an active part to reflect on the reading during the conversation as indicated in the comments: "everyone participated well in our discus-

sion" or "I thoroughly enjoy bouncing my ideas off of others, and hearing about others' experiences in SL".

2. **Enhanced Understanding:** The conversations played a key role in assisting students understanding the readings as indicated in the comments: "they are really helping me get a handle on the readings," "was able to form my own ideas off of what others said" or "the conversation starter gives the class the opportunity to link the issues and events we face in life to our experiences in SL".

3. **Improved Communication with Voice and Text Chat:** Students definitely enjoyed having the option of both voice and text as indicated in the comments: "Using the chat feature was the best way to create an order to when each individual got to use their voice feature to add to the conversation".

Challenging Experiences

The main challenge was in keeping track of the conversation. Students thought that it was hard to follow the dialogue and to express thoughts at the right moments as indicated in the following comments: "I'd be typing something, but by the time I was ready to hit the 'enter' button, the conversation had already moved to a different topic so I simply refrained from submitting it".

Interventions

Interestingly, in a further review of the reflection journals, the incidences of challenging experiences reduced significantly during the second half of the class. There was not a negative view of the conversation starter and only one negative view of the field trip due to technical issue at the last week. The instructors implemented the following interventions to minimize the barriers to student participation in the tasks: (1) introduced ground rules for conversation starter; (2) made the computer lab available for students who did

not have access to the SL clients; (3) loaned headsets to students who have technical issues; and (4) provided immediate feedback to students (less than 24 hours), who had any difficulties with the tasks. As a result, the incidences of negative experiences with both conversation starters and the field trips are significantly reduced as shown in Table 4 and 5.

CONCLUSION AND FUTURE DIRECTIONS

The aim of this chapter was to understand student experiences of interactive learning tasks in the virtual world of SL, and how instructor-led interventions minimized the barriers to student participation. A case study in which two specific learning tasks, conversation starters and SL field trips, were implemented yielded the finding that student experiences of the learning task were primarily positive with some challenges. Regarding the field trips, of the positive experiences, par-

Table 4. Field trips: Number of comments by weeks

	Challenging	Neutral	Positive	Totals
Week 1	0	1	13	14
Week 2	7	9	20	36
Week 3	1	2	14	17
Week 4	1	4	4	9
Subtotals (%)	9 (12%)	16 (21%)	51 (67%)	75 (100%)

Table 5. Conversation starter: Number of comments by weeks

	Challenging	Neutral	Positive	Totals
Week 1	4	4	4	12
Week 2	3	4	13	20
Week 3	1	0	12	13
Week 4	0	5	14	19
Subtotals (%)	8 (13%)	13 (20%)	43 (67%)	63 (100%)

ticipants found the field trips exciting, increasing their confidence, motivating them to learn, and enhancing their knowledge in the application of virtual worlds for learning and development. Of the challenging experiences, participants found that the field trips could interrupt learning due to technical glitches or losing contact with the groups. With respect to the conversation starters, the positive experiences are reinforced through active participation, enhanced understanding of the readings, and a combination of voice and text chats. The challenging experiences are mostly related to the management of the flow of the conversation.

The two activities, conversation starters and field trips, served well in providing students the events to fully immerse in the 'experiential learning cycle'. They acquired concrete experiences through field trip exploration, and conversation starter preparation (reading and posing questions), reflected on their learning through the weekly journal entries, gained a broader understanding through the conversation starter dialogue, and applied the course materials in their final case study projects. Their perceptions of the learning experiences as reflected in the weekly journals are consistent with recent studies on virtual world learning (Leong, Joseph, & Boulay, 2010; Mason, 2007). Students demonstrated strong interest initially and the interest can be worn off by technical glitches. Instructor interventions and continuing support are crucial in creating a social space for learning. 3D virtual worlds open up an exciting venue for experiential learning. Participants in this study demonstrated strong interest in learning the course materials through virtual worlds. Yet the time that it took to learn and the technical issues could remain the main barriers to a wider acceptance of the learning platform.

This study is significant by contributing to the knowledge and literature of virtual world research in the following ways: (1) providing clear descriptions on strengths and challenges of virtual world teaching that can be useful for virtual worlds' educators; (2) offering useful intervention recommendations for reducing entry barriers for students; and (3) suggesting pedagogically sound activities to engage students.

For future research, student satisfaction of a course and evidence of knowledge construction through the conversation starters or other virtual world-related activities should be examined. The 'experiential learning model' provides the framework in designing student-centered learning activities. Further studies on how these activities can help student in achieving learning goals and stay engaged would help to researchers, educators, and developers of 3D virtual worlds to find common ground in facilitating 3D immersive learning activities.

REFERENCES

Aldrich, C. (2009). Virtual worlds, simulations, and games for education: A unifying view. *Innovate, 5*(5). Retrieved from http://www.innovateonline.info/pdf/vol5_issue5/Virtual_Worlds,_Simulations,_and_Games_for_Education-__A_Unifying_View.pdf

Anderson, C. (2010). *Learning theories and Second Life*. Retrieved from http://www.cathyandersonblog.com/?p=235

Barab, S., Thomas, M., Dodge, T., Carteaux, R., & Tuzun, H. (2005). Making learning fun: Quest Atlantis, a game without guns. *Educational Technology Research and Development, 53*(1), 86–107. doi:10.1007/BF02504859

Berge, Z. L. (1999). Interaction in post-secondary web-based learning. *Educational Technology, 39*(1), 5–11.

Broadribb, S., & Carter, C. (2009). Using Second Life in human resource development. *British Journal of Educational Technology, 40*(3), 547–550. doi:10.1111/j.1467-8535.2009.00950.x

Bruner, J. S. (1966). *Towards a theory of instruction*. New York, NY: Norton.

Bull, G., Bull, G., & Kajder, S. (2004). Tapped in. *Learning and Leading with Technology*, *31*(5), 34–37.

Chou, C. C., & Hart, R. K. (2012). The pedagogical considerations in the design of virtual worlds for organization learning. In Yang, H., & Yuen, S. (Eds.), *Handbook of research on practices and outcomes in virtual worlds and environment* (pp. 561–569). Hershey, PA: Information Science Reference/IGI Global.

Clarke, J., Dede, C., Ketelhut, D. J., & Nelson, B. (2006). A design-based research strategy to promote scalability for educational innovations. *Educational Technology*, *46*(3), 27–36.

Dieterle, E., & Clarke, J. (in press). Multi-user virtual environments for teaching and learning. In Pagani, M. (Ed.), *Encyclopedia of multimedia technology and networking* (2nd ed.). Hershey, PA: Idea Group, Inc. doi:10.4018/978-1-60566-014-1.ch139

Elliott, J. L. (2005). *AquaMOOSE 3D: A constructionist approach to math learning motivated by artistic expression*. Unpublished Doctoral Dissertation, Georgia Institute of Technology, Atlanta, GA.

Galarneau, L. (2005). *Spontaneous communities of learning: Learning ecosystems in massively multiplayer online gaming environments*. Retrieved from http://papers.ssrn.com/sol3/papers.cfm?abstract_id=810064

Heiphetz, A., & Woodill, G. (2010). *Training and collaboration with virtual worlds: How to create cost-saving, efficient, and engaging programs*. New York, NY: McGraw Hill.

Hewett, T. T., Baecker, R., Card, S., Carey, T., Gasen, J., & Mantei, M. Verplank, W. (1996). *Curricula for human-computer interaction*. Retrieved from http://old.sigchi.org/cdg/cdg2.html#2_1

Jarmon, L. (2008). Learning in virtual world environments: Social presence, engagement, & pedagogy. In Rogers, P., Berg, G., Boettcher, J., Howard, C., Justice, L., & Schenk, K. (Eds.), *Encyclopedia of distance and online learning*. Hershey, PA: IGI Global.

Jenlink, P., & Carr, A. A. (1996). Conversation as a medium for change in education. *Educational Technology*, *36*(1), 31–38.

Jin, L., & Ingram, A. (2008). Constructing online conversation to support learning. In Luppicini, R. (Ed.), *Handbook of conversation design for instructional applications* (pp. 218–236). IGI Global. doi:10.4018/978-1-59904-597-9.ch014

Kafai, Y. B. (2006). Playing and making games for learning: Instructionist and constructionist perspectives for game studies. *Games and Culture*, *1*(1), 36–40. doi:10.1177/1555412005281767

Ketelhut, D., Dede, C., Clarke, J., Nelson, B., & Bowman, C. (in press). Studying situated learning in a multi-user virtual environment. In Baker, E., Dickieson, J., Wulfeck, W., & O'Neil, H. (Eds.), *Assessment of problem solving using simulations*. Mahwah, NJ: Lawrence Erlbaum Associates.

Kolb, D. A. (1984). *Experiential learning: Experience as the source of learning and development*. Englewood Cliffs, NJ: Prentice-Hall, Inc.

Kolb, D. A., Boyatzis, R. E., & Mainemelis, C. (2009). Experiential learning theory: Previous research and new directions. In Sternberg, R. J., & Zhang, L. F. (Eds.), *Perspectives on cognitive, learning, and thinking styles* (pp. 193–200). Lawrence Erlbaum.

Leong, P., Joseph, S. R., & Boulay, R. (2010). Applying constant comparative and discourse analyses to virtual worlds research. *Journal of Virtual Worlds Research*, *3*(1), 3–26.

Lucke, U., & Zender, R. (2011). 3D interactions between virtual worlds and real life in an e-learning community. *Advances in Human-Computer Interaction*, *2011*, 1–11. doi:10.1155/2011/684202

Mason, H. (2007). Experiential education in Second Life. In D. Livingstone & J. Kemp (Eds.), *Proceedings of the Second Life Education Workshop* (pp. 14-18). Retrieved from www.simteach.com/slccedu07proceedings.pdf

Messinger, P. R., Stroulia, E., & Lyons, K. (2008, July). A typology of virtual worlds: Historical overview and future directions. *Journal of Virtual Worlds Research, 1*(1), 1–18.

Michels, P. (2008). Universities use Second Life to teach complex concepts. *Government Technology.* Retrieved from http://www.govtech.com/gt/252550

Riedl, R., Bronack, S., & Tashner, J. (2005). *Innovation in learning assumptions about teaching in a 3-D virtual world.* Paper presented at International College Teaching Methods and Styles Conference, Reno, NV.

Romiszowski, A. J. (1981). *Designing instructional systems: Decision making in course planning and curriculum design.* New York, NY: Nichols Publishing Company.

Sanchez, J. (2009). Barriers to student learning in Second Life. *Library Technology Reports, 45*(2), 29–34.

Schlager, M. S., Fusco, J., & Schank, P. (2002). Evolution of an online education community of practice. In Renninger, K. A., & Shumar, W. (Eds.), *Building virtual communities: Learning and change in cyberspace* (pp. 129–158). Cambridge, UK: Cambridge University Press. doi:10.1017/CBO9780511606373.010

Shaffer, D. W., Squire, K. R., Halverson, R., & Gee, J. P. (2005). Video games and the future of learning. *Phi Delta Kappan, 87*(2), 104–111.

Shneiderman, B. (1998). *Designing the user interface: Strategies for effective human-computer interaction* (3rd ed.). Reading, MA: Addison-Wesley.

Squire, K., Barnett, M., Grant, J. M., & Higginbotham, T. (2004). Electromagnetism supercharged!: Learning physics with digital simulation games. *International Conference on Learning Sciences,* (pp. 513-520). International Society of the Learning Sciences. Retrieved from http://portal.acm.org/citation.cfm?id=1149126.1149189

Squire, K. R., & Jenkins, H. (2003). Harnessing the power of games in education. *Insight (American Society of Ophthalmic Registered Nurses), 3*(1), 5–33.

Warburton, S. (2009). Second Life in higher education: Assessing the potential for and the barriers to deploying virtual worlds in learning and teaching. *British Journal of Educational Technology, 40*(3), 414–426. doi:10.1111/j.1467-8535.2009.00952.x

Wenger, E. (1998). *Communities of practice: Learning as a social system.* Retrieved from http://www.co-i-l.com/coil/knowledge-garden/cop/lss.shtml

Yin, R. K. (2003). *Case study research: Design and methods* (2nd ed.). Thousand Oaks, CA: Sage Publications.

ADDITIONAL READING

Alarifi, S. A. (2009). An exploratory study of higher education virtual campuses in Second Life. Retrieved from http://www.4shared.com/file/105077350/c1603541/Sultan__Sam6__dissertation_in_SL.html

Aldrich, C. (2005). *Learning by doing: A comprehensive guide to simulations, computer games, and pedagogy in e-Learning and other educational experiences.* San Francisco, CA: John Wiley & Sons, Inc.

Antonacci, D. M., & Modress, N. (2008). Envisioning the educational possibilities of user-created virtual worlds. *AACE Journal, 16*(2), 115–126.

Bessiere, K., Ellis, J. B., & Kellogg, W. A. (2009, April 4-9). Acquiring a professional 'Second Life:' Problems and prospects for the use of virtual worlds in business. *Proceedings of ACM CHI 2009 Conference on Human Factors in Computing Systems: Case Study.* Retrieved from jellis. org/work/vw-chi2009.pdf

Brandon, B. (2007, October 8). Give your e-Learning some (Second) life: Simulation made easy. *Learning Solutions e-Magazine.*

Broadribb, S., & Carter, C. (2009). Using Second Life in human resource development. *British Journal of Educational Technology, 40*(3), 547–550. doi:10.1111/j.1467-8535.2009.00950.x

Chang, V., Gütl, C., Kopeinik, S., & Williams, R. (2009). Evaluation of collaborative learning settings in 3D virtual worlds. *International Journal of Emerging Technologies in Learning, 4*(3), 6–17.

Damer, B. (2008, July). Meeting in the ether: A brief history of virtual worlds as a medium for user-created events. *Journal of Virtual Worlds Research, 1*(1). Retrieved from http://www.jvwresearch.org/index.php/past-issues/volume1issue1

Davis, A., Murphy, J., Owens, D., Khazanchi, D., & Zigurs, I. (2009). *Avatars, people, and virtual worlds: Foundations for research in metaverses.* Business Source Premier database.

DeMers, M. N. (2008). *Second Life fireside chats: Social presence in online GIS education.* Retrieved from http://proceedings.esri.com/library/user-conf/educ08/educ/abstracts/a1063.html

Dieterle, E., & Clarke, J. (2007). Multi-user virtual environments for teaching and learning. In Pagani, M. (Ed.), *Encyclopedia of multimedia technology and networking* (2nd ed.). Hershey, PA: Idea Group.

Ellis, J. B., Luther, K., Bessiere, K., & Kellogg, W. A. (2008, February 25-27). *Games for virtual team building.* Paper presented at the 7th ACM conference on designing interactive systems, Cape Town, South Africa.

Esteves, M., Antunes, R., Fonseca, B., Morgado, L., & Martins, P. (2008). *Using Second Life in programming's communities of practice.* Retrieved from http://home.utad.pt/~leonelm/papers/CRIWG/MicaelaCRIWG.pdf

Fortney, K. (2007). *Using Second Life to provide corporate blended learning solutions SimTeach.* Retrieved February 10, 2011, from http://www.simteach.com/slccedu07proceedings.pdf

Gibson, D., Aldrich, C., & Prensky, M. (2007). *Games and simulations in online learning: Research and development frameworks.* Hershey, PA: IGI Global.

Herrington, J., Reeves, T. C., & Oliver, R. (2007). Immersive learning technologies: Realism and online authentic learning. *Journal of Computing in Higher Education, 19*(1), 65–84. doi:10.1007/BF03033421

Hudson, K., & Degast-Kennedy, K. (2009). Canadian border simulation at Loyalist College. *Journal of Virtual Worlds Research, 2*(1), 1–11. Retrieved from http://www.jvwresearch.org/index.php/past-issues/21-pedagogy-education-and-innovation

Kapp, K. M., & O'Driscoll, T. (2010). *Learning in 3D: Adding a new dimension to enterprise learning and collaboration.* San Francisco, CA: Pfeiffer.

Oliver, M., & Carr, D. (2009). Learning in virtual worlds: Using communities of practice to explain how people learn from play. *British Journal of Educational Technology, 40*(3), 444–457. doi:10.1111/j.1467-8535.2009.00948.x

Omale, N., Hung, W.-C., Luetkehans, L., & Cooke-Plagwitz, J. (2009). Learning in 3-D multiuser virtual environments: Exploring the use of unique 3-D attributes for online problem-based learning. *British Journal of Educational Technology, 40*(3), 480–495. doi:10.1111/j.1467-8535.2009.00941.x

Twining, P. (2009). Exploring the educational potential of virtual worlds: Some reflections from the SPP. *British Journal of Educational Technology, 40*(3), 496–514. doi:10.1111/j.1467-8535.2009.00963.x

Wexler, S., Corti, K., Derryberry, A., Quinn, C., & Barneveld, A. v. (2008). *Immersive learning simulations: The demand for, and demands of, simulations, scenarios, and serious games: The eLearning Guild.*

Yoder, M. B. (2009). Walk, fly, or teleport to learning: Virtual worlds in the classroom. *Learning and Leading with Technology, 37*(2), 16–20.

Zielke, M. A., Roome, T. C., & Krueger, A. B. (2009, April). A composite adult learning model for virtual world residents with disabilities: A case study of the virtual ability Second Life Island. *Journal of Virtual Worlds Research, 2*(1).

KEY TERMS AND DEFINITIONS

3D Avatar: A persona representing a user in a 3D virtual world can walk, move, gesture, and communicate with other avatars.

3D Learning Environment: Three-dimensional learning environments that allow participants to represent themselves with an avatar to interact with other avatar and offer opportunities to create authentic learning contexts.

3D Virtual Worlds: Similar to 3D learning environments, 3D virtual worlds allow multiple users to interact with each other for a wide variety of purposes, e.g., meetings, simulation, public relations, e-commerce, games, social interaction, etc.

3D Immersive Learning: Learning principles that encourage learners to immerse in 3D learning environment through an authentic context and include, but are not limited to, demonstration, simulation, collaborative learning, and communities of practice with a strong emphasis on experiential learning.

Community of Practice (CoP): CoP are characterized by a group of professionals who have share interests in specific domains join together to engage in discussion, share resources, or learn about something.

Conversation Starter: A synchronous chat activity that is designed to encourage student interaction and gain a broader understanding of the impact of virtual worlds in society, groups and interpersonal interaction.

Field Trip: A 3D virtual world activity that is designed to assist the participant to become proficient in navigating in virtual worlds and learn about various virtual world sites for educational and training purposes.

Second Life: A virtual world that is developed by Linden Lab and launched in 2003 and that is accessible from the Internet through a free Second Life or other compatible client.

Compilation of References

Aballay, L. (2011). *A model for the teaching of usability from a collaborative perspective. Final work for obtaining the Bachelor of Science in Information.* National University of San Juan Argentina.

Abrahamsson, P., Salo, O., Ronkainen, J., & Warsta, J. (2002). *Agile software development methods: Review and analysis.* Technical Report # 408. Espoo, Finland: VTT Publications.

Abu, Z. A., & Fong, S. F. (2010). *Lurking as learning in online discussions: A case study.* Paper presented at the Global Learn Asia Pacific 2010.

ACER. (2011). *Dropout DNA, and the genetics of effective support.* Australian Council for Educational Research: Research Briefing 11. Retrieved from http://www.acer.edu.au/documents/AUSSE_Research_Briefing_Vol11.pdf

ACER. (2011). *Australasian survey of student engagement (AUSSE).* Australian Council for Educational Research. Retrieved from http://www.acer.edu.au/research/ausse

ACS. (2005). *Policy statement on computer literacy.* Australian Computer Society. Retrieved from http://www.acs.org.au/acs_policies/docs/2005/ComputerLiteracy.pdf

Ågerfalk, P. J., Fitzgerald, B., Holmström, H., Lings, B., Lundell, B., & O'Conchuir. (2005). A framework for considering opportunities and threats in distributed software development. In *International Workshop on Distributed Software Development 2005,* (pp. 47–61).

Ågerfalk, P. J., & Fitzgerald, B. (2006). Flexible and distributed software processes: OLD petunias in new bowls? *Communications of the ACM, 49*(10), 27–34.

Ahanchian, M. R., & McCormick, J. (2009). Culture and the processes of virtual teaming for training. *Journal of Computer Assisted Learning, 25*(4), 386–396. doi:10.1111/j.1365-2729.2009.00314.x

Aiken, M., Garner, B., Ghosh, K., & Vanjani, M. (2008). Dot.com boom and bust effects on MIS college enrollments: 1995-2006. *Communications of the IIMA, 8*(1), 31–42.

Alam, S. L. (2008). *To wiki or to blog: Piloting social software technologies for assessment in a large first year information systems class.* Paper presented at the 19th Australasian Conference on Information Systems, Christchurch.

Alam, S. L., & McLoughlin, C. (2010). Using digital tools to connect learners: Present and future scenarios for citizenship 2.0. In C. H. Steel, M. J. Keppell, P. Gerbic, & S. Housego (Eds.), *Curriculum, Technology & Transformation for an Unknown Future: Proceedings ASCILITE Sydney 2010* (pp. 13-24). Retrieved from http://ascilite.org.au/conferences/sydney10/procs/Alam-full.pdf

Alam, S. L., & Campbell, J. (2009). Using social software to support assessment tasks in information systems: Trialing wiki and blog technologies. *Journal of Informatics Education Research, 11,* 1–28.

Aldrich, C. (2009). Virtual worlds, simulations, and games for education: A unifying view. *Innovate, 5*(5). Retrieved from http://www.innovateonline.info/pdf/vol5_issue5/Virtual_Worlds,_Simulations,_and_Games_for_Education-__A_Unifying_View.pdf

Alton-Lee, A. (2008). *Designing and supporting teacher professional development to improve valued student outcome.* Paper presented at the Education of Teachers Symposium, International Academy of Education Meeting.

Alvino, S., Asensio-Perez, J. I., Dimitriadis, Y., & Hernandez-Leo, D. (2009). Supporting the reuse of effective CSCL learning designs through social structure representations. *Distance Education, 30*(2), 239–258. doi:10.1080/01587910903023215

Anderson, C. (2010). *Learning theories and Second Life.* Retrieved from http://www.cathyandersonblog.com/?p=235

Anderson, L. S., & Hildenbrand, E. K. (2009). Can Facebook replace face-to-face? *Learning and Leading with Technology, 37*(2), 8–9.

Anderson, T. (2003). Getting the mix right again: An updated and theoretical rationale for interaction. *International Review of Research in Open and Distance Learning, 4*(2). Retrieved from http://www.irrodl.org/index.php/irrodl/article/view/149/230

Anderson, T., & Elloumi, F. (Eds.). (2004). *Theory and practice of online learning.* Athabasca University.

Angeli, C., & Valanides, N. (2009). Epistemological and methodological issues for the conceptualization, development, and assessment of ECT-TPCK: Advances in technological pedagogical content knowledge (TPCK). *Computers & Education, 52,* 154–168. doi:10.1016/j.compedu.2008.07.006

Arapi, P., Moumoutzis, N., Mylonakis, M., & Christodoulakis, S. (2007). *A pedagogy-driven personalization framework to support adaptive learning experiences.* Paper presented at the IEEE International Conference on Advanced Learning Technologies, ICALT 2007., Niigata, Japan.

Arceo, F. D. B., & Rojas, G. H. (2002). *Estrategias docentes para un aprendizaje significativo: Una interpretación constructivista.* Mc Graw Hill.

Arnold, N., Ducate, L., & Kost, C. (2009). Collaborative writing in wikis: Insights from culture projects in German classes. In Lomicka, L., & Lord, G. (Eds.), *The next generation: Social networking and online collaboration in foreign language learning* (pp. 115–144). San Marcos, TX: Computer Assisted Language Instruction Consortium.

Arsham, H. (2002). Impact of the internet on learning and teaching. *USDLA Journal, 6*(3).

Attwell, G. (2007). *Personal learning environments – The future of eLearning?* eLearning Papers, 2. Retrieved from http://www.elearningeuropa.info/files/media/media11561.pdf

Australian Government AusAid (2007). *Australian agency for international development: Indonesia education program strategy 2007ystem.*

Autor, D., Levy, F., & Murnane, R. (2003). The skill content of recent technological change: An empirical exploration. *The Quarterly Journal of Economics, 118*(4), 1279–1333. doi:10.1162/003355303322552801

Azra, A., Afrianty, D., & Hefner, R. (2007). *Pesantren* and madrasa: Muslim schools and national ideals in Indonesia. In Hefner, R., & Zaman, M. Q. (Eds.), *Schooling Islam: The culture and politics of modern Muslim education* (pp. 172–199). Princeton, NJ: Princeton University Press.

Bagley, C., & Chou, C. (2007). Collaboration and the importance for novices in learning Java computer programming. *ACM SIGCSE Bulletin, 39*(3), 211–215. doi:10.1145/1269900.1268846

Barab, S., Thomas, M., Dodge, T., Carteaux, R., & Tuzun, H. (2005). Making learning fun: Quest Atlantis, a game without guns. *Educational Technology Research and Development, 53*(1), 86–107. doi:10.1007/BF02504859

Barak, M., & Doppelt, Y. (2000). Using portfolio to enhance creative thinking. *The Journal of Technology Studies, 26*(2), 16–25.

Bareisa, E., Karciauskas, E., Macikenas, E., & Motiejunas, K. (2007). Research and development of teaching software engineering processes. *Proceedings of the 2007 International Conference on Computer Systems and Technologies,* (p. 75). ACM Press.

Barkley, E. F. (2010). *Student engagement techniques: A handbook for faculty.* San Francisco, CA: Jossey-Bass.

Barkley, E., Cross, K., & Major, C. H. (2005). *Collaborative learning techniques - A handbook for college faculty.* The Jossey-Bass Higher and Adult Education Series.

Barrows, H. S. (1985). *How to design a problem-based curriculum for the preclinical years.* New York, NY: Springer Publishing Company.

Barrows, H. S. (1996). Problem-based learning in medicine and beyond: A brief overview. *New Directions for Teaching and Learning, 68,* 3–11. doi:10.1002/tl.37219966804

Barrows, H., & Kelson, A. (1998). *Problem-based learning: A total approach to education.* Springfield, IL: SIU School of Medicine, Department of Medical Education Springfield.

Barton, G. (1996). The liberal, progressive roots of Abdurrahman Wahid's thought. In Barton, G., & Fealy, G. (Eds.), *Nadhlatul Ulama, traditional Islam and modernity in Indonesia* (pp. 190–226). Clayton, Australia: Monash Asia Institute.

Barton, G. (1997). Indonesia's Nurcholish Madjid and Abdurrahman Wahid as intellectual Ulama: The meeting of Islamic traditionalism and modernism in neo-modernist thought. *Islam & Christian-Muslim Relations, 83,* 323. doi:10.1080/09596419708721130

BBC. (2010). *George Osborne outlines detail of £6.2bn spending cuts.* Retrieved from http://news.bbc.co.uk/2/hi/uk_news/politics/8699522.stm

Becker, J. H. (1999). *Internet use by teachers: Conditions of professional use and teacher-directed student use.* Retrieved from http://www.eric.ed.gov/ERICWebPortal/search/detailmini.jsp?_nfpb=true&_&ERICExtSearch_SearchValue_0=ED429564&ERICExtSearch_SearchType_0=no&accno=ED429564

Belawati, T. (2007). Open and distance education in the Asia Pacific region: Indonesia. In Shive, G., Jegebe, O., Haynes, P., & Smith, J. L. (Eds.), *Online learning and teaching in higher education: Indonesia* (pp. 171–188). Hong Kong: Open University of Hong Kong.

Bellows, S., & Jankowski, J. (2009). Live and learn. *Contract (New York, N.Y.), 50*(2), 32–33.

Bender, T. (2005). *Role playing in online education: A teaching tool to enhance student engagement and sustained learning.* Retrieved from http://www.innovateonline.info/index.php?view=article&id=57

Bennett, W. L., Wells, C., & Rank, A. (2008). *Young citizens and civic learning: Two paradigms of citizenship in the digital age.* Report from the Civic learning online project.

Bennett, R. E., Jenkins, F., Persky, H., & Weiss, A. (2003). Assessing complex problem solving performances. *Assessment in Education, 10*(3), 347–359. doi:10.1080/0969594032000148181

Benson, R., & Samarawickrema, G. (2009). Addressing the context of e-learning: Using transactional distance theory to inform design. *Distance Education, 30*(1), 5–21. doi:10.1080/01587910902845972

Berge, Z. L. (1999). Interaction in post-secondary web-based learning. *Educational Technology, 39*(1), 5–11.

Berrett, C. (2012, February 5). Harvard conference seeks to jolt university teaching. *The Chronicle of Higher Education.*

Bhabha, H. (1992). The third space: Interview with Homi Bhabha. In Rutherford, J. (Ed.), *Identity: Community, culture, difference* (pp. 207–221). London, UK: Lawrence and Wishart.

Bhabha, H. (1994). *The location of culture.* London, UK: Routledge.

Bigum, C. (1998). Boundaries, barriers and borders: Teaching science in a wired world. *Australian Science Teachers Journal, 44*(1), 13–24.

Bloom, B. (1956). *Taxonomy of educational objectives: The classification of educational goals.* London, UK: Longman.

Boettcher, J. V. (2006, 28 February). The rise of student performance content. *Campus Technology.* Retrieved from http://campustechnology.com/articles/2006/02/the-rise-of-student-performance-content.aspx

Boler, M. (1999). *Feeling power: Emotions and education.* London, UK: Routledge.

Bonk, C., & Dennen, V. (2003). Frameworks for research, design, benchmarks, training, and pedagogy in web-based distance education. In Moore, M. G., & Anderson, W. G. (Eds.), *Handbook of distance education* (pp. 329–348). Mahwah, NJ: L. Erlbaum Associates.

Boudett, K., City, E., & Murnane, R. (Eds.). (2005). *Data Wise: A step-by-step guide to using assessment results to improve teaching and learning.* Cambridge, MA: Harvard University Press.

Boulos, M., Maramba, I., & Wheeler, S. (2006). Wikis, blogs and podcasts: A new generation of web-based tools for virtual collaborative clinical practice and education. *BMC Medical Education, 6*(41). Retrieved from http://www.biomedcentral.com/1472-6920/6/41

Bower, M., Hedberg, J., & Kuswara, A. (2009). Conceptualizing Web 2.0 enabled learning designs. In *Same Places, Different Spaces: Proceedings Ascilite* Auckland 2009. Retrieved from http://www.ascilite.org.au/conferences/auckland09/procs/bower.pdf

Boyle, D., Nackerud, L., & Kilpatrick, A. (1997). The road less traveled: Cross-cultural, international experiential learning. *International Social Work, 42*(2), 201–214. doi:10.1177/002087289904200208

Bradley, D., Noonan, P., Nugent, H., & Scales, B. (2008). *Review of Australian higher education: Final report.* Australian Government: Department of Education, employment and workplace Relations. Retrieved from http://www.deewr.gov.au/HigherEducation/Review/Pages/default.aspx

Bratitsis, T., & Dimitracopoulou, A. (2006). Monitoring and analysing group interactions in asynchronous discussions with the DIAS system. In *Proceedings of the 12th International Workshop on Groupware, GRIWG' 2006, in: Lecture Notes in Computer Science, vol. 4154,* (pp. 54–61). Berlin, Germany: Springer.

Brézillon, P., & Araujo, R. M. D. (2005). Reinforcing shared context to improve collaboration. In *Proceedings of Revue d'Intelligence Artificielle* (pp. 537-556).

Broadribb, S., & Carter, C. (2009). Using Second Life in human resource development. *British Journal of Educational Technology, 40*(3), 547–550. doi:10.1111/j.1467-8535.2009.00950.x

Brown, D., & Warschauer, M. (2006). From the university to the elementary classroom: Students' experiences in learning to integrate technology in instruction. *Journal of Technology and Teacher Education, 14*(3), 599–621.

Bruner, J. S. (1966). *Towards a theory of instruction.* New York, NY: Norton.

Brusilovsky, P. (2004). *Knowledge tree: A distributed architecture for adaptive e-learning.* Paper presented at the International World Wide Web Conference - Proceedings of the 13th international www conference - Session: Adaptive e-learning systems, New York.

Brusilovsky, P. (2001). Adaptive hypermedia. *User Modeling and User-Adapted Interaction, 11,* 87–110. doi:10.1023/A:1011143116306

Brusilovsky, P., & Millan, E. (2007). User models for adaptive hypermedia and adaptive educational systems. In Brusilovsky, P., Kobsa, A., & Nejdl, W. (Eds.), *The adaptive Web.* Berlin, Germany: Springer. doi:10.1007/978-3-540-72079-9_1

Bryant, T. (2006). Social software in academia. *EDUCAUSE Quarterly, 29*(2), 61–64.

Bull, G., Bull, G., & Kajder, S. (2004). Tapped in. *Learning and Leading with Technology, 31*(5), 34–37.

Bunt, G. (2009). *iMuslims: Rewiring the house of Islam.* Chapel Hall, NC: University of North Carolina Press.

Bunt, G. (2000). *Virtually Islamic: Computer mediated communication and cyber Islamic environments.* Cardiff, UK: University of Wales Press.

Bunt, G. (2003). *Islam in the digital age: E-jihad, online fatwas and cyber Islamic environments.* London, UK: Pluto Press.

Burdett, J. (2003). A switch to online takes time: academics' experiences of ICT innovation. In G. Crisp, D. Thiele, I. Scholten, S. Barker, & J. Baron (Eds.), *Interact, Integrate, Impact: Proceedings of the 20th Annual Conference of the Australasian Society for Computers in Learning in Tertiary Education* (pp. 84-93). Adelaide, 7-10 December.

Burgos, D., Tattersall, C., & Koper, R. (2006). *Representing adaptive eLearning strategies in IMS learning design.* Paper presented at the Workshop Learning Networks for Lifelong Competence Development, Sofia, Bulgaria.

Burgos, D., Tattersall, C., & Koper, R. (2007). How to represent adaptation in e-learning with IMS learning design. *Interactive Learning Environments, 15*(2), 161–170. doi:10.1080/10494820701343736

Capauno, N., Miranda, S., & Ritrovato, P. (2009). *Creation and delivery of complex learning experiences: the ELeGI approach.* Paper presented at the Internation Conference on Complex, Intelligent and Software Intensive Systems, Japan.

Care, E., & Griffin, P. (2009). Assessment is for teaching. *Independence, 34*(2), 56-59.

Carmel, E. (2009). *Global software teams: Collaborating across borders and time zones.* NJ: Prentice-Hall.

Carnaby, P. (2009). *Citizen-centric content, digital equity and the preservation of community memory.* World library and Information Congress:75th IFLA General Conference and Council, 23-27 August 2009, Milan, Italy. Retrieved from http://www.ifla.org/annual-conference/ifla75/index.htm

Carr, N. (2008, July/August). Is Google making us stupid?' *Atlantic Magazine.*

Carr, N. (2009). New media mayhem. *The American School Board Journal, 196*(10), 45–47.

Carter, T. (2004). Recipe for growth. *ABA Journal.* Retrieved from http://www.abajournal.com/magazine/article/recipe_for_growth/

Caruana, V., & Hanstock, J. (2003). *Internationalising the curriculum: From policy to practice.* Retrieved from www.edu.salford.ac.uk/her/proceedings/papers/vc

Castells, M. (1996). *The rise of the network society.* Cambridge, MA: Blackwell Publishers.

Central Intelligence Agency. (2010). World fact book: Australia. Retrieved from https://www.cia.gov/library/publications/the-world-factbook/geos/as.html

Chalfoun, P., & Frasson, C. (2011). Subliminal cues while teaching: HCI techniques for enhanced learning. *Advances in Human-Computer Interaction.* doi:10.1155/2011/968753

Chang Lai, M. L., & Yang, K. Y. (2006). *A study of biodiversity problem-based learning portfolio for college freshmen.* Paper presented at the 22nd Annual Conference of Science Education.

Chang, A., & Kannan, P. (2008). *Leveraging Web 2.0 in government.* Industry research paper. Retrieved from http://www.businessofgovernment.org/

Chang, C. C., & Chou, P. N. (2006). Development, implementation and effect of a competency-based web learning system. *Chinese Journal of Science Education, 14*(2), 209–235.

Chang, C. C., & Tung, Y. H. (2000). Constructing an e-learning portfolio on World Wide Web. *Instructional Technology & Media, 51,* 37–45.

Charskey, D., Kish, M., Briskin, J., Hathaway, S., Walsh, K., & Barajas, N. (2009). Millennials need training too: Using communication technology to facilitate teamwork. *TechTrends, 53*(6).

Chen, D. L. (2002). *Design and implementation of a web-based portfolio supporting system.* Unpublished Master's Thesis. National Sun Yat Sen University, Kaohsiung, Taiwan.

Chen, Y. C. (2011). *The influence of problem-based learning on primary school senior students' scientific attitude and learning strategy.* Unpublished Master's thesis. National Pingtung University of Education, Pingtung, Taiwan.

Chen, F., & Wang, T. (2009). Social conversation and effective discussion in online group learning. *Education Tech Research, 57*(5), 587–612. doi:10.1007/s11423-009-9121-1

Cherbakov, L., Brunner, R., Smart, R., & Liu, C. (2009). Enable far-reaching enterprise collaboration with virtual spaces, Part 1: Introduction to the opportunities and tchnologies. *Convergence,* 1–22.

Chickering, A. W., & Gamson, Z. F. (1987). Seven principles for good practice in undergraduate education. *American Association for Higher Education Bulletin,* March.

Chickering, A., & Ehrmann, S. C. (1996). Implementing the seven principles: technology as a lever. *American Association for Higher Education Bulletin,* October, 3-6.

Chiu, B., & Yu, Y. (2002). Promoting the use of information technology in education via lightweight authoring tools. *Proceedings of the International Conference on Computers in Education* (ICCE '02), Auckland, New Zealand.

Chiu, H. D. (2003). *A comparative study of establishing the basic concepts in junior high school electromagnetism by subject-based learning and problem-based learning.* Unpublished Master's thesis. National Chiao Tung University, Hsinchu, Taiwan.

Chou, C. C., & Hart, R. K. (2012). The pedagogical considerations in the design of virtual worlds for organization learning. In Yang, H., & Yuen, S. (Eds.), *Handbook of research on practices and outcomes in virtual worlds and environment* (pp. 561–569). Hershey, PA: Information Science Reference/IGI Global.

Chung, C. J., Rodriguez, M., & O'Hara, S. (2005). Building a community of practice in electronic portfolios. *Proceeding of SITE 2005—Society for Information. Technology & Teacher Education International Conference,* Phoenix, AZ, USA, (pp. 2188-2192).

Cifuentes, L., Sharp, A., Bulu, S., Benz, M., & Stough, L. (2010). Developing a Web 2.0-based system with user-authored content for community use and teacher education. *Educational Technology Research and Development*, *58*(4), 377–398. doi:10.1007/s11423-009-9141-x

Clarke, J., Dede, C., Ketelhut, D. J., & Nelson, B. (2006). A design-based research strategy to promote scalability for educational innovations. *Educational Technology*, *46*(3), 27–36.

Clark, R. (2004). What works in distance learning: Instructional strategies. In O'Neil, H. (Ed.), *What works in distance learning: Guidelines*. Greenwich, CT: Information Age Publishers.

Cogan, J., & Derricott, R. (1988). *Citizenship for the 21st century: An international perspective on education.*

Coldwell, J., Craig, A., & Goold, A. (2011). Using e technologies for active learning. *Interdisciplinary Journal of Information. Knowledge and Management*, *6*, 1–12.

Coldwell, J., & Newlands, D. A. (2004). Deakin online: An evolving case study. *Journal of Issues in Informing Science and Information Technology*, *1*, 1–10.

Collazos, C., Giraldo, F., Zapata, S., Ochoa, S., Lund, M., Aballay, L., & Clunie, G. (2010). *CODILA: A collaborative and distributed learning activity applied to software engineering courses in Latin American Universities*. International Conference on Collaborative Computing COLLABORATECOM.

Commonwealth of Australia. (2009). *Transforming Australia's higher education system*. Canberra, Australia.

Coniam, D., & Lee, M. (2008). Incorporating wikis into the teaching of English writing. *Hong Kong Teachers'. Centre Journal*, *7*, 52–67.

Conole, G., & Oliver, M. (Eds.). (2007). *Contemporary perspectives in e-learning research: Themes, methods and impact on practice. The Open and Flexible Learning Series*. UK: Routledge.

Cooke, M., & Lawrence, B. B. (Eds.). (2005). *Muslim networks from Hajj to hip hop*. Chapel Hill, NC: University of North Carolina Press.

Council of Europe. (2010). *Communication from the Commission: Europe 2020 – A strategy for smart, sustainable and inclusive growth*. COM(2010). Retrieved from http://ec.europa.eu/education/llp/doc/call12/part1_en.pdf

Courus, G. (2011). Why social media can and is changing education. *Connected Principals*. Retrieved from http://www.connectedprincipals.com/archives/3024

Craig, A., Coldwell, J., & Goold, A. (2009). The role of the online teacher in supporting student learning: A case study. In T. Bastiaens, J. Dron, & C. Xin (Eds.), *World Conference on E-Learning in Corporate, Government, Healthcare, and Higher Education* (pp. 1181 – 1187). Vancouver, Canada: AACE.

Craig, A., Goold, A., Coldwell, J., & Mustard, J. (2008). Perceptions of roles and responsibilities in online learning: A case study. *Interdisciplinary Journal of E-Learning and Learning Objects*, *4*, 205–223.

Crook, C., Fisher, T., Graber, R., Harrison, C., & Lewin, C. (2008, September). *Implementing Web 2.0 in secondary schools: Impacts, barriers and issues*. Retrieved from http://decra.ioe.ac.uk/148/

Csapó, B., Ainley, J., Bennett, R., Latour, T., & Law, N. (2011). Technological issues for computer-based assessment. In Griffin, P., Care, E., & McGaw, B. (Eds.), *Assessment and teaching of 21st century skills*. New York, NY: Springer.

Damian, D., & Zowghi, D. (2003). Requirements engineering challenges in multi-site software development organizations. *Requirements Engineering Journal*, *8*(1), 149–160. doi:10.1007/s00766-003-0173-1

Danaher, P. A., Danaher, G. R., & Moriarty, B. J. (2003). Space invaders and pedagogical innovators: Regional educational understandings from Australian occupational travellers. *Journal of Research in Rural Education*, *18*(3), 164–169.

Darhower, M. (2002). Interactional factors of synchronous computer-mediated communication in the intermediate L2 class: A sociocultural case study. *CALICO Journal*, *19*(2), 249–277.

Darling-Hammond, L. (1990). *Teacher supply, demand and quality*. Washington, DC: National Board for Professional Standards.

De Wert, M. H., Babinski, L. M., & Jones, B. D. (2003). Safe passages: Providing online support to beginning teachers. *Journal of Teacher Education, 54*(4), 311–320. doi:10.1177/0022487103255008

De Wever, B., Van Keer, H., Schellens, T., & Valcke, M. (2009). Structuring asynchronous discussion groups: The impact of role assignment and self-assessment on students' levels of knowledge construction through social negotiation. *Journal of Computer Assisted Learning, 25*(2), 177–188. doi:10.1111/j.1365-2729.2008.00292.x

Deakin University. (2008). *Student charter*. Retrieved from http://theguide.deakin.edu.au/TheDeakinGuide.nsf/7264c32fe71924374a2566f3000a65de/60045aea1a0c4d47ca2574d3008361c1?OpenDocument&Highlight=0,student,charter

Delfino, M., & Manca, S. (2007). The expression of social presence through the use of figurative language in a web-based learning environment. *Computers in Human Behavior, 23*, 2190–2211. doi:10.1016/j.chb.2006.03.001

Delisle, R. (2003). *How to use problem-based learning in the classroom* (Chou, T. S., Trans.). Taipei, Taiwan: Psychological.

DeValenzuela, J. (2007, August 22). *Sociocultural theory*. Retrieved from http://www.unm.edu/~devalenz/handouts/sociocult.html

Dewey, J. (1938). *Experience and education*. New York, NY: Collier Books.

Dey, E. L., Burn, H. E., & Gerdes, D. (2009). Bringing the classroom to the web: Effects of using new technologies to capture and deliver lectures. *Research in Higher Education, 50*(4), 377–393. doi:10.1007/s11162-009-9124-0

Dieterle, E., & Clarke, J. (in press). Multi-user virtual environments for teaching and learning. In Pagani, M. (Ed.), *Encyclopedia of multimedia technology and networking* (2nd ed.). Hershey, PA: Idea Group, Inc. doi:10.4018/978-1-60566-014-1.ch139

DiGiovanni, E., & Nagaswami, G. (2001). Online peer review: An alternative to face-to-face? *ELT Journal, 55*(3), 263–272. doi:10.1093/elt/55.3.263

Dillenbourg, P. (1999). What do you mean by 'collaborative learning. In Dillenbourg, P. (Ed.), *Collaborative-learning: Cognitive and computational approaches* (pp. 1–19). New York, NY: Elsevier Science, Inc.

Dillenbourg, P. (2005). Designing biases that augment socio-cognitive interactions. In Bromme, R., Hesse, W., & Spada, H. (Eds.), *Barriers and biases in computer-mediated knowledge communication - and how they may be overcome* (pp. 243–264). Dordrecht, The Netherlands: Kluwer. doi:10.1007/0-387-24319-4_11

Dix, A., Roselli, T., & Sutinen, E. (Eds.). (2006). eLearning and human-computer interaction: Exploring design synergies for more effective learning experience. *Journal of Educational Technology & Society, 9*(4), 1–2.

Donnelly, R., & O'Rourke, K. (2007). What now? Evaluating e-learning CPD practice in Irish third-level education. *Journal of Further and Higher Education, 31*(1), 31–40. doi:10.1080/03098770601167864

Downes, S. (2005, October). E-learning 2.0. *ELearn*. Retrieved from http://www.elearnmag.org/subpage.cfm?section=articles&article=29-1

Dreyfus, S., & Dreyfus, H. (1980). *A five-stage model of the mental activities involved in directed skill acquisition*. Washington, DC: Storming Media.

Dron, J. (2007). Designing the undesignable: Social software and control. *Journal of Educational Technology & Society, 10*(3), 60–71.

Eberhardt, D. M. (2007). Facing up to Facebook. *About Campus, 12*(4), 18–26. doi:10.1002/abc.219

Ebner, M., Lienhardt, C., Rohs, M., & Meyer, I. (2010). Microblogs in higher education- A chance to facilitate informal and process oriented education? *Computers & Education, 55*, 92–100. doi:10.1016/j.compedu.2009.12.006

Edirisingha, P., Nie, M., Pluciennik, M., & Young, R. (2009). Socialisation for learning at a distance in a 3-D multi-user virtual environment. *British Journal of Educational Technology, 40*(3), 458–479. doi:10.1111/j.1467-8535.2009.00962.x

Elliott, J. L. (2005). *AquaMOOSE 3D: A constructionist approach to math learning motivated by artistic expression*. Unpublished Doctoral Dissertation, Georgia Institute of Technology, Atlanta, GA.

Enriquez, J. G. (2009). Discontent with content analysis of online transcripts. *Association for Learning Technology Journal, 17*(2), 101–113. doi:10.1080/09687760903033066

Ericsson, K. A., & Simon, H. A. (1993). *Protocol analysis: Verbal reports as data (rev. ed.).* Cambridge, MA: The MIT Press.

Fáber, F. D., & César, C. A. (2011). *Red latinoamericana de investigación aplicada en ingeniería de software experimental: Un esfuerzo de integración latinoamericano para la investigación y cooperación en ingeniería de software.* Editorial Universidad del Quindío.

Facer, K., & Sandford, R. (2009). The next 25 years? Future scenarios and future directions for education and technology. *Journal of Computer Assisted Learning, 26,* 74–93. doi:10.1111/j.1365-2729.2009.00337.x

Fanning, E. (2009). Instructional design factors as they relate to the creation of a virtual learning environment. *Journal of Interactive Instruction Development, 21*(2), 24–42.

Farrell, G. (Ed.). (2001). *The changing face of virtual education.* Vancouver, Canada: Commonwealth of Learning.

Fitze, M. (2006). Discourse and participation in ESL face-to-face and written electronic conferences. *Language Learning & Technology, 10*(1), 67–86.

Følstad, A., & Knutsen, J. (2010). Online user feedback in early phases of the design process: Lessons learnt from four design cases. *Advances in Human-Computer Interaction, 9.* Retrieved from doi:10.1155/2010/956918

Foss, J., & Cristea, A. (2009). *Adaptive hypermedia content authoring using MOT3.0.* Paper presented at the 7th International Workshop on Authoring of Adaptive and Adaptable Hypermedia, Nice, France.

Fowler-Finn, T. (2009). *Instructional Rounds Australia.* Paper presented at the Instructional Rounds Conference, Harvard University, May.

Franzoni, A., & Asar, S. (2009). Student learning styles adaptation method based on teaching strategies and electronic media. *Journal of Educational Technology & Society, 12*(4), 15–29.

Frohberg, D., Goth, C., & Schwabe, G. (2009). Mobile learning projects: A critical analysis of the state of the art. *Journal of Computer Assisted Learning, 25*(4), 307–331. doi:10.1111/j.1365-2729.2009.00315.x

Frydenberg, M. (2006). Principles and pedagogy: The two P's of podcasting in the information technology classroom. In D. Colton, W. J. Tastle, M. Hensel, & A. A. Abdullat (Eds.), *Proceedings of ISECON 2006,* Vol. 23 (Dallas) (§3354). Chicago, IL: AITP. Retrieved from http://proc.isecon.org/2006/3354/ISECON.2006.Frydenberg.pdf

Fullan, M., Hill, P., & Crévola, C. (2006). *Breakthrough.* Thousand Oaks, CA: Corwin Press.

Fuller, J. (2009). Engaging students in large classes using Elluminate. In T. Robinson, T. Tang and A. Fletcher (Eds.), *Proceedings of Australasian Teaching Economics Conference,* School of Economics and Finance, Queensland University of Technology, Brisbane, Queensland, (pp. 84-97).

Gaide, S. (2006). E-portfolios supercharge performance-based student assessment. *Distance Education Report,* 4-6.

Galarneau, L. (2005). *Spontaneous communities of learning: Learning ecosystems in massively multiplayer online gaming environments.* Retrieved from http://papers.ssrn.com/sol3/papers.cfm?abstract_id=810064

Garrison, D. R., Anderson, T., & Archer, W. (2000). Critical inquiry in a text-based environment: Computer conferencing in higher education. *The Internet and Higher Education, 2*(2-3), 87–105. doi:10.1016/S1096-7516(00)00016-6

Gaver, W. W., Smets, G., & Overbeeke, K. (1995). A virtual window on media space. In I. R. Katz, R. L. Mack, L. Marks, M. B. Rosson, & J. Nielsen (Eds.), *Proceedings of the ACM CHI 95 Human Factors in Computing Systems Conference,* May 7-11, 1995.

Geertz, C. (1960). The Javanese Kijaji: The changing role of a cultural broker. *Comparative Studies in Society and History, 2*(2), 228–249. doi:10.1017/S0010417500000670

Geertz, C. (1988). *Works and lives: The anthropologist as author.* Cambridge, UK: Polity Press.

Gibson, A., Courtney, N., Ward, A., Wilcox, D., & Holtham, C. (2009). *Social by social: A practical guide to using new technologies to deliver social impact.*

Gilroy, M. (2009, September 21). Higher education migrates to YouTube and social networks. *The Hispanic Outlook in Higher Education, 19*, 12–14.

Giraldo, F. D., Collazos, C. A., Ochoa, S. F., Zapata, S., & Torres de Clunie, G. (2010). Teaching software engineering from a collaborative perspective: Some Latin-American experiences. *Proceedings of DEXA Workshops, 2010*, 97–101.

Glaser, R. (2007). *Personal communication*, 28 June.

Glaser, R. (1963). Instructional technology and the measurement of learning outcomes: Some questions. *The American Psychologist, 18*, 519–521. doi:10.1037/h0049294

Glaser, R. (1991). Expertise and assessment. In Wittrock, M. C., & Baker, E. L. (Eds.), *Testing and cognition* (pp. 17–30). Englewood Cliffs, NJ: Prentice Hall.

Godwin, B. (2008). *Matrix of Web 2.0 technology tools and government.* U.S. GSA Office of Citizen Services and Innovative Technologies. Retreived from http://www.usa.gov/webcontent/documents/Web_Technology_Matrix.pdf

Gordon-Murnane, L. (2010). We need your input. *Searcher, 18*(3), 26–88.

Government 2.0 Taskforce Report. (2009). *Engage: Getting on with Government 2.0.* Retrieved from http://www.finance.gov.au/publications/gov20taskforcereport/index.html

Greci, L., Ramloll, R., Hurst, S., Garman, K., Beedasy, J., & Pieper, E. Agha, Z. (2009). *Disaster planning.* Best practice poster session presented at the California Hospital Association's Fifth Annual Disaster Planning for California Hospitals Workshop, Sacramento.

Greci, L., Ramloll, R., Hurst, S., Garman, K., Beedasy, J., Pieper, E., et al. (2010). *Pandemic flu patient surge planning and practice in a virtual environment.* 2010 Integrated Training Summit, Las Vegas, Nevada.

Greenfield, P. (2009). Technology and informal education: What is taught, what is learned. *Science Magazine*, 323-69.

Greenhow, C., Robelia, B., & Hughes, J. (2009). Learning, teaching and scholarship in a digital age. [ProQuest Hospital Collection.]. *Educational Researcher, 38*(4), 246–259. doi:10.3102/0013189X09336671

Griffin, P. (2000). *ARC learning profiles: User's manual.* Unpublished manuscript, Melbourne.

Griffin, P. (2007). The comfort of competence and the uncertainty of assessment. *Studies in Educational Evaluation, 33*, 87–99. doi:10.1016/j.stueduc.2007.01.007

Griffin, P. (2009). Teacher's use of assessment data. In Wyatt-Smith, C., & Cumming, J. (Eds.), *Educational assessment in the 21st cenutry.* Dordrecht, The Netherlands: Springer. doi:10.1007/978-1-4020-9964-9_10

Griffin, P., Care, E., & McGaw, B. (2011). The changing role of education and schools. In Griffin, P., Care, E., & McGaw, B. (Eds.), *Assessment and teaching of 21st century skills.* New York, NY: Springer. doi:10.1007/978-94-007-2324-5_1

Griffin, P., Murray, L., Care, E., Thomas, A., & Perri, P. (2010). Developmental assessment: Lifting literacy through professional learning teams. *Assessment in Education: Principles. Policy & Practice, 17*(4), 383–397.

Griffin, P., & Nix, P. (1991). *Educational assessment and reporting: A new approach.* Victoria, Australia: Harcourt Brace.

Grodzinsky, F. S., & Wolf, M. J. (2008). Ethical interest in free and pen source software. In Himma, K. E., & Tavani, H. T. (Eds.), *The handbook of information and computer ethics.* New Jersey: John Wiley & Sons. doi:10.1002/9780470281819.ch10

Groff, J., & Mouza, C. (2008). A framework for addressing challenges to classroom technology use. *Association for the Advancement of Computing in Education Journal, 16*(1), 21–46.

Grosseck, G. (2009). *To use or not to use Web 2.0 in higher education?* Procedia - Social and Behavioral. doi:10.1016/j.sbspro.2009.01.087

Guldberg, K., & Mackness, J. (2009). Foundations of communities of practice: Enablers and barriers to participation. *Journal of Computer Assisted Learning, 25*(6), 528–538. doi:10.1111/j.1365-2729.2009.00327.x

Gunawardena, C. N., Lowe, C. A., & Anderson, T. (1997). Analysis of a global online debate and the development of an interactive analysis model for examining social construction of knowledge in computer conferencing. *Journal of Educational Computing Research*, *17*(4), 397–431. doi:10.2190/7MQV-X9UJ-C7Q3-NRAG

Gunawardena, C., Hermans, M., Sanchez, D., Richmonds, C., Bohley, M., & Tuttle, R. (2009). A theoretical framework for building online communities of practice with social networking tools. *Educational Media International*, *46*(1), 3–16. doi:10.1080/09523980802588626

Gunawardena, C., & Zittle, F. (1997). Social presence as a predictor of satisfaction within a computer-mediated conferencing environment. *American Journal of Distance Education*, *11*(3), 8–26. doi:10.1080/08923649709526970

Guo, Z. Y. (2009). *A study on effectiveness of applying problem-based learning to electronics course for the electronic information department in vocational high schools*. Unpublished master's thesis. National Taiwan Normal University, Taipei, Taiwan.

Gustin, S. (2011, February 11). *Social media sparked, accelerated Egypt's revolutionary fire*. Retrieved from http://www.wired.com/epicenter/2011/02/egypts-revolutionary-fire/

Gutiérrez, K. D. (2008). Developing a sociocritical literacy in the third space. *Reading Research Quarterly*, *43*(2), 148–164. doi:10.1598/RRQ.43.2.3

Gutiérrez, K. D., Baquedano-Lopez, P., & Turner, M. G. (1997). Putting language back into language arts: When the radical middle meets the third space. *Language Arts*, *75*(5), 368–378.

Hackos, J. T., & Redish, J. C. (1998). *User and task analysis for interface design*. John Wiley & Sons, Inc.

Haddad, S. G. F. (2005). Seek knowledge as far as china. *Living Islam: Islamic Tradition*. Retrieved August 8, 2012, from http://www.livingislam.org/n/skx_e.html

Hall, G. E. (2010). Technology's Achilles heel: Achieving high-quality implementation. *Journal of Research on Technology in Education*, *42*(3), 231–253.

Halverson, R., Grigg, J., Prichett, R., & Thomas, C. (2005). *The new instructional leadership: Creating data-driven instructional systems in schools*. Madison, WI: University of Wisconsin-Madison, Wisconsin Center for Education Research.

Hanewald, R., & White, P. (2008). What, how and why Web 2.0? *Australian Educational Computing*, *23*(2), 3–6.

Hannafin, R., & Sullivan, H. (1995). Learner control in full and lean CAI programs. *Educational Technology Research and Development*, *43*, 19–30. doi:10.1007/BF02300479

Hansen, L. (2009). *What ever happened to Second Life?* Retrieved from http://news.bbc.co.uk/2/hi/8367957.stm

Hara, N., Bonk, C., & Angeli, C. (2000). Content analysis of on-line discussion in an applied educational psychology course. *Instructional Science*, *28*(2), 115–152. doi:10.1023/A:1003764722829

Harris, J. (2005). Our agenda for technology integration: It's time to choose. *Contemporary Issues in Technology & Teacher Education*, *5*(2). Retrieved from http://www.citejournal.org/vol5/iss2/editorial/article1.cfm

Harris, L. (2009). Electronic classroom, electronic community: Designing elearning environments to foster virtual social networks and student learning. In Martin, J., & Hawkins, L. (Eds.), *Information communication technologies for human services education and delivery: Concepts and cases* (pp. 87–104). Hershey, PA: IGI Global. doi:10.4018/978-1-60566-735-5.ch006

Hattie, J. (2009). *Visible learning: A synthesis of over 800 meta-analyses relating to achievement*. London, UK: Routledge.

Hatti, J., & Timperley, H. (2007). The power of feedback. *Review of Educational Research*, *77*(1), 81–112. doi:10.3102/003465430298487

Hauger, D., & Köck, M. (2007). *State of the art of adaptivity in e-learning platforms*. Paper presented at the 15th Workshop on Adaptivity and User Modeling in Interactive Systems, Halle/Saale, Germany.

Haverback, H. R. (2009). Facebook: Uncharted territory in a reading education classroom. *Reading Today*, *27*(2), 34–34.

Hawkins, L., & Pattanayak, S. (2009). Virtual communication for field education placements in a global context. In Martin, J., & Hawkins, L. (Eds.), *Information communication technologies for human services education and delivery: Concepts and cases* (pp. 133–151). Hershey, PA: IGI Global. doi:10.4018/978-1-60566-735-5.ch009

Heiphetz, A., & Woodill, G. (2010). *Training and collaboration with virtual worlds: How to create cost-saving, efficient, and engaging programs*. New York, NY: McGraw Hill.

Helium.com. (2011). *Debate: Is the use of laptops in the classroom beneficial or a distraction?* Retrieved from http://www.helium.com/debates/180273-is-the-use-of-laptops-in-the-classroom-beneficial-or-a-distraction

Hemmi, A., Bayne, S., & Land, R. (2009). The appropriation and repurposing of social technologies in higher education. *Journal of Computer Assisted Learning, 20*(1), 19–30. doi:10.1111/j.1365-2729.2008.00306.x

Henri, F. (1992). Computer conferencing and content analysis. In Kaye, A. R. (Ed.), *Collaborative learning through computer conferencing: The Najaden papers* (pp. 117–136). Berlin, Germany: Springer-Verlag. doi:10.1007/978-3-642-77684-7_8

Herbsleb, J., & Grinter, R. (1999). Coordination, and distance: Conway's law and beyond. *IEEE Software, 16*(5), 63–70. doi:10.1109/52.795103

Herrington, A., Herrington, J., Kervin, L., & Ferry, B. (2006). The design of an online community of practice for beginning teachers. *Contemporary Issues in Technology & Teacher Education, 6*(10), 120–132.

Hewett, T. T., Baecker, R., Card, S., Carey, T., Gasen, J., & Mantei, M. Verplank, W. (1996). *Curricula for human-computer interaction*. Retrieved from http://old.sigchi.org/cdg/cdg2.html#2_1

Hibbets, J. (2010, April 11). *A chat with Cheryl McKinnon*. Retrieved from http://opensource.com/life/10/4/leadership-culture-innovation-with-cheryl-mckinnon

Hidayatullah, S., & Dharmawan, Z. (2003). *Islam virtual: Keberadaan Dunia Islam di Internet*. Ciputat, Indonesia: Penerbit Mifta.

Hill, P., & Crévola, C. (1997). The literacy challenge in Australian primary schools. *IARTV Seminar Series, 69*.

Hill, P., Crévola, C., & Hopkins, D. (2000). Teaching and learning as the heartland of school improvement. *IARTV Seminar Series, 100*.

Hillbrick, A. (2004). *Tuning in with task cards: Middle primary*. Carlton, Australia: Curriculum Corporation.

Hiltz, S. R. (1994). *The virtual classroom: Learning without limits via computer networks*. Norwood, NJ: Ablex Publishing Corporation.

Hollan, J., Hutchins, E., & Kirsh, D. (2000). Distributed cognition: Toward a new foundation for human-computer interaction research. *ACM Transactions on Computer-Human Interaction, 7*(2), 174–194. doi:10.1145/353485.353487

Holmstrom, H., Fitzgerald, B., Agerfalk, P. J., & Conchuir, E. O. (2006). Agile practices reduce distance in global software development. *Information Systems Management*, 7–26. doi:10.1201/1078.10580530/46108.23.3.20060601/93703.2

Ho, M., & Savignon, S. (2007). Face-to-face and computer-mediated peer review in EFL writing. *CALICO Journal, 24*(2), 269–290.

Homer, B., Plass, J., & Blake, L. (2008). The effects of video on cognitive load and social presence in multimedia-learning. *Computers in Human Behavior, 24*(3), 786–797. doi:10.1016/j.chb.2007.02.009

Honeycutt, L. (2001). Comparing e-mail and synchronous conferencing in online peer response. *Written Communication, 18*(1), 26–60. doi:10.1177/0741088301018001002

Hong, H., & Sullivan, F. (2009). Towards an idea-centered, principle-based design approach to support learning as knowledge creation. *Educational Technology Research and Development, 57*(5), 613–627. doi:10.1007/s11423-009-9122-0

Hong, J. J., & Lin, C. L. (2006). *Theory and practice of problem-based learning curriculum development*. Taipei, Taiwan: Shtabook.

Hossain, E., Babar, A. M., Paik, H., & Verner, J. (2009). Risk identification and mitigation processes for using Scrum in global software development: A conceptual framework. In *Proceeding of the Asia Pacific Software Engineering Conference, APSEC 2009*, (pp. 457–464).

Hossain, E., Babar, A. M., & Paik, H. (2009). Using Scrum in global software development: A systematic literature review. *Proceedings of ICGSE, 2009*, 175–184.

Hossain, E., Babar, M. A., & Verner, J. (2009). How can agile practices minimize global software development co-ordination risks? In O'Connor, R. V., Baddoo, N., Cuadrago Gallego, J., Rejas Muslera, R., Smolander, K., & Messnarz, R. (Eds.), *EuroSPI 2009: Communications in Computer and Information Science* (Vol. 42, pp. 81–92). Heidelberg, Germany: Springer. doi:10.1007/978-3-642-04133-4_7

Hossain, E., Bannerman, P., & Jeffery, D. (2011). Scrum practices in global software development: A research framework. In Caivano, D. (Eds.), *Product-focused software process improvement* (pp. 88–102). Berlin, Germany: Springer. doi:10.1007/978-3-642-21843-9_9

Hsu, W. C. (2008). *A study of problem-based learning strategy on energy cognition and conservation for fourth graders*. Unpublished Master's thesis. National Taipei University of Education, Taipei, Taiwan.

Hudson, A. (2011). *Grouputer report: Five ways to improve work group collaboration in virtual meetings*. Technical Report. Retrieved from http://www.grouputer.com/papers/5_ways_to_improve_work_group_collaboration.pdf

Hulme, R., Cracknell, D., & Owens, A. (2009). Learning in third spaces: Developing trans-professional understanding through practitioner enquiry. *Educational Action Research, 17*(4), 537–550. doi:10.1080/09650790903309391

Indonesian Telematics Coordinating Team. (2001). *Five-year action plan for the development and implementation of information and communication technologies (ICT) in Indonesia*.

Ingram, A. L., & Hathorn, L. G. (2004). Methods for analyzing collaboration in online communications. In Roberts, T. S. (Ed.), *Online collaborative learning: Theory and practice* (pp. 215–241). Hershey, PA: Information Science Publishing.

Iqbal, A., Kankaanranta, M., & Neittaanmäki, P. (2010). Engaging learners through virtual worlds. *Procedia - Social and Behavioral Sciences, 2*(2), 3198-3205. Retrieved from http://www.sciencedirect.com/science/journal/18770428

ISTE. (2007). *National educational technology standards and performance indicators for students*. Retrieved from http://www.iste.org/standards/nets-for-students/nets-student-standards-2007.aspx

Iyengar, S., & Jackman, S. (2003). *Technology and politics: Incentives for youth participation*. International Conference on Civic Education Research — 16-18 November, New Orleans.

Jabali, F., & Jamhari. (Eds.). (2003). *The modernization of Islam in Indonesia: an Impact Study on the Cooperation between the IAIN and McGill University*. Jakarta, Indonesia: Indonesia-Canada Islamic Higher Education Project.

Jarmon, L. (2008). Learning in virtual world environments: Social presence, engagement, & pedagogy. In Rogers, P., Berg, G., Boettcher, J., Howard, C., Justice, L., & Schenk, K. (Eds.), *Encyclopedia of distance and online learning*. Hershey, PA: IGI Global.

Jaworski, B. (1996). *Constructivism and teaching: The socio-cultural context*. Retrieved from http://www.grout.demon.co.uk/Barbara/chreods.htm

Jenlink, P., & Carr, A. A. (1996). Conversation as a medium for change in education. *Educational Technology, 36*(1), 31–38.

Jih, H. J., & Chang, H. F. (2001). The instructional design model for problem-based learning. *Instructional Technology & Media, 55*, 17–30.

Jimenez, M., Piattini, M., & Vizcaino, A. (2009). Challenges and improvements in distributed software development: A systematic review. *Advances in Software Engineering*, 1–14. doi:10.1155/2009/710971

Jin, L., & Ingram, A. (2008). Constructing online conversation to support learning. In Luppicini, R. (Ed.), *Handbook of conversation design for instructional applications* (pp. 218–236). IGI Global. doi:10.4018/978-1-59904-597-9.ch014

JISC. (2009). *Higher education in a Web 2.0 world*. Retrieved from http://www.jisc.ac.uk/publications/documents/heWeb2.aspx

Johnson, D., & Johnson, R. (1986). *Circles of learning: Cooperation in the classroom*. Edina, MN: Interaction Book Company.

Johnson, L., Levine, A., Smith, R., & Stone, S. (2010). *The 2010 horizon report*. Austin, TX: The New Media Consortium.

Johnson, L., Smith, R., Willis, H., Levine, A., & Haywood, K. (2011). *The 2011 horizon report*. Austin, TX: The New Media Consortium.

Junco, R., Heiberger, G., & Loken, E. (2010). The effect of Twitter on college student engagement and grades. *Journal of Computer Assisted Learning, 27*(2). doi:doi:10.1111/j.1365-2729.2010.00387.x

Jung, Y. (2008). Influence of sense of presence on intention to participate in a virtual community. *Proceedings of the 41st Hawaii International Conference on System Science*, Vol. 325. Retrieved from http://www.computer.org/comp/proceedings/hicss/2008/3075/00/30750325.pdf

Kafai, Y. B. (2006). Playing and making games for learning: Instructionist and constructionist perspectives for game studies. *Games and Culture, 1*(1), 36–40. doi:10.1177/1555412005281767

Kankaanranta, M., & Neittaanmaki, P. (Eds.). (2009). *Design and use of serious games*. New York, NY: Springer. doi:10.1007/978-1-4020-9496-5

Kaplan, A., & Haenlein, M. (2010). Users of the world, unite! The challenges and opportunities of social media. *Business Horizons, 53*(1), 59–68. doi:10.1016/j.bushor.2009.09.003

Kearsley, G., & Lynch, W. (1996). Structural issues in distance education. *Journal of Education for Business, 71*(2), 167–191.

Kessler, S. (2010, 5 November). Twitter increases student engagement. Mashable/Social Media blog. Retrieved from from http://www.mashable.com/2010/11/04/twitter-student-engagement//r:t

Kessler, G. (2009). Student-initiated attention to form in wiki-based collaborative writing. *Language Learning & Technology, 13*(1), 79–95.

Kessler, G., & Bikowski, D. (2010). Developing collaborative autonomous learning abilities in computer-mediated language learning: Attention to meaning among students in wiki space. *Computer Assisted Language Learning, 23*(1), 41–58. doi:10.1080/09588220903467335

Ketelhut, D., Dede, C., Clarke, J., Nelson, B., & Bowman, C. (in press). Studying situated learning in a multi-user virtual environment. In Baker, E., Dickieson, J., Wulfeck, W., & O'Neil, H. (Eds.), *Assessment of problem solving using simulations*. Mahwah, NJ: Lawrence Erlbaum Associates.

Ketelhut, D., Nelson, B., Clarke, J., & Dede, C. (2009). A multiuser virtual environment for building and assessing higher order inquiry skills in science. *British Journal of Educational Technology, 41*(1), 56–68. doi:10.1111/j.1467-8535.2009.01036.x

Khan, S. (2000). *Muslim women: Crafting a North American identity*. Gainesville, FL: University Press of Florida.

Kirschner, P. (2002). Cognitive load theory: Implications of cognitive load theory on the design of learning. *Learning and Instruction, 12*(1), 1–10. doi:10.1016/S0959-4752(01)00014-7

Knauf, R., Sakurai, Y., Takada, K., & Tsuruta, S. (2010). *Personalised learning processes by data mining*. Paper presented at the 10th IEEE International Conference on Advanced Learning Technologies (ICALT 2010), Sousse, Tunisia.

Kolb, D. A. (1984). *Experiential learning: Experience as the source of learning and development*. Englewood Cliffs, NJ: Prentice-Hall, Inc.

Kolb, D. A., Boyatzis, R. E., & Mainemelis, C. (2009). Experiential learning theory: Previous research and new directions. In Sternberg, R. J., & Zhang, L. F. (Eds.), *Perspectives on cognitive, learning, and thinking styles* (pp. 193–200). Lawrence Erlbaum.

Krathwohl, A., Bloom, B., & Masia, B. (1964). *Taxonomy of educational objectives: The classification of educational goals. Handbook II: The affective domain*. New York, NY: Longman Green.

Kreijns, K., Kirschner, P., & Jochems, W. (2002). The sociability of computer-supported collaborative learning environments. *Journal of Educational Technology & Society, 5*(1), 8–22.

Kreijns, K., Kirschner, P., & Jochems, W. (2003). Identifying the pitfalls for social interaction in computer-supported collaborative learning environments: A review of the research. *Computers in Human Behavior, 19*, 335–353. doi:10.1016/S0747-5632(02)00057-2

Krishna, S., Sahay, S., & Walsham, G. (2004). Managing cross-cultural issues in global software outsourcing. *Communications of the ACM, 47*(4), 44–47. doi:10.1145/975817.975818

Kumar, V. (2007, July 18-20). *Innovations in e-pedagogy.* Paper presented at the Seventh IEEE International Conference on Advanced Learning Technologies (ICALT 2007), Niigata, Japan.

Kumar, D. D. (2010). Approaches to interactive video anchors in problem-based science learning. *Journal of Science Education and Technology, 19*(1), 13–19. doi:10.1007/s10956-009-9154-6

Kundra, V. (2009). The nation's new chief information officer speaks. *New York Times Business and Technology Blog, Bits.*

Kussmaul, C., Jack, R., & Sponsler, B. (2004). Outsourcing and offshoring with agility: A case study. In *Proceedings of XP* (pp. 147–154). Agile Universe. doi:10.1007/978-3-540-27777-4_15

Kvavik, R. B., & Caruso, J. B. (2005). ECAR study of students and information technology. *Convenience, Connection, Control, and Learning.* Boulder, CO: EDUCAUSE. Retrieved from http://www.educause.edu/ir/library/pdf/ers0506/rs/ERS0506w.pdf

Lai, Y. C., Chang, Y. F., & Liu, Z. F. (2009). *Motives of using Facebook and its influence on making-friends and learning performance.* Paper presented at the International Conference of Web 2.0 and Education (ICWE 2009), Taoyuan, Taiwan.

Lamy, M. N., & Hampel, R. (2007). *Online communication in language learning and teaching.* Palgrave Macmillan. doi:10.1057/9780230592681

Lankshear, C., Snyder, I., & Green, B. (2000). *Teachers and techno-literacy: Managing literacy, technology and learning in schools.* St Leonards, Australia: Allen and Unwin.

Lantholf, J., & Thorne, S. (2000). *Sociocultural theory and second language learning.* New York, NY: Oxford University Press.

Lantolf, J. P. (2000). Introducing sociocultural theory. In Lantolf, P. J. (Ed.), *Sociocultural theory and second language learning* (pp. 1–26). Oxford, UK: Oxford University Press.

Lantolf, J. P., & Thorne, S. L. (2007). Sociocultural theory and second language learning. In VanPatten, B., & Williams, J. (Eds.), *Theories in second language acquisition: An introduction* (pp. 197–221). Mahwah, NJ: Lawrence Erlbaum Associates.

Lara, S., & Naval, C. (2009). Educative proposal of Web 2.0 for the encouragement of social and citizenship competence. In G. Siemens & C. Fulford (Eds.), *Proceedings of World Conference on Educational Multimedia, Hypermedia and Telecommunications 2009* (pp. 47-52). Chesapeake, VA: AACE.

Larach, U., & Cabra, J. (2010). Creative problem-solving in Second Life: An action research study. *Creativity and Innovation Management, 19*(2), 167–179. doi:10.1111/j.1467-8691.2010.00550.x

Latham, T. (2011, July 16). The Google effect: Is our reliance on the internet making us dumber? *Psychology Today, Blogs.*

Lave, J., & Wenger, E. (1991). *Situated learning: Legitimate peripheral participation.* Cambridge, UK: Cambridge University Press. doi:10.1017/CBO9780511815355

Law, C., Jaeger, P., & McKay, E. (2010). User-centred design in universal design resources? *Universal Access in the Information Society, 9*(4), 327–335. doi:10.1007/s10209-009-0182-z

Lee, M. J. W., Chan, A., & McLoughlin, C. (2006). Students as producers: Second year students' experiences as podcasters of content for first year undergraduates. In *Proceedings of the 7th Conference on Information Technology Based Higher Education and Training* (pp. 832-841). Sydney, Australia: University of Technology, Sydney.

Lee, H., & Rha, I. (2009). Influence of structure and interaction on student achievement and satisfaction in web-based distance learning. *Journal of Educational Technology & Society, 12*(4), 372–382.

Lee, L. (2010). Exploring wiki-mediated collaborative writing: A case study in an elementary Spanish course. *CALICO Journal, 27*(2), 260–276.

Lee, M. J. W., & McLoughlin, C. (Eds.). (2010). *Web 2.0-based e-learning: Applying social informatics for tertiary teaching.* Hershey, PA: Information Science Reference. doi:10.4018/978-1-60566-294-7

Leighton, J., & Gierl, M. J. (2007). Verbal reports as data for cognitive diagnostic assessment. In Leighton, J., & Gierl, M. J. (Eds.), *Cognitive diagnostic assessment for education* (pp. 146–172). Cambridge, UK: Cambridge University Press. doi:10.1017/CBO9780511611186.006

Leong, P., Joseph, S. R., & Boulay, R. (2010). Applying constant comparative and discourse analyses to virtual worlds research. *Journal of Virtual Worlds Research*, *3*(1), 3–26.

Liang, Y., Zhao, Z., & Zeng, Q. (2007). *Mining user's interest from reading behavior in e-learning system.* Paper presented at the Eighth ACIS International Conference on Software Engineering, Artificial Intelligence, Networking, and Parallel/Distributed Computing, Qingdao, China.

Liang, M. Y. (2010). Using synchronous online peer review response groups in EFL writing: Revision-related discourse. *Language Learning & Technology*, *14*(1), 45–64.

Lin, C., Chou, C., & Bagley, C. (2007). APEC cyber academy: Integration of pedagogical and HCI principles in an international networked learning environment. In McKay, E. (Ed.), *Enhancing learning through human-computer interaction* (pp. 154–177). Hershey, PA: Idea Group Publishing, Inc.doi:10.4018/978-1-59904-328-9.ch009

Link, S., Schuster, T., Hoyer, P., & Abeck, S. (2008). *Focusing graphical user interfaces in model-driven software development.* Paper presented at the First International Conference on Advances in Computer-Human Interaction, Sainte Luce, Martinique.

Lin, L. J. (2002). Apply problem-based learning to Internet resource-based learning. *Instructional Technology & Media*, *60*, 42–53.

Liou, H.-C., & Peng, Z.-Y. (2009). Training effects on computer-mediated peer review. *System*, *37*(3), 514–525. doi:10.1016/j.system.2009.01.005

Lipowicz, A. (2010). vGov for feds aims to be a more engaging online environment. *Federal Computer Week.* Retrieved from http://fcw.com/Articles/2010/07/12/FEAT-QandA-Paulette-Robinson-NDU-vGov.aspx

Littlejohn, A. (2009). Key issues in the design and delivery of technology-enhanced learning. In Lockyer, L., Bennett, S., Agostinho, S., & Harper, B. (Eds.), *Handbook of research on learning design and learning objects: Issues, applications, and technologies* (pp. 1–1018). Hershey, PA: IGI Global.

Liu, J., & Sadler, R. W. (2003). The effect and affect of peer review in electronic versus traditional modes on L2 writing. *Journal of English for Academic Purposes*, *2*(3), 193–227. doi:10.1016/S1475-1585(03)00025-0

Lloyd, M. (2008). Finding the 'on' switch: Being a digital teacher in the 21st century. In Millwater, J., & Beutel, D. (Eds.), *Transitioning to the real world of education* (pp. 97–119). Sydney, Australia: Pearson.

Losey, S. (2010). Government to launch 'Fedspace,' a social media site for feds. *FederalTimes.com.* Retrieved from http://www.federaltimes.com/article/20100427/DEPARTMENTS07/4270302/-1/RSS?sms_ss=email

Lucke, U., & Zender, R. (2011). 3D interactions between virtual worlds and real life in an e-learning community. *Advances in Human-Computer Interaction*, *2011*, 1–11. doi:10.1155/2011/684202

Lund, A. (2008). Wikis: A collective approach to language production. *ReCALL*, *20*(01), 35–54. doi:10.1017/S0958344008000414

Lundy, K. (2010). *Open submission to the National Curriculum Consultation.* Retrieved from http://www.katelundy.com.au/2010/04/22/open-submission-to-the-national-curriculum-consultation/

Ma, L., Wang, Y.-S., & Sun, H.-Y. (2009). Construction and practice for interaction in networked learning situation. International Forum on Information Technology and Applications, Vol. 1, (pp. 447-452).

Mackenzie, O. J. (2001). Tacit knowledge in action: basic notions of knowledge sharing in computer supported work environments. In M. Jacovi, A. Ribak & A. Woodcock (Eds.), *Proceedings of the European CSCW Workshop on Managing Tacit Knowledge,* Bonn.

MacKinnon, D., & Manathunga, C. (2003). Going global with assessment: What to do when the dominant culture's literacy drives assessment. *Higher Education Research & Development*, *22*(2), 131–144. doi:10.1080/07294360304110

Magnolda, P., & Platt, G. (2009). Untangling Web 2.0's influences on student learning. [Academic Search Premier.]. *About Campus*, *14*(3), 10–16. doi:10.1002/abc.290

Makinen, M. (2006). Digital empowerment as a process for enhancing citizens' participation. *E-learning*, *3*(3), 381–395. doi:10.2304/elea.2006.3.3.381

Mangenot, F., & Nissen, E. (2006). Collective activity and tutor involvement in e-learning environments for language teachers and learners. *CALICO Journal, 23*(3), 601–621.

Martínez-Monés, A., Harrer, A., & Dimitriadis, Y. (2011). An interaction-aware design process for the integration of interaction analysis into mainstream CSCL practices. In Puntambekar, S., Erkens, G., & Hmelo-Silver, C. (Eds.), *Analyzing interactions in CSCL* (pp. 269–291). Springer, US. doi:10.1007/978-1-4419-7710-6_13

Martin, J., & McKay, E. (2009). Developing information communication technologies for the human services: Mental health and employment. In Martin, J., & Hawkins, L. (Eds.), *Information communication technologies for human services education and delivery: Concepts and cases* (pp. 152–166). Hershey, PA: IGI Global. doi:10.4018/978-1-60566-735-5.ch010

Martin, J., & Tan, D. (2010). Freeware solutions and international work integrated learning in higher education. In Burton Browning, J. (Ed.), *Open-source solutions in education: Theory and practice.* California, USA: Informing Science Press.

Marzano, R. J., Marzano, J. S., & Pickering, D. J. (2003). *Classroom management that works.* Alexandria, VA: ASCD.

Mason, H. (2007). Experiential education in Second Life. In D. Livingstone & J. Kemp (Eds.), *Proceedings of the Second Life Education Workshop* (pp. 14-18). Retrieved from www.simteach.com/slccedu07proceedings.pdf

Mawlawi Diab, N. (2010). Effects of peer- versus self-editing on students' revision of language errors in revised drafts. *System, 38*(1), 85–95. doi:10.1016/j.system.2009.12.008

Maxwell, T. W., Harrington, I., & Smith, H. J. (2010). Supporting primary and secondary beginning teachers online: Key findings of the education alumni support project. *Australian Journal of Teacher Education, 35*(1), 42–58.

McGinnis, T., Bustard, D., Black, M., & Charles, D. (2008). *Enhancing e-learning engagement using design patterns from computer games.* Paper presented at the First International Conference on Advances in Computer-Human Interaction, Sainte Luce, Martinique.

McInnis, C., Griffen, P., James, R., & Coates, H. (2000). *Development of the course experience questionnaire (CEQ).* Department of Education, Training and Youth Affairs. Retrieved from http://www.dest.gov.au/archive/highered/eippubs/eip01_1/01_1.pdf

McIntyre, S. (2011). *Teaching with Web 2.0 technologies: Twitter, wikis & blogs- Case study.* Retrieved from http://online.cofa.unsw.edu.au/learning-to-teach-online/ltto-episodes?view=video&video=229

McIsaac, M., & Gunawardena, C. (1996). Research in distance education. In Jonassen, D. (Ed.), *Handbook of research for educational communications and technology* (pp. 403–437). New York, NY: Scholastic Press.

McKay, E., & Merrill, M. D. (2003). Cognitive skill and web-based educational systems. Paper presented at the *eLearning Conference on Design and Development: Instructional Design - Applying first principles of instruction.* Informit Library: Australasian Publications. Retrieved from http://www.informit.com.au/library/

McKay, E. (2008). Human-dimensions of human-computer interaction: Balancing the HCI equation. In Balacheff, J. B. N. (Ed.), *The future of learning series* (*Vol. 3*). Amsterdam, The Netherlands: IOS Press.

McKenzie, W., & Murphy, D. (2000). "I hope this goes somewhere": Evaluation of an online discussion group. *Australian Journal of Educational Technology, 16*(3), 239–257.

McLoughlin, C., & Alam, S. L. (2011). Digital literacy and e-citizenship skills: A case study in applying Web 2.0 tools. In T. Bastiaens & M. Ebner (Eds.), *Proceedings of World Conference on Educational Multimedia, Hypermedia and Telecommunications 2011* (pp. 3505-3510). Chesapeake, VA: AACE. Retrieved from http://www.editlib.org/p/38361

McLoughlin, C., & Lee, M. J. W. (2007). *Social software and participatory learning: Pedagogical choices with technology affordances in the Web 2.0 era.* Paper presented at the Ascilite 2007: ICT: Providing Choices for Learners and Learning.

McLoughlin, C., & Lee, M. J. W. (2008). The three p's of pedagogy for the networked society: Personalization, participation, and productivity. *International Journal of Teaching and Learning in Higher Education, 20*(1), 10–27.

McLoughlin, C., & Lee, M. J. W. (2009). Pedagogical responses to social software in universities. In Hatzipanagos, S., & Warburton, S. (Eds.), *Handbook of research on social software and developing community ontologies* (pp. 269–284). doi:10.4018/978-1-60566-208-4.ch023

Means, B., Toyama, Y., Murphy, R., Bakia, M., & Jones, K. (2009). *Evaluation of evidence-based practices in online learning: A meta-analysis and review of online-learning studies*. Washington, DC: U.S. Department of Education. Retrieved from http://ctl.sri.com/publications/displayPublication.jsp?ID=770

Meier, A., Spada, H., & Rummel, N. (2007). A rating scheme for assessing the quality of computer-supported collaboration process. *Computer-Supported Collaborative Learning, 2*, 63–86. doi:10.1007/s11412-006-9005-x

Meister, J., & Willyerd, K. (2010). Looking ahead at social learning: Ten predictions. *T+D, 64*(7), 34-41.

Mejias, U. (2005). A nomad's guide to learning and social software. *The Knowledge Tree: An E-Journal of Learning Innovation, 7*. Retrieved from http://knowledgetree.flexiblelearning.net.au/edition07/download/la_mejias.pdf

Messinger, P. R., Stroulia, E., & Lyons, K. (2008, July). A typology of virtual worlds: Historical overview and future directions. *Journal of Virtual Worlds Research, 1*(1), 1–18.

Michels, P. (2008). Universities use Second Life to teach complex concepts. *Government Technology*. Retrieved from http://www.govtech.com/gt/252550

Mills, C. N., Potenza, M. T., Fremer, J. J., & Ward, W. C. (2002). *Computer-based testing: Building the foundation for future assessments*. New Jersey: Laurence Erlbaum Associates, Inc.

Mislevy, R. J., Steinberg, L. S., Breyer, F. J., Almond, R. G., & Johnson, L. (1999). A cognitive task analysis with implications for designing simulation-based performance assessment. *Computers in Human Behavior, 15*(3-4), 335–374. doi:10.1016/S0747-5632(99)00027-8

Moe, N. B., & Šmite, D. (2008). Understanding a lack of trust in global software teams: A multiple case study. *Software Process Improvement and Practice, 13*(3), 217–231. doi:10.1002/spip.378

Moje, E., Ciechanowski, K., Kramer, K., Ellis, L., Carrillo, R., & Collazo, T. (2004). Working toward third space in content area literacy: An examination of everyday funds of knowledge and discourse. *Reading Research Quarterly, 39*(1), 38–70. doi:10.1598/RRQ.39.1.4

Moll, R., & Krug, D. (2009). Using Web 2.0 for education programs on global citizenship: Addressing moral and ethical issues. Retrieved from http://www.policyalternatives.ca/sites/default/files/uploads/publications/Our_Schools_Ourselve/13_Moll_Krug_using_web_2.pdf

Monasor, M. J., Vizcaíno, A., & Piattini, M. (2010). An educational environment for training skills for global software development. In *Proceedings of the 2010 10th IEEE International Conference on Advanced Learning Technologies* (ICALT '10), (pp. 99-101). Washington, DC: IEEE Computer Society. DOI=10.1109/ICALT.2010.35

Morville, P., & Rosenfeld, L. (2007). *Information architecture for the World Wide Web*, 3rd ed. O' Reilly.

Muñoz-Merino, P., Kloos, C., Muñoz-Organero, M., Wolpers, M., & Friedrich, M. (2010). *An approach for the personalization of exercises based on contextualized attention metadata and semantic Web technologies*. Paper presented at the 10th IEEE International Conference on Advanced Learning Technologies, Athens, Greece.

Murphy, E., & Ciszewska-Carr, J. (2007). Instructor's experiences of web based synchronous communication using two way audio and direct messaging. *Australasian Journal of Educational Technology, 23*(1), 68–86.

Murray, L., & Rintoul, K. (2008). *The literacy assessment project: An initiative of the Catholic Education Office for continuous school improvement in literacy*. Paper presented at the Australian Councol for Educational Leaders.

NDLR (National Digital Learning Repository). (n.d.). Retrieved from http://www.ndlr.ie/

Newell, A., & Simon, H. A. (1961). *GPS, a program that simulates human thought*. Los Angeles, CA: Rand Corporation.

Newlands, D. A., & Coldwell, J. (2004). Managing student expectations online. *Lecture Notes in Computer Science, 3583*, 355–363. doi:10.1007/11528043_37

Nguyen, L. V. (2008). Computer mediated communication and foreign language education: Pedagogical features. *International Journal of Instructional Technology and Distance Learning, 5*(12), 23–44.

Nguyen, L. V. (2010). Computer mediated collaborative learning within a communicative language teaching approach: A sociocultural perspective. *The Asian EFL Journal Quarterly, 12*(1), 202–233.

Nguyen, L. V., & White, C. (2011). The nature of 'talk' in synchronous computer-mediated communication in a Vietnamese tertiary EFL context. *International Journal of Computer-Assisted Language Learning and Teaching, 1*(3), 14–36. doi:10.4018/ijcallt.2011070102

Nielsen, J. (2006). *Ten usability heuristics.* Retrieved from http://www.useit.com/papers/heuristic/heuristic_list.html

Nitko, A. (1980). Distinguishing the many varieties of criterion-referenced tests. *Review of Educational Research, 50*(3), 14.

NMC. (2005). *The 2005 horizon report.* Austin, TX: The New Media Consortium.

Noor, F. A. (2007). *Ngruki revisited: Modernity and its discontents at the pondok pesantren al-Mukmin of Ngruki. Surakarta, S.* Singapore: Rajaratnam School of International Studies.

Northedge, A. (2003). Rethinking teaching in the context of diversity. *Teaching in Higher Education, 8*(1), 17–32. doi:10.1080/1356251032000052302

O' Reilly, T. (2009). Gov 2.0: Promise of innovation. In Gotze, J., & Pedersen, C. (Eds.), *State of the eUnion: Government 2.0 and onwards. 21Gov.net.*

O'Reiley, T. (2005). *What is Web 2.0?* Retrieved from http://oreilly.com/Web2/archive/what-is-Web-20.html

Oblinger, D. G., & Oblinger, J. L. (2005). Is it age or IT: First steps toward understanding the NET Generation. In Oblinger, D. G., & Oblinger, J. L. (Eds.), *Educating the net generation* (pp. 3.1–3.7). EDUCAUSE.

O'Brien, J. (2008). *Are we preparing young people for 21st-century citizenship with 20th century thinking? A case for a virtual laboratory of democracy.* Contemporary Issues in Technology and Teacher.

Ochoa, T., & Robinson, J. (2005). Revisiting group consensus: Collaborative learning dynamics during a problem-based learning activity in education. *Teacher Education and Special Education, 28*(1), 10–20. doi:10.1177/088840640502800102

O'Donnell, E. (2008). *Can e-learning be used to further improve the learning experience to better prepare students for work in industry.* Masters in Information Systems for Managers, Dublin City University, Dublin. Retrieved from http://arrow.dit.ie/buschmanoth/1

O'Donnell, E. (2010). *E-learning can improve learning: Preparing students for work.* Saarbrücken, Germany: Lambert Academic Publishing AG & Co. KG.

Ohta, A. S. (2001). *Second language acquisition processes in the classroom: Learning Japanese.* Mahwah, NJ: Lawrence Erlbaum Associates.

Okamoto, T. (2003). *E-collaborative learning technologies and e-pedagogy.* Paper presented at the The 3rd IEEE International Conference on Advanced Learning Technologies (ICALT '03), Athens, Greece.

Okamoto, T. (2004, August 30 - September 1). *Collaborative technology and new e-pedagogy.* Paper presented at the IEEE International Conference on Advanced Learning Technologies (ICALT '04), Joensuu, Finland.

Orlando, J. (2009). Understanding changes in teachers' ICT practices: A longitudinal perspective. *Technology, Pedagogy and Education, 18*(1), 33–44. doi:10.1080/14759390802704030

Ortega, L. (2009). *Understanding second language acquisition.* London, UK: A Hodder Arnold Publication.

Osimo, D. (2008). *Web 2.0 in government: Why and how*, vol. 23358. Institute for Prospective Technological Studies (IPTS), JRC, European Commission, EUR.

Paasivaara, M., Durasiewicz, S., & Lassenius, C. (2008). Distributed agile development: Using Scrum in a large project. *Software Process Improvement and Practice, 13*(6), 527–544. doi:10.1002/spip.402

Paavola, S., & Hakkarainen, K. (2005). The knowledge creation metaphor – An emergent epistemological approach to learning. *Science and Education, 14*, 535–557. doi:10.1007/s11191-004-5157-0

Pachler, N., & Daly, C. (2009). Narrative and learning with Web 2.0 technologies: Towards a research agenda. *Journal of Computer Assisted Learning, 25*(1), 6–18. doi:10.1111/j.1365-2729.2008.00303.x

Padda, H., Mudur, S., Seffah, A., & Joshi, Y. (2008). *Comprehension of visualization systems - Towards quantitative assessment.* Paper presented at the First International Conference on Advances in Computer-Human Interaction, Sainte Luce, Martinique.

Paireekreng, W., & Wong, K. W. (2010). *Mobile content personalisation using intelligent user profile approach.* Paper presented at the Third International Conference on Knowledge Discovery and Data Mining.

Palvia, S., & Pancaro, R. (2010). Promises and perils of Internet-based networking. *Journal of Global Information Technology Management, 13*(3).

Parker, D., & Rossner-Merill, V. (1998). *Socialization of distance education: The web as enabler.* WebNet '98, Association for the Advancement of Computing in Education, Orlando, Florida, Nov. 7-12.

Parrish, P. E. (2009). Aesthetic principles for instructional design. *Educational Technology Research and Development, 57*, 511–528. doi:10.1007/s11423-007-9060-7

Parry, M. (2012, March 7). Could many universities follow borders bookstores into oblivion? *The Chronicle of Higher Education.* Retrieved from http://chronicle.com/blogs/wiredcampus/could-many-universities-follow-borders-bookstores-into-oblivion/35711?utm_source=twitterfeedandutm_medium=twitter

Parshall, C. G., & Harmes, J. C. (2009). Improving the quality of innovative item types: Four tasks for design and development. *Journal of Applied Testing Technology, 10*(1), 1–20.

Pelligrino, J., Chudowsky, N., & Glaser, R. (Eds.). (2001). *Knowing what students know: The science and design of educational assessment.* Washington, DC: National Academy Press.

Pence, H. E. (2007). The homeless professor in Second Life. *Journal of Educational Technology Systems, 36*(2), 171–177. doi:10.2190/ET.36.2.e

Pettys, G., Panos, P., Cox, S., & Oosthuysen, K. (2005). Four models of international field placement. *International Social Work, 48*(3), 277–288. doi:10.1177/0020872805051705

Phelps, R., Hase, S., & Ellis, A. (2005). Competency, capability, complexity and computers: Exploring a new model for conceptualising end-user computer education. *British Journal of Educational Technology, 36*(1), 67–84. doi:10.1111/j.1467-8535.2005.00439.x

Pohl, F. (2007). Islamic education and civil society: Reflections on the *pesantren* tradition in contemporary Indonesia. In Kadi, W., & Billeh, V. (Eds.), *Islam and education: Myths and truths.* Chicago, IL: University of Chicago Press.

Powers, S., Janz, K., & Ande, T. (2006). Using theories of social presence and transactional distance to understand technology enhanced instruction. In C. Crawford, et al., (Eds.), *Proceedings of Society for Information Technology & Teacher Education International Conference 2006* (pp. 502-505). Chesapeake, VA: AACE. Retrieved from http://www.editlib.org/p/22087

Prebble, T., Hargraves, H., Leach, L., Naidoo, K., Suddaby, G., & Zepke, N. (2005). *Impact of student support services and academic development programmes on student outcomes in undergraduate tertiary study: A synthesis of the research.* Report to the Minister.

Preece, J., Rogers, Y., & Sharp, H. (2002). *Interaction design: Beyond human computer interaction.* John Wiley & Sons, Inc.

Preston, C., & Mowbray, L. (2008). Use of SMART boards for teaching, learning and assessment in kindergarten science. *Teaching Science, 54*(2), 50–53.

Punie, Y., & Cabrera, M. (2006). *The future of ICT and learning in the knowledge society.* Luxembourg: European Communities. Retrieved from http://www.eenet.org/upload/File/Vision%202015/ThefutureofIctandlearningintheknowledgesociety.pdf

Rafael, D., Rodríguez, M. L., Hurtado, M. V., Bravo, C., & Rodríguez-Domínguez, C. (2012). Integration of collaboration and interaction analysis mechanisms in a concern-based architecture for groupware systems. *Science of Computer Programming, 77*(1), 29-45. ISSN 0167-6423

Rai, G. (2004). International fieldwork experience: A survey of US schools. *International Social Work, 47*(2), 213–226. doi:10.1177/0020872804034138

Raizen, S., Binkley, M., Erstad, O., Herman, J., Ripley, M., Miller-Ricci, M., & Rumble, M. (2011). Defining 21st century skills. In Griffin, P., Care, E., & McGaw, B. (Eds.), *Assessment and teaching of 21st century skills.* New York, NY: Springer.

Rasch, G. (1960). *Probablistic models for some intelligence and attainment tests.* Copenhagen, Denmark: Danish Institute for Education Research.

Razack, N. (2002). A critical examination of international student exchanges. *International Social Work, 45*(2), 251–265.

Rheingold, H. (2008). Invitation to the social media classroom and collabatory. *Social Media Classroom.* Retrieved from http://socialmediaclassroom.com/

Rheingold, H. (2008). Using participatory media and public voice to encourage civic engagement. In W. L. Bennett (Ed.), *Civic life online: Learning how digital media can engage youth,* (pp. 97–118). The John D., & Catherine T. MacArthur Foundation Series on Digital Media and Learning. Cambridge, MA: The MIT Press.

Rheingold, H. (2012 April). *Howard home.* Retrieved from http://rheingold.com

Richards, R. (2010). Digital citizenship and Web 2.0 tools. *MERLOT Journal of Online Learning and Teaching, 6*(2).

Richardson, W. (2006). *Blogs, wikis, podcasts, and other powerful web tools for classrooms.* Thousand Oaks, CA: Corwin Press.

Riedl, R., Bronack, S., & Tashner, J. (2005). *Innovation in learning assumptions about teaching in a 3-D virtual world.* Paper presented at International College Teaching Methods and Styles Conference, Reno, NV.

Roberts, G. (2005). Technology and learning expectations of the net generation. In Oblinger, D. G., & Oblinger, J. L. (Eds.), *Educating the net generation* (pp. 3.1–3.7). EDUCAUSE.

Rogers, E. M. (2003). *Diffusion of innovations* (5th ed.). New York, NY: The Free Press.

Romiszowski, A. J. (1981). *Designing instructional systems: Decision making in course planning and curriculum design.* New York, NY: Nichols Publishing Company.

Rossiter, D., Petrulis, R., & Biggs, C. A. (2010). A blended approach to problem-based learning in the freshman year. *Chemical Engineering Education, 44*(1), 23–29.

Rourke, L., Anderson, T., Garrison, D. R., & Archer, W. (2001). Methodological issues in the content analysis of computer conference transcripts. *International Journal of Artificial Intelligence in Education, 12*(1), 8–22.

Saeed, N., Yang, Y., & Sinnappan, S. (2009). Emerging web technologies in higher education: A case of incorporating blogs, podcasts, and social bookmarks in a web programming course based on students' learning styles and technology preferences. *Journal of Educational Technology & Society, 12*(4), 98–109.

Salomon, G. J. (1984)... *Education Psychology, 76,* 647. doi:10.1037/0022-0663.76.4.647

Sanchez, J. (2009). Barriers to student learning in Second Life. *Library Technology Reports, 45*(2), 29–34.

Scardamalia, M., & Bereiter, C. (2003). Knowledge building. In Guthrie, J. W. (Ed.), *Encyclopaedia of education* (2nd ed., pp. 1370–1373). New York, NY: Macmillan.

Schlager, M. S., Fusco, J., & Schank, P. (2002). Evolution of an online education community of practice. In Renninger, K. A., & Shumar, W. (Eds.), *Building virtual communities: Learning and change in cyberspace* (pp. 129–158). Cambridge, UK: Cambridge University Press. doi:10.1017/CBO9780511606373.010

Schnotz, W., & Kürschner, C. (2007). A reconsideration of cognitive load theory. *Educational Psychology Review, 19,* 469–508. doi:10.1007/s10648-007-9053-4

Schramm, W. (Ed.). (1954). *The process and effects of communication.* Urbana, IL: University of Illinois Press.

Schroeder, A., Minocha, S., & Schneider, C. (2010). The strengths, weaknesses, opportunities and threats of using social software in higher and further education teaching and learning. *Journal of Computer Assisted Learning, 26*(3), 159–174. doi:10.1111/j.1365-2729.2010.00347.x

Schuck, S. (2003). Getting help from the outside: Developing a support network for beginning teachers. *Journal of Educational Enquiry, 4*(1), 49–67.

Selwyn, N. (2002). *Telling tales on technology: Qualitative studies of technology and education.* Hampshire, UK: Ashgate Publishing Limited.

Settouti, L., Prié, Y., Marty, J., & Mille, A. (2009, July 15-17). *A trace-based system for technology-enhanced learning systems personalisation.* Paper presented at the Ninth IEEE International Conference on Advanced Learning Technologies, Riga.

Sfard, A. (1998). On two metaphors for learning and the dangers of choosing just one. [Academic Search Premier.]. *Educational Researcher, 27*(2), 4–13.

Shaffer, D. W., Squire, K. R., Halverson, R., & Gee, J. P. (2005). Video games and the future of learning. *Phi Delta Kappan, 87*(2), 104–111.

Shank, P. (2008). Web 2.0 and beyond: The changing needs of learners, new tools, and ways to learn. In Carliner, S., & Shank, P. (Eds.), *The e-learning handbook: Past promises, present challenges. Pfeiffer - Essential resources for training and HR professionals* (pp. 241–278). San Francisco, CA: Pfeiffer.

Shneiderman, B. (1998). *Designing the user interface: Strategies for effective human-computer interaction* (3rd ed.). Reading, MA: Addison-Wesley.

Shrestha, M., Wilson, S., & Singh, M. (2008). Knowledge networking: A dilemma in building social capital through non formal education, *Adult Education Quarterly, 58*(2), 129 58.

Siemens, G. (2005, January). Connectivism: A learning theory for the digital age. *International Journal of Instructional Technology & Distance Learning.* Retrieved from http://www.itdl.org/Journal/Jan_05/article01.htm

Simmons, D. B. (2006). Software engineering education in the new millennium. *Proceedings of the 30th Annual International Computer Software and Applications Conference* (COMPSAC'06). IEEE Press.

Skerrett, A. (2010). Lolita, facebook, and the third space of literacy teacher education. *Educational Studies, 46*(1), 67–84.

Slagter van Tryon, P., & Bishop, M. (2009). Theoretical foundations for enhancing social connectedness in online learning environments. *Distance Education, 30*(3), 291–337. doi:10.1080/01587910903236312

Smith, M. K. (2001). David A. Kolb on experiential learning. In *Encyclopaedia of informal education.* Retrieved from http://www.infed.org/encyclopaedia.htm

Smith, R., Bagley, C., & Greci, L. (2010). *Disaster emergency medical personnel system (DEMPS) selection of a virtual world platform to address human performance requirements.* Retrieved from http://ntsa.metapress.com/app/home/contribution.asp?referrer=parent &backto=issue,52,170;journal,1,18;linkingpublicationresults,1:113340,1

Snyder, I. (1993). Writing with word processors: A research overview. *Educational Research, 35*(1), 49–68. doi:10.1080/0013188930350103

So, H., & Brush, T. (2009). Student perceptions of collaborative learning, social presence, and satisfaction in a blended learning environment: Relationships and critical factors. [Academic Search Premier.]. *Computers & Education, 51*(1), 318–336. doi:10.1016/j.compedu.2007.05.009

Soja, E. W. (1996). *Thirdspace: Journeys to Los Angeles and other real and imagined places.* Malden, MA: Blackwell.

Sonwalkar, N. (2008). Adaptive individualization: The next generation of online education. *Horizon, 16*(1), 44–47. doi:10.1108/10748120810853345

Sorcinelli, M. D. (1991). Research findings on the seven principles. *New Directions for Teaching and Learning, 47*, 13–25. doi:10.1002/tl.37219914704

Squire, K., Barnett, M., Grant, J. M., & Higginbotham, T. (2004). Electromagnetism supercharged!: Learning physics with digital simulation games. *International Conference on Learning Sciences*, (pp. 513-520). International Society of the Learning Sciences. Retrieved from http://portal.acm.org/citation.cfm?id=1149126.1149189

Squire, K. R., & Jenkins, H. (2003). Harnessing the power of games in education. *Insight (American Society of Ophthalmic Registered Nurses), 3*(1), 5–33.

Stacey, E., & Gerbic, P. (2008). Success factors for blended learning. In R. Atkinson & C. McBeath (Eds.), *Hello! Where are you in the landscape of educational technology? Proceedings Australasian Society for Computers in Learning in Tertiary Education (ASCILITE) Conference*, Melbourne 2008.

Stahl, G. (2006). *Group cognition: Computer support for building collaborative knowledge*. MIT Press. ISBN 0-2-19539-9

Stahl, G. (2010). *Global introduction to CSCL*. Philadelphia, PA: Gerry Stahl at Lulu.

Swan, K. (2002). Building learning communities in online courses: The importance of interaction. *Education Communication and Information*, 2(1), 23–49. doi:10.1080/1463631022000005016

Sweller, J. (1988). Cognitive load during problem-solving: Effects on learning. [Academic Search Premier.]. *Cognitive Science*, 12(2), 257–285. doi:10.1207/s15516709cog1202_4

Tapscott, D. (2009). *Grown up digital: How the Web is changing your world*. McGraw Hill US.

Tapscott, D., Williams, A. D., & Herman, D. (2007). *Government 2.0: Transforming government and governance for the 21st century, new paradigm's government 2.0: Wikinomics, government and democracy program*.

Tapscott, D., & Williams, A. D. (2008). *Wikinomics: How mass collaboration changes everything (expanded edition)*. Penguin.

Tapscott, D., & Williams, A. D. (2010). *Macrowikinomics: Rebooting business and the world*. Penguin.

Taylor, B. M., Pearson, P. D., Peterson, D. S., & Rodriguez, M. C. (2005). The CIERA school change framework: An evidenced-based approach to professional development and school reading improvement. *Reading Research Quarterly*, 40(1), 40–69. doi:10.1598/RRQ.40.1.3

Tennyson, R., & Bagley, C. (1992). Structured versus constructed instructional strategies for improving concept acquisition by domain-competent and domain-novice learners. *Journal of Structural Learning*, 11(3), 255–263.

Terenzini, P., Springer, L., Pascarella, E. T., & Nora, A. (1995)... *Research in Higher Education*, 36, 23. doi:10.1007/BF02207765

Terrell, J., Richardson, J., & Hamilton, M. (2011). Using Web 2.0 to teach Web 2.0: A case study in aligning teaching, learning and assessment with professional practice. *Australasian Journal of Educational Technology*, 27(special issue, 5), 846-862.

Tesoriero, F., & Rajaratnam, A. (2001). Partnership in education. An Australian school of social work and a South Indian primary health care project. *International Social Work*, 44(1), 31–41. doi:10.1177/0020872801044000104

Thompson, J. (2007). Is education 1.0 ready for Web 2.0 students? *Innovate: Journal of Online Education*, 3(4). Retrieved from http://www.innovateonline.info/vol3_issue4/Is_Education_1.0_Ready_for_Web_2.0_Students

Tidwell, J. (2006). *Designing interfaces*. O' Reilly.

Timperley, H. (2008). *Teacher professional learning and development. Education Practices Series-18*. Paris, France: International Bureau of Education.

Timperley, H., Parr, J., & Bertanees, C. (2009). Promoting professional inquiry for improved outcomes for students in New Zealand. *Professional Development in Education*, 35(2), 227–245. doi:10.1080/13674580802550094

Tingling, P., Gemino, A., & Parker, D. (2011). Changing channels: The impact of web 2.0 on supply chain management. *Production and Inventory Management Journal*, 47(2), 31–44.

Torp, L., & Sage, S. M. (1998). *Problems as possibilities: Problem-based learning for K-12 education*. Virginia: Association for Supervision and Curriculum Development.

Traub, R., & Wolfe, R. (1981). Latent trait theories and the assessment of educational achievement. *Review of Research in Education*, 9, 377–435.

Tsai, M. F. (2001). *Designing an analysis system for e-learning portfolio*. Unpublished Master's thesis. National Sun Yat Sun University, Kaohsiung, Taiwan.

Tseng, C. H. (2003). *The implementation and evaluation of networked portfolio system for individual and group*. Unpublished master's thesis. National Chiao Tung University, Hsinchu, Taiwan.

Tyack, D., & Cuban, L. (2000). Teaching by machine. In Pea, R. D. (Ed.), *Jossey-Bass reader on technology and learning* (pp. 247–254). San Francisco, CA: Jossey-Bass.

Tzou, H. Y. (2000). Project-based learning for curriculum, teaching, and evaluation. *Journal of National Tainan Teachers College*, 34, 3–9.

Väljataga, T., & Fiedler, S. (2009). Supporting students to self-direct intentional learning projects with social media. *Journal of Educational Technology & Society*, 12(3), 58–69.

Veletsianos, G. (Ed.). (2010). *A definition for emerging technologies in education, emerging technologies in distance education.* Athabasca University Press.

Vygotsky, L. (1978). *Mind and society: The development of higher psychological processes.* Cambridge, MA: Harvard University Press.

Vygotsky, L. S. (1981). The instrumental method in psychology. In Wertsch, J. (Ed.), *The concept of activity in Soviet psychology* (pp. 143–184). Armonk, NY: M.E. Sharpe.

Wagner, E. (2005). Enabling mobile learning. *EDUCAUSE Review, 40*(3), 40–53.

Waluyo, H. (2006). *General ICT overview: Data and information centre.* Ministry of Culture and Tourism, Republic of Indonesia.

Wang, Q. (2007). Designing a web-based constructivist learning environment. *Interactive Learning Environments, 17*(1), 1–13. doi:10.1080/10494820701424577

Wang, S., & Hsu, H. (2009). Using the ADDIE model to design Second Life activities for on-line learners. *TechTrends, 53*(6), 76–81. Retrieved from http://edtc6325teamone2ndlife.pbworks.com/f/6325+Using+the+ADDIE+Model.pdfdoi:10.1007/s11528-009-0347-x

Wang, S., & Susilo, A. (2009). Using Facebook to develop network learning communities. *Journal of Tianjin Radio & Television University, 13*(1), 17–18.

Warburton, S. (2009). Second Life in higher education: Assessing the potential for and the barriers to deploying virtual worlds in learning and teaching. *British Journal of Educational Technology, 40*(3), 414–426. doi:10.1111/j.1467-8535.2009.00952.x

Ware, P. D., & O'Dowd, R. (2008). Peer feedback on language form in telecollaboration. *Language Learning & Technology, 12*(1), 43–63.

Warschauer, M. (1996). Comparing face-to-face and electronic discussion in the second language classroom. *CALICO Journal, 13*(2), 7–26.

Warschauer, M. (2010). Invited commentary: New tools for teaching writing. *Language Learning & Technology, 14*(1), 3–8.

Warshauer, M. (1997). Computer-mediated collaborative learning: Theory and practice. *Modern Language Journal, 81*(3), 470–481. doi:10.1111/j.1540-4781.1997.tb05514.x

Waycott, J., & Sheard, J. (2011). Editorial: Preface to the special issue. *Australasian Journal of Educational Technology, 27*(Special issue, 5), iii-ix. Retrieved from http://www.ascilite.org.au/ajet/ajet27/editorial27-5.html

Wegner, S. B., Holloway, K., & Crader, A. (1998). *Utilizing a problem-based approach on the World Wide Web.* ERIC: ED414262.

Wegner, D., & Vallacher, R. (1977). *Implicit psychology: An introduction to social cognition.* New York, NY: Oxford University Press.

Wei, D., Chen, C. S., & Chang, Y. Y. (1998). Statistics of biological species in Taiwan. *Accounting and Statistics Monthly Report, 85*(4), 20–53.

Wellington, C. A., Briggs, T., & Girard, C. D. (2005). Examining team cohesion as an effect of software engineering methodology. *Proceedings of the 2005 Workshop on Human and Social Factors of Software Engineering,* (pp. 1- 5). ACM Press.

Wenger, E. (1998). *Communities of practice: Learning as a social system.* Retrieved from http://www.co-i-l.com/coil/knowledge-garden/cop/lss.shtml

Wenger, E. (1998). *Communities of practice: Learning, meaning and identity.* Cambridge, UK: Cambridge University Press.

Westheimer, J., & Kahne, J. (2004). What kind of citizen? The politics of educating for democracy. *American Educational Research Journal, 41*(2). doi:10.3102/00028312041002237

Wheeler, S., Yeomans, P., & Wheeler, D. (2008). The good, the bad and the wiki: Evaluating student-generated content for collaborative learning. *British Journal of Educational Technology, 39*(6), 987–995. doi:10.1111/j.1467-8535.2007.00799.x

White, C. (2007). Focus on the language learner in an era of globalization: Tensions, positions and practices in technology-mediated language teaching. *Language Teaching, 40*(4), 321–326. doi:10.1017/S026144480700451X

Wilczenski, F. L., Bontrager, T., Ventrone, P., & Correia, M. (2001). Observing collaborative problem-solving processes and outcomes. *Psychology in the Schools*, *38*(3), 269–278. doi:10.1002/pits.1017

Williams, B. T. (2007). I'm ready for my close-up now: Electronic portfolios and how we read identity. *Journal of Adolescent & Adult Literacy*, *50*, 500–504. doi:10.1598/JAAL.50.6.7

Williamson, D. M., Bauer, M., Steinberg, L. S., Mislevy, R. J., Behrens, J. T., & DeMark, S. F. (2004). Design rationale for a complex performance assessment. *International Journal of Testing*, *4*(4), 303–332. doi:10.1207/s15327574ijt0404_2

Williamson, D. M., Mislevy, R. J., & Bejar, I. I. (2006). *Automated scoring of complex tasks in computer-based testing*. New Jersey: Lauwrence Erlbaum Associates, Inc.

Wilson, G., & Stacey, E. (2004). Online interaction impacts on learning: Teaching the teachers to teach online. *Australasian Journal of Educational Technology*, *20*(1), 33-48. Retrieved from http://www.ascilite.org.au/ajet/ajet20/wilson.html

Wilson, M., Bejar, I., Scalise, K., Templin, J., Wiliam, D., & Irribarra, D. T. (2011). Perspectives on methodological issues. In Griffin, P., Care, E., & McGaw, B. (Eds.), *Assessment and teaching of 21st century skills*. New York, NY: Springer.

Wirth, J., & Klieme, E. (2003). Computer-based assessment of problem solving competence. *Assessment in Education*, *10*(3), 329–345. doi:10.1080/0969594032000148172

Woods, K., & Griffin, P. (2010). *Teachers' use of developmental assessment to support communication proficiency for students with additional needs*. Paper presented at the AARE International Education Research Conference - 2010, Melbourne, Australia.

Wu, C. S., & Lin, T. Y. (2002). Creative-thinking teaching. *Journal of Educational Resources and Research*, *60*, 46.

Wu, M., Adams, R. J., & Wilson, M. (1998). *ConQuest: Generalised item response modelling software*. Melbourne, Australia: ACER Press.

Yamada, M. (2009). The role of social presence in learner-centered communicative language learning using synchronous computer-mediated communication: Experimental study. [Academic Search Premier.]. *Computers & Education*, *52*(4), 820–833. doi:10.1016/j.compedu.2008.12.007

Yang, Z., & Liu, Q. (2004). Research and development of web-based virtual online classroom. [Academic Search Premier.]. *Computers & Education*, *48*(2), 171–184. doi:10.1016/j.compedu.2004.12.007

Yee, N. (2006). Motivations for play in online games. *Cyberpsychology & Behavior*, *9*(6), 772–775. Retrieved from http://www.liebertonline.com/toc/cpb/9/6doi:10.1089/cpb.2006.9.772

Yew, R. S. (2001). *An action research of electronic portfolio in six-grade science course*. Unpublished master's thesis. National Taichung University, Taichung, Taiwan.

Yin, R. K. (2003). *Case study research: Design and methods* (2nd ed.). Thousand Oaks, CA: Sage Publications.

Yoshitaka, S. Kinshuk, Graf, S., Zarypolla, A., Takada, K., & Tsuruta, S. (2009). Enriching web based computer supported collaborative learning systems by considering misunderstandings among learners during interactions. *ICALT, Ninth IEEE International Conference on Advanced Learning Technologies*, (pp. 306-310).

Yueh, H. P., & Wang, Y. C. (2000). A study of students' attitudes toward the electronic portfolio practice. *Bulletin of Educational Psychology*, *31*(2), 65–84.

Zeng, G., & Takatsuka, S. (2009). Text-based peer-peer collaborative dialogue in a computer-mediated learning environment in the EFL context. *System*, *37*(3), 434–446. doi:10.1016/j.system.2009.01.003

Zhao, Y., Pugh, K., Sheldon, S., & Byers, J. L. (2002). Conditions for classroom technology innovations. *Teachers College Record*, *104*(3), 482–515. doi:10.1111/1467-9620.00170

Zhao, Y., & Rop, S. (2001). A critical review of the literature on electronic networks as reflective discourse communities for inservice teachers. *Education and Information Technologies*, *6*(2), 81–94. doi:10.1023/A:1012363715212

Zoanetti, N. P. (2010). Interactive computer based assessment tasks: How problem-solving process data can inform instruction. *Australasian Journal of Educational Technology*, *26*(5), 585–606.

About the Contributors

Elspeth McKay is Associate Professor of Business IT & Logistics at RMIT University, Australia. She earned her PhD in Computer Science and Information Systems and her Graduate Certificate of Applied Science in Instructional Design from Deakin University, Australia, her Graduate Diploma of Education in Computer studies from Hawthorn Institute of Education, and her Bachelor of Business with Distinction in Business Information Systems from RMIT University, Australia. Her current research includes learning/training modules online and standalone PC application, vocational training, rehabilitation programmes (cultural and learning style variation), and multi-media interface development, including animation.

* * *

Sultana Lubna Alam is a Lecturer in the Faculty of Information Sciences and Engineering at the University of Canberra. She has over 10 years of teaching experience in the area of IT. Her research interests include technology enabled education, digital citizenship, government 2.0 and crowdsourcing. She is currently pursuing a PhD in the area of crowdsourcing in Australian government. She has published scholarly papers in refereed conferences and journals.

Nafisa Awwal has a Bachelor of Computer Science (MIS) and completed her Master's of Information Management and Systems from Monash University. At present in her role in the Assessment Research Centre, University of Melbourne, she is involved in the design and development of web-based educational assessment and reporting tools. She has also worked on projects that have included data management and analysis for some studies, item writing, and test and scale development.

Carole A. Bagley, PhD, has 25+ years in the instructional technology and learning field as President and Team Leader of The Technology Group, Inc. and Distinguished Service Professor for the University of St Thomas, St. Paul, MN, USA. Dr. Bagley has made significant contributions to the field by providing eLearning strategic planning, advising, training and curriculum design, workshops, seminars, publications, and keynote presentations within the US and internationally for the business and educational community. Dr. Bagley has advised several international law firms, corporations, and US govt. agencies in the telecommunications, medicine, banking, and technology sectors as they engaged in and built their eLearning offerings and several school districts in building communities of learners who integrate technology into their restructured classrooms. Dr. Bagley has been the recipient of numerous honors including: Outstanding International ISPI member, Outstanding Computer Based Education Professional for ASTD, Digital Learning Forum (DLF): Founder, and Who's Who among America's Teachers.

Siew Mee Barton is a Lecturer in Business Communication and Campus Coordinator for Business Communication at the School of Management and Marketing, Deakin University, Melbourne. She coordinates and manages the Burwood on-campus core unit MMH299 Business Communication (a very large unit with a total of approximately 1800 enrolled students over two semesters). During this period, she had successfully trialed an alternative intensive marking system involving 22 markers over three days to mark final exam papers, preceded by a marking workshop session. She had also successfully introduced the use of the social networking tool, the blog, as a component of the assessment. Her PhD dissertation examines the role of culture and social networks in the adoption and development of eLearning systems by tertiary academics in Singapore, Malaysia, Indonesia, and Turkey. Her current research interests are on women's leadership and entrepreneurship in South East Asia; and she is also looking at academics use of mobile technology devices to enhance their teaching.

Myvan Bui has a Bachelor of Economic (Social Sciences) with first class honours in Psychology, and PhD in Psychology from the University of Sydney. She has many years experience in teaching and conducting statistical analysis of psycho-educational test data and experience with psycho-educational assessment in schools. Myvan has worked on national and large scale international education research and consultancy projects focused on English, mathematics, general ability, and 21st century skills. Currently, she is a Research Fellow at the Assessment Research Centre, University of Melbourne.

Esther Care is an Associate Processor with the University of Melbourne, and specializes in assessment. She is a Fellow of the Australian Psychological Society and coordinates the educational psychology programs at the University. Her doctoral work was focused around measurement of vocational interests and aptitudes and since that time she has extended her psychometric interest in the area of educational assessment, assessment of early literacy, and in collaborative problem solving.

Chientzu Candace Chou is an Associate Professor of the Learning Technology Program at the University of St. Tomas. She oversees the eLearning graduate certificate program and serves as the co-program director for the Master of Arts in Technology for Learning, Development, and Change program. Her research has focused on computer-mediated communication, online interaction, instructional design of learning environments, student learning experiences, technology integration in K-16 systems, pedagogy of virtual world education, and computer-supported collaborative learning. She teaches online and blended learning course on technology integration, online teaching and evaluation, instructional design for eLearning, immersive training and learning through virtual worlds, and web-based curriculum development.

Jo Coldwell is currently Associate Head of School (Teaching and Learning) in the School of Information Technology at Deakin University. Before becoming an academic Jo had extensive industrial experience in the UK and Australia as a programmer, analyst, and project leader. Her teaching revolves around foundation skills in IT and professional practice. Jo's research expertise is in eLearning in general but focuses on the use of educational technologies to support, and the impact on learning and teaching. Jo also has an interest in: factors that impact on, and developing strategies to support, students-at-risk; and exploring the gender imbalance in the IT sector and developing, implementing and evaluating strategies to encourage females to participate in IT education and training.

Cesar A. Collazos received his degree in System Engineer at Universidad de los Andes (Bogota-Colombia). PhD in Computer Science at Universidad de Chile. Full Professor at University of Cauca (Colombia), head of the IDIS Research Group. His research areas are CSCL, CSCW, and HCI.

William H. Creswell III, M.Ed., is Instructional Design Specialist/Multimedia Project Lead on eLearning projects for the Technology Group, Inc. As an award-winning video, web, and new media director-producer, he has 20+ years experience in providing project direction for corporate, institutional and non-profit clients including American Express Financial Advisors Group, Cargill, Land O'Lakes, the National Center for Supercomputing Applications, Grant Thornton LLP, the American Heart Association (Dallas), the University of Illinois and the University of Minnesota.

Judith Crigan completed a Bachelor of Applied Sciences (Psychology) at Deakin University. She then completed Honours in Psychology and a Master's of Educational Psychology at the University of Melbourne. She is currently working on her PhD at the University of Melbourne, examining a range of factors relating to teachers' collaborative use of data to inform teaching. The resulting model will be used to determine the operative elements that lead to improvement in student literacy learning. In her current role as Research Officer at the Assessment Research Centre, University of Melbourne, she is working on a range of projects relating to developmental learning and the use of data to inform teaching and literacy learning.

Jennifer Elsden-Clifton is a Lecturer in the School of Education at RMIT University. As an experienced school teacher and university educator, she teaches in teacher preparation programs in the areas of health education, professional issues in teaching, diversity and curriculum. She also has an interest in professional experience through her role of Academic Director (Professional Practice).

Fáber D. Giraldo, System and Computer Engineer at University of Quindío (Colombia), Ms.Eng. EAFIT University, PhD (C) in Informatics at Universitat Politècnica de València (Spain), is Full professor at University of Quindío and researcher of the SINFOCI Research Group. His research areas are software engineering, software architecture, model driven engineering, CSCW-L, and HCI.

Patrick Griffin holds the Chair of Education (Assessment) at the University of Melbourne and is Deputy Dean of the Graduate School of Education and Associate Dean for Knowledge Transfer. He is the Director of the Assessment Research Centre. He has published widely on assessment and evaluation topics that include competency, language proficiency, industrial literacy, school literacy and numeracy profile development, portfolio assessment, and online assessment and calibration.

Rama Kaye Hart is an Assistant Professor in the Department of Organizational Learning and Development at the University of St. Tomas in Minneapolis, Minnesota. Her research interests include group dynamics and leadership, organization development, virtual/global teams, and interpersonal relationships and communication in groups. She has served as a consultant to organizations in the areas of leadership and organizational development, strategic planning, and team effectiveness for a variety of Fortune 500 and non-profit/non-governmental clients. She holds a PhD from Case Western Reserve University and an MBA in Management from Rutgers University.

Kathy Jordan is a Senior Lecturer in Literacy in the School of Education at RMIT University. She is an experienced secondary school teacher and university educator and teaches in teacher preparation programs in the areas of English Method, teaching principles and practices, and integrating curriculum. As well, Kathy supervisors research students around the teaching of literacy, and the use of ICT in school and higher education settings.

Min -Yeuan Lan is a teacher of Nei-Pu Vocational High School in Pingtung County, and has been involved in vocational high school teaching for over five years. His teaching subjects are mainly about animal sciences. He received his Master's degree from National Pingtung University of Technology and Science in Taiwan. His interests are teaching, reading, and sports.

Shi-Jer. Lou is a professor of the Graduate Institute of Technological and Vocational Education at National Pingtung University of Technology and Science in Taiwan. He received his Ph.D. from Iowa State University. His academic research focus is on computer application in education, knowledge management, vocational education, and engineering education.

Catherine McLoughlin is currently Coordinator of SIMERR ACT, the Research Centre for Science, Information Technology and Mathematics Education for Rural and regional Australia (SiMERR) at the School of Education, Canberra. Dr. McLoughlin teaches at undergraduate and postgraduate levels in the areas of educational psychology, learning design and research methods. Catherine is the author of over 200 refereed publications, including journal articles, book chapters and conference papers on a wide range of topics related to eLearning, design of culturally relevant learning environments, evaluation of learning technologies, innovative pedagogy, and learner engagement.

Catherine Mulwa is a PhD. Research Candidate working with the Knowledge and Data Engineering Research Group (KDEG) in the School of Computer Science and Statistics, The University of Dublin Ireland (TCD). Catherine graduated with a Honours B.Sc. Degree in Computer Science from Dublin Institute of Technology, School of Computing (DIT). In 2008, she received her M.Sc. Degree in Computing Knowledge Management (Grade - 2.1 Upper Class) from the School of Computing (Comp DIT). The same year, she was awarded the Postgraduate Research Studentship by Trinity College Dublin. Currently she is actively researching in the areas of Adaptive Hypermedia and Personalised Adaptive Technology Enhanced Learning as Part of Research being carried out at the Centre for Next Generation Localisation (CNGL).

Long V. Nguyen is currently Head of Academic Affairs in the College of Foreign Languages, University of Danang, where he has been working as a Lecturer since the late 90s. He received his MA in TESOL Studies from the University of Queeensland in 2005 and his PhD in Applied Linguistics (Specialized in Computer-Assisted Language Learning- CALL) at Massey University in 2011. Long has received a number of outstanding grants for his contributions in research. He has published widely in the areas of educational technology and communication in foreign language learning and teaching, sociocultural perspectives in languages education, digital literacy, collaborative learning, and language teacher education.

Eileen O'Donnell was conferred by Dublin City University with an Honours (2.1) BSc Degree in Information Technology and a First Class MSc in Business Information Systems for Managers. While lecturing on the Post Graduate Diploma in Business Information Systems in the Dublin Institute of Technology a research interest in Technology Enhanced Learning (TEL) commenced. This interest evolved into the pursuit of research conducted with the Knowledge and Data Engineering Group, School of Computer Science & Statistics, College of Engineering, Trinity College Dublin, Ireland. Research interests include: technology enhanced learning, personalised eLearning, adaptive simulations, user profiling, and human computer interaction.

Drew Parker is an Associate Professor in the Management Information Systems area at Simon Fraser University. He teaches Information Technology topics, and crafted a new course exploring Social Media's impact on Business Administration in the summer of 2008. The experience impacted not only the topic, but also the pedagogy of the course itself, and ultimately the way Drew teaches and thinks about teaching. The 'power of the crowd' can be effectively brought into the classroom setting, and completely change the teaching and learning process.

Masa Pavlovic (MSc) has been working in the fields of educational assessment, test development, data management and analysis, neurosciences and software development for the last ten years. Her primary role within the Assessment Research Centre (ARC) is working on test development including item writing and banking for a number of projects undertaken by ARC requiring assessments in numeracy, literacy, and problem solving. She has also undertaken work on a variety of projects that have included research design, data management and analysis for large-scale studies, as well as test and scale development. Ms. Pavlovic has been working on the Assessment and Learning Partnerships research program since 2009.

Pam Robertson worked for many years as a secondary teacher of Maths and Science. In her current role at the Assessment Research Centre, University of Melbourne, she has worked on projects relating to developmental learning and the use of assessment data to inform teaching. For her Master's thesis, Pam developed an instrument to measure the functioning of professional learning teams and a developmental progression of team functioning. She also provides professional development for teachers in the areas of assessment use and professional learning teams.

Mary Sharp is an Assistant Professor and Tutor in the School of Computer Science & Statistics, Trinity College Dublin lecturing on undergraduate and graduate programmes. She is the Chair of the School's Ethics Committee and Erasmus co-ordinator for the school. She is involved at EU level evaluating projects. Mary's research interests include: the evaluation of eLearning systems, medical informatics, and ethics in Information Technology.

María Lilí Villegas, System and Computer Engineer at University of Quindío (Colombia), Ms.Eng. EAFIT University, is Full professor at University of Quindío and Researcher of the SINFOCI Research Group. Her research areas are Software Engineering and HCI.

Vincent P. Wade is Professor and Head of Intelligent Systems in the School of Computer Science and Statistics, in Trinity College Dublin (TCD) University. He is Deputy Director of CNGL, a world leading multi-institutional research centre focusing on multilingual, multi modal globalisation of digital content. In 2002 Vincent was awarded Fellowship of Trinity College (FTCD) for his contribution to research in the areas of knowledge management, web based personalisation and adaptive learning technologies. Vincent was a visiting scientist at IBM (2006-9) and holds multiple patents in the area of personalisation and adaptive digital content. He has authored over two hundred and fifty scientific papers in peer reviewed research journals and international conferences and he has received seven 'best paper' awards for IEEE, ACM, and IFIP conferences. He has a H index is 24 (Google scholar). In 2010 he received the European Award of Language Technology.

Hsiu-Ling Yen I is a Chinese teacher in a vocational high school. She has been a teacher for over eighteen years. She likes to take every challenge, and is eager for various kinds of knowledge. Facing the advancements in information technologies, she has deep sympathy for the saying "It's not too late to learn," and "always encourages to move forwards instead of fooling around." She received the Master degree from National Pingtung University of Technology and Science in Taiwan, and did the research about vocational high school composition teaching combining with blended learning. It not only enriches her teaching compositions, makes composition classes interesting, but also get students love composition writing.

Nathan Zoanetti completed his Bachelor of Science degree at the University of Adelaide and on student exchange at Leeds University. Since then he has completed a Master of Assessment and Evaluation, and a PhD, both at the University of Melbourne. His Master's thesis reported on the application of Item Response Theory to identify and account for suspect rater-submitted data his PhD focused on the design and automated scoring of computer-based assessment tasks. Dr. Zoanetti has extensive experience in applied measurement research in school assessment, medical education assessment, and language testing. His current research interests include computer-based assessment design and the application of educational measurement techniques to support assessment validation efforts.

Index